Basic Administrative Law
for Paralegals

ASPEN PUBLISHERS

Basic Administrative Law for Paralegals

Fourth Edition

Anne Adams

Wolters Kluwer
Law & Business

AUSTIN   BOSTON   CHICAGO   NEW YORK   THE NETHERLANDS

To contact Customer Care, e-mail customer.care@aspenpublishers.com, call 1-800-234-1660, fax 1-800-901-9075, or mail correspondence to:

Aspen Publishers
Attn: Order Department
PO Box 990
Frederick, MD 21705

Printed in the United States of America.

1 2 3 4 5 6 7 8 9 0

ISBN 978-0-7355-7773-2

Library of Congress Cataloging-in-Publication Data

Adams, Anne, date
   Basic administrative law for paralegals / Anne Adams. — 4th ed.
      p. cm.
   Includes index.
   ISBN 978-0-7355-7773-2 (pbk.)
   1. Administrative law — United States.   2. Legal assistants — United States — Handbooks, manuals, etc.   I. Title.
   KF5402.A75 2009
   342.73′06 — dc22

                                                                            2009018403

About Wolters Kluwer Law & Business

Wolters Kluwer Law & Business is a leading provider of research information and workflow solutions in key specialty areas. The strengths of the individual brands of Aspen Publishers, CCH, Kluwer Law International, and Loislaw are aligned within Wolters Kluwer Law & Business to provide comprehensive, in-depth solutions and expert-authored content for the legal, professional, and education markets.

CCH was founded in 1913 and has served more than four generations of business professionals and their clients. The CCH products in the Wolters Kluwer Law & Business group are highly regarded electronic and print resources for legal, securities, antitrust and trade regulation, government contracting, banking, pension, payroll, employment and labor, and healthcare reimbursement and compliance professionals.

Aspen Publishers is a leading information provider for attorneys, business professionals, and law students. Written by preeminent authorities, Aspen products offer analytical and practical information in a range of specialty practice areas from securities law and intellectual property to mergers and acquisitions and pension/benefits. Aspen's trusted legal education resources provide professors and students with high-quality, up-to-date, and effective resources for successful instruction and study in all areas of the law.

Kluwer Law International supplies the global business community with comprehensive English-language international legal information. Legal practitioners, corporate counsel, and business executives around the world rely on the Kluwer Law International journals, loose-leafs, books, and electronic products for authoritative information in many areas of international legal practice.

Loislaw is a premier provider of digitized legal content to small law firm practitioners of various specializations. Loislaw provides attorneys with the ability to quickly and efficiently find the necessary legal information they need, when and where they need it, by facilitating access to primary law as well as state-specific law, records, forms, and treatises.

Wolters Kluwer Law & Business, a unit of Wolters Kluwer, is headquartered in New York and Riverwoods, Illinois. Wolters Kluwer is a leading multinational publisher and information services company.

To Mary, Emily, and Mulligan

Summary of Contents

Contents

3 AGENCY DISCRETION   65

4 CLIENT RIGHTS   101

5 AGENCY RULES AND REGULATIONS 141

6 INVESTIGATIONS AND INFORMATION GATHERING 175

7 INFORMAL PROCEEDINGS 205

8 ADMINISTRATIVE AGENCY HEARINGS 237

9 JUDICIAL REVIEW   275

10 PARALEGALISM IN ADMINISTRATIVE LAW   325

Preface

Administrative law is valuable to all paralegals because administrative agencies interact with all of the other paralegal fields. Today's competitive professionals demand paralegals with knowledge and practical experience.

For the instructor, the teaching resources include reinforcement tools: fill-in worksheets, key terms crosswords, take-home exams, and research projects that may be completed in the book. There are also projects for library and Internet research.

To enhance the paralegal's legal studies, this revised text highlights the practical experience of Internet administrative agency websites with their individual news, rules, documents, and forms. There are also cites with documents in the *Federal Register* and access to court case decisions.

The readers of this textbook will discover well-thought-out reinforcement exercises to enhance their knowledge of administrative law. Readily available references to topics and pages ease the mastery of the subject. Also provided are exercises and examples of the practical aspects of the paralegal's work life. The Fourth Edition includes the updated **Electronic Workbook on CD**, as a classroom and home study aid. This workbook focuses on Internet-based exercises exploring laws, rules, and agencies. It also includes information on agency websites, agency organization, and possible career options.

There are several features in the text to further illustrate and explain administrative law. **STUDENT PRACTICE** is an enhancement exercise that may be performed in the classroom, as a written assignment or as voluntary practice for individual students. The **CONCEPTS JOURNAL** is a practical experience that enables each student to observe, analyze, and write on a pertinent topic in administrative law. The **ADVANCED STUDIES** is an entirely separate section at the end of each chapter that may be assigned in or outside of class. This expansive section offers a hands-on approach to documents and concepts and presents an opportunity for more in-depth study.

May 2009

Anne Adams

1

Administrative Law and Administrative Agencies

ARTICLE ONE

All Legislative Powers herein granted shall be vested in a Congress of the United States, which shall consist of a Senate and a House of Representatives . . .

The Congress shall have power to *lay and collect taxes . . . provide for the common defense and general welfare of the United States . . . regulate commerce . . .* **make rules for the government . . . make all laws** *which shall be necessary and proper for carrying into execution the foregoing powers, and all other powers vested by this Constitution in the government of the United States, or in any Department or Officer thereof.*

—United States Constitution

CHAPTER OBJECTIVES

Administrative law defines the legal powers of government agencies. Questions answered in this chapter include:

- What is administrative law?
- What is an administrative (government) agency?
- What are the major areas of administrative law?
- What are substantive and procedural laws?
- Why do legislatures create administrative agencies?
- What is an enabling act/statute?
- What are the powers of agencies?

1

CHAPTER OVERVIEW

Congress may pass a new statute creating agencies (sometimes called departments or commissions) to solve problems. For example, to solve widespread environmental pollution, Congress passed a law in 1970 creating the United States Environmental Protection Agency (EPA). Prior to the creation of the EPA, environmental problems were handled by five different federal agencies. As part of the law creating the EPA, the Department of Agriculture's registration of pesticides and the Department of Interior's water pollution control programs became functions of the EPA. Modern agencies are often formed by transferring some of the powers in the statutes of established agencies to the new agency. The authority to register pesticides was contained in the statute creating the Department of Agriculture and transferred to the EPA through a reorganization plan within the law of 1970, which created the EPA.

A new agency, such as the EPA, then follows the established laws in its area of expertise (environmental protection for EPA) and develops new standards and makes new rules and regulations. Agencies on state and local levels operate in similar fashion; the state legislature passes a law creating the agency and the agency upholds laws in its area of expertise and makes rules and regulations to implement the laws. The laws creating agencies and the laws upheld by agencies are referred to as administrative laws; the government agencies as administrative agencies. Administrative law and administrative agencies are important in the daily operation of federal, state, and local governments for matters ranging from national defense to changing electric utility rates to licensing drivers.

A. Explanation of Administrative Law

The laws that define the legal powers of government agencies and the limits of these powers are collectively called **administrative law.** The administrative law sets out the means agencies may pursue to apply these powers and the remedies people may seek if injured by an action or decision of an agency using these powers.

1. Acts and Statutes

The administrative authority is derived from the **enabling act** (also called **statute** or **law**), which creates the agency. The enabling act defines the agency's role or mission. The Department of Agriculture was created by an enabling act passed by Congress cited as 7 USC §2201, which is presented in the following example.

Example 1.1

7 USC §2201: Establishment of Department

There shall be at the seat of government a Department of Agriculture, the general design and duties of which shall be to acquire and to diffuse among the people of the United States useful information on subjects connected with agriculture, rural development, aquaculture, and human nutrition in the most general and comprehensive sense of these terms and to procure, propagate, and distribute among the people new and valuable seeds and plants.

The **statute** creates the agency; it is an administrative law. Accountability of agency action is a major facet of the statute. In a sense, administrative law equalizes the vast power of the government and the lesser powers of individuals and organizations working with government agencies; agencies are bound by rules, just as citizens are bound by the rules that agencies make. Any action an agency takes that is not mandated by the powers in the statute may be appealed. The Department of Agriculture cannot make rules upholding education laws, nuclear energy laws, or laws relating to other areas of government; it only may make rules upholding any law on agriculture that is stated in its enabling act or amendments. Legislatures pass this authority to agencies because legislatures do not have the time and resources to make all the laws necessary to implement the general laws that legislatures enact. The federal government has one administrative law system and each state has its own administrative law system. Therefore, there are federal agencies and state and local agencies.

Figure 1.1 illustrates the powers of the enabling statute that creates the agency.

Figure 1.1 **Powers of Enabling Statute (Act/Law)**

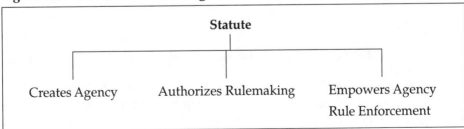

2. Substantive Laws and Procedural Laws

In addition to creating specific agencies, administrative laws guide all agencies in their treatment of individuals. Some of the laws concentrate on personal protections while others stress proper procedures to be followed in any agency action. The administrative laws that protect rights and liberties are considered **substantive law;** the administrative laws that define the legal procedures and methods to be followed are considered **procedural law.**

The notable procedural law is the **Federal Administrative Procedure Act.** This statute standardizes the procedures of the various federal administrative agencies. In stating standards for the making of rules by agencies, the Act says: "the agency shall give interested persons an opportunity to participate. . . ." (5 USC §553(c))

Example 1.2 illustrates substantive and procedural laws.

Example 1.2

Substantive Law

The United States Constitution states the basic rights of citizens. ". . . nor shall any state deprive any person of life, liberty, or property, without due process of law;" (Amendment XIV) Agencies must extend the protections of law or their decisions will not be enforceable.

Procedural Law

The Federal Administrative Procedure Act states the standards for the making of rules (regulations): "General notice of proposed rule making shall be published in the Federal Register, unless persons subject thereto are named and either personally served or otherwise have actual notice thereof in accordance with law." (5 USC §553b) Agencies must notify individuals of impending rules and regulations, if notification is not given, the rule will not have the effect of a law because the legislature limited the power of the agency by requiring notification.

3. The Range of Administrative Laws

Administrative laws include: the enabling acts (statute/laws), the procedural laws, the substantive laws, and the laws within an agency's field of expertise. Figure 1.2 illustrates these areas of administrative laws as they relate to the EPA.

Figure 1.2 **Areas of Administrative Law**

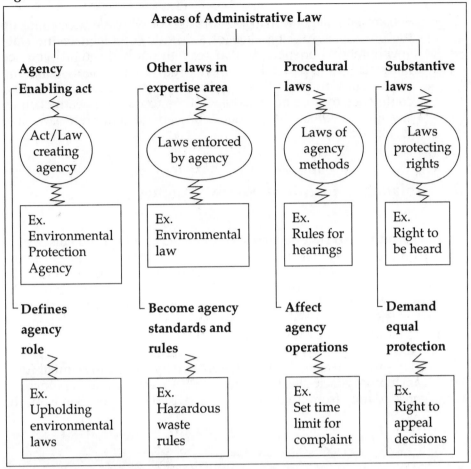

Figure 1.3 **Creating Agencies through a Statute**

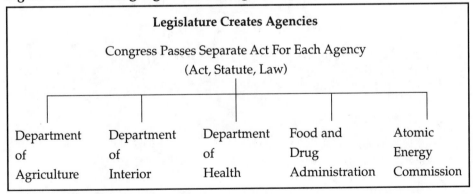

PARALEGAL PRACTICE EXAMPLE

You are a paralegal working for an attorney who asks you to look up the proper cites for his draft of a client's complaint to the state environmental agency. As you read through the draft, you see both state and federal laws and regulations mentioned; you know your firm keeps the state laws and regulations in its library/ conference room. You schedule in time to visit the nearby county law library, which has updates on federal and state laws and regulations.

B.   Explanation of Administrative Agency

Originally, **administrative agencies** were created to solve problems of public interest quickly and inexpensively. An administrative agency is a government body or organization created by legislatures to serve citizens by overseeing and administering laws in designated areas of expertise; the legislature begins the enactment or creation of an agency. Welfare services, police departments, national defense agencies, and health commissions are examples of administrative agencies.

Figure 1.3 depicts creating agencies by statute.

Today's modern agencies are often created by combining similar functions from many agencies into one agency. EPA's environmental functions were consolidated from five agencies and departments. Some of the

The EPA is a well-known government agency — can you
think of others?

programs transferred to the EPA were: air pollution control, solid waste management, radiation control, and the drinking water program.

Figure 1.4 illustrates creating an agency by transferring functions of established agencies to a new agency.

Figure 1.4   **Creating Agencies by Reorganization**

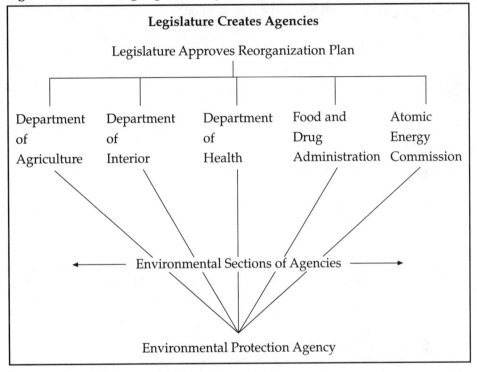

1. Reasons for Creating Agencies

An agency is created to solve a set of specific problems and/or to provide services to individuals. For example, complaints of workplace injuries brought about the formation of the Occupational Safety and Health Agency (OSHA); a federal agency mandated to check safety and health hazards in the workplace.

If mandated by a legislature, an agency has diverse powers to:

1. Set standards.
2. Make rules and regulations.
3. Prosecute against those who refuse to obey the regulations.
4. Make decisions on those actions that come before it in claims and hearings.
5. Investigate complaints.

Agencies are given this power, because legislatures determine that the expertise of each agency is the best means of serving the people.

The Department of Homeland Security was proposed and introduced in October of 2001 by Senator Joseph Lieberman, D-Conn., as a result of the 9/11 attacks. Some functions and personnel of agencies, such as U.S. Customs, the Border Patrol, and the U.S. Coast Guard, were transferred to the new agency.

Exhibit 1.1   **Homeland Security Act of 2002**

DHS | Homeland Security Act of 2002

 Homeland Security

Homeland Security Act of 2002

Title I - Department of Homeland Security

Sec. 101. Executive Department; Mission

> (a) Establishment. - "There is established a Department of Homeland Security, as an executive department of the United States within the meaning of title 5, United States Code.
>
> (b) Mission
>> (1) In General. - The primary mission of the Department is to
>> (A) prevent terrorist attacks within the United States;
>> (B) reduce the vulnerability of the United States to terrorism; and
>> (C) minimize the damage, and assist in the recovery, from terrorist attacks that do occur within the United States."

From the *Homeland Security Act of 2002*

Read the entire text of the <u>Homeland Security Act of 2002</u> *(PDF, 187 pages - 526 KB).*

This page was last reviewed/modified on November 28, 2008.

PARALEGAL PRACTICE EXAMPLE

On your first day of your paralegal internship in a state motor vehicle/driver licensing agency, your supervisor tells you to spend your morning re-filling the form files. This includes opening boxes of forms and placing them on the shelves; a dull job until you realize you are actually understanding the processes of the agency as you review the forms as suggested by your supervisor. This helped in the afternoon conference you attended with agency lawyers who were reviewing license revocation cases that were being appealed.

Agencies do make rules and regulations that are enforceable as laws. But isn't that a violation of the United States Constitution, Article I, which states "all legislative powers herein granted shall be vested in a Congress of the United States"? Although the legislative is the only branch of government vested with the power to enact laws, the Supreme Court has ruled that the legislatures may **delegate** limited powers to agencies that allow the agencies to make rules and regulations that will implement the intentions of the laws in the agency's area of expertise. The enabling statute delineates the exact powers and limitations to the agency mandated by the legislature. The time constraints in passing the required detailed laws, as well as the increasing level of expertise necessary to solve various problems (i.e., toxic waste disposal), have prompted the legislatures to create more & more agencies to deal with specific problem areas. See Figure 1.5.

Figure 1.5   **Why Legislatures Give Power to Agencies**

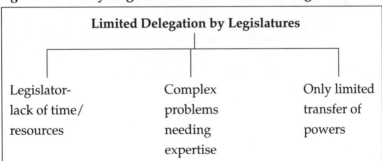

2.   Extent of Administrative Agencies

Under the authority of the federal, state, and local governments, the categories of agencies include: social welfare (e.g., social security), regulatory (e.g., commerce), independent (e.g., environment), and executive (e.g., national defense). The titles of the agencies are determined by their duties and by their manner of appointing and removing agency staff members. Most administrative laws that paralegals study do not include the major federal government agencies handling defense and foreign affairs. Focusing on the administrative agency's impact on the private citizen or private business, modern administrative law concentrates on the procedures of **regulatory** and **social welfare** agencies of both the federal and state systems. Because of the 2008/2009 economic stock and banking woes, the nation's focus is on regulatory agencies and their impact on economic and social welfare issues.

The major concentration of administrative agencies are in the areas illustrated in Figure 1.6.

Figure 1.6   **Major Concentration of Administrative Agencies**

a. *Regulatory Agency*

Regulatory agencies direct or regulate certain areas of public and private interests. For example, licensing of motor vehicle drivers is part of the regulatory state agency (or department) of motor vehicles that protects the public highways. There are also licensing agencies for professions and occupations such as doctors and electricians. On the national level all forms of transportation — aviation, boat, truck, rail — are regulated.

Federal and state regulatory agencies have the following powers to:

1. Define and establish regulations.
2. Monitor compliance with regulations.
3. Prosecute if regulations are violated.

So in a regulated occupation such as the electricians' field, all electricians are required to adhere to license eligibilities or risk losing their licenses; they are also liable for violations.

The staff members of regulatory commissions are often people in the occupational fields being regulated; the theory being they are the experts in the field area, and better able to understand the problems or requirements to be addressed.

b. Social Welfare Agency

Instead of regulating, **social welfare agencies** administer and provide assistance on both federal and state levels. Disability, old age benefits, and workers' compensation are just a few of these agencies' programs. Administrative law has greatly expanded in these areas because so many individuals are affected by the rules and regulations that these agencies administer. This social legislation is now encroaching into other areas such as consumer protection and environmental protection.

 PARALEGAL PRACTICE EXAMPLE

You, a paralegal in a social service agency, assist families by selecting the proper background information each family needs to write on the forms in order to become eligible for benefits; previously these families had been denied benefits because they were unable to follow the instructions that were developed, based on agency rules and statutes. Your ability to encourage the family to use both the agency and community standards saves the agency's legal department the costs of appeals because the initial claim simply did not properly identify the problem and agency resource sought.

c. Independent Agency

A board of five to seven members of each **independent agency** makes decisions on matters that effect the economy, such as stocks. They have a direct effect on commerce and are often called commissions; their purpose is usually a specific task and their staffs are specialists in the field. They are called independent agencies because the commission members may only be removed by just cause.

d. Executive Agency

Executive agencies are part of the executive branches of federal and state governments. Executive agencies may both regulate and provide assistance, for example, the Department of Labor regulates workplace standards; the Department of Health and Human Services dispenses aid. The head of the department is appointed by the executive, therefore the agency is not independent of political influences. Often, a politician is appointed as the department head and usually is not an expert in the field. The head also is easily removed by the executive.

This list is a small sample of some executive agencies:

Commission of Civil Rights
Consumer Product Safety Commission
Environmental Protection Agency
Equal Employment Opportunity Commission
National Labor Relations Board
Occupational Safety and Health Review Commission

Securities and Exchange Commission
Small Business Administration

CONCEPTS JOURNAL

Role Playing

Begin by separating the class into two groups. Group 1 should choose a student, an instructor, and members of the student support group. Group 2 should choose a student, an instructor, and members of the student/instructor conflict committee.

Problem — Group 1

The instructor fails a student's project. This is the last course of the student's degree program and qualifications for a paralegal certificate. There is no established appeals process to deal with this situation. The student seeks assistance from a student support group.

Student, Support Group:
1. Analyze the situation — list the exact problem areas.
2. Develop a possible avenue to favorably solve the situation.

Problem — Group 2

Same situation as Group 1's problem, *except* there is a committee overseeing student/instructor conflict. This group has access to school rules for this type of situation.

Student, Committee
1. Analyze the situation — list the exact problem areas.
2. Create rules that the committee might have access to in this type of scenario.
3. Advise the student on the best manner to handle the situation.

Presentation

Each group should present its resolution to the entire class.

1. Group 1 — Student and instructor meet; student from support group presents methods developed to class. Instructor gives answer.
2. Group 2 — Student and instructor meet; student from committee offers written list of rules. Instructor gives answer after committee student presents any alternatives.

Journal Keeping

1. Take notes on class presentations as groups rejoin.
   a. List problems.
   b. List solutions of each group.
2. Write down what works best and why.

> 3. Compare the committee to an agency with rules.
>   a. Are the rules fair to all (student/instructor)?
>   b. Is there a process to implement the rules?
>   c. Did both sides have an input into the rules?
>
> Compare the committee to an agency and then write a definition of what an agency's role and functions are.

CHAPTER SUMMARY

Administrative law is a collection of laws that guide government agencies; substantive law defines rights while procedural law defines the methods to uphold those rights. Legislatures enact statutes that create agencies and empower the agencies to make rules and regulations and to enforce those rules and regulations.

Administrative agencies are created to solve problems. In the past, agencies were primarily created to regulate the economy in areas such as commerce and transportation; many modern agencies attempt to solve social welfare problems. Some of today's agencies are quasi-regulatory and quasi-social, such as the consumer protection agencies. The types of agencies are: social welfare, regulatory, independent, and executive.

Key Terms

administrative agency
administrative law
administrative procedure acts
delegation
executive agency
independent agency

procedural law
regulatory agency
social welfare agency
statute
substantive law

Use these Key Terms for the Key Terms Crossword on the next page — it's a **reinforcement study aid.**

Key Terms Crossword

Across
1. Laws of agency methods
5. Agency providing assistance programs
6. Collection of agency laws
8. Agency making decisions on the economy
9. Agency headed by politician, not expert
10. Laws protecting personal rights

Down
2. Agency monitoring licenses
3. Enabling act or _____
4. Transfer of authority to agency
7. Government organizations serving the people

Statements

Student Study Time Hints: Look for answers under Chapter / Section.

Chapter 1 / Section A. Correction of an agency decision or action: r_____

Section A.1. Acts or statutes: l_____

Section B.2. Regulatory agency powers: e_____

_____, _____,

and _____ _____.

No Hints:

Two major types of agency laws: _____ or _____.

Powers all agencies have: _____ _____ and _____ _____.

Web Resources

www.house.gov   U.S. Congress, House of Representatives
http://thomas.loc.gov   U.S. Congress and Administrative Agencies
www.doi.gov   Department of the Interior
www.epa.gov   Environmental Protection Agency

Advanced Studies

This section more fully illustrates the creation of an administrative agency and more fully defines administrative laws. To facilitate understanding, one agency has been chosen — the EPA.

Once created, the agency sets standards, some of which become rules and regulations. The following steps indicate the possible extent of an agency such as the EPA:

1. Congress passes environmental laws.
2. The EPA sets standards to carry out these laws.
3. Individual states create programs to establish these standards in each state.
4. The EPA reviews and approves the state's program.
5. The state establishes monitoring of programs to ascertain that standards are being met.
6. The EPA shares technical information with the states.
7. The EPA provides some funding.

Various documents and charts pertaining to the EPA have been included to aid in your understanding of what administrative agencies are and how they work. These are:

Document 1 — EPA Reorganization Plan No. 3 of 1970
Document 2 — Solid Waste Disposal/Resource Conservation and Recovery Act (RCRA) 42 USC 6901 Table of Contents
Document 3 — Section 6921 of RCRA
Document 4 — EPA 40 CFR ch. 1 — rules and regulations implementing RCRA in Code of Federal Regulations
Chart 1 — Establishment of the EPA
Document 5 — EPA website questions

Document 2 is a partial table of contents of the various sections of RCRA, cited as 42 USC 6901. The hazardous waste section of this act is Subchapter III, Section 6921 "Identification and listing of hazardous waste." Document 3 is an actual section of the hazardous waste topic in the law that Congress passed. The EPA makes the rules and regulations to implement the hazardous waste section of RCRA. These rules and regulations are printed in the Code of Federal Regulations (CFR), cited as 40 CFR 261. A section of the CFR is given in Document 4. Section 6291 (Document 3) is quite typical of a law passed by Congress for which an agency develops rules and regulations to implement the legislative law. This same type of action occurs on the state level with state and local agencies. Document 5 is a website from the Environmental Protection Agency with links to hazardous waste and other topics.

Outline and/or List

1. Document 1 (EPA Reorganization Plan No. 3) is a portion of the law (statute) creating the Environmental Protection Agency (EPA) from other agencies. In Document 1, list the functions transferred to the Environmental Protection Agency (EPA) by the Environmental Control Administration. (page 20, Document 1, §2(3)(ii))

2. Document 2 is the Solid Waste Disposal Section of Hazardous Waste. In Document 2, list the section titles of §§6333, 6334, 6335. (page 23)

3. Document 3 is a section of the law identifying the criteria for defining hazardous waste. Outline how and where the administrator sends his decision. (page 25, Document 3, §6921(b)(2)(C))

4. Document 4 shows some of the rules and regulations to carry out the EPA law (which is in Document 3). List the two types of waste being discussed in §261.3(a)(2). (page 27)

Analyzing Documents and Practices

1. In Document 1, which department functions were transferred in §2(7)? (page 21)

2. In Document 2, which section refers to public vessels? How would you cite this section? (page 23)

3. In Document 3, what does the administrator publish in *Federal Register*? (page 25, §6921(b)(2)(B))

4. Document 4 is a portion of the statute (law) establishing the EPA. Describe the rule that defines hazardous waste. How do you cite this rule? (page 26)

Take Home Exam

True/False   1. Administrative laws define the legal powers of administrative agencies.

True/False   2. A law is also called an act or a statute.

True/False   3. Administrative substantive laws protect citizens' rights.

True/False   4. The Executive Branch of government creates an agency.

True/False   5. Procedural laws explain methods and procedures.

True/False   6. Social Security makes rules for national security.

True/False   7. Administrative laws define the limits of agency powers.

True/False   8. Administrative procedural laws protect citizens' rights to drive.

True/False   9. The Supreme Court creates administrative agencies.

True/False   10. Administrative procedural laws protect citizens' liberties.

Complete Diagrams

1. **Diagram** two types of Administrative Law. (page 4)

2. **Diagram** the powers of regulatory agencies. (page 10)

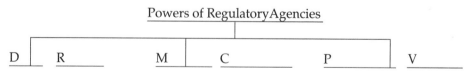

3. **Diagram** the three bureaus *not* transferred to EPA in Document 1 (Sec. 2(3)(ii)(C)(i)(ii)(iii)). (pages 20–21)

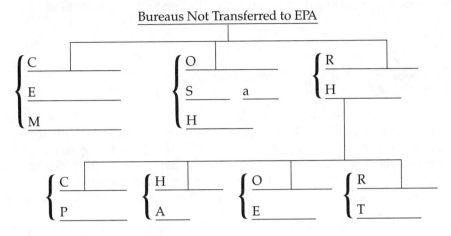

Three Venues for Research

1. **In Book**   Research in the text chapter what the Department of Agriculture can and cannot do. Use examples from 7 USCS §2201 and text. (page 3)

2. **At Library**   (a) Choose a news magazine. Summarize an article that mentions a government agency's activities.
(b)   Research and write a brief history of the Department of Homeland Security today.

3. **On Internet**   Look up the Environmental Protection Agency at *www.epa.gov.* Explain one of the top stories on the home page. (page 29)

Internship

Today you begin working as a paralegal for a three-lawyer law firm. Your lawyer tells you that she is working on a possible hazardous waste case. A homeowner believes his property has been polluted by a machine shop next door to him, possibly from waste that spills onto his land.

The lawyer tells you to find the website for the United States Code that cites the Environmental Protection Agency (*http://thomas.loc.gov*). This is the Library of Congress site. She tells you to summarize what 42 USC §6901 emphasizes.

She also asks you to see if the EPA website at *www.epa.gov* has any useful information on waste spills.

In a third memo, list the websites for the state and federal environmental agencies. Also, list any environmental agencies' telephone numbers, e-mail and mailing addresses; list pertinent department heads.

Documents

Document 1: EPA Reorganization Plan No. 3 of 1970
(5 USCS §903)

... (d) There shall be in the Agency not to exceed five Assistant Administrators of the Environmental Protection Agency who shall be appointed by the President, by and with the advice and consent of the Senate. Each Assistant Administrator shall perform such functions as the Administrator shall from time to time assign or delegate.

Sec. 2. Transfers to Environmental Protection Agency. (a) There are hereby transferred to the Administrator:

(1) All functions vested by law in the Secretary of the Interior and the Department of the Interior which are administered through the Federal Water Quality Administration, all functions which were transferred to the Secretary of the Interior by Reorganization Plan No. 2 of 1966 (80 Stat. 1608), and all functions vested in the Secretary of the Interior or the Department of the Interior by the Federal Water Pollution Control Act or by provisions of law amendatory or supplementary thereof.

(2)(i) The functions vested in the Secretary of the Interior by the Act of August 1, 1958, 72 Stat. 479, 16 USC 742d-1 (being an Act relating to studies on the effects of insecticides, herbicides, fungicides, and pesticides upon the fish and wildlife resources of the United States), and (ii) the functions vested by law in the Secretary of the Interior and the Department of the Interior which are administered by the Gulf Breeze Biological Laboratory of the Bureau of Commercial Fisheries at Gulf Breeze, Florida.

(3) The functions vested by law in the Secretary of Health, Education, and Welfare or in the Department of Health, Education, and Welfare which are administered through the Environmental Health Service, including the functions exercised by the following components thereof:

(i) The National Air Pollution Control Administration,

(ii) The Environmental Control Administration:

(A) Bureau of Solid Waste Management,

(B) Bureau of Water Hygiene,

(C) Bureau of Radiological Health,

except that functions carried out by the following components of the Environmental Control Administration of the Environmental Health Service are not transferred: (i) Bureau of Community Environmental Management, (ii) Bureau of Occupational Safety and Health, and (iii) Bureau of Radiological Health, insofar as the functions carried out by the latter Bureau pertain to (A) regulation of radiation from consumer products, including electronic product radiation, (B) radiation as used in the healing arts, (C) occupational exposures to radiation, and (D) research, technical assistance, and training related to clauses (A), (B), and (C).

(4) The functions vested in the Secretary of Health, Education, and Welfare of establishing tolerances for pesticide chemicals under the Federal Food, Drug, and Cosmetic Act, as amended, 21 USC 346, 346a, and 348, together with authority, in connection with the functions transferred, (i) to monitor compliance with the tolerances and the effectiveness of surveillance and enforcement, and (ii) to provide technical assistance to the States and conduct research under the Federal Food, Drug, and Cosmetic Act, as amended and the Public Health Service Act, as amended.

(5) So much of the functions of the Council on Environmental Quality under section 204(5) of the National Environmental Policy Act of 1969 (Public Law 91–190, approved January 1, 1970, 83 Stat. 855), as pertains to ecological systems. . . .

(6) The functions of the Atomic Energy Commission under the Atomic Energy Act of 1954, as amended, administered through its Division of Radiation Protection Standards to the extent that such functions of the Commission consist of establishing generally applicable environmental standards for the protection of the general environment from radioactive material. As used herein, standards mean limits on radiation exposures, or levels, or concentrations or quantities of radioactive material, in the general environment outside the boundaries of locations under the control of persons possessing or using radioactive material.

(7) All functions of the Federal Radiation Council (42 USC 2021(h)).

(8)(i) The functions of the Secretary of Agriculture and the Department of Agriculture under the Federal Insecticide, Fungicide, and Rodenticide Act, as amended (7 USC 135–135k), (ii) the functions of the Secretary of Agriculture and the Department of Agriculture under section 408(*l*) of the Federal Food, Drug, and Cosmetic Act, as amended (21 USC 346a(*l*)), and (iii) the functions vested by law in the Secretary of Agriculture and the Department of Agriculture which are administered through the Environmental Quality Branch of the Plant Protection Division of the Agricultural Research Service.

(9) So much of the functions of the transferor officers and agencies referred to in or affected by the foregoing provisions of this section as is incidental to or necessary for the performance by or under the Administrator of the functions transferred by those provisions or relates primarily to those functions. The transfers to the Administrator made by this section shall be deemed to include the transfer of (1) authority, provided by law, to prescribe regulations relating primarily to the transferred functions, and (2) the functions vested in the Secretary of the Interior and the Secretary of Health, Education and Welfare by section 169(d)(1)(B) and (3) of the Internal

Revenue Code of 1954 (as enacted by section 704 of the Tax Reform Act of 1969, 83 Stat 668); but shall be deemed to exclude the transfer of the functions of the Bureau of Reclamation under section 3(b)(1) of the Water Pollution Control Act (33 USC 466a(b)(1)).

(b) There are hereby transferred to the Agency:

(1) From the Department of the Interior, (i) the Water Pollution Control Advisory Board (33 USC 466f), together with its functions, and (ii) the hearing boards provided for in sections 10(c)(4) and 10(f) of the Federal Water Pollution Control Act, as amended (33 USC 466g(c)(4); 466g(f)). The functions of the Secretary of the Interior with respect to being or designating the Chairman of the Water Pollution Control Advisory Board are hereby transferred to the Administrator.

(2) From the Department of Health, Education, and Welfare, the Air Quality Advisory Board (42 USC 1857e), together with its functions. The functions of the Secretary of Health, Education, and Welfare with respect to being a member and the Chairman of that Board are hereby transferred to the Administrator. . . .

Advantages of Reorganization

This reorganization would permit response to environmental problems in a manner beyond the previous capability of our pollution control programs. The EPA would have the capacity to do research on important pollutants irrespective of the media in which they appear, and on the impact of these pollutants on the total environment. Both by itself and together with other agencies, the EPA would monitor the condition of the environment — biological as well as physical. With these data, the EPA would be able to establish quantitative "environmental baselines" — critical if we are to measure adequately the success or failure of our pollution abatement efforts.

As no disjoined array of separate programs can, the EPA would be able — in concert with the States — to set and enforce standards for air and water quality and for individual pollutants. This consolidation of pollution control authorities would help assure that we do not create new environmental problems in the process of controlling existing ones. Industries seeking to minimize the adverse impact of their activities on the environment would be assured of consistent standards covering the full range of their waste disposal problems. As the States develop and expand their own pollution control programs, they would be able to look to one agency to support their efforts with financial and technical assistance and training. . . .

Roles and Functions of EPA

The principal roles and functions of the EPA would include:

— The establishment and enforcement of environmental protection standards consistent with national environmental goals.

—The conduct of research on the adverse effects of pollution and on methods and equipment for controlling it, the gathering of information on pollution, and the use of this information in strengthening environmental protection programs and recommending policy changes. . . .

Ultimately, our objective should be to insure that the nation's environmental and resource protection activities are so organized as to maximize both the effective coordination of all and the effective functioning of each. . . .

The Congress, the Administration and the public all share a profound commitment to the rescue of our natural environment, and the preservation of the Earth as a place both habitable by and hospitable to man. With its acceptance of these reorganization plans, the Congress will help us fulfill that commitment.

RICHARD NIXON

THE WHITE HOUSE,
July 9, 1970.

Document 2: Solid Waste Disposal/Resource Conservation and Recovery Act (RCRA) 42 USC 6901 Table of Contents

42 USC	Section Title	Solid Waste Disposal/ Resource and Conservation and Recovery Act (as amended)
Subchapter I	General Provisions	Subtitle A
	. . . .	
Subchapter III	Hazardous Waste Management	Subtitle C
6921	Identification and listing of hazardous waste	sec. 3001*
6922	Standards applicable to generators of hazardous waste	sec. 3002*
6923	Standards applicable to transporters of hazardous waste	sec. 3003*
6924	Standards applicable to owners and operators	sec. 3004*
6925	Permits for treatment, storage, or disposal of hazardous waste	sec. 3005*
6926	Authorized State hazardous waste programs	sec. 3006*
6927	Inspections	sec. 3007*
6928	Federal enforcement	sec. 3008*
6929	Retention of State authority	sec. 3009*
6930	Effective date	sec. 3010*
6931	Authorization of assistance to States	sec. 3011*
6932	Transferred restrictions on recycled oil	sec. 3012*
6933	Hazardous waste site inventory	sec. 3012++
6934	Monitoring, analysis, and testing	sec. 3013++
6935	Restrictions on recycled oil	sec. 3014+
6936	Expansion during interim status	sec. 3015+

Document 3: Section 6921 of RCRA

§6921. Identification and listing of hazardous waste.

(a) Criteria for identification or listing

Not later than eighteen months after October 21, 1976, the Administrator shall, after notice and opportunity for public hearing, and after consultation with appropriate Federal and State agencies, develop and promulgate criteria for identifying the characteristics of hazardous waste, and for listing hazardous waste, which should be subject to the provisions of this subchapter, taking into account toxicity, persistence and degradability in nature, potential for accumulation in tissue, and other related factors such as flammability, corrosiveness, and other hazardous characteristics. Such criteria shall be revised from time to time as may be appropriate.

(b) Identification and listing

(1) Not later than eighteen months after October 21, 1976, and after notice and opportunity for public hearing, the Administrator shall promulgate regulations identifying the characteristics of hazardous waste, and listing particular hazardous wastes (within the meaning of section 6903(5) of this title), which shall be subject to the provisions of this subchapter. Such regulations shall be based on the criteria promulgated under subsection (a) of this section and shall be revised from time to time thereafter as may be appropriate.

(2)(A) Notwithstanding the provisions of paragraph (1) of this subsection, drilling fluids, produced waters, and other wastes associated with the exploration, development, or production of crude oil or natural gas or geothermal energy shall be subject only to existing State or Federal regulatory programs in lieu of this subchapter until at least 24 months after October 21, 1980, and after promulgation of the regulations in accordance with subparagraphs (B) and (C) of this paragraph. It is the sense of the Congress that such State or Federal programs should include, for waste disposal sites which are to be closed, provisions requiring at least the following:

(i) The identification through surveying, platting, or other measures, together with recordation of such information on the public record, so as to assure that the location where such wastes are disposed of can be located in the future; except however, that no such surveying, platting, or other measure identifying the location of a disposal site for drilling fluids and associated wastes shall be required if the distance from the disposal site to the surveyed or platted location to the associated well is less than two hundred lineal feet; and

(ii) A chemical and physical analysis of a produced water and a composition of a drilling fluid suspected to contain a hazardous material, with such information to be acquired prior to closure and to be placed on the public record.

(B) Not later than six months after completion and submission of the study required by section 6982(m) of this title, the Administrator shall, after public hearings and opportunity for comment, determine either to promulgate regulations under this subchapter for drilling fluids, produced waters, and other wastes associated with the exploration, development, or production of crude oil or natural gas or geothermal energy or that such regulations are unwarranted. The Administrator shall publish his decision in the Federal Register accompanied by an explanation and justification of the reasons for it. In making the decision under this paragraph, the Administrator shall utilize the information developed or accumulated pursuant to the study required under section 6982(m) of this title.

(C) The Administrator shall transmit his decision, along with any regulations, if necessary, to both Houses of Congress. Such regulations shall take effect only when authorized by Act of Congress.

(3)(A) Notwithstanding the provisions of paragraph (1) of this subsection, each waste listed below shall, except as provided in subparagraph (B) of this paragraph, be subject only to regulation under other applicable provisions of Federal or State law in lieu of this subchapter until at least six months after the date of submission of the applicable study required to be conducted under subsection (f), (n), (o), or (p) of section 6982 of this title and after promulgation of regulations in accordance with subparagraph (c) of this paragraph:

(i) Fly ash waste, bottom ash waste, slag waste, and flue gas emission control waste generated primarily from the combustion of coal or other fossil fuels.

(ii) Solid waste from the extraction, beneficiation, and processing of ores and minerals, including phosphate rock and overburden from the mining of uranium ore.

(iii) Cement kiln dust waste.

(B)(i) Owners and operators of disposal sites for wastes listed in subparagraph (A) may be required by the Administrator, through regulations prescribed under authority of section 6912 of this title —

(I) as to disposal sites for such wastes which are to be closed, to identify the locations of such sites through surveying, platting, or other measures, together with recordation of such information on the public record, to assure that the locations where such wastes are disposed of are known and can be located in the future, and

(II) to provide chemical and physical analysis and composition of such wastes, based on available information, to be placed on the public record.

Document 4: EPA 40 CFR Ch.1 — Rules and Regulations Implementing RCRA

Part 261 — Identification and Listing of Hazardous Waste

Subpart A — General

Sec.
261.1   Purpose and scope.
261.2   Definition of solid waste.
261.3   Definition of hazardous waste.
261.4   Exclusions.
261.5   Special requirements for hazardous waste generated by conditionally exempt small quantity generators.
261.6   Requirements for recyclable materials.
261.7   Residues of hazardous waste in empty containers.
261.8   PCB wastes regulated under Toxic Substance Control Act.
261.9   Requirements for Universal Waste.

§261.1 Purpose and scope.

(a) This part identifies those solid wastes which are subject to regulation as hazardous wastes under parts 262 through 265, 268, and parts 270, 271, and 124 of this chapter and which are subject to the notification requirements of section 3010 of RCRA. In this part:

(1) Subpart A defines the terms "solid waste" and "hazardous waste", identifies those wastes which are excluded from regulation under parts 262 through 266, 268, and 270 and establishes special management requirements for hazardous waste produced by conditionally exempt small quantity generators and hazardous waste which is recycled.

(2) Subpart B sets forth the criteria used by EPA to identify characteristics of hazardous waste and to list particular hazardous wastes.

(3) Subpart C identifies characteristics of hazardous waste.

(4) Subpart D lists particular hazardous wastes.

(b)(1) The definition of solid waste contained in this part applies only to wastes that also are hazardous for purposes of the regulations implementing subtitle C of RCRA. For example, it does not apply to materials (such as non-hazardous scrap, paper, textiles, or rubber) that are not otherwise hazardous wastes and that are recycled.

(2) This part identifies only some of the materials which are solid wastes and hazardous wastes under sections 3007, 3013, and 7003 of RCRA. A material which is not defined as a solid waste in this part, or is not a hazardous waste identified or listed in this part, is still a solid waste and a hazardous waste for purposes of these sections if:

(i) In the case of sections 3007 and 3013, EPA has reason to believe that the material may be a solid waste within the meaning of section 1004(27) of RCRA and a hazardous waste within the meaning of section 1004(5) of RCRA; or

(ii) In the case of section 7003, the statutory elements are established.

(c) For the purposes of §§261.2 and 261.6:

(1) A "spent material" is any material that has been used and as a result of contamination can no longer serve the purpose for which it was produced without processing:

(2) "Sludge" has the same meaning used in §260.10 of this chapter; . . . .

§261.3 Definition of hazardous waste.

(a) A solid waste, as defined in §261.2, is a hazardous waste if:

(1) It is not excluded from regulation as a hazardous waste under §261.4 (b); and

(2) It meets any of the following criteria:

(i) It exhibits any of the characteristics of hazardous waste identified in subpart C of this part. However, any mixture of a waste from the extraction, beneficiation, and processing of ores and minerals excluded under §261.4(b)(7) and any other solid waste exhibiting a characteristic of hazardous waste under subpart C of this part only if it exhibits a characteristic that would not have been exhibited by the excluded waste alone if such mixture had not occurred or if it continues to exhibit any of the characteristics exhibited by the non-excluded waste prior to mixture. Further, for the purposes of applying the Toxicity Characteristic to such mixtures, the mixture is also a hazardous waste if it exceeds the maximum concentration for any contaminant listed in Table I to §261.24 that would not have been exceeded by the excluded waste alone if the mixture had not occurred or if it continues to exceed the maximum concentration for any contaminant exceeded by the nonexempt waste prior to mixture.

(ii) It is listed in subpart D of this part and has not been excluded from the lists in subpart D of this part under §§260.20 and 260.22 of this chapter. . . .

(iv) It is a mixture of solid waste and one or more hazardous wastes listed in subpart D of this part and has not been excluded from paragraph (a)(2) of this section under §§260.20 and 260.22 of this chapter; however, the following mixtures of solid wastes and hazardous wastes listed in subpart D of this part are not hazardous wastes (except by application of paragraph (a)(2)(i) or (ii) of this section) if the generator can demonstrate that the mixture consists of wastewater the discharge of which is subject to regulation under either section 402 or section 307(b) of the Clean Water Act. . . .

Chart 1: Establishment of the EPA

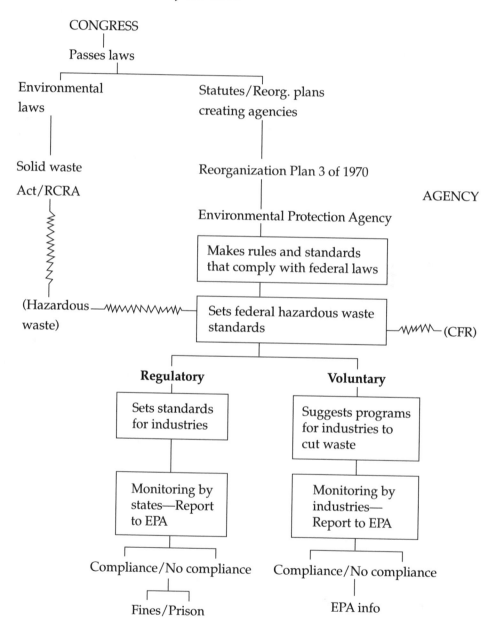

Document 5: EPA Website on Waste

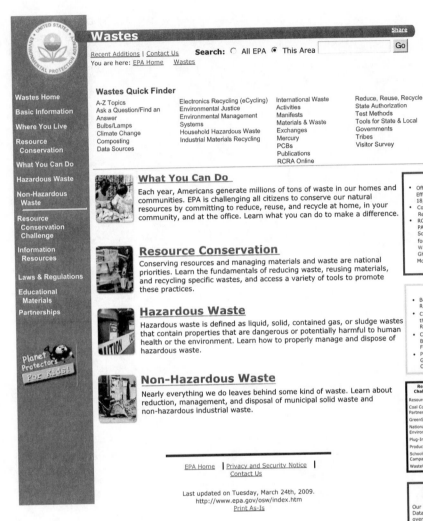

This document will now print as it appears on screen when you use the File » Print command.
Use View » Refresh to return to original state.

2

Development of Administrative Law

GOVERNMENT AND . . .
* forests
* taxes
* business
* horse racing
* communications
* health
* government budget

* oceans
* coal
* prisons
* oil
* poultry
* labor

CHAPTER OBJECTIVES

Administrative law includes laws made by legislatures and rules made by agencies to enact these laws. This chapter discusses:

- A brief history of administrative law.
- How administrative laws grant executive, legislative and judicial powers to administrative agencies.
- Which safeguards stop agencies from abusing the powers of the three branches of government.
- Why agencies are called the fourth branch of government.
- How the Delegation Doctrine relates to agencies.
- How the Separation of Powers is upheld by agencies.
- Why some agency rules have the power of laws.
- Which guidelines agencies follow.

CHAPTER OVERVIEW

The various interests of the people of the nation, such as business, health, communications, freedom, taxes, forests, and more, encompass the legal system, which was developed and continues to evolve to protect these interests. The nation, through the Constitution, established the legislature to pass laws to oversee these interests. To further carry out these interests, the legislature delegates authority and powers to administrative agencies; administrative laws then guide agency actions. In addition to these legislative powers, the agencies also assume executive and judicial roles. Yet, the agencies' powers are limited by the separation of powers of government: Executive, legislative and judicial branches. This limitation of power is expressed in administrative laws that protect the powers of each branch of government if those powers overlap in the administrative agencies. Administrative laws also are subject to the reality of government: political manuevering and philosophical conflicts.

A. History of Administrative Law

The enabling act establishing the Interstate Commerce Commission (ICC) in 1887 is regarded as the first actual administrative law, although legal principles guiding the American bureaucracy of government have existed since the beginnings of the nation. Prior to 1887, Congress delegated extremely limited powers to agencies. Unique to the ICC in its era was the power to make rules and regulations for private industries. This power was necessitated by the direct influence on the national economy of private industries such as the railroads; most of the early ICC regulations monitored the railroads.

The actual term, administrative law, did not come into common usage until the twentieth century when the laws that comprised the term, administrative law, developed as the administrative system of government agencies grew.

The following is a brief chronological outline of the growth of administrative law:

1776–1886
Administrative legal principles guide government bureaucracy.
1887
First actual administrative law — establishing the ICC.
- Enforcement power for rules
- Power to make rules for private industries

1887–1929
>   Agencies created with similar rulemaking as ICC.
>   Administrative Law becomes legal term in twentieth century.

1930–1950
>   Courts review administrative laws.
>   Courts limit powers of agencies.

1951–Present
>   Agency powers extended.

After creating the ICC in 1887 Congress established other agencies with similar enabling acts and similar rulemaking powers. Most agencies modeled themselves and their rulemaking on the ICC. In the 1930's administrative law greatly expanded as Congress created new agencies to solve the problems of the Great Depression. Court challenges to the extent of the powers of administrative laws and to the actions of administrative agencies were made by a diverse group of individuals and industries. In this era, some powers of administrative agencies were limited and some administrative laws were invalidated and declared unconstitutional. The Supreme Court did protect the rights of individuals by limiting the extent of the procedures of agency administrators to the rules of the Administrative Procedure Act, in this way retaining the supremacy of the legislator over the agency official. In the 1980s and 1990s the Supreme Court often stressed the public interest over the interests of private industries as crucial and has continued to stress the technical expertise of agencies in making their rules.

Because our complex society demands experts to quickly solve some of its technical and cultural problems, the administrative agencies and administrative law continue to expand. No matter how tedious the red-tape of agencies, the solution of problems would be even slower if the legislatures had to solve them without delegating authority to agencies and without relying on agency expertise.

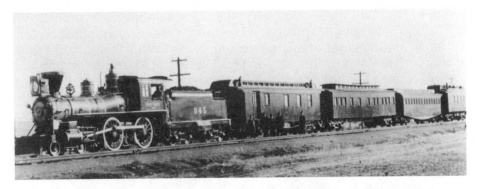

**Administrative laws are rooted in the nation's young
beginnings.**

B. Delegation Doctrine

The Delegation Doctrine is a legal theory; it is not a written document like the U.S. Constitution or the Declaration of Independence. This theory proposes that the legislature may make laws and that the legislature may convey this power of law-making to others *sparingly*. This legal theory upholds the precepts of democracy with the practicality of governing. The writers of the U.S. Constitution based their ideas on John Locke's *Second Treatise of Civil Government*, 1690. John Locke was an English philosopher and legal theorist who was widely read by the founders of this nation.

Locke states,

> . . . the legislative cannot transfer the power of making laws to any other hands; for it being a delegated power from the people, they who have it cannot pass it over to others; . . . the legislative can have no power to transfer their authority of making laws and placing it in other hands.

In essence, the Delegation Doctrine theorizes, like Locke, that Congress is delegated power from the people; but the Delegation Doctrine allows a limited transfer of powers.

By applying the Delegation Doctrine the legislators adapt the tenets of the U.S. Constitution by transferring (or delegating) the power to make laws, within strict limitations, to the administrative agencies.

Article I of the United States Constitution states,

> Section 1. All legislative powers herein granted shall be vested in a Congress of the United States, which shall consist of a Senate and a House of Representatives.
> Section 8. The Congress shall have power . . .
>   To make rules for the government . . .
>   To make all laws which shall be necessary and proper for carrying into execution the foregoing powers. . . .

The Delegation Doctrine adapts Article I into the practical functions of governing. Without this adaptation it would be impossible to answer the question, how will the government take actions on the daily problems of individuals? Without adaptation, who would process an application for a workmen's compensation claim—a legislator? Who would process an application for a dog license—a legislator? Could the legislator who helps to create a law be accountable for processing the various daily aspects of the law?

Figure 2.1 depicts the Delegation Doctrine as the pure theory based on Locke and the practical theory in our government.

PARALEGAL PRACTICE EXAMPLE

You work as a paralegal in the General Counsel's office of a state agency and have volunteered to help some of the lawyers with a presentation on how agencies work to local junior high students coming to the agency next week. You are immersed in your topic, history of the legal philosophy of administrative agencies. Sarcastically, you think that the only paralegal on the project has the most time consuming and most difficult part of the presentation — to make it interesting and understandable.

Figure 2.1   **Delegation Doctrine: Pure Theory v. Practical Theory**

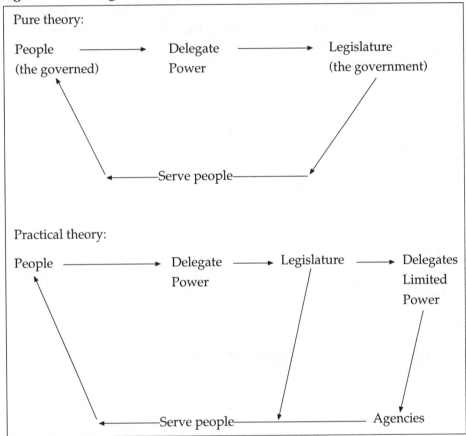

1. Delegation to an Agency

Delegation to an administrative agency occurs when the agency receives legislative powers of rule-making and the judicial powers of hearing cases and making decisions. As discussed in Chapter 1, the reason agencies receive these powers is the inability of the legislature and the courts to handle this tremendous volume of daily work; and the need for administrative agencies to develop an expertise in their area of specialty.

With their accumulation of executive, legislative, and judicial functions, the administrative agencies are sometimes referred to as the fourth branch of government as they are quasi-executive, quasi-legislative, and quasi-judicial. Having survived derogatory viewpoints and many challenges in the courts, the delegation of power to agencies is apparently the best manner to accomplish much of the work of government.

Some reasons for the challenges to agency power are the beliefs that agencies usurp the legitimate powers of the three branches of government, as illustrated in Figure 2.2.

Figure 2.2   **Powers of Government and of Agencies**

	Manage programs	Make laws or rules	Review legal disputes
Executive	✓		
Legislative		✓	
Judicial			✓
Agencies	✓	✓	✓

STUDENT PRACTICE

Problem
There are tax violations by businesses that this state agency must address.

Solution
Split the class into the following three sections:

1. The official administrator and staff of the agency;
2. The employees who helped draft the tax violation rules to implement the tax violation statute; and
3. The hearing officers who make decisions at the tax violation hearings.

> As you see, the agency has the three powers of the executive, legislative and judicial branches. The staff is going to meet to draft some guidelines to speed up the process of bringing these violators into compliance with agency rules. The staff is under heavy scrutiny from the media who are claiming little is done in this area.
>
> Write up some guidelines.

2. Delegation of Quasi-Judicial Powers

The judicial function of government is delegated to an administrative agency when Congress allows the agency to conduct hearings. It is impracticable for the courts to hear all matters that come before administrative agencies; however the action the agency takes and the procedures used before, during, and after the hearings may later be appealed through the court system in judicial review. The judicial power is the decision-making over disputed cases and the legislative power is the making of rules and regulation that become part of the administrative law system. As long as the right to judicial review by the courts is provided, the administrative agencies may utilize judicial (adjudicatory) functions.

3. Application of the Delegation Doctrine

The Delegation Doctrine is actually the redelegation of the powers given to the legislature in the Constitution to administrative agencies. As stated previously, some of the dramatic applications of (delegation of power to agencies) the Doctrine occurred during the Depression recovery era of the 1930s. A less dramatic application of the Delegation Doctrine took place between two states in the 1960s—Arizona and California. The U.S. Department of the Interior was under orders by the U.S. Congress to regulate the Colorado River, which runs between Arizona and California; this regulation included establishing flood control, developing irrigation, aiding water consumption, and providing power production. The two states disagreed with the apportionments allotted by the Secretary of the Interior. In *Arizona v. California*, 373 US 546 (1963), the U.S. Supreme Court allowed the delegation of power to the Secretary of the Interior because Congress had set an order of priorities—a standard—for the Secretary of the Interior to follow, even though the Secretary was allowed much discretion in managing the system that came under the Boulder Canyon Project Act.

Some delegation is applicable to handling the sports and entertainment industries. For example, the New York State Harness and Racing Commission was delegated with the power to regulate the harness racing industry by the New York State Legislature. Sufficient standards were given that allowed the Commission to issue licenses in the public interest.

(*Sullivan County Harness Racing Ass'n v. Glasser*, 30 NY2d 269 (1972))
Similar delegation is given to the Federal Communications Commission
in granting licenses to television stations. The delegating legislature offers
standards that are guidelines from which the agencies develop their own
standards that become rules.

a. Guidelines from Legislatures

Legislatures direct the agencies in enacting laws by establishing
guidelines that must be followed, thus limiting the powers of the agencies.
If the legislative standards are too broad, the agencies and the executive
branch that manage the agencies have great powers with little limits on
their authority. The lack of definite guidelines in recent legislatures has
reflected the politics of the legislators who may be deflecting criticism
from their constituents.

b. Standards from Agencies

The agencies develop standards through rules and regulations using
the legislative guidelines. An example is the *United States v. Grimaud*, 220
US 506 (1911) case, which involved the saving of land for the nation's
forests. Congress had provided for regulation of these forests by stating
that the agency head, the Secretary of Agriculture,

> ... may make such rules and regulations and establish such service as will
> insure the objects of such reservations; namely, to preserve the forests therein
> from destruction. . . .
> 　　Under these act, the Secretary of Agriculture . . . established certain
> rules for the purpose of regulating the use . . . of the public forest reserva-
> tions . . . among those established was the following: [Regulation 45] All
> person(s) must secure permits before grazing any stock in a forest
> reserve. . . . (*Grimaud*)

In *Grimaud* the defendants were accused of violating Regulation 45 by
grazing sheep without the permit ordered by the regulations. The Court
upheld the Department of Agriculture's right to make these rules and
regulations by stating that the Congress did not establish specific detailed
guidelines because each forest area has distinct local features; therefore, the
agency needed to develop the standards particular to each forest.

4. Disputed Delegation

The U.S. Supreme Court concluded that a correct or legal delegation
occurs when the delegation to an agency is accomplished with standards
established by Congress and these standards are followed by the agency
(*Yakus v. United States*, 321 US 414 (1944)). In recent years the Court has
stood by sufficient standards as a criteria, "A Congressional delegation of
power . . . must be accompanied by discernible standards, so that the

delegate's actions may be measured by fidelity to the legislative will."
Eastlake v. Forest City Enters., 426 US 668 (1976) There have been three
major cases in which the Court struck down delegation; these cases were
litigated during the 1930s as the government strove to regain the nation's
economic footing.

> *Panama Refining — 1935*
>   Reason: Legislative powers delegated without sufficient stan-
>   dards and limitations
> *Schecter — 1935*
>   Reason: Legislative powers delegated without standards
> *Carter — 1936*
>   Reason: Legislative powers delegated to private persons

These cases resulted from the enactment of the National Industrial
Recovery Act (NIRA), an act passed to speed recovery by addressing
both industrial and labor problems. The previous idea of stab-in-the-
back competition was discouraged, to be replaced with the concept of
fair competition in industries; the minimum wage was introduced as a
labor incentive. The NIRA was powerful; breaking a business cycle in
the nation that harbored overproduction and resulted in lower wages for
workers. Vast numbers of citizens were thrown out of work, creating a fear
that the nation was heading to revolution; a fear addressed by the presence
of troops on guard at the inauguration in Washington, D.C. of President
Franklin D. Roosevelt in 1932.

The month after the NIRA was enacted, oil companies attempted
to stop an executive order ceasing overproduction of oil by seeking an
injunction against Section 9c of the act. Section 9c stated, "The President
is authorized to prohibit the transportation . . . of petroleum . . . from
storage in excess of the amount permitted to be produced." The US
Supreme Court invalidated Section 9c of the act and the delegation,
stating standards had to be set by Congress *Panama Refining Co. v. Ryan*,
293 US 388 (1935). Driven by the zeal to bring the nation out of the
Depression, Congress had not set sufficient standards or limits when
delegating its powers.

Another section of the NIRA, Section 3, allowed the President to
approve a fair competition code developed by the industries. This was
declared unconstitutional because it lacked standards set by Congress.
Schecter Poultry Corp. v. United States, 295 US 495 (1935)

During this period the Bituminous Coal Conservation Act of 1935 was
invalidated because it delegated powers to private coal producers, a violation of government delegation theory. The Court stated, "The power
conferred upon the majority is, in effect, the power to regulate the affairs
of an unwilling minority. This is legislative delegation in its most obnox-
ious form. . . ." *Carter v. Carter Coal Co.*, 298 US 238 (1936). These three cases
are the only significant instances in which delegation was invalidated, but
the criteria for determining proper delegation has been greatly debated
over the years.

C. Separation of Powers

The Separation of Powers is a theory of government in which powers are separated into three branches: executive, legislative, and judicial. This theory prevents the usurpation of power by one group or one person.

Under our Constitution the **legislative branch** creates the laws, the **judicial branch** settles disputes concerning the laws, and the **executive branch** manages the staff and programs necessary in carrying out the laws. This **tripartite** functioning of government is the **separation of powers**.

Figure 2.3   **Separation of Powers**

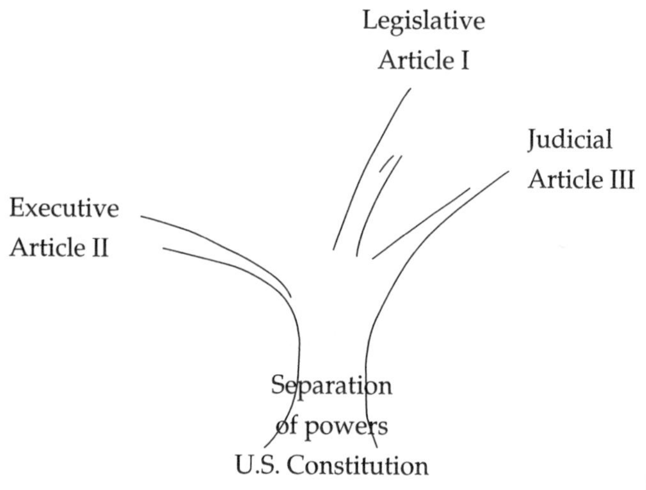

Legislative
Article I

Judicial
Article III

Executive
Article II

Separation
of powers
U.S. Constitution

Article I:	All legislative powers herein granted shall be vested in a Congress . . .
Article II:	The executive power shall be vested in a President . . .
Article III:	The judicial power . . . shall be vested in one Supreme Court, and . . . inferior courts

Why was the power to make or create the laws granted to the legislative branch? The legislature is directly elected by the people and each legislator represents a small but significant number of individuals; for example a state if a national senator, or a district if a state senator; unlike the judiciary, who are appointed on the national level and in many states.

Why give separate powers to each branch? Each branch of government is given only the amount of power necessary to perform responsibilities the people believe are best carried out by the government. All other powers are in the hands of the citizens. The Constitution separates these powers to avoid absolute control of power by any one group.

In addition to requiring that the powers of government be split into three branches, the Constitution requires two distinct forms of government that will be equal: A national (federal) and state government system. The state governments are equal to the federal government according to the Constitution's Tenth Amendment which states, "The powers not **delegated** to the United States by the Constitution, nor prohibited by it to the states, are reserved to the states respectively, or to the people." The states theoretically possess more powers than the national government, but states often yield to the federal government's standards when offered economic incentives, such as subsidies. Nevertheless, the national and local governments are completely separate in many areas; this division is called **federalism.** Because of the concept of federalism, there is a national (federal) system of administrative laws and 50 state systems of administrative laws.

Figure 2.4 depicts the organizational division of government into two systems. Each system has its own set of administrative laws.

Figure 2.4 **Federalism in the United States**

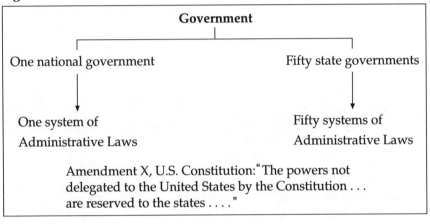

1. **Role of Each Branch in Administrative Agencies**

It is inevitable that some of the functions of each branch overlap; this is exhibited in administrative agencies. It is the legislative branch that creates the agency by statute or act, determines the powers of the agency, and sets the guidelines for the standards to be developed by the agency. The executive branch appoints the people to administer the agency, while the judicial branch reviews the decisions of the agency.

a. Independence of the Branches

The **executive branch** of government manages government programs, administers government agencies, and implements the laws. Nationally, the President is the head of the federal executive branch, which also consists of the President's assistants, cabinet, agencies, and departments and their respective staffs. The governor is the head of the executive branch of a state.

The **legislative branch** makes the laws.

The **judicial branch** interprets the laws by settling disputes about the laws in the various court systems — federal, state, and local.

STUDENT PRACTICE

Split the class into three sections.

1. The President and staff
2. Members of Congress
3. Judges

Premise: The U.S. Constitution has been accepted. This group is meeting to draft a treason law in anticipation of an attempt to overthrow the new government.

1. The executive's staff will administer and appoint the officials to handle the treasonists. This group will offer suggestions in that area.
2. The legislators will draft the law, making sure they have the executive and judicial support.
3. The judges will look for both the practical and theoretical means of examining any decisions made by the executive branch in carrying out this law.

Remember: No agencies in this area exist and this group will not be forming an agency to carry out this law. These three branches of government are separate.

Write the treason law.

---

b. Checks and Balances on the Branches

Because government is composed of humans, the founders considered human nature in designing controls against the usurpation of power. By natural instinct, each human protects its own turf. This has always been evident in government. As Madison stated in *The Federalist Papers, No. 51,*

> Ambition must be made to counteract ambition. The interest of the man must be connected with the constitutional right of the place . . . In framing a government which is to be administered by men over men, the great difficulty lies in this: you must first enable the government to control the governed; and in the next place oblige it to control itself.

By protecting its own turf, each branch of government acts as a check against encroaching power-grabbing by another branch, and keeps a balance of power.

Another Action — "Delegation"

Congress must establish an intelligible principle if an agency such as EPA is to set standards.

Whitman v. American Trucking Associations, Inc.

531 U.S. 457 (2001)

Justice SCALIA delivered the opinion of the Court.

Section 109(b)(1) of the CAA instructs the EPA to set "ambient air quality standards the attainment and maintenance of which in the judgment of the Administrator, based on [the] criteria [documents of §108] and allowing an adequate margin of safety, are requisite to protect the public health." The Court of Appeals . . . found that the EPA's interpretation (but not the statute itself) violated the nondelegation doctrine. We disagree.

[In] a delegation challenge, the constitutional question is whether the statute has delegated legislative power to the agency. Article 1, §1, of the Constitution vests "[a]ll legislative Powers herein granted . . . in a Congress of the United States." This text permits no delegation of those powers, and so we repeatedly have said that when Congress confers decisionmaking authority upon agencies *Congress* must "lay down by legislative act an intelligible principle to which the person or body authorized to [act] is directed to conform." We have never suggested that an agency can cure an unlawful delegation of legislative power by adopting in its discretion a limiting construction of the statute. . . . The idea that an agency can cure an unconstitutionally standardless delegation of power by declining to exercise some of that power seems to us internally contradictory.

We agree with the Solicitor General that the text of §109(b)(1) of the CAA at a minimum requires that "[f]or a discrete set of pollutants and based on published air quality criteria that reflect the latest scientific knowledge, [the] EPA must establish uniform national standards at a level that is requisite to protect public health from the adverse effects of the pollutant in the ambient air." Requisite, in turn, "mean[s] sufficient, but not more than necessary." These limits on the EPA's discretion are strikingly similar to the ones we approved in *Touby v. United States*, 500 U.S. 160 (1991), which permitted the Attorney General to designate a drug as a controlled substance for purposes of criminal drug enforcement if doing so was " 'necessary to avoid an imminent hazard to the public safety.' " They also resemble the Occupational Safety and Health Act provision requiring the agency to " 'set the standard which most adequately assures, to the extent feasible, on the basis of the best available evidence, that no employee will suffer any impairment of health' " — which the Court upheld . . .

. . . Section 109(b)(1) of the CAA, which to repeat we interpret as requiring the EPA to set air quality standards at the level that is "requisite" — that is, not lower or higher than is necessary — to protect the public health with an adequate margin of safety, fits comfortably within the scope of discretion permitted by our precedent.

We therefore reverse the judgment of the Court of Appeals remanding for reinterpretation that would avoid a supposed delegation of legislative power.

2.   Conflict of Overlapping Power

The legislative branch supplies the money to the agencies. In this manner, legislators do wield power over who is employed by the agencies in the realm of political patronage in exchange for a full budget.

The executive branch develops programs and seeks legislation to solve problems. The most famous case of an executive requesting Congress's implementation is President Franklin Roosevelt and the NIRA. Although many of the programs under the NIRA were essential to recovery, some sections gave arbitrary powers to administrative agencies and were ruled illegal and unconstitutional.

The judicial branch cautiously decides if a matter brought to its attention is subject to judicial review. Not all matters seeking judicial examination meet the courts' standards for acceptance. If the court oversteps its powers, the court has assumed a legislative function and not a judicial one.

 PARALEGAL PRACTICE EXAMPLE

A client makes an appointment at the law firm where you are working as a paralegal. This client represents a volunteer citizen group to which your law firm offers pro bono advice. The attorney you're working with asks you to look up rulings on agency regulations regarding rivers and estuaries. She also wants the pertinent federal cases reviewed, because this group is disputing the amount of power an energy commission has over the allocation of money to improve dams.

D.   Intelligible Principle

Legislators may protect their jobs by specifically not writing clear laws, because a general law may offend fewer voters than a specific law that restricts the actions of certain groups. Legislators also claim that broad laws are necessary because of the complexities involved and the lack of necessary time to make detailed laws that only agencies can do properly. Therefore, the **"intelligible principle"** test demands that the legislature give an agency guidelines from which to make specific laws and criteria to set standards. This principle was established by the U.S. Supreme Court in *Mistretta v. United States*, 488 US 361 (1989). *Mistretta* is a major case often cited in intelligible principle issues.

1. Starting Point

By designating a starting point, the sentencing commission in *Mistretta v. United States*, 488 US 361 (1989), proved the intelligible principle test. The United States Sentencing Commission is an agency set up to research and draft standards for sentencing that federal judges may use as guidelines. Current sentences were mandated by the statute as the starting point for the Commission. The agency also was limited by the minimum sentences prescribed by current laws. Along with the starting point, the goals and maximum limits were included in the instructions to the agency in the enabling statutes.

Mistretta questioned Congress' delegation of authority to the U.S. Sentencing Commission to research prison sentences and to draft prison sentence guidelines for federal judges. This delegation was challenged on the grounds that sentencing is a discretionary function of the legislature. The Court upheld the delegation on three major grounds:

1. Congress had created a "starting point" of current sentencing averages;
2. Congress determined the sentencing goals; and
3. Congress ordered statutory minimums and maximums to be followed as guidelines.

The following is the legislation creating the United States Sentencing Commission:

28 USCS §994

§994. Duties of the Commission

(a) The Commission, by affirmative vote of at least four members of the Commission, and pursuant to its rules and regulations and consistent with all pertinent provisions of any federal statute, shall promulgate and distribute to all courts of the United States and to the United States Probation System —

(1) guidelines, as described in this section, for use of a sentencing court in determining the sentence to be imposed in a criminal case, including —

(A) a determination whether to impose a sentence to probation, a fine, or a term of imprisonment;

(B) a determination as to the appropriate amount of a fine or the appropriate length of a term of probation or a term of imprisonment;

(C) a determination whether a sentence to a term of imprisonment should include a requirement that the defendant be placed on a term of supervised release after imprisonment, and, if so, the appropriate length of such a term; and

(D) a determination whether multiple sentences to terms of imprisonment should be ordered to run concurrently or consecutively;

(b)(1) The Commission, in the guidelines promulgated pursuant to subsection (a)(1), shall, for each category of offense involving each category of defendant, establish a sentencing range that is consistent with all pertinent provisions of title 18, United States Code.

(2) If a sentence specified by the guidelines includes a term of imprisonment, the maximum of the range established for such a term shall not exceed the minimum of that range by more than the greater of 25 percent or 6 months, except that, if the minimum term of the range is 30 years or more, the maximum may be life imprisonment. . . .

(h) The Commission shall assure that the guidelines specify a sentence to a term of imprisonment at or near the maximum term authorized for categories of defendants in which the defendant is eighteen years old or older and —

(1) has been convicted of a felony that is —

(A) a crime of violence; or

(B) an offense described in section 401 of the Controlled Substances Act (21 U.S.C. 841), sections 1002(a), 1005, and 1009 of the Controlled Substances Import and Export Act (21 U.S.C. 952(a), 955, and 959), and the Maritime Drug Law Enforcement Act (46 U.S.C. App. 1901 et seq.); and

(2) has previously been convicted of two or more prior felonies, each of which is —

(A) a crime of violence; or

(B) an offense described in section 401 of the Controlled Substances Act (21 U.S.C. 841), sections 1002(a), 1005, and 1009 of the Controlled Substances Import and Export Act (21 U.S.C. 952(a), 955, and 959), and the Maritime Drug Law Enforcement Act (46 U.S.C. App. 1901 et seq.). . . .

(n) The Commission shall assure that the guidelines reflect the general appropriateness of imposing a lower sentence than would otherwise be imposed, including a sentence that is lower than that established by statute as a minimum sentence, to take into account a defendant's substantial assistance in the investigation or prosecution of another person who has committed an offense.

Any standard established by the Commission would have to fall within the range already created by legislative statute; the intelligible principle is upheld because the guidelines are clear and comprehensive, or intelligible.

The intelligible principle test established another way to examine delegation besides the sufficient standards test (previously discussed). In the sufficient standards test, the guidelines set by the legislature are examined. In the intelligible principle test, the criteria for setting standards as established by the legislature are examined.

 PARALEGAL PRACTICE EXAMPLE

At the litigation department staff meeting in the law firm where you are a paralegal intern, you notice that certain staff members frequently allude to basic historical cases to either back up or refute another staff member's analysis of a present case. Your paralegal supervisor responds to your comments by telling you he thinks it's professional to be knowledgeable of prominent cases. You make a note to re-familiarize yourself with textbook cases and to keep a list of cases mentioned frequently in meetings.

2. Guidelines and Standards

Much of the right of administrative agencies to their delegated power is upheld constitutionally by the requirement that agencies adhere to statutory standards on both the federal and state levels. "... clear legislative standards must be provided to guide the officer in exercising the delegated authority in accordance with legislative policy. ..." was an answer given by the Supreme Judicial Court of Massachusetts in 1984 to a question asked by the Massachusetts legislature. 393 Mass. 1209, *Opinions of the Justices*. It is these legislative standards and guidelines that are evaluated under the intelligible principle test.

Legislatures do not have the abilities to make technical decisions that are necessary to protect the public interest. The "intelligible principle" test requires that the legislature set standards that are specific enough on which an agency can base detailed, fair rules. An example of this is the federal government's control of drugs that are considered to be hazardous for public use. Congress passed a law that states a drug must show a potential for abuse and a potential for dependence as requirements before it is considered to be hazardous. Although broad, they are guidelines that meet the intelligible principle test.

CONCEPTS JOURNAL

Role Playing

1. Split the class into two sections: delegation and separation of powers.

2. Each group develops two "buzz" lists (commonly used in the field).
   "Legal Jargon"
   "Buzz Cases"
3. Use this chapter in the textbook and choose which legal words and theories are important. Choose the same for cases. Limit the list to your group's specialty; either delegation or separation of powers.
4. Explain each topic on your list by definition. Examine why it is important. Summarize any cases.
5. Both groups rejoin and have each member present either a word or a case.

Journal Notebook

Take notes on what the role playing defined and the reasons for its importance.

Keep this list as pertinent topics you should know in your field. Add to it as necessary.

E. Enactment of Statutes

The legislature passes a statute (act/law) to create an agency to solve a problem of public interest. In 1913 the Department of Labor was created by the passage of 29 USCS §551. Its purpose is to improve working conditions. Until the Department of Labor was established, labor problems were intermingled with business and commerce problems.

Section 551 follows:

§551. Establishment of Department; Secretary; seal

There is hereby created an executive department in the Government to be called the Department of Labor, with a Secretary of Labor, who shall be the head thereof, to be appointed by the President, by and with the advice and consent of the Senate; and who shall receive a salary [of twelve thousand dollars per annum], and whose tenure of office shall be like that of the heads of the other executive departments; [and section one hundred and fifty-eight of the Revised Statutes is hereby amended to include such department,] and the provisions of title four of the Revised Statutes, including all amendments thereto, are hereby made applicable to said department; and the Department of Commerce and Labor shall hereafter be called the Department of Commerce, and the Secretary thereof shall be called the Secretary of Commerce, and the Act creating the said Department of Commerce and Labor is hereby amended accordingly. The purpose of the Department of Labor shall be to foster, promote, and develop the welfare of the wage earners of the United States, to improve their working conditions, and to advance their opportunities for profitable employment. The said Secretary shall cause a seal of office to be made for the said department of such device as the President shall approve and judicial notice shall be taken of the said seal.

(March 4, 1913, ch 141, §1, 37 Stat. 736.)

In a similar vein, Congress sought to protect the health and safety of workers by enacting 29 USCS §651, which formed the Occupational Safety and Health Agency.
Section 651 follows:

§651. Congressional statement of findings and declaration of purpose and policy

[(a)] The Congress finds that personal injuries and illnesses arising out of work situations impose a substantial burden upon, and are a hindrance to, interstate commerce in terms of lost production, wage loss, medical expenses, and disability compensation payments.

(b) The Congress declares it to be its purpose and policy, through the exercise of its powers to regulate commerce among the several States and with foreign nations and to provide for the general welfare, to assure so far as possible every working man and woman in the Nation safe and healthful working conditions and to preserve our human resources—

(1) by encouraging employers and employees in their efforts to reduce the number of occupational safety and health hazards at their places of employment, and to stimulate employers and employees to institute new and to perfect existing programs for providing safe and healthful working conditions;

Just as Congress may pass a statute creating an agency, it may pass a statute abolishing an agency. This happened to the oldest administrative agency, the ICC, in 1996. The ICC Termination Act of 1995 became effective on January 1, 1996. The following is a copy of the ICC termination.

PUBLIC LAW 104–88 [H.R. 2539]; December 29, 1995
ICC TERMINATION ACT OF 1995

An Act to abolish the Interstate Commerce Commission, to amend subtitle IV of title 49, United States Code, to reform economic regulation of transportation, and for other purposes.

Be it enacted by the Senate and House of Representatives of the United States of America in Congress assembled,

TITLE 1—ABOLITION OF INTERSTATE COMMERCE COMMISSION

SEC. 101. ABOLITION

The Interstate Commerce Commission is abolished.

CHAPTER SUMMARY

Administrative law developed as the government spread its powers among agencies. Although applicable to the nation since its origins, the term administrative law came into usage after 1887 when the Interstate Commerce Commission was created and given the power to make rules and regulations. It became apparent that a system of laws unique to governing the public interest was growing separately from the constitutional, tort, and criminal systems of laws. Administrative laws result from Congress delegating some of its powers to agencies in order to solve society's complex problems and from state legislatures delegating authority to their agencies. A control on this power is contained in the tripartite separation of powers of government into executive, legislative, and judicial branches, with each branch acting as a check and balance over each other's powers and agency powers. Because the Delegation Doctrine theory of government, which allows transfer of power from the people to the legislature but frowns upon the legislature transferring its powers, legislatures must establish guidelines that meet the sufficient standards test and provide criteria for setting standards that meets the intelligible principle test. Although the Delegation Doctrine is not strictly followed in practice, the theory is upheld because it hinders any autocratic control of government by one person or group. A safeguard developed to protect individuals who appear before the delegated agencies is the Administrative Procedure Act, which codifies procedural rights for federal agencies; most states have similar acts.

Key Terms

adjudicatory
checks and balances
Delegation Doctrine
federalism
intelligible principle
private rights

public rights
quasi
separation of powers
sufficient standards
tripartite

Key Terms Crossword

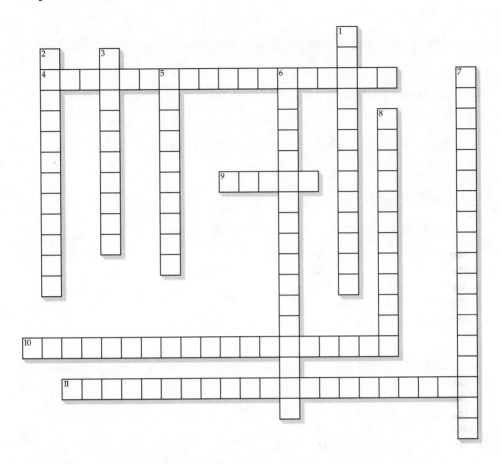

Across
4. Transfer of power to legislature
9. Resembling, almost
10. Adequate guidelines
11. Appropriate criteria given by agency

Down
1. Individual rights
2. Resolving disputes
3. Division into federal/state governments
5. Having three parts
6. Safeguards of government power
7. Three branches of government
8. The people's rights

Statements

Student Study Time Hints: Look for answers under Chapter / Section

Chapter 2 / Section A. Interests stressed by Supreme Court: _____

Section B. Transfers a limited amount of power to agencies: _____

Section C. Three branches of government: _____, _____, and _____

Section D. Under Intelligible Principle, the legislature gives agencies: _____.

Section E. Labor Department was established to: _____.

No Hints:

Makes laws: _____ Makes rules: _____

Separation of Power is a _____

Web Resources

http://newdeal.feri.org   History of New Deal (1930s)
www.sec.gov   Securities and Exchange Commission
www.pbs.org/wgbh/pages/amex/dustbowl   History of Dust Bowl (1930s)

Advanced Studies

Delegation and Separation of Powers are concepts that are inherent in the forms and documents individuals utilize in dealing with agencies. This section uses state and federal documents as well as a famous historical tract to further illuminate these two concepts.

The documents are:

Document 1 — Texas — Application for Permit
Document 2 — California — Notice of Intent
Document 3 — Small Business Administration 15 USCS §§631–633
Document 4 — James Madison, The Federalist Papers, No. 51 (1788)

Documents 1 and 2 are good illustrations of the practical application of the delegation of authority to agencies by both the state and federal governments. Two states, Texas and California, allow businesses access by a permit system; these businesses are attempting to alleviate a severe problem — lack of water. The Department of Resources from each state must approve the applications for businesses to initiate precipitation by altering cloud formations (Document 1). This weather control may have vast environmental consequences to businesses and individuals in the target areas. Because of this potential impact, the state prints notification of the application for all concerned to register their opinions (Document 2). The agencies are making judgments on the expertise of the applicants. Because both states have similar processes for regulating weather control in the applications and notices of intent, only an application from one state is provided.

When creating agencies through enabling acts, Congress generally explains the reasons for the agencies. Section 631 of Document 3 sets out Congress' justification for the delegation of legislative authority in creating the Small Business Administration.

Document 4 expresses James Madison's views on the separation of powers set out in the Constitution. Included in paper No. 51 is the basis of the bicameral philosophy and the checks and balances theory. In 1787 the Constitutional Convention in Philadelphia adjourned leaving delegates with the demanding task of convincing the various states to ratify this new constitution. New York was a crucial state with much opposition to the new constitution — three of its four delegates to the convention had protested and walked out of the Philadelphia convention. To garner New York's vote, a series of articles were sent to the New York papers explaining the rationale behind the Constitution; these are called the Federalist Papers, authored by Alexander Hamilton, John Jay, and James Madison. Hamilton later became Secretary of the Treasury, Jay excelled in foreign affairs, and Madison became the fourth President of the United States (1809–1817).

Outline and/or List

1. In Document 1, businesses need a permit to solve a severe water shortage problem. List the specifics in Section V, Evaluation. (page 58)

2. In Document 2, California publishes the notice of intent. Outline the purpose of the project. (page 58)

3. In Document 3, list five purposes of the policy in 15 USCS §631. (page 59)

4. In the last eight sentences in Document 4, James Madison discusses government controls. List three controls over government. (page 63)

Analyzing Documents and Practices

1. In Document 1, Texas application permit, list some of the topics the agency requests. (page 57)

2. In Document 3, how will the agency fulfill its role? (page 60)

3. On page 39, the Supreme Court invalidated §9c of the NIRA because of insufficient standards. Do you think the Small Business Administration is supplied sufficient standards in Document 3, §§631–633? (pages 60–62)

4. In Document 4, how does James Madison think each department should be constructed? (page 62)

Take Home Exam

True/False 1. Administrative Law defines legal powers and limits of agencies.

True/False 2. The judicial branch creates administrative agencies.

True/False 3. A Reorganization Plan creates a new agency by transferring powers from other agencies.

True/False 4. The first administrative law established the Justice Department.

True/False 5. The Delegation Doctrine is the legislature giving some powers to agencies.

True/False 6. In *Panama Refining* (1935), delegation was struck down by the Supreme Court during recovery from the Great Depression.

True/False 7. The first administrative law established the Interstate Commerce Commission (ICC).

True/False 8. Congress creates administrative agencies.

True/False 9. Administrative laws define an agency's legal limits.

True/False 10. The executive branch supplies money to agencies.

Complete Diagrams

1. **Diagram** a timeline of Administrative Law's growth. (pages 32–33)

Administrative Law Timeline

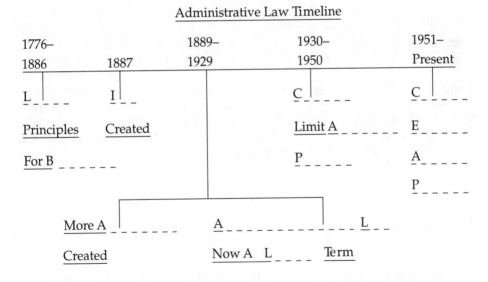

2. **Diagram** the four problems the NIRA addressed. (page 39)

3. **Diagram** the interests 15 USCS §631 addresses. (page 60)

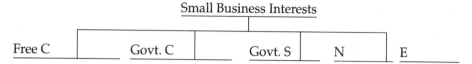

Small Business Interests

| Free C | | Govt. C | | Govt. S | N | E |

Three Venues for Research

1. **In Book**   Explain the roles of the three branches of government.

2. **At Library**   (a) Count the number of mentions of agencies in two newspapers and one news magazine.
(b) Pick two of the reports and write a summary.

3. **On Internet**   Look up the Securities and Exchange Commission and its role in the 2008/2009 Stock Market collapse. Consult the following website:

   www.sec.gov

Internship

A hardware store owner is seeking assistance from your lawyer because of the slowing economy. Your lawyer tells you to research the Small Business Administration Statute, particularly 15 USCS §631(d). Write a memo on what you find. The store is in a low income area. (page 61)
Then try to find any facts and statistics about the national economy of the last few years — stock market, labor figures, unemployment, construction figures, bankruptcies. Have they gone up or down? Is the national economy in a slowdown or is it just the hardware business, or this particular hardware store? Write anything that is pertinent to showing the national economy's condition in your memo.

Documents

Document 1: Texas — Application for Permit

Project Operations Plan*

To Be Submitted by Texas Weather Modification Permit Applicants

The reason for requiring an applicant for a weather modification permit to submit a Project Operations Plan with the application is to provide

---

*Form furnished courtesy of the Texas Department of Water Resources.

Department staff and the Weather Modification Advisory Committee with a clear description of the proposed method of operation to be used in the weather modification project to achieve expected overall results. This plan is intended to serve as an operational guide to the Department. Its submission to the Department is not intended to impose operational restrictions on the project unless so stated in the permit.

The Project Operations Plan for the proposed weather modification project is expected to be detailed and to include the following topics:

I.   Type of Weather Modification Activity
  A.   State the reason for implementing the proposed weather modification project and fully describe the overall intended results.
  B.   If the project is multi-purpose, i.e., rainfall augmentation and hail-suppression, state which purpose is "expected" to be the primary purpose for conducting cloud-seeding operations during the season. For example, a dual-purpose project designed to benefit agricultural interests during the growing season *may expect* to conduct cloud-seeding operations for hail-suppression about 70 percent of the time (dependent on location) and operations for rainfall augmentation about 30 percent of the time.

II. Equipment and Personnel
  A.   Provide a list of equipment to be used in support of the weather modification project operation. Manufacturer's specifications may be substituted for the description of weather radar units, aircraft, rain gauges, meteorological instruments, and telecommunication equipment.
  B.   Include a list and schedule of meteorological data which will be obtained and used in support of the weather modification project. For example, daily rawinsonde data obtained through the National Weather Service.
  C.   Include a list and description of all equipment that produces and dispenses the nucleating material to the cloud and all the expendable weather modification supplies to be used in the project. Specify the type of nucleating agent(s) to be used.
  D.   Describe briefly the responsibilities of key personnel with regard to the conduct of the weather modification operation.

III. Seeding Situation
  A.   Describe the various types of synoptic weather situations for the region which are expected to provide seedable clouds during the operational season.
  B.   For each synoptic weather situation, state the threshold conditions the seedable cloud usually achieves prior to the time the decision to seed is made. Some cloud parameters to consider for this description include: cloud base and cloud top temperatures; cloud growth rate; updraft characteristics; cloud appearance from the ground and aloft; radar echo

> return level; cloud liquid-water content; cloud vertical shear; heights of cloud base and top; rate of cloud movement across the project area.

IV. Seeding Methodology
  A. For each synoptic situation describe proposed procedures for applying the nucleating material to the seedable cloud.
  B. For each synoptic situation describe the seeding rates and expected total amounts as determined by observed cloud parameters.
  C. For each synoptic situation, state the anticipated cloud behavior subsequent to the application of the nucleating agent.

V. Evaluation
  Provide a realistic evaluation design, a priori, which may provide some insight into the anticipated cloud behavior. Include with this design: the proposed statistical approach; the controls to be used; the types of data to be collected; the period of the data base; data stratifications; and, the expected results.

Document 2: California — Notice of Intent

Published notice of intent to engage in operations — California.*

Notice of Intention to Modify Precipitation by Artificial Means

Notice is hereby given that Northern River Water Supply District of 1234 Boulder Road, Smalltown, California 93333, plans to conduct a continuing program of weather modification by artificial nucleation of clouds with silver iodide compounds and carbon dioxide (dry ice), with other substances considered appropriate to this project under acceptable scientific practices. The project will be supervised by Carla Lopez, Lopez Weather Associates, Inc., 701 Pebble Lane, Smalltown, California 93334, holder of weather resources management license number X45 of the State of California.

The purpose of the project is to increase precipitation in the Northern River Watershed above Winslow Dam in order to increase available water supply for the Northern River Water Supply District. The program will include both winter orographic and summer cumulous cloud seeding activities.

Weather modification equipment may be operated in parts of Stone, Pyrite, and Flint Counties, California.

The target area is the 425 sq. mile total watershed of the Northern River above Winslow Dam in Stone and Pyrite Counties, California. An area which may also be affected is the adjacent Granite Valley Watershed in Flint County, California.

---

*Sample notice furnished courtesy of the California Department of Water Resources.

The project operations may extend from October 1, 1981 through September 30, 1985.

A complete project description and a full environmental impact report may be reviewed by public agencies and the general public at the offices of Lopez Weather Associates, Inc., 701 Pebble Lane, Smalltown, CA 93334, Northern River Water Supply District, 1234 Boulder Road, Smalltown, CA 93333, and the Smalltown Public Library.

Comments on the proposed project should be sent to the Department of Water Resources, Weather Resources Management Group, P.O. Box 388, Sacramento, California 95802.

Dated _____, 19____.

S.A. Morris, Director
Northern River Water Supply District
1234 Boulder Road
Smalltown, CA 93333

Document 3: Small Business Administration 15 USCS §§631–633

CHAPTER 14A.   AID TO SMALL BUSINESS

Section
   631.   Declaration of policy
      (a) Aid, counsel, assistance, etc., to small business concerns.
      (b) Assistance to compete in international markets.
      (c) Aid for agriculturally related industries; financial assistance.
      (d) Use of assistance programs to establish, preserve, and strengthen small business concerns.
      (e) Assistance to victims of floods, etc., and those displaced as result of federally aided construction programs.
      (f) Participation in free enterprise system by socially and economically disadvantaged persons.
      (g) Assistance to disaster victims under disaster loan program.
      (h) Assistance to women owned business.
      (i) Prohibition on the use of funds for individuals not lawfully within the United States.
      (j) Contract bundling.
  631a. Congressional declaration of small business economic policy
      (a) Foster small business.
      (b) Capital availability to small business.
  631b. Reports to Congress; state of small business
      (a) Report on Small Business and Competition.
      (b) Appendix to report.
      (c) Supplementary reports.
      (d) Referral to congressional committees.
      (e) Small business concerns owned by disadvantaged individuals and by women.

632. Small-business concern
    (a) Criteria.
    (b) "Agency" defined.
    (c) Qualified employee trust; eligibility for loan guarantee; definition; regulations for treatment of trust as qualified employee trust.
    (d) "Qualified Indian tribe" defined.
    (e) "Public or private organization for the handicapped" defined.
    (f) "Handicapped individual" defined.
    (g) "Energy measures" defined.
    (h) "Credit elsewhere" defined.
    (i) "Homeowners" defined.
    (j) "Small agricultural cooperative" defined.
    (k) "Disaster" defined.
    (l) "Computer crime" defined.
  (m) "Simplified acquisition threshold" defined.
    (n) "Small business concern" defined.
    (o) Definitions of bundling of contract requirements and related terms.
    (p) Definitions relating to HUBZones.
    (q) Definitions relating to veterans.

633. Small Business Administration
    (a) Creation; principal, branch, and regional offices.

§631. Declaration of policy

(a) Aid, counsel, assistance, etc., to small business concerns. The essence of the American economic system of private enterprise is free competition. Only through full and free competition can free markets, free entry into business, and opportunities for the expression and growth of personal initiative and individual judgment be assured. The preservation and expansion of such competition is basic not only to the economic well-being but to the security of this Nation. Such security and well-being cannot be realized unless the actual and potential capacity of small business is encouraged and developed. It is the declared policy of the Congress that the Government should aid, counsel, assist, and protect, insofar as is possible, the interests of small-business concerns in order to preserve free competitive enterprise, to insure that a fair proportion of the total purchases and contracts or subcontracts for property and services for the Government (including but not limited to contracts or subcontracts for maintenance, repair, and construction) be placed with small-business enterprises, to insure that a fair proportion of the total sales of Government property be made to such enterprises, and to maintain and strengthen the overall economy of the Nation.

(b) Assistance to compete in international markets. (1) It is the declared policy of the Congress that the Federal Government, through the Small Business Administration, acting in cooperation with the

Department of Commerce and other relevant State and Federal agencies, should aid and assist small businesses, as defined under this Act, to increase their ability to compete in international markets. . . .

(c) Aid for agriculturally related industries; financial assistance. It is the declared policy of the Congress that the Government, through the Small Business Administration, should aid and assist small business concerns which are engaged in the production of food and fiber, ranching, and raising of livestock, aquaculture, and all other farming and agricultural related industries; and the financial assistance programs authorized by this Act are also to be used to assist such concerns.

(d) Use of assistance programs to establish, preserve, and strengthen small business concerns. (1) The assistance programs authorized by sections [636(i) and 636(j)] are to be utilized to assist in the establishment, preservation, and strengthening of small business concerns and improve the managerial skills employed in such enterprises, with special attention to small business concerns (1) located in urban or rural areas with high proportions of unemployed or low-income individuals; or (2) owned by low-income individuals; and to mobilize for these objectives private as well as public managerial skills and resources.

(2)(A) With respect to the programs authorized by section [§636(j)], the Congress finds —

(i) that ownership and control of productive capital is concentrated in the economy of the United States and certain groups, therefore, own and control little productive capital;

(ii) that certain groups in the United States own and control little productive capital because they have limited opportunities for small business ownership;

(iii) that the broadening of small business ownership among groups that presently own and control little productive capital is essential to provide for the well-being of this Nation by promoting their increased participation in the free enterprise system of the United States;

(iv) that such development of business ownership among groups that presently own and control little productive capital will be greatly facilitated through the creation of a small business ownership development program, which shall provide services, including, but not limited to, financial, management, and technical assistance.[;]

(v) that the power to let sole source Federal contracts pursuant to section [§637(a)] can be an effective procurement assistance tool for development of business ownership among groups that own and control little productive capital; and

(vi) that the procurement authority under section [§637(a)] shall be used only as a tool for developing business ownership among groups that own and control little productive capital.

(B) It is, therefore, the purpose of the programs authorized by section 7(j) of this Act [15 USCS §636(j)] to —

(i) foster business ownership by individuals in groups that own and control little productive capital; and

(ii) promote the competitive viability of such firms by creating a small business and capital ownership development program to provide such available financial, technical, and management assistance as may be necessary.

§632. Small-business concern

(a) Criteria. (1) For the purposes of this Chapter, a small-business concern, including but not limited to enterprises that are engaged in the business of production of food and fiber, ranching and raising of livestock, aquaculture, and all other farming and agricultural related industries, shall be deemed to be one which is independently owned and operated and which is not dominant in its field of operation: *Provided*, that notwithstanding any other provision of law, an agricultural enterprise shall be deemed to be a small business concern if it (including its affiliates) has annual receipts not in excess of $750,000.

§633. Small Business Administration

(a) Creation; principal, branch, and regional offices. In order to carry out the policies of this Act there is hereby created an agency under the name "Small Business Administration" (herein referred to as the Administration),

Document 4: *James Madison*, The Federalist Papers, *No. 51 (1788)*

To the People of the State of New York:

To what expedient, then, shall we finally resort, for maintaining in practice the necessary partition of power among the several departments, as laid down in the Constitution? The only answer that can be given is, that as all these exterior provisions are found to be inadequate, the defect must be supplied, by so contriving the interior structure of the government as that its several constituent parts may, by their mutual relations, be the means of keeping each other in their proper places. Without presuming to undertake a full development of this important idea, I will hazard a few general observations, which may perhaps place it in a clearer light, and enable us to form a more correct judgment of the principles and structure of the government planned by the convention.

In order to lay a due foundation for that separate and distinct exercise of the different powers of government, which to a certain extent is admitted on all hands to be essential to the preservation of liberty, it is evident that each department should have a will of its own; and consequently should be so constituted that the members of each should have as little agency as possible in the appointment of the members of the others. Were this principle rigorously adhered to, it would require that all the appointments for the supreme executive, legislative, and judiciary magistracies should be drawn from the same fountain of authority, the people, through channels having no communication whatever with one another. Perhaps such a plan of constructing the several departments would be less difficult in practice than it may in contemplation appear. Some difficulties, however, and some additional expense would attend the execution of it. Some deviations, therefore, from the principle must be admitted. In the constitution of the judiciary department in particular, it might be inexpedient to insist rigorously on the principle: first, because peculiar qualifications being essential in the members, the primary consideration ought to be to select that mode of choice which best secures these qualifications; secondly, because the permanent tenure by which the appointments are held in that department, must soon destroy all sense of dependence on the authority conferring them.

It is equally evident, that the members of each department should be as little dependent as possible on those of the others, for the emoluments annexed to their offices. Were the executive magistrate, or the judges, not independent of the legislature in this particular, their independence in every other would be merely nominal.

But the great security against a gradual concentration of the several powers in the same department, consists in giving to those who administer each department the necessary constitutional means and personal motives to resist encroachments of the others. The provision for defense must in this, as in all other cases, be made commensurate to the danger of attack. Ambition must be made to counteract ambition. The interest of the man must be connected with the constitutional rights of the place. It may be a reflection on human nature, that such devices should be necessary to control the abuses of government. But what is government itself, but the greatest of all reflections on human nature? If men were angels, no government would be necessary. If angels were to govern men, neither external nor internal controls on government would be necessary. In framing a government which is to be administered by men over men, the greatest difficulty lies in this: you must first enable the government to control the governed; and in the next place oblige it to control itself. A dependence on the people is, no doubt, the primary control on the government; but experience has taught mankind the necessity of auxiliary precautions.

3

Agency Discretion

* reasonable choice
* expertise
* past practices

* options
* compliance
* penalties

CHAPTER OBJECTIVES

Agency discretion is the power of the agency to use its expertise in making choices among different actions.
You will discover in this chapter:

- Why agencies have discretion.
- When agencies use discretion.
- The effect of discretionary choices.
- The dangers of discretion.
- The safeguards legislatures create.
- The impact of past practices on discretion.
- How discretion may be abused.
- How abuses of discretion may be appealed.

CHAPTER OVERVIEW

An agency's discretion is the ability and opportunity for an agency to make choices between alternative agency actions, such as the agency deciding to levy fines against an individual violating a rule instead of choosing to issue a warning. Informal agency actions often allow much discretion, which, if properly utilized, is highly effective in an agency's daily operations. Yet, if the agency's discretionary powers are abused, the agency may become arbitrary and domineering. However, most agency discretion is properly administered and reasonable choices are made in processing claims; receiving and implementing individual input for new rules and policies; and in deciding to levy fines or pursue incarceration. Discretion is only reviewed by the courts for abuse, therefore it is a powerful agency tool. It is limited, however, by Constitutional safeguards, statutes, and political manuevering.

A.   Explanation of Discretion

Discretion is the power to make a choice among different actions or alternatives. An agency makes this choice based on its expertise.

Agency discretion is necessary because the laws enacted by the legislatures are not detailed and specific enough to apply to an individual action that presents itself before the agency. Conversely, agency statutes do not delineate each and every decision an agency administrator must make because agencies need the ability and flexibility to adapt to the changing conditions of society and technology without constantly seeking statute revisions. Inherent in discretion is the agency ability to choose between reasonable options.

Agencies use discretion primarily for informal agency processes such as processing claims, informal hearings, and negotiations. Discretion also is important in policy and rulemaking, as well as in the levying of penalties for noncompliance with agency rules.

Figure 3.1 outlines the concept of discretion and how it applies to an agency decision.

Figure 3.1   **Discretion**

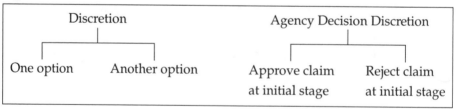

B.   Effect of Discretion on Agency Decisions

What are the dangers of an agency exercising discretion? If there is too much discretion, an agency may become arbitrary and dictatorial in its unlimited power. If there is too little discretion, the agency may become ineffective in the daily decision-making. At times, an administrator may need to choose between alternatives such as the necessity to simply instruct an individual or business to comply with an agency rule or to strictly enforce the rule by imposing penalties. If the agency regularly imposes overburdening penalties, the agency becomes domineering. If the agency makes no discretionary decisions to impose penalties, quite possibly no one will comply with the rules. It is presumed that discretionary decisions of agencies will follow a regularity; a client may assume that decisions on his/her situation today will follow similar decisions made by the agency in the past. Because many agency processes are informal and the daily decisions discretionary, discretion may be quite powerful. Although not considered abusive, a potential problem exists when agency personnel identify with their consistent clients, such as minorities at the Equal Opportunity agencies. Agencies are wary that this constant contact does not influence decisions and choices.

There are three major safeguards against agency discretion for individuals: (1) constitutional protections, (2) statutes, and (3) politics. The United States Constitution protects an individual's basic rights with due process, fairness, and search warrants. A second safeguard is the general boundaries of the enabling statute/act that specified the agency's mission. An agency's discretionary power is limited to its expertise; for example, a driver licensing agency may only make decisions on specific requirements for an individual to qualify for a driving license. The third limitation on agency discretion is the political scene. If too many agency decisions are viewed unfavorably by the public, a politician, in order not to lose an upcoming election, will exert pressure on the agency. Even with these safeguards, individuals still are subject to the daily discretionary power of agency personnel and their standards in solving and processing most agency functions.

 PARALEGAL PRACTICE EXAMPLE

As a paralegal in a workers' compensation case, you contact your state workers' compensation agency to determine the criteria that the agency has established for clients to receive benefits. You also check to see the amount the agency has allowed previously for the type of claim your client is filing.

1. Informal Actions

The daily work of administrative agencies encompasses mostly informal actions. There are two primary methods in which discretion affects these informal agency decisions:

1. the agency's adaptation to chronological, societal, and technological changes in areas delegated to the agency in the enabling statute and

2. the agency's choice of which process to use to adapt to these changes that may become problems needing agency solutions.

For instance, in the last twenty years computers have given individuals greater access to the communications industry, which is regulated by the Federal Communications Commission (FCC). The FCC adapts its policies to this new technology just as it adapted when television entered the communications arena. Perhaps the FCC will ask a user to stop interfering with fellow user's access to computer networks, or order the user to cease and desist, and threaten penalties.

Figure 3.2 outlines discretion in handling a complaint made to an administrative agency.

There are other decisions an agency could make in Figure 3.2: phone the company to solve the situation, or immediately inspect the premises for fear of hazardous health conditions. Whatever decision the agency makes is a matter of discretion based on the agency's expertise.

These informal decisions by the agency follow precedents established by the original discretionary decision of the agency when it began its functioning as an agency. "... [I]t is equally, if not more important, that

Figure 3.2   **Administrative Agency and Discretion**

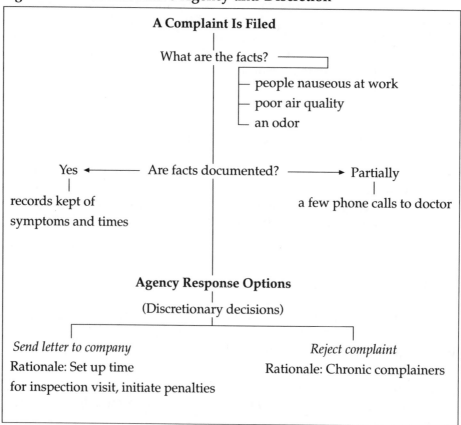

the procedure for informal decision, which will affect by far the greater number, be swift, simple and fair." (Report of the Attorney General's Committee on Administrative Procedure 38, 1941). Keep in mind that the agency's discretionary power is subject to inquiry by the clients of the agency; therefore, informal actions decided by discretion continue on the basis of mutual consent between the agency and the clients. If there is not mutual consent, the actions are subject to scrutiny to determine if they are reasonable. This questioning and review of informal agency actions has been upheld by the U.S. Supreme Court. "The reviewing court should always be able to determine that the discretion has not been exercised in a manner in which no reasonable administrator would act." (*Heckler v. Chaney*, 470 US 821, 1985)

This ability to have informal actions reviewed enables an agency to use discretion in a reasonable manner when making decisions. An example of discretion of an agency is its decision to issue a complaint when requested; the agency may request a complaint, as shown in the previous Figure 3.2. The following two figures summarize when discretion may be introduced in agency decisions.

Figure 3.3   **Agency Discretion**

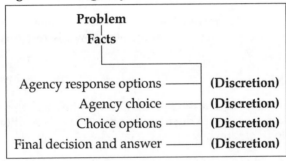

Figure 3.4   **Agency Discretion — Another View**

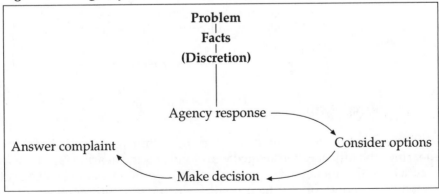

PARALEGAL PRACTICE EXAMPLE

You begin your job at a state welfare agency by sorting the claims filed by type of aid requested: age, education, gender. In tallying a month of claims, you realize the diversity; you also realize why your supervisor told you the qualities he seeks in paralegals are: adaptability, patience, and manners in handling clients.

CONCEPTS JOURNAL

Role Playing

Your instructor has assigned your paralegal class a lengthy research paper due the week of final exams. Your class objects.

Divide the class into three student teams who role play as members of the student agency that suggests rules.

Team 1 (Flexibility) develops rules that allow discretion in decision-making for the exam and report schedules.
Team 2 (Domineering) develops rules that are inflexible.
Team 3 (Ineffective) develops nebulous rules.

After the rules are developed and written, a member from each team reads them to the class, and states how discretion is used in each rule.

Journal Keeping

Each individual student should take notes on the team presentations to the class, and keep them under the title, "Discretion." Seek answers to the following:

1. Flexibility: Is there any in the presentations? Does flexibility work or fail?
2. Regularity: Which rules will last a long time and why?
3. Safeguards: Is there mutual consent or access for review?

Copy down the rule that best illustrates the opportunity for discretion to be utilized fully and correctly in the timing for the research reports.

---

2. Formal Actions

Discretion also is part of formal actions within agencies. For example, at hearings the officer of the agency who conducts the hearing is not always the officer of the agency who makes the final decision. Some hearing officers write a report of the hearing that includes a presentation of the evidence and the issues along with a recommendation for a decision. This is a discretionary procedure created by the agency because statutes do not require such a procedure. The agency has the discretionary power to make a report or not make a report of the evidence considered. Even in agencies in which it is normal procedure to make such reports, the decision of an agency officer not to make a report has been upheld by court decisions. "The Fifth Amendment guarantees no particular form of procedure; it protects substantial rights." (*Morgan II,* 304 US 1, 21 (1938))

This type of discretion has been changed by agencies following the Administrative Procedure Act, which requires administrative law judges to write a recommendation for a final decision; even though in their hearing officer function, they do not make the final decision. Remember, the statutes give the decision-making power to the head of the agency, not the entire agency staff.

Agencies, such as the National Labor Relations Board and the Securities Exchange Commission, have used discretionary powers in their formal actions by allowing staff members to review evidence from a hearing and make a recommendation. Attempts by clients to have these agency memoranda and recommendations put into the record have been denied by the courts. These reviews by members other than the hearing officer are considered to be part of the agency process if so desired by the agency.

PARALEGAL PRACTICE EXAMPLE

The new head of the environmental agency where you are a paralegal thinks the hearing officers' decisions on hazardous waste have been veering too far afield of the original statutes. You are to find the basis of the statute and work forward. You start by searching the index of the U.S. Code.

C. Past Practice and Discretion

The agency enforces the enabling statute by making decisions; these decisions are repeated in similar situations. This reoccurrence of the same decision-making creates past practice, which allows for the predictability in similar future cases. Some of these discretionary decisions will become rules of the agency.

There is a presumption toward regularity of agency decisions that is based on the expertise of the agency staff in making professional choices. Following previous decisions not only allows regularity in decisions, but also forestalls duplication of time and effort. Even though resources may be limited, the agency must follow its own rules in each individual action it addresses. The courts uphold this. "For once an agency exercises its discretion and creates the procedural rules under which it desires to have its actions judged, it denies itself the right to violate these rules. If an agency in its proceedings violates its rules and prejudice results, any action taken as a result of the proceedings cannot stand." *Pacific Molasses Co. v. FTC*, 356 F2d 386, 387, 390 (5th Cir. 1966) accord, *Kelly v. Railroad Retirement Board,* 625 F2d 486, 492-493 (3d Cir. 1980).

Following past practices can create a present result that appears not to follow past practices. For example, a company has used information gathered from past practices in awarding its annual bonuses; but when the national economy was in a slump, there was grumbling and poor morale concerning the bonus program; workers made accusations that the department heads were keeping the bonuses for themselves. The company realized it had to fully explain its rationale for its bonus program. The company issued the following written (and obviously, long overdue) explanation of its bonus policy:

1. bonuses are linked to company profits
2. 20% of profits go to bonuses
3. the hourly wage of each employee and the years of service determine the percentage of the bonus.

Even though the bonus program followed past practice, the employees had been part of a growing company for years; not one in a slump therefore the bonuses were now down. In a similar way, agencies base their present solutions on past practices that have proved successful, but the agencies must be ready to explain their actions.

1.   Examples of Discretion in Agency Decisions

An agency, such as a licensing board, is established by a statute. The licensing board makes decisions based on the expertise of its staff and determines the criteria for attaining, and retaining, a professional license. Much of the minute detailing is based on the discretionary decision-making of the board of experts, because each level of criteria is not written, either in the statute or in the agency rules. Therefore, the original members of the agency licensing board, by having the discretionary power to make decisions, begin to establish conduct requirements that are followed by subsequent agency boards in similar situations. These past practices of discretionary decision-making may become standards and rules.

Why were these decisions left to discretion and not written in the rules? Rules can be rigid and take a lengthy time to be adopted, or later adapted and changed. A criteria for professional conduct may change; for example, advertising in the legal profession. Today lawyers may advertise with quite visible, large ads, while a decade ago many states considered that type of advertising to be unprofessional attorney conduct. The agency licensing board has the discretionary powers to adapt to this newly accepted conduct without changing the enabling statute. Flexibility is paramount for successful performance by agencies. Discretion allows agencies to conform to acceptable conduct for today; conduct that may have been considered unacceptable in previous decades.

PARALEGAL PRACTICE EXAMPLE

It is time for license renewal at the insurance firm where you are a paralegal. You contact the licensing agency to see if the criteria has changed for insurance brokers' licenses.

One agency that utilizes discretion is the Internal Revenue Service (IRS). If the IRS decides tax fillings are wrong or fraudulent, it can take a monetary action, demanding money with a late fee; can take a monetary-penalty action, seeking money owed with interest, costs and penalties; can take a monetary action and file charges that lead to imprisonment. Even though the broad powers are part of the discretionary power of the IRS, the agency must adhere to reasonable, non-arbitrary decision-making. This decision-making is not only based on the violation's seriousness, but also on the deterrent value to other taxpayers who may make similar incorrect filings.

Figure 3.5 shows the various discretionary decisions the IRS can make if a tax filing is incorrect.

Figure 3.5   **IRS — Discretionary Decisions**

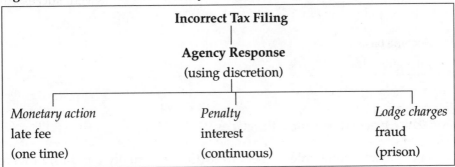

Discretion and past practice is used also by the Federal Trade Commission (FTC) as it has accumulated decisions on unfair competition over the years. The past practice discretionary decisions have become precedents for many of the standards the FTC uses to determine and establish the criteria for denoting unfair competition.

Figure 3.6 illustrates how the pattern of past practice and discretionary decisions may become the basis for new rules and future decisions.

PARALEGAL PRACTICE EXAMPLE

Your attorney's client wants to assess her chances of winning before the local zoning board in order to decide whether to pay a great deal of money for plans and legal advice. As a paralegal, you visit your local zoning board to ascertain how to compile a list of the zoning board decisions on your client's type of problem. A clerk explains how the computer program will facilitate your search for information.

Figure 3.6   **Past Practice and Discretion**

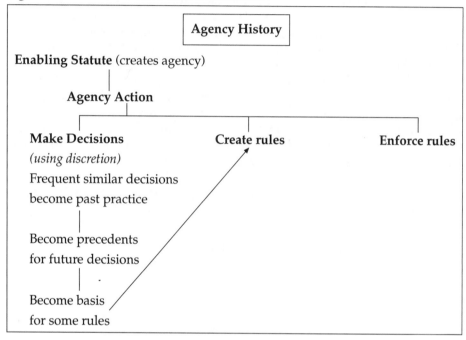

2. Effect of Agency Practices

People and companies expect to be treated equally and fairly by the government; when they believe they are being treated unfairly, they become concerned, even angry. Over the years the television industry has had its share of concerns with agency treatment. In 1990, the Children's Television Act was passed, ordering television stations to have at least three hours of educational children programs each week. This change was to happen before the stations received their license renewal. Initially, the stations argued for their First Amendment rights, but have dropped this argument. In 1996, it appeared that either the stations would voluntarily accept the federal regulation or the Federal Communications Commission (FCC) would take mandatory steps to ensure enforcement of the regulations, based on the power that stations promise public service for the use of the public airwaves. As in other licensing agencies, the FCC has the power to refuse to grant license renewal and the power to revoke licenses.

Earlier in the 1960s, the FCC established new proceedings for license renewal; prior to this change stations had their operating licenses renewed on the basis of each individual application. The new proceedings changed from this individual approach to a comparative approach—judging the renewal license with other licensee applications. The television industry protested this, claiming that a renewal applicant, and present holder of a license, was being treated in a similar manner to a new applicant.

In this case, *Greater Boston Television Corp. v. FCC*, 444 F2d 841 (D.C. Cir. 1970), cert. denied, 403 US 923 (1971), the FCC cited it powers of discretion in clarifying that the case was an unusual situation, and that the FCC had the discretionary power to change its proceedings. The industry appealed to the courts. In *Greater Boston*, Judge Harold Leventhal stated,

> . . . the Commission's policies are in flux. An agency's view of what is in the public interest may change, either with or without a change in circumstances. But an agency changing its course must supply a reasoned analysis indicating that prior policies and standards are being deliberately changed, not casually ignored, and if an agency glosses or swerves from prior precedents without discussion it may cross the line from the tolerably terse to the intolerably mute.

Discretion, and decisions based on discretion, do not have to be agreed on by all the parties; but, they must be reasonable and based on a rational process. The court upheld the FCC's right to adapt its proceedings based on its power of discretion. Agency reasoning should

> promote results in the public interest by requiring the agency to focus on the values served by its decision, and hence releasing the clutch of unconscious preference and irrelevant prejudice. It furthers the broad public interest of enabling the public to repose confidence in the process as well as the judgment of its decision-makers. (*Greater Boston*)

If agency discretion is not backed by reasonableness, it will be questioned and brought into court actions and placed under scrutiny. The effect of this is increased judicial review of agency decisions.

Figure 3.7 depicts how discretionary decisions and agency treatment must be based on reasonableness.

Figure 3.7   **Effect of Reasonableness on Past Practice**

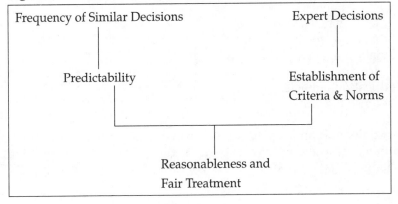

PARALEGAL PRACTICE EXAMPLE

You are a real estate paralegal; or in school studying to be in that field of law. What a fall in home prices, and jobs!

What do administrative agencies have to do with that, your job crisis?

You may be surprised to know that the U. S. Federal Trade Commission is right on top of the fraud that has been discovered in this home mortgage economic quagmire. And you can keep of top of it right in your local newspapers.

The *Boston Sunday Herald,* January 18, 2009, reports on "foreclosure fix-it firms" that are being investigated for actions like accepting $1200 from a home owner to save their homes, and doing nothing. The home and the $1200 is lost! And this is after they have guaranteed their services to these frightened home owners.

In the article "Feds Target Foreclosure Fix-it Firms," author Kenneth R. Harvey writes that Federal Trade Commission spokeswoman Cindy Liebes says these schemes to supposedly rescue foreclosure home owners are increasing across the nation. One firm agreed to pay $1.2 million to settle a lawsuit.

The article lists ways to avoid these schemes.

D.   Expertise and Agency Decisions

Agencies function because of the expertise of their personnel. Just a sample list of the types of agencies indicates the vastness of the subjects handled by government experts:

> environment agencies
> commerce agencies
> transportation agencies
> drug and alcohol agencies
> welfare agencies
> police agencies
> housing agencies
> aviation agencies
> space agency
> education agencies
> defense agency

In their daily operations agencies come in contact with diverse members of the public; some themselves experts in their fields and others with little knowledge. It falls upon the agency to adapt itself to the complexities of such a vast, diverse clientele. It is through the agency's discretionary powers and by relying on the technical knowledge of experts that the agency accomplishes this feat. Equally important is the experience of the agency personnel with similar situations. Of course, agency personnel need to be vigilant against adopting attitudes of indifference or of cronyism with clients who utilize agency services often.

Perhaps, you or someone you know may become an expert. Below is a list of possible experts:

Agency	*Expert*
Water resources	engineer
Hazardous waste	chemist
Aid to elderly	physician
Aid to children	social worker
Attorney licensing board	attorney
Plumber licensing board	plumber
Commerce commission	businessman
Labor department	union official
All agencies	experienced employees

1. Different Standards in Each Agency

Each agency develops its own standards. Agencies regulating public safety and security have more stringent standards than an agency regulating the licensing of contractors. An agency with stringent standards has less discretion in its decision-making. Yet, even if standards are stringent, agencies must exhibit fairness in the discretion allowed for their decisions. For example, a utility company must show that there is a proper correlation between service given and compensation charged.

Agencies involved in public morality usually develop standards that conform to the public view in order not to be charged with censorship. Professional licensing agencies establish standards of competence by following the advice of their own and other experts in their field.

PARALEGAL PRACTICE EXAMPLE

As you compile your documents, a rush job, your attorney tells you to be certain that the compliance with safety standards documents are attached because the Occupational Safety and Health Agency (OSHA) will not allow any further processing without them. The agency time limit that you must meet will not allow you to list and doublecheck all the documents to be submitted. You decide to take the time to check and doublecheck the safety standard compliance documents.

2. Complexities in Decisions

The agency officer has to read or hear the claim/complaint, consider the facts, decide which facts are pertinent, and make a determination based on agency regulations after all the options have been considered. Unfortunately options are not necessarily provable; this is the reason agency decisions are complex and require discretion.

Although it might seem more appropriate and fair to have tightly written rules adhering to any situation an agency might encounter, in actuality the fairness often lies in discretion. With discretion government authority is individualized, and more able to adapt to the vagaries of individuals. This flexibility allows government to curtail the seemingly endless list of requirements for individuals. In many areas greater access is given to more individuals for government programs because the variety of their needs are met through fewer standards and more discretion.

Of course, there is the possibility of an unknown bias held by the individual making the decision. This bias may not even be perceived by that individual. Usually the appeal system in the agencies corrects this situation. Discretion must be founded in reasonableness and decisions supported by a rational examination of the facts.

 ## PARALEGAL PRACTICE EXAMPLE

You decide you would like to work for a state agency, helping people with your skills. Perhaps helping people with the information and forms they would need if they have lost their jobs.

Your supervisor tells you to think of this scenario to understand the clients of this state unemployment agency:

> You start work and suddenly you are 'let go'—lose your job; business at your place is bad. Layoffs are happening. The administrative agency you will visit is the state Division of Unemployment Assistance. You will have to fill out forms to qualify for aid to get through this period.
>
> If you qualify, you'll receive a weekly check (your benefit) which will be less than 50% of your regular pay. You must file a claim every week, stating any income you earned. Some states offer health insurance. Some states demand you attend employment seminars where you will be trained to operate a computer to look for jobs. Many states have these types of career centers.

As a paralegal you could seek a career at these state unemployment agencies because you have training to look up the facts that people coming into the centers need to file a claim. You can read forms and help people with filling them out. You have telephone finesse to call around for other information needed.

E. Abuse of Discretionary Power

What if a client believes an agency has abused its power of discretion? First, the client goes through the appeal process set up within the agency to try and rectify the situation. Before it will review any agency action or decision, the agency requires reasons supporting the client's request for review; this includes the rejection of an initial application or claim. After the client has exhausted the agency's appeal process, the abusive action can be appealed through the courts. Both questions of law and fact may be appealed to the courts for judicial review; but all agency appeals must be utilized or the courts will not accept the case.

The Administrative Procedure Act (APA) explains the appeal process in 5 USC §557(c)(1)(2) and (3):

> (c) Before a . . . decisions on agency review of the decision . . . the parties are entitled to a reasonable opportunity to submit for the consideration . . .
> (1) proposed findings and conclusions; or
> (2) exceptions to the decisions . . .
> (3) supporting reasons for the exceptions or proposed findings or conclusions.

If the agency appeal process has been exhausted, the client may file a petition with the appropriate court, depicting what the abuse is and what law they are citing. The courts decide if there is abuse. If the court decides in the affirmative, the case is remanded back to the agency to be reassessed according to guidelines set by the court.

Questions of fact are more difficult for a court to review. The courts are the experts in law; the agencies are the experts in facts. The agencies base their right of discretion on being experts on facts. Still, the courts have heard cases on abuse of discretion concerning questions of facts; such as the validity attributed to certain facts presented as evidence.

Discretion is not reviewable by the courts; *the abuse* of discretion is reviewed. The APA states:

> To the extent necessary to a decision and when presented, the reviewing court shall decide all relevant questions of law, interpret constitutional and statutory provisions, and determine the meaning or applicability of the terms of an agency action. The reviewing court shall—
> (2) hold unlawful and set aside agency actions, findings, and conclusions found to be—
> (A) arbitrary, capricious, and abuse of discretion, or otherwise not in accordance with law; (§706)

Therefore, in a practical sense, all agency actions are reviewable if agency powers are being abused. Courts review abuse of discretion of law according to the Constitution, statutes and cases; courts review facts according to the weight of the evidence for the agency to make its decision.

Often, the case is sent back (remanded) to the agency, but the court may substitute its own opinion in place of the agency decision. The usual procedure, however, is for the court to limit itself to the record of the agency and to return the case to the agency for it to reconsider and amend its decision.

 PARALEGAL PRACTICE EXAMPLE

As a paralegal for a zoning board attorney, you have to gather information from the construction industry about the structural power of some wooden planks. The zoning board had ruled against their use in construction; but the building company had appealed through the courts, supplying the same evidence on the strength of the planks. The court sent the case back to the zoning board for reconsideration of the case and ruling. Your attorney wants you to gain a consensus from experts in the field on whether they agree with the zoning board ruling on the evidence or the court's ruling.

1. Appeals within Agencies

If a claim is filed and rejected by an agency, the claimant may ask for review of the rejection. Different agency personnel than those who rejected the claim will review the action. If this decision is unfavorable, the claimant may seek a hearing before a hearing officer, usually called an administrative law judge. If the hearing results in an unfavorable decision the claimant may request that it be reviewed. If this is another ruling against the claimant, the claimant may make a written request for appeal within a certain time period (usually 60 days). With this request the claimant files evidence. Some agencies will allow a longer time period to supply evidence.

If the appeals council dismisses the case, the claimant may appeal to the courts. If the appeals council accepts the case for review, it does one of two things:

1. Reviews the evidence and gives a decision.
2. Sets up a hearing, may request additional evidence. If the appeals council rules unfavorably on the hearing, the claimant may then appeal to the courts.

All agency avenues of appeal have to be exhausted before the appellate courts will hear the case.

Examples of these types of actions are reported on television, radio, and in the newspapers regularly. For instance, in May 1996, the Chrysler Corporation asked to have an administrative law judge review an order from a California state agency that stopped Chrysler from selling cars for sixty days in California. The agency had investigated a complaint and found that Chrysler was reselling "lemon cars" — cars found to be faulty and returned to Chrysler.

Figure 3.8 is an outline of an appeal process of an agency.

Figure 3.8   **An Agency Appeal Process**

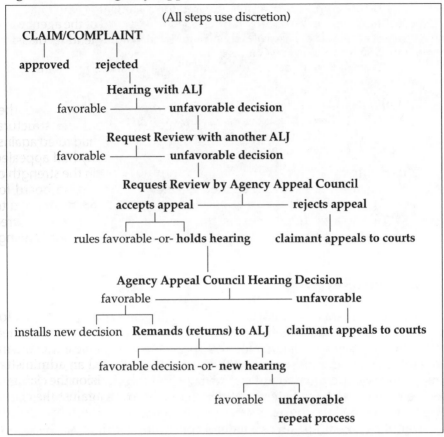

(All steps use discretion)

CLAIM/COMPLAINT
  | |
approved   rejected
                       |
                 Hearing with ALJ
        favorable ———|——— unfavorable decision
                                |
                 Request Review with another ALJ
        favorable ———|——— unfavorable decision
                                |
                 Request Review by Agency Appeal Council
        accepts appeal ———|——— rejects appeal
              | |
    rules favorable -or- holds hearing   claimant appeals to courts
                      |
                 Agency Appeal Council Hearing Decision
        favorable ———|——— unfavorable
              | |
installs new decision Remands (returns) to ALJ   claimant appeals to courts
                              |
                 favorable decision -or- new hearing
                                    |
                             favorable unfavorable
                                        repeat process

10 minutes:
> Team 1: Prepare plausible excuses for a student accused of cheating; keep the list.
> Teams 2 and 3: Take rules from Team 1 and Team 4 and prepare your case for the Review Council.
> Team 4: Take rule from Team 1 and decide criteria to look for in the hearing.

20 minutes:
> Team 3: Present case before Review Council.
> Team 4: Listen and decide if you wish to question Team 2; make decision and write it down.

10 minutes:
> Team 4: Tell class your decision.
> Team 1: Tell class your plausible excuse list; compare with Team 4's decision.

2. Court Review

After a claimant has exhausted all the agency processes of review and appeal, the claimant may then seek judicial review, which is a court examination of the agency decision. Not all appeals are accepted by the courts; claimants need to demonstrate that they are injured by the agency action. Jurisdiction is imperative to judicial review; social security cases, by statute, are reviewed by the federal district courts; other federal agencies are reviewed in appellate courts. State agencies have review in state courts, however, if a claimant believes a federal constitutional right has been violated by a state agency, the claimant should seek review in a federal court. Timing is another factor that influences the courts' accepting appeals; there is a deadline (usually 60 days) set by agencies in which the claimant may seek court review. Any petitions for appeal filed beyond the deadline are not accepted.

If the petition to the court is accepted, the court reviews the record of the case, the evidence presented to the agency, and the reasons for the agency decision. Issues that were not raised during the agency proceedings may not be raised by a lawyer at the trial. If new evidence is presented, the court sends the case back to the agency for a ruling on the new evidence. When the final court decision is made, the court often remands that decision to the agency to implement the court recommendations.

PARALEGAL PRACTICE EXAMPLE

You are a paralegal working on the appeal of a major case for your law firm. There are five other paralegals in the office, working on different cases. You've noticed constant loud talking and other noises by one paralegal that disturbs your concentration. What should you do? Nothing.

This is a common ploy to get your case or job. Remember those students that are loud in the library during exam preparation time, disturbing the studying of those around them? It's the same game. If you are involved in a big stakes cases—money, business, drugs—other paralegals may join in the action. By doing nothing, you learn who are your possible career attackers. If one of these paralegals offers to xerox and hand in your work on a day you are ill or wish to leave early, you are prepared not to take this "helpful assistance."

In a big enough case, the loud paralegal may go so far as to put a microphone in your office to ensure you are hearing and being disturbed. Even though your part in the case may not seem to be important enough to warrant any of this, getting closer to your lawyer may be important to another paralegal.

How do you handle this problem? (1) Focus on your work. (2) Think this . . . you've arrived professionally! (At least your office competition thinks you have!)

F. Cases Upholding Discretion

Two Supreme Court cases are notable for their rulings on discretion and administration agencies. One (*Overton*) examines discretion when an agency takes an action; the other (*Chaney*) when an agency refuses to take an action.

In *Citizens to Preserve Overton Park, Inc. v. Volpe*, 401 US 402 (1971), the citizens appealed the Secretary of Transportation's decision to build a highway through a public park. He claimed his discretion gave him the power to choose that route over alternate routes. The citizens claimed this case was an exception to agency discretion. The Court said, ". . . the Secretary's decision here does not fall within the exception for action 'committed to agency discretion.' This is a very narrow exception."

In *Heckler v. Chaney*, 470 US 821 (1985), prisoners appealed the use of lethal drugs for executions, claiming the Federal Food and Drug Administration should investigate because they were not safe for human execution. The FDA refused to investigate according to their discretionary powers. The Court said, ". . . an agency's decision not to prosecute, or enforce, whether through civil or criminal process, is a decision generally committed to an agency's absolute discretion." The ". . . agency decision not to institute proceedings" was upheld.

STUDENT PRACTICE

"Jargon Bee"

This operates as a spelling bee, only the words are defined not spelled.

Rules:
1. Divide into two teams.
2. No answer longer than ten words.
3. Ten seconds allowed to begin answer.
4. Incorrect answerer must sit down.
5. Team with fewest members sitting down wins!

Instructor and/or judge may add or delete from list.

1. discretion	16. standard
2. ALJ	17. determination
3. expert	18. norm
4. review	19. enabling act
5. past practice	20. FCC
6. administrator	21. proceedings
7. complaint	22. hearing officer
8. APA	23. rule
9. precedent	24. FTC
10. claim	25. appeal council
11. writ of certiori	26. bias
12. appeal	27. board
13. law	28. statute
14. criteria	29. administrative agency
15. petition	30. professional conduct

CHAPTER SUMMARY

Discretion is the power of an agency to choose options and make decisions based on its staff's expertise. This expertise is necessary, because legislatures pass broad laws that must be applied to the individual situations that come before an agency. The agency rules and regulations are flexible enough to allow agency staff to adapt to changing conditions. To curtail abuse of discretion, agencies must explain their decisions, based on reasonableness and past practices. A claimant who objects to an agency decision may seek review of the decision through the agency appeal processes and the court review. Figure 3.9 charts the various components of agency discretion discussed in this chapter.

Figure 3.9   **Review of Agency Discretion**

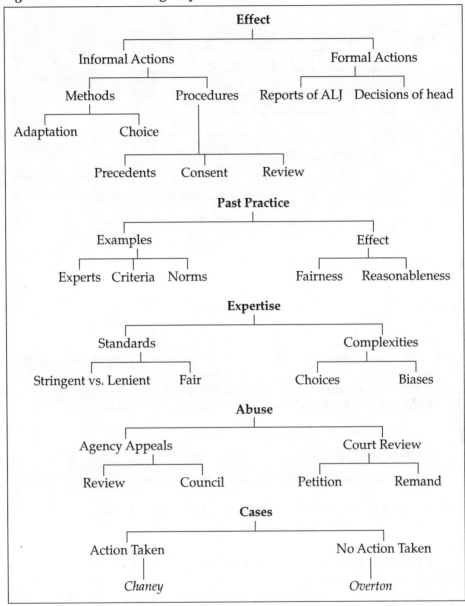

Key Terms

ALJ
appeal
appeal council
bias
board
criteria

discretion
expert
past practice
precedent
review

Key Terms Crossword

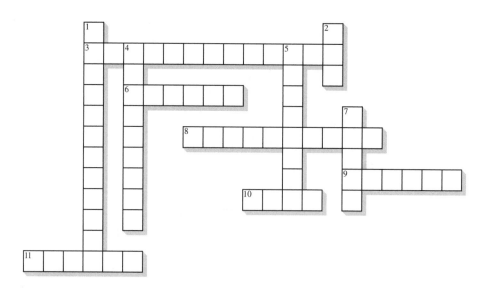

Across
3. Board reviewing decisions
6. Qualified person
8. Right to reasonable actions
9. Examination
10. Partiality, prejudice
11. Write request for review

Down
1. Similar past decisions
2. A hearing officer
4. Decision forming legal basis for future cases
5. Requirements
7. Agency executives

Statements

Student Study Time Hints: Look for answers under Chapter / Section

Chapter 3 / Section A. Discretion is the power to make a
c_____ between different actions.

Agency discretion is necessary because the laws of Congress
and legislatures are not d_____ and not
s_____ enough to apply to every situation.

P_____ c_____ and
c_____ are informal agency actions.

Section B.   The dangers of agency discretion are:
too much agency discretion — agency becomes _____.
too little agency discretion — agency becomes _____.

Section B.1./Figure 3.4   An agency uses discretion in informal actions when it decides its response by c_____

_____, _____ _____,

and _____ _____.

Section B.2.   Formal actions include h_____.

Section C.   _____ _____ is the repeating of agency decisions in similar situations.

Section C.1./Figure 3.5   The _____

_____ _____ uses discretion in agency decisions.

Section D.1.   Each agency develops its own _____.

Section E.   There is an a_____ _____ for the abuse of agency discretionary power.

Web Resources

www.whitehouse.gov   Access to federal government web pages
www.fcc.gov   Federal Communications Commission
www.gpoaccess.gov   Code of Federal Regulations

Advanced Studies

Agency discretion embodies freedom of action and responsibility. These actions affect both the agency and the people interacting with the agency. To further examine this topic and its implications, the following documents are presented in this section:

Document 1 — Representation of Parties at Social Security Administration 20 CFR §§404.1700 et seq.

Document 2 — *Dixon, Secretary of State of Illinois v. Love*, 431 US 105 (1972)

Document 3 — Illinois Statute 625 ILCS 5/6 206

Document 4 — Illinois Regulation 6–206

Document 5 — James O. Freedman, *Summary Actions by Administrative Agencies*, 40 U. Chi. L. Rev. I, 44–49 (1972)

Paralegals and legal assistants may represent clients at Social Security hearings. Document 1 provides the rules to follow in representing a party at the Social Security Administration, excerpted from the Code of Federal Regulations (CFR).

The *Dixon v. Love* decision (Document 2) is often studied for its due process issue; a claim that a statute (and subsequent rule) does not allow a hearing prior to a driver's license revocation is in violation of the Fourteenth Amendment. For this chapter on discretion, students should focus on the discretion decisions that are illustrated by this case and the accompanying statute (Document 3. Notice that the statute begins with discretion.), rule (Document 4), and article (Document 5) cited by the U.S. Supreme Court in the decision. In *Dixon* the government addressed its powers of discretion in creating more concrete rules and regulations; it actually limited some of its own powers of discretion.

Please note the following when reading the case (which is often cited in other cases, pro and con):

1. Using his discretion, the Illinois Secretary of State (an executive department and therefore an administrative agency) created a rule which does not allow hearings before suspension or revocation of licenses.

2. At issue is whether the driver received his constitutional protections.
3. Regulations and rules define procedures for discretionary suspension.
4. These regulations limit discretionary power.
5. The Secretary of State had broad discretionary powers with which he created rules that limit his discretionary powers. The court applauds this and cites the Freedman article. (Document 5. This article is cited in the footnotes of *Dixon*. The Court comments on the narrowing of discretion by making rules. Summary action may be temporary or emergency action, which is applicable to drivers' licenses being suspended or revoked.)
6. Although the District Court upheld the driver's argument, the U.S. Supreme Court favored the Secretary of State and reversed the U.S. District Court's ruling.

Outline and/or List

1. Outline the three major safeguards of agency discretion. (page 67)

2. Document 2 illustrates agency discretion in an agency action that is appealed on a due process issue. List some of the actions that the Secretary of State took. (Paragraph 1, page 94)

3. In Document 1, list three rules of conduct and standards. (§§404 and 1740, page 93)

4. In Document 4, list the steps the Illinois Secretary of State must take after suspending or revoking a license. (§6–206(c)(1), page 97)

Analyzing Documents and Practices

1. In Document 1, analyze the difference between a lawyer representative and a non-lawyer representative. (§404.1705, page 91)

2. In Document 2, the Supreme Court stresses the public interest in agency informal hearings. Compare this view to the Attorney General's view on pages 68 and 69.

3. In Document 4, what does the Secretary of State take into consideration in making the decision? (page 96)

4. Summary actions are decisions, not fully explained by agencies, which rely on agency expertise. In Document 4, explain the two procedures in §6–206(c)(1). (page 97)

Take Home Exam

True/False   1.   Agency discretion is used in informal actions.

True/False   2.   Discretion is used in processing claims.

True/False   3.   Driving license agencies also license consumer groups.

True/False   4.   Agency claimants may not appeal to the courts.

True/False   5.   All agencies have the same standards.

True/False   6.   Discretion allows cases to be individualized.

True/False   7.   In *Greater Boston,* a change of agency policy is allowed if reasonable analysis is shown.

True/False   8.   Agencies are adaptable because of expert's technical knowledge.

True/False   9.   Past practice often becomes a precedent in agencies.

True/False   10.   In Document 1, your representative at a Social Security hearing may submit evidence.

Complete Diagram

Diagram the different levels of standards on page 77.

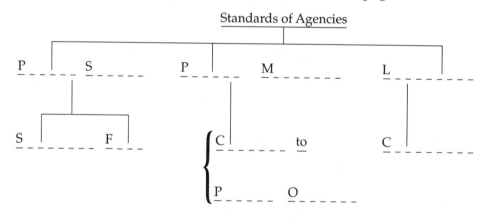

Three Venues of Research

1. **In Book** (a) In Document 1, explain the actions taken if the representative violates §§404.1740(c)(1) and (b) Examine §§404.1745 and 404.1750. (pages 93 and 94)

2. **At Library** (a) Choose an agency in the Code of Federal Regulations. Explain which rules are stringent and which rules are lenient, *or*

(b) Research the history of the Federal Communications Commission.

3. **On Internet** Look up the Code of Federal Regulations (CFR) for the Environmental Protection Agency (*www.epa.gov*). Explain §261.6 (40 CFR).

Internship

Your lawyer is preparing a case disputing a Federal Communications Commission decision. He instructs you to find the statute creating the FCC in the U.S. Codes. Then he wants you to find the rules in the Code of Federal Regulations (CFR).

He tells you to do the following:

(1) Write an outline of the FCC statute with detailed specifics
(2) Write a general outline of the FCC in the CFR; so he can decide which sections he may want researched at a later date

Documents

Document 1: Representation of Parties at Social Security Administration — 20 CFR §404.1700 et seq.

Subpart R — Representation of Parties
Authority: Secs. 205(a), 206, and 702(a)(5) of the Social Security Act (42 U.S.C. 405(a), 406, and 902(a)(5)).
Source: 45 FR 52090, Aug. 5, 1980, unless otherwise noted.

§404.1700 Introduction.

You may appoint someone to represent you in any of your dealings with us. This subpart explains, among other things —

(a) Who may be your representative and what his or her qualifications must be;

(b) How you appoint a representative;

(c) The payment of fees to a representative;

(d) Our rules that representatives must follow; and

(e) What happens to a representative who breaks the rules.

§404.1705 Who may be your representative.

(a) *Attorney.* You may appoint as your representative in dealings with us, any attorney in good standing who —

(1) Has the right to practice law before a court of a State, Territory, District, or island possession of the United States, or before the Supreme Court or a lower Federal court of the United States;

(2) Is not disqualified or suspended from acting as a representative in dealings with us; and

(3) Is not prohibited by any law from acting as a representative.

(b) *Person other than attorney.* You may appoint any person who is not an attorney to be your representative in dealings with us if he or she—

(1) Is generally known to have a good character and reputation;

(2) Is capable of giving valuable help to you in connection with your claim;

(3) Is not disqualified or suspended from acting as a representative in dealings with us; and

(4) Is not prohibited by any law from acting as a representative.

§404.1707 Appointing a representative.

We will recognize a person as your representative if the following things are done:

(a) You sign a written notice stating that you want the person to be your representative in dealings with us.

(b) That person signs the notice, agreeing to be your representative, if the person is not an attorney. An attorney does not have to sign a notice of appointment.

(c) The notice is filed at one of our offices if you have initially filed a claim or have requested reconsideration; with an administrative law judge if you requested a hearing; or with the Appeals Council if you have requested a review of the administrative law judge's decision.

§404.1710 Authority of a representative.

(a) *What a representative may do.* Your representative may, on your behalf—

(1) Obtain information about your claim to the same extent that you are able to do;

(2) Submit evidence;

(3) Make statements about facts and law; and

(4) Make any request or give any notice about the proceedings before us.

(b) *What a representative may not do.* A representative may not sign an application on behalf of a claimant for rights or benefits under title II of the Act unless authorized to do so under §404.612.

§404.1715 Notice or request to a representative.

(a) We shall send your representative—

(1) Notice and a copy of any administrative action, determination, or decision; and

(2) Requests for information or evidence.

(b) A notice or request sent to your representative, will have the same force and effect as if it had been sent to you.

§404.1720 Fee for a representative's services.

(a) *General.* A representative may charge and receive a fee for his or her services as a representative only as provided in paragraph (b) of this section.

(b) *Charging and receiving a fee.*

(1) The representative must file a written request with us before he or she may charge or receive a fee for his or her services.

(2) We decide the amount of the fee, if any, a representative may charge or receive.

§404.1740 Rules of conduct and standards of responsibility for representatives.

(a) *Purpose and scope.* (1) All attorneys or other persons acting on behalf of a party seeking a statutory right or benefit shall, in their dealings with us, faithfully execute their duties as agents and fiduciaries of a party. A representative shall provide competent assistance to the claimant and recognize the authority of the Agency to lawfully administer the process. . . .

(2) All representatives shall be forthright in their dealings with us and with the claimant . . .

(b) *Affirmative duties.* . . .

(1) Act with reasonable promptness to obtain the information and evidence that the claimant wants to submit in support of his or her claim. . . .

(2) Assist the claimant in complying as soon as practicable, with our requests for information or evidence . . .

(3) Conduct his or her dealings in a manner that furthers the efficient, fair and orderly conduct of the administrative decisionmaking process. . . .

(c) *Prohibited actions.* A representative shall not:

(1) In any manner or by any means threaten, coerce, intimidate, deceive or knowingly mislead a claimant, or prospective claimant or beneficiary, regarding benefits or other rights under the Act: . . .

(6) Attempt to influence, directly or indirectly, the outcome of a decision, determination or other administrative action by offering or granting a loan, gift, entertainment or anything of value to a presiding official. . . .

§404.1745 Violations of our requirements, rules, or standards.

When we have evidence that a representative fails to meet our qualification requirements or has violated the rules governing dealings with us, we may begin proceedings to suspend or disqualify that individual from acting in a representational capacity before us. We may file charges seeking such sanctions when we have evidence that a representative:

(a) Does not meet the qualifying requirements described in §404.1705;

(b) Has violated the affirmative duties or engaged in the prohibited actions set forth in §404.1740; or

(c) Has been convicted of a violation under section 206 of the Act.

[As amended, 71 FR 2876, Jan. 18, 2006]

§404.1750 Notice of charges against a representative.

(a) The Deputy Commissioner for Disability and Income Security Programs (or other official the Commissioner may designate), or his or her designee, will prepare a notice containing a statement of charges that constitutes the basis for the proceeding against the representative.

(b) We will send this notice to the representative either by certified or registered mail, to his or her last known address, or by personal delivery.

(c) We will advise the representative to file an answer, within 30 days from the date of the notice, or from the date the notice was delivered personally, stating why he or she should not be suspended or disqualified from acting as a representative in dealings with us.

Document 2: Dixon, Secretary of State of Illinois v. Love, *431 US 105 (1972)*

Appeal from the United States District Court for the Northern District of Illinois

The case centers on §6–206 of the Illinois Driver Licensing Law (c. 6 of the Illinois Vehicle Code). The section is entitled "Discretionary authority to suspend or revoke license or permit." It empowers the Secretary of State to act "without preliminary hearing upon a showing by his records or other sufficient evidence" that a driver's conduct falls into any one of 18 enumerated categories. Ill. Rev. Stat., c. 95½, §6–206 (a) (1975). Pursuant to his rulemaking authority under this law, §6–211 (a), the Secretary has adopted administrative regulations that further define the bases and procedures for discretionary suspensions. These regulations generally provide for an initial summary determination based on the individual's driving record. The Secretary has established a comprehensive system of assigning "points" for various kinds of traffic offenses, depending on severity, to provide an objective means of evaluating driving records.

. . . the Secretary has limited his broad statutory discretion by an administrative regulation.

Appellee Love, a resident of Chicago, is employed as a truck-driver. His license was suspended in November 1969, under §6–206 (a)(2), for three convictions within a 12-month period. He was then convicted of a charge of driving while his license was suspended, and consequently another suspension was imposed in March 1970 pursuant to §6–303 (b). Appellee received no further citation until August 1974, when he was arrested twice for speeding. He was convicted of both charges and then received a third speeding citation in February 1975. On March 27, he was notified by letter that he would lose his driving privileges if convicted of a third offense. On March 31 appellee was convicted of the third speeding charge.

On June 3, appellee received a notice that his license was revoked effective June 6. The stated authority for the revocation was §6–206 (a)(3); the explanation, following the language of the statute, was:

This action has been taken as a result of: Your having been repeatedly convicted of offenses against laws and ordinances regulating the movement of traffic, to a degree which indicates disrespect for the traffic laws. App. 13.

Appellee, then aged 25, made no request for an administrative hearing. Instead, he filed this purported class action on June 5 against the Illinois Secretary of State in the United States District Court for the Northern District of Illinois. His complaint sought a declaratory judgment that §6–206 (a)(3) was unconstitutional, an injunction against enforcement of the statute, and damages. Appellee's application for a temporary restraining order was granted on condition that he apply for a hardship driving permit. He applied for that permit on June 10, and it was issued on July 25.

A three-judge District Court was convened to consider appellee's claim that the Illinois statute was unconstitutional. On cross-motions for summary judgment, the court held that a license cannot constitutionally be suspended or revoked under §6–206 (a)(3) until after a hearing is held to determine whether the licensee meets the statutory criteria of "lack of ability to exercise ordinary and reasonable care in the safe operation of a motor vehicle or disrespect for the traffic laws and the safety of other persons upon the highway." The court regarded such a prior hearing as mandated by this Court's decision in *Bell v. Burson*, 402 US 535 (1971). Accordingly, the court granted judgment for appellee and enjoined the Secretary of State from enforcing §6–206 (a)(3). The Secretary appealed, and we noted probable jurisdiction *sub nom. Howlett v. Love*, 429 US 813 (1976).

It is clear that the Due Process Clause applies to the deprivation of a driver's license by the State:

Suspension of issued licenses . . . involves state action that adjudicates important interests of the licensees. In such cases the licenses are not to be taken away without that procedural due process required by the Fourteenth Amendment. *Bell v. Burson*, 402 US, at 539.

. . . We therefore conclude that the nature of the private interest here is not so great as to require us "to depart from the ordinary principle, established by our decisions, that something less than an evidentiary hearing is sufficient prior to adverse administrative action." *Mathews v. Eldridge*, 424 US, at 343. See *Arnett v. Kennedy*, 416 US 134 (1974).

Moreover, the risk of an erroneous deprivation in the absence of a prior hearing is not great. Under the Secretary's regulations, suspension and revocation decisions are largely automatic.

Finally, the substantial public interest in administrative efficiency would be impeded by the availability of a pretermination hearing in every case. Giving licensees the choice thus automatically to obtain a delay in the effectiveness of a suspension or revocation would encourage drivers routinely to request full administrative hearings. See *Mathews v. Eldridge,* 424 US, at 347. Far more substantial than the administrative burden, however, is the important public interest in safety on the roads and highways, and in the prompt removal of a safety hazard. See *Perez v. Campbell,* 402 US 637, 657, 671 (1971) (opinion concurring in part and dissenting in part). This factor fully distinguishes *Bell v. Burson, supra,* where the "only purpose" of the Georgia statute there under consideration was "to obtain security from which to pay any judgments against the licensee resulting from the accident." 402 US, at 540.[11]

The present case is a good illustration of the fact that procedural due process in the administrative setting does not always require application of the judicial model. When a governmental official is given the power to make discretionary decisions under a broad statutory standard, case-by-case decisionmaking may not be the best way to assure fairness. Here the Secretary commendably sought to define the statutory standard narrowly by the use of his rulemaking authority.[12]

The judgment of the District Court is reversed.

It is so ordered.

Mr. Justice Blackmun delivered the opinion of the Court.

Document 3: Illinois Statute 625 ILCS 5/6 206

5/6–206. Discretionary authority to suspend or revoke license or permit — Right to a hearing

§6–206. Discretionary authority to suspend or revoke license or permit; Right to a hearing.

(a) The Secretary of State is authorized to suspend or revoke the driving privileges of any person without preliminary hearing upon a showing of the person's records or other sufficient evidence that the person:

1. Has committed an offense for which mandatory revocation of a driver's license or permit is required upon conviction;

2. Has been convicted of not less than 3 offenses against traffic regulations governing the movement of vehicles committed within

---

[11]Since *Bell v. Burson* was decided, courts have sustained suspension or revocation of driving privileges, without prior hearing, where earlier convictions were on the record. See, e.g., *Cox v. Hjelle,* 207 N.W.2d 266, 269–270 (N.D. 1973); *Stauffer v. Weedlun,* 188 Neb. 105, 195 N.W.2d 218, appeal dismissed, 409 US 972 (1972); *Horodner v. Fisher,* 38 N.Y.2d 680, 345 N.E.2d 571, appeal dismissed, 429 US 802 (1976); *Wright v. Malloy,* 373 F. Supp. 1011, 1018–1019 (Vt.), summarily aff'd, 419 US 987 (1974); *Scott v. Hill,* 407 F. Supp. 301, 304 (E.D. Va. 1076).

[12]See K. Davis, Discretionary Justice, c. III, 52–96 (1969). The promulgation of rules may be of particular value when it is necessary for administrative decisions to be made summarily. See Freedman, Summary Action by Administrative Agencies, 40 U. Chi. L. Rev. 1, 44–49 (1972).

any 12 month period. No revocation or suspension shall be entered more than 6 months after the date of last conviction;

3. Has been repeatedly involved as a driver in motor vehicle collisions or has been repeatedly convicted of offenses against laws and ordinances regulating the movement of traffic, to a degree that indicates lack of ability to exercise ordinary and reasonable care in the safe operation of a motor vehicle or disrespect for the traffic laws and the safety of other persons upon the highway;

4. Has by the unlawful operation of a motor vehicle caused or contributed to an accident resulting in death or injury requiring immediate professional treatment in a medical facility or doctor's office to any person, except that any suspension or revocation imposed by the Secretary of State under the provisions of this subsection shall start no later than 6 months after being convicted of violating a law or ordinance regulating the movement of traffic, which violation is related to the accident, or shall start not more than one year after the date of accident, whichever date occurs later;

5. Has permitted an unlawful or fraudulent use of a driver's license, identification card, or permit;

6. Has been lawfully convicted of an offense or offenses in another state, including the authorization contained in Section 6–203.1, which if committed within this State would be grounds for suspension or revocation;

7. Has refused or failed to submit to an examination provided for by Section 6–207 or has failed to pass the examination;

8. Is ineligible for a driver's license or permit under the provisions of Section 6–103;

9. Has made a false statement or knowingly concealed a material fact or has used false information or identification in any application for a license, identification card, or permit;

10. Has possessed, displayed, or attempted to fraudulently use any license, identification card, or permit not issued to the person;

11. Has operated a motor vehicle upon a highway of this State when the person's driving privilege or privilege to obtain a driver's license or permit was revoked or suspended unless the operation was authorized by a judicial driving permit, probationary license to drive, or a restricted driving permit issued under this Code;

12. Has submitted to any portion of the application process for another person or has obtained the services of another person to submit to any portion of the application process for the purpose of obtaining a license, identification card, or permit for some other person;

13. Has operated a motor vehicle upon a highway of this State when the person's driver's license was invalid under the provisions of Section 6–110. Provided that for the first offense the Secretary of State may suspend the driver's license for not more than 60 days, for the second offense not more than 90 days, and for the third offense not more than one year;

14. Has committed a violation of Section 6–301, 6–301.1, or 6–301.2 of this Act, or Section 14, 14A, or 14B of the Illinois Identification Card Act;

15. Has been convicted of violating Section 21–2 of the Criminal Code of 1961 relating to criminal trespass to vehicles in which case, the suspension shall be for one year;

16. Has been convicted of violating Section 11–204 of this Code relating to fleeing from a police officer; . . . .

Document 4: Illinois Regulation 6–206

Rule 6–206 (a) (1975) provides in part:

"The Secretary of State is authorized to exercise discretionary authority to suspend or revoke the license or permit of any person without a preliminary hearing, or to decline to suspend or revoke such driving privileges. In making a determination of the action to be taken, the Secretary of State shall take into consideration the severity of the offense and conviction, the number of offenses and convictions, and prior suspensions or revocations on the abstract of the driver's record. The Secretary may also take into consideration the points accumulated by the driver and noted on his driving record.

"For the purpose of this Rule and its companion rules, a conviction is the final adjudication of 'guilty' by a court of competent jurisdiction, either after a bench trial, trial by jury, plea of guilty, order of forfeiture, or default, as reported to the Secretary of State, and the Secretary of State is not authorized to consider or inquire into the facts and circumstances surrounding the conviction."

Rule 6–206 (a)2 (1975) provides:

"A person who has been convicted of three (3) or more offenses against traffic regulations, governing the movement of vehicles, with the exception of those offenses excluded under provisions of Section 6–204 (2) and whose violations have occurred within a twelve (12) month period may be suspended as follows:

Number of points	Action
20 to 44	Suspension up to 2 months
45 to 74	Suspension up to 3 months
75 to 89	Suspension up to 6 months
90 to 99	Suspension up to 9 months
100 to 109	Suspension up to 12 months
Over 110	Revocation for not less than 12 months.

"A person who has accumulated sufficient points to warrant a second suspension within a 10-year period may be either suspended or revoked, depending on the number of points. In the event of a second suspension in the 10-year period, the length of suspension, determined by the point total, is doubled to arrive at the type and duration of action."

Rule 6–206 (a)3 (1975) provides:

"A person repeatedly involved in collisions or convictions to a degree which indicates the lack of ability to exercise ordinary and reasonable care in the safe operation of a motor vehicle, or whose record indicates disrespect for traffic laws and the safety of other persons on the highway, and who has accumulated sufficient points to warrant a second suspension within a 5 year period, may either be suspended or revoked by the Secretary of State, based upon the number of points in his record. A person who has been suspended thrice within a 10 year period shall be revoked."

Section 6–206 (c)(1): "Upon suspending or revoking the license or permit of any person as authorized in this Section, the Secretary of State shall immediately notify such person in writing of the order revoking or suspending the license or permit. Such notice to be deposited in the United States mail, postage prepaid, to the last known address of such person."

Document 5: James O. Freedman, Summary Action by Administrative Agencies, 40 U. Chi. L. Rev. I, 44–49 (1972)

> In framing a government which is to be administered by men over men, the great difficulty lies in this: you must first enable the government to control the governed; and in the next place oblige it to control itself.
>
> James Madison, *The Federalist No. 51*

2. *Rules and Reasons.* Two procedures commonly used to structure formal administrative processes are the promulgation of rules for the exercise of a particular discretionary power and the provision of a statement explaining the agency's reasons in each instance for its discretionary acts. The existence of a body of standards tends to encourage greater deliberation, self-consciousness, and consistency in the exercise of administrative discretion and thereby reduces the likelihood that an agency will act arbitrarily. By promulgating rules and providing statements of reasons, an administrative agency creates a body of standards against which its performance can be measured by Congress, the courts, and the public, and thereby tends to make the law more democratic.

These arguments have found renewed expression during the last decade in scholarly criticism and judicial decisions urging administrative agencies to make greater use of rules and reasons. . . .

. . . Most decisions to take summary action, it is said, are based on a highly developed expertise that gives the agency confidence in the refined quality of what are, essentially, educated guesses and hunches. To articulate criteria for taking summary action—the type of harm, the magnitude of the violation, the seriousness of the threat to the public interest, the substantiality of the agency's evidence, the availability of alternate relief, and the special characteristics of the individual involved, including his prior record of violations, his degree of culpability, and his vulnerability to successful action—would be, in the view of many administrators, to do

no more than announce obvious generalities that would neither standardize an agency's decision-making processes nor provide the public with
reliable information on how future cases, each of them turning on individual facts, are likely to be decided.

Although this explanation has some validity, it is not wholly persuasive. Some administrative agencies have managed to formulate and publish rules defining the circumstances in which they take summary action.

... In most instances the requirement that administrative agencies
state the reasons for their decisions has been of judicial origin, based
both on the desirability of refining the exercise of administrative discretion
and on the necessity of facilitating judicial review.

The substantial number of judicial decisions requiring administrative
agencies to state the reasons for their decisions are, however, limited almost
entirely to formal agency proceedings. Although the purposes underlying
the requirement of reasons — improvement of the exercise of discretion
and prevention of arbitrary administrative action — are probably more in
need of vindication when an agency acts informally than when it uses the
formal hearing process, courts have only recently begun to require administrative agencies to provide a statement of reasons when they act
informally.

By promulgating rules describing generally the criteria that guide its
discretion in taking summary action and by providing an informative statement of reasons whenever it does act summarily, an administrative agency
can make one of its most significant informal processes more visible. These
reforms would be an important step toward strengthening the fairness of
the process by which summary action is taken. Sunlight, as Justice Brandeis
said, is the best of disinfectants.

4

Client Rights

* Declaration of
  Independence
* U.S. Constitution
* life, liberty, property
* Bill of Rights
* Sunshine Act
* Fifth Amendment
* State Constitutions

* due process
* Privacy Act
* equal treatment
* Fourteenth Amendment
* procedural safeguards
* Trade Secrets Act
* Freedom of Information
  Act

CHAPTER OBJECTIVES

Individuals and corporations, the "clients" of government agencies, retain all of their Constitutional rights in agency actions. This chapter discusses:

- What due process rights are in agency actions.
- How agencies enforce the due process rights.
- Which Constitutional amendments are cited in agency procedures.
- Which rules address client rights.
- How government programs complicate the interpretation of client rights.
- How costs impact client rights.
- What is meant by public rights, or freedoms.
- How immunity protects agencies.

CHAPTER OVERVIEW

Individuals maintain all their rights in agency actions, whether they are the "clients" seeking agency services or the employees of the agency. Agencies safeguard these rights in the procedures and rules that incorporate the constitutional rights—primarily, the due process rights of life, liberty, and property, and the right to fair and equal treatment. Through the Fifth and Fourteenth Amendments of the U.S. Constitution, the rights are applicable to both federal and state agencies. Along with these Amendment rights—to ensure protection of information gathered on clients and others—agencies are guided by: Statutes that allow individuals to see information the agency gathers (the Freedom of Information Act), statutes that protect the privacy of information gathered (the Privacy Act), statutes that order public access to government meetings (the Sunshine Act), and statutes that protect the information gathered on businesses (the Trade Secrets Act). Because gathering and analyzing information are significant to agency decision-making, these acts are meaningful to due process and fair treatment.

A. Introduction

1. What Are Client Rights?

A person or organization seeking services from an agency is also called a client of the agency. Client rights are the protections these citizens have in all agency actions. Some of the protections are in the actual procedures of the agencies; other protections are within the national and state constitutional laws that agencies must uphold.

2. Which Constitutional Rights Are Primary?

The primary constitutional rights are due process and fair and equal treatment, the Fifth and Fourteenth Amendments. Due Process in the Fifth Amendment protects life, liberty, and property of individuals. Fair and equal treatment in the Fourteenth Amendment ensures that each individual will be treated fairly, and without bias.

3. When Are These Rights Upheld by Agencies?

These rights are inherent in every agency action, from the filing and receiving of claims and complaints, through the decision process, and to any appeal. If any of these rights are denied or violated by any agency action, clients may follow established procedures to protest or appeal, then later rectify any threat to their due process, and fair and equal treatment rights.

Figure 4.1 outlines how these protections operate.

Figure 4.1 **Client Rights**

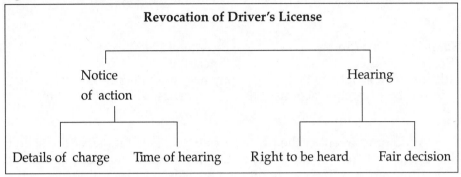

B. Constitutional Grounds

Due process, and fair and equal treatment, are the mainstays of client rights in agencies; these rights are delineated for federal agencies in the Fifth Amendment and for state agencies in the Fourteenth Amendment. Both due process and equal treatment demand that an individual be vested with certain protections and be treated fairly. Due process protects a person's right to life, liberty, and property. If a person is threatened with the denial of life, liberty, or property, due process and equal protection rights take precedent over any agency rules. Although these may seem to be extreme issues for agencies, agencies deal with these issues everyday: If individuals do not receive their government benefits and supplements, they may not eat, may not have heat, and may even die; prisoners seeking parole may not be released from prison; a motor vehicle driver may have her car impounded because of a driving offense.

Think of the power of licensing and registration. If you need to drive to work, or if driving is a necessity in your work, the denial of a driver's license can mean no food on your table. What if you attempt to improve your income and become a master plumber, a realtor, a doctor, and need to be licensed or registered? In each case, the denial of a license or registration drastically alters your life. Equal protection and fairness are important to the due process awarded each individual.

1. Effect on Procedures

The two major areas in which due process, and fair and equal treatment, are addressed are in the procedural and substantive rules in agencies. Substantive due process underlines the rules that address the rights an individual or industry has when interacting with an agency, and are considered broad rules. Procedural due process dictates the rules that determine agency procedures and are considered specific rules.

Substantive Due Process	*Procedural Due Process*
(Broad)	(Specific)
citizens have a right to be informed of agency actions	agency must mail notice of hearing to parties with specific date, time, and action to be taken

At no time, in either the procedures that clients follow, or the actions that agencies take, should client rights be violated. Agency actions and procedures are just, if they are rational and reasonable; any agency action that is irrational or unreasonable will violate the constitutional protections of due process and/or fair and equal treatment.

 PARALEGAL PRACTICE EXAMPLE

You, a paralegal for a small law firm, are assigned the zoning board case that your attorney received by phone this morning. Your client abuts property on which a four car garage is being built. Your client had not been given notice of the zoning board hearing that occurred last week; therefore, did not attend to voice his objection. You have to look up state and local regulations for procedural rules in the law library. Also, your attorney wants you to look up the requirement distance buildings must be from the property line in private dwelling areas. This information should be at the town hall.

 PARALEGAL PRACTICE EXAMPLE

As a paralegal working for the town counsel's office, you join in with the group at work who are having a bit of fun by hiding records from a few townspeople who come to the assessor's office Thursday mornings to look up neighbor's, and others', property records. You keep the records on your desk in the town counsel's office. Your attorney stops by your desk, telling you an irate person just called claiming that he is being denied access to the public records. Your attorney tells you that town rules uphold the broad substantive laws and constitutional rights of the public to view public records. You immediately return the records to the town assessor's office.

2. Constitutional Amendments

Although all sections of the U.S. Constitution are applicable to agencies, it is the Fifth and Fourteenth Amendments that are most often cited in court cases. The Fifth Amendment applies to the federal government and federal agencies; the Fourteenth Amendment governs state agencies.

a. Fifth Amendment

No person shall be held to answer for a capital, or otherwise infamous crime, unless on a presentment or indictment of a Grand Jury, except in cases arising in the land or naval forces, or in the Militia, when in actual danger; nor shall any person be subject for the same offence to be twice put in jeopardy of life or limb; nor shall be compelled in any criminal case to be a witness against himself, *nor be deprived of life, liberty, or property, without due process of law;* nor shall private property be taken for public use, without just compensation. (Emphasis added.)

Due Process in the Fifth Amendment as applied to agencies is concerned with government actions; procedural due process, inherent in the Fifth Amendment, demands proper procedures if government action affects a citizen's rights of life, liberty, and property.

b. Fourteenth Amendment, Section 1

All persons born or naturalized in the United States, and subject to the jurisdiction thereof, are citizens of the United States and of the State wherein they reside. No State shall make or enforce any law which shall abridge the privileges or immunities of citizens of the United States; *nor shall any State deprive any person of life, liberty, or property, without due process of law; nor deny to any person within its jurisdiction the equal protection of the laws.*

The Fourteenth Amendment was passed after the Civil War, with the intention of alleviating the concerns of racial discrimination after the abolishment of slavery. This concept extended to equal protection in the economic and political areas in the states by the 1900s; at that time, the courts also increased judicial review of government programs. Today the courts review equal protection rights that relate to both substantive and procedural law. "... the Fourteenth Amendment protects against deprivations of property without due process, ..." *Richardson v. Town of Eastover*, 922 F2d 1152, 1156 (4th Cir. 1991)

STUDENT PRACTICE

The Fifth and Fourteenth Amendments protect due process of life, liberty, and property.

1. Brainstorm some actions a government may take to help or punish a citizen (for example, food stamps, imprisonment, licensing). Make a list of actions.
2. Separate this list of actions into three columns:

Life   *Liberty*   *Property*

In order to claim lack of due process if an agency rules unfavorably on an individual's complaint, a person has to illustrate that an agency violated a situation that comes under one of the three categories — life, liberty, or property.

C.   Due Process

Due process has become more complex as the original concepts of the words life, liberty, and property have expanded just as have government programs and agencies. Life involves quality of life as well as freedom from death; liberty could be reputation as well as bodily restraints; property may be government benefits, such as welfare benefits as well as land or possessions. As upheld by the courts in *Kelm v. Hyatt*, 44 F3d 415, 421 (6th Cir. 1995), a person has a right to life, liberty, and property and may be denied those rights only with the proper procedures established by the government. Both due process and equal protection are fundamental rights. Questions asked and answered by governmental procedures are: Is there a reason for the government to be involved in this person's life? Is there adequate procedure for this person to remedy any wrong that might be committed?

Figure 4.2 illustrates the due process amendments impact on administrative agencies.

Figure 4.2   **Due Process Amendments**

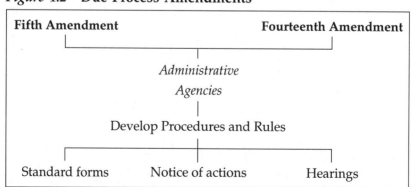

Goldberg v. Kelly, is a landmark case discussing a person's right to due process in agency actions. *Its major issue — the need for a hearing before relief benefits are denied —* has been consistently upheld by courts for over twenty years in cases of severe deprivation. In many agencies, hearings are held after an action is taken; for example, a driver may have his license revoked and then a hearing is held. Yet, *Goldberg* has been upheld because it alleviates the distress and deprivation in cases in which due process necessitates a pre-determination hearing. "Only in 'extraordinary situations' may notice and a hearing be postponed until after the deprivation." *Bendiburg v. Dempsey,* 909 F2d 463, 470 (11th Cir. 1990), cert. denied, 500 US 932 (1991) "Post-deprivation remedies do not provide due process if pre-deprivation remedies are practicable." *Jackson Water Works, Inc. v. Public Utilities Comm'n of Cal.,* 793 F2d 1090, 1097 (9th Cir. 1986), cert. denied, 479 US 1102 (1987)

CASE ABSTRACT

Please note when reading the case:
1. Procedural due process of the Fourteenth Amendment is the issue in this case which emanates from New York State and New York City.
2. The appellant is New York City. The appellees are the families receiving aid, who won the case in the U.S. District Court; the District Court said termination of benefits denied a "brutal need."
3. The program in question is a federal program, but is administered by the City and State of New York.
4. Even though many regulations are cited, the Court only addresses Procedural Regulation No. 68-18, which is formulated on New York Social Welfare Law §351.26(b).
5. Included in the above regulation and law is a seven-day notice of an action and review by a welfare official of termination of aid. Included is a letter stating that a hearing is available *after* termination.
6. The State and City uphold hearings after termination, but the recipients believe this is a violation of their due process rights.
7. The issue is whether a hearing before termination is required or whether a hearing after termination of benefits, which could result in severe deprivation to the families, meets the due process standard.

Goldberg, Commissioner of Social Services of the City of New York v. Kelly
397 US 254 (1970)

Mr. Justice Brennan delivered the opinion of the Court.

The question for decision is whether a State that terminates public assistance payments to a particular recipient without affording him the opportunity for an evidentiary hearing prior to termination denies the recipient procedural due process in violation of the Due Process Clause of the Fourteenth Amendment.

This action was brought in the District Court for the Southern District of New York by residents of New York City receiving financial aid under the federally assisted program of Aid to Families with Dependent Children (AFDC) or under New York State's general Home Relief program. Their complaint alleged that the New York State and New York City officials administering these programs terminated, or were about to terminate, such aid without prior notice and hearing, thereby denying them due process of law. . . .

The State Commissioner of Social Services amended the State Department of Social Services' Official Regulations to require that local social services officials proposing to discontinue or suspend a recipient's financial aid do so according to a procedure that conforms to either subdivision (a) or subdivision (b) of §351.26 of the regulations as amended. . . .

Pursuant to subdivision (b), the New York City Department of Social Services promulgated Procedure No. 68-18. A caseworker who has doubts about the recipient's continued eligibility must first discuss them with the recipient. If the caseworker concludes that the recipient is no longer eligible, he recommends termination of aid to a unit supervisor. If the latter concurs, he sends the recipient a letter stating the reasons for proposing to terminate aid and notifying him that within seven days he may request that a higher official review the record, and may support the request with a written statement prepared personally or with the aid of an attorney or other person. If the reviewing official affirms the determination of ineligibility, aid is stopped immediately and the recipient is informed by letter of the reasons for the action. Appellees' challenge to this procedure emphasizes the absence of any provisions for the personal appearance of the recipient before the reviewing official, for oral presentation of evidence, and for confrontation and cross-examination of adverse witnesses. However, the letter does inform the recipient that he may request a post-termination "fair hearing." . . .

The constitutional issue to be decided, therefore, is the narrow one whether the Due Process Clause requires that the recipient be afforded an evidentiary hearing *before* the termination of benefits. The District Court held that only a pre-termination evidentiary hearing would satisfy the constitutional command, and rejected the argument of the state and city officials that the combination of the post-termination "fair hearing" with the informal pre-termination review disposed of all due process claims. The court said: "While post-termination review is relevant, there is one overpowering fact which controls here. By hypothesis, a welfare recipient is destitute, without funds or assets. . . . Suffice it to say that to cut off a welfare recipient in the face of . . . 'brutal need' without a prior hearing of some sort is unconscionable, unless overwhelming considerations justify it." *Kelly v. Wyman*, 294 F. Supp. 893, 899, 900 (1968). The court rejected the argument that the need to protect the public's tax revenues supplied the requisite "overwhelming consideration." "Against the justified desire to protect public funds must be weighed the individual's over-powering need in this unique situation not to be wrongfully deprived of assistance. . . . While the problem of additional expense must be kept in mind, it does not justify denying a hearing meeting the ordinary standards of due process. Under all the circumstances, we hold that due process requires an adequate hearing before termination of welfare benefits, and the fact that there is a later constitutionally fair proceeding does not alter the result." *Id.*, at 901. Although state officials were party defendants in the action, only the Commissioner of Social Services of the City of New York appealed. . . .

. . . The extent to which procedural due process must be afforded the recipient is influenced by the extent to which he may be "condemned to suffer grievous loss," *Joint Anti-Fascist Refugee Committee v. McGrath*, 341 US 123, 168 (1951) (Frankfurter, J., concurring), and depends upon whether the recipient's interest in avoiding that loss outweighs the governmental interest in summary adjudication. . . .

It is true, of course, that some governmental benefits may be administratively terminated without affording the recipient a pre-termination evidentiary hearing. But we agree with the District Court that when welfare is discontinued, only a pre-termination evidentiary hearing provides the recipient with procedural due process. Cf. *Sniadach v. Family Finance Corp.*, 395 US 337 (1969). For qualified recipients, welfare provides the means to obtain essential food, clothing, housing, and medical care. Cf. *Nash v. Florida Industrial Commission*, 389 US 235, 239 (1967). Thus the crucial factor in this context — a factor not present in the case of the blacklisted government contractor, the discharged government employee, the taxpayer denied a tax exemption, or virtually anyone else whose governmental entitlements are ended — is that termination of aid pending resolution of a controversy over eligibility may deprive an *eligible* recipient of the very means by which to live while he waits. Since he lacks independent resources, his situation becomes immediately desperate. His need to concentrate upon finding the means for daily subsistence, in turn, adversely affects his ability to seek redress from the welfare bureaucracy.

Moreover, important governmental interests are promoted by affording recipients a pre-termination evidentiary hearing. From its founding the Nation's basic commitment has been to foster the dignity and well-being of all persons within its borders. We have come to recognize that forces not within the control of the poor contribute to their poverty. . . .

Appellant does not challenge the force of these considerations but argues that they are outweighed by countervailing governmental interests in conserving fiscal and administrative resources. . . .

We agree with the District Court, however, that these governmental interests are not overriding in the welfare context. The requirement of a prior hearing doubtless involves some greater expense, and the benefits paid to ineligible recipients pending decision at the hearing probably cannot be recouped, since these recipients are likely to be judgment-proof. But the State is not without weapons to minimize these increased costs. Much of the drain on fiscal and administrative resources can be reduced by developing procedures for prompt pre-termination hearings and by skillful use of personnel and facilities. . . .

We also agree with the District Court, however, that the pre-termination hearing need not take the form of a judicial or quasi-judicial trial. . . .

. . . In the present context these principles require that a recipient have timely and adequate notice detailing the reasons for a proposed termination, and an effective opportunity to defend by confronting any adverse witnesses and by presenting his own arguments and evidence orally. . . .

The opportunity to be heard must be tailored to the capacities and circumstances of those who are to be heard. . . .

Written submissions are an unrealistic option for most recipients, who lack the educational attainment necessary to write effectively and who cannot obtain professional assistance. . . .

We do not say that counsel must be provided at the pre-termination hearing, but only that the recipient must be allowed to retain an attorney if he so desires. . . .

. . . We agree with the District Court that prior involvement in some aspects of a case will not necessarily bar a welfare official from acting as a decision maker. He should not, however, have participated in making the determination under review.

Affirmed.

1. Due Process and Agency Authority

The agency receives its authority through the statute creating the agency; a legislated power delegated to the agency. Due process is based on the Constitution and supported by legislative laws. Just as agencies have the authority to make decisions, clients have the right to due process. This client right may conflict with the daily running of agencies; as crass as it may sound, costs are often a determining factor. Both the benefit to the client and the cost to the government are weighed. (See *Goldberg v. Kelly*) The balance of any possible injury to a client and the costs of supplying procedural protections is considered.

This cost analysis is clarified in notices and hearings. "Notice" is the informing of the client that an action is to take place. The notice must include information about the time of the action, the place, and other details of the action. Cost analysis is used in deciding the manner in which to give notice to the client. Personal contact is, of course, best, but generally much too expensive. Mailing a notice is usually sufficient, although a requirement may state that it be sent certified or registered mail. Hearings are affected by cost analysis as well. Most clients prefer a jury, but the reality of costs enter the picture and usually a hearing officer or administrative law judge hears the issues.

2. Due Process Requirements for Violations

A claimant may believe her right to due process has been denied by an agency and may appeal the action citing the due process procedural requirements that have been violated. The requirements of such a due process claim are founded in the theory of procedural due process required in the Fifth Amendment. To initiate a violation claim, the claimant has to show that the government agency has developed procedures to deprive the person of the right to life, liberty, and property.

In order to claim a due process violation, one must show:

1. this is a *protected interest* — life, liberty, property;
2. the government deprived one of that interest — false imprisonment where the interest is liberty;
3. it is a *state action* — the government or agency action did not use proper procedures.

The *protection* of interests is founded in the Constitution, but the *actual* interests may be created by the statutes, agency rules, and municipal ordinances that support the Constitution:

Property interests. The right to welfare aid is created by statutes. The protection of these rights is in the U.S. Constitution's Fifth Amendment. Even with this protection, a person has to have "more than an abstract need or desire or a unilateral hope" to prove a valid property interest. (*Gaston v. Taylor*, 945 F2d 340, 344 (4th Cir. 1991))

Liberty interests. These extend beyond bodily restraint. The destruction of a reputation may destroy one's liberty. If the agency says a person bidding for a government contract is dishonest, that person may be stigmatized. (*ATL, Inc. v. United States*, 736 F2d 677 (Fed. Cir. 1984)). Other cases have discussed liberty interests. "Liberty interests are both broader and more difficult to define than property interests. While property exists in concrete entitlement secured by independent sources of law, liberty interests cannot be so easily characterized." (*Bank of Jackson County v. Cherry*, 966 F2d 1406, 1410 (11th Cir. 1992))

Life interests. These have been upheld in case law as well as in the Constitution. Medical treatment to sustain the life of an incompetent patient was deemed a procedural due process right in *Cruzan v. Director, Missouri Dept. of Health*, 497 US 261, 281 (1990).

CONCEPTS JOURNAL

Analyzing *Goldberg v. Kelly*

Develop three teams.
Team 1 — Prepare an outline of the appellant's case.
Team 2 — Prepare an outline of the appellee's case.
Team 3 — Prepare an outline of the court's reasoning.

> After the outlines are prepared, each team should decide how
> due process is shown in their outlines. Select one person from each
> team to present their outline and their explanation of due process.
>
> **Journal Keeping**
>
> Take notes as the team presenter is outlining the section of the case
> and explaining due process. Keep the notes under the title "Due
> Process." After taking notes, write a sentence or two explaining
> what due process is.

D.   Right to Know and Right to Privacy

All constitutional rights are available to individuals or organizations interacting with government. In addition to the primary rights of due process
and equal treatment, people rely on certain rights or "freedoms" that
facilitate their pursuits. Clients have the right to participate in agency
actions by having knowledge of the activity; this includes records and
meetings. At the same time, a client has the right to be protected
from others acquiring knowledge of some private information that the
agency has gathered. Both of these—the right to know and the right
to privacy—are enveloped in our public rights, which are written in
statutes such as the:

1. Freedom of Information Act (FOIA), 5 USC §552—access to
   information
2. Privacy Act, 5 USC §552(a)—privacy of information
3. Sunshine Act, 5 USC §552(b)—access to government meetings
4. Trade Secrets Act, 5 USC §552b(e)(4)—privacy of business
   information

These acts afford the freedom for people to gather helpful information and
restrain the release of injurious information. The right to know and the
right to privacy are so essential they are included in the Federal Administrative Procedure Act 5 USC §§551–557. They have an effect on the substantive and procedural rules of agencies just as the Fifth and Fourteenth
Amendments do. Each of these four acts instructs government agencies to
construct rules that will fulfill the intent of the act.

The following cases cite the FOIA and the Privacy Act. The first
case, *Mayock v. Immigration and Naturalization Service*, depicts the plight
of immigrants; the second case, *Katz v. National Archives*, the plight of a
family of an assassinated U.S. President. As you read these cases, you will
realize the obstacles agencies encounter in attempting to relate to the needs
of different personalities and their beliefs. In these two cases, agencies must

supply information in acceptable time frames and balance the right to know of some individuals with the right of privacy of other individuals.

CASE ABSTRACT

Please note when reading the case:
1. Case is in the U.S. District Court, California.
2. The FOIA sets a ten-day period to reply to request.
3. Plaintiff states the Immigration and Naturalization Service (INS) pattern not to follow the ten-day time limit.
4. The FOIA statute is 5 USC §552; INS rule/regulation is 8 CFR §103.10(c)
5. Congress adopted ten-day limit in 1974 because delay "is often tantamount to denial."
6. Does the INS's backlog constitute "exceptional circumstances"?

James R. Mayock v. Immigration and Naturalization Service, et al.
714 F. Supp. 1558 (ND Cal. 1989)

LEGGE, District Judge.

Plaintiff James R. Mayock is an immigration attorney. He originally filed this suit to require the Immigration and Naturalization Service ("INS") to comply with certain Freedom of Information Act, 5 USC §552, (FOIA) requests which he made on behalf of clients. Many of the clients were involved in deportation or exclusion proceedings and were faced with immediate deportation. Plaintiff requested a permanent injunction: (1) requiring the INS to release certain requested FOIA information, (2) staying deportation or exclusion proceedings pending compliance with FOIA requests, and (3) requiring the INS to comply with the FOIA requests within the 10-day period provided by statute.

In earlier proceedings in this case, the specific FOIA requests were resolved by the parties and by the court. This case has become a "pattern and practice" case. That is, plaintiff contends that the INS has a pattern and practice of failing to produce certain categories of FOIA information, and of failing to comply with FOIA requests within the statutory 10-day period. Plaintiff claims that this pattern and practice deprives his clients and other aliens of information necessary to enable them to resist deportation before they are actually deported and their requests are rendered moot.

The INS deportation procedures are governed by 8 USC §1252(b). This statute provides that an alien has the right to present evidence, and to receive a "reasonable opportunity to examine the evidence against him." However, there are no discovery procedures provided by the INS regulations. FOIA is essentially the only procedure which aliens can use to obtain from the INS information relevant to their cases.

Plaintiff seeks injunctive relief requiring the INS to 1) make a determination on an alien's FOIA requests within ten working days of receipt, 2) give notice if a ten working day extension of time is required, 3) search certain electronic data systems in response to FOIA requests for "all records," and 4) sufficiently describe the documents withheld from production and correlate the withheld documents with the statutory FOIA exemptions.

Plaintiff has presented substantial and uncontroverted evidence that lengthy delays are systematic, . . . and that aliens have been excluded or deported before the INS's FOIA replies are received. There is also no dispute as to the form in which the INS office denies requests for information. The denial merely indicates how many pages will not be disclosed, and cites the relevant statutory exemptions. Finally, there is also no dispute that the INS did not, until recently, search any of its computer databases in response to requests for "all records."

The basic disputes between the parties are therefore ones of law and not of fact. The issue is whether the practices of the INS are in compliance with the requirements of FOIA. . . .

Plaintiff's primary claim is that the INS does not process FOIA information requests in the time period prescribed by the statute, the regulations, and the agency guidelines.

The 10-day rule was a 1974 amendment to FOIA, prompted in response to administrative agency delay. "[E]xcessive delay by the agency in its response is often tantamount to denial. It is the intent of this bill that the affected agencies be required to respond to inquiries and administrative appeals within specific time limits." H. Rep. No. 876, 93d Cong., 2d Sess., *reprinted in* 1974 U.S. Code Cong. & Admin. News, 6267, 6271. . . .

. . . the number of requests made to the INS had risen in the past few years, resulting in a larger backlog. . . .

[T]he INS has made no showing that it has unsuccessfully sought more FOIA resources from Congress or attempted to redirect its existing resources. . . .

Nor does it seem to accord with requirements of "due diligence" that the INS gives no special priority to requests needed in time for deportation or exclusion proceedings. Courts have been sensitive to the claimants' needs for information, . . .

[2] Plaintiff also complains that the aliens do not even receive the appropriate notice of the §552(a)(6)(B) 10-day extension, and the reasons therefor. The INS practice is initially to acknowledge receipt of the request, but it does not send separate notice invoking the §552(a)(6)(B) extension. This practice also violates the legislative mandate.

[4] Plaintiff also complains that the INS's procedure for invoking FOIA exemptions states too little about what types of documents are being withheld. The agency's current practice is to reveal only the number of pages withheld, and to list the statutory exceptions on which it relies.

IT IS THEREFORE ORDERED, ADJUDGED, AND DECREED that:

1. Plaintiff's motion for summary judgment is granted in part, and defendant's motion for summary judgment is denied.

2. Pursuant to the Declaratory Judgment Act, this court declares that:
    a. Title 5, USC, section 552(a)(6)(C) may not be invoked by the INS as a general exemption from the time requirements of FOIA. In order to invoke that exemption properly, the INS must demonstrate "exceptional circumstances" other than the number or backlog of applications. The exemption is applicable primarily to individual requests which are large or complicated.
    b. The INS must issue the appropriate notices of extension of time required by section 552(a)(6)(B).
3. The San Francisco District Office of the INS is hereby ordered to:
    a. Refrain from failing to comply with the time requirements set forth in 5 USC §552(a)(6)(A), (B), and (C);
    b. Give due consideration for priority to the requests for information by aliens who have urgent need for the information in pending deportation or exclusion proceedings.
    c. Search relevant electronic databases as a part of responses to requests for "all records."

Mayock was appealed to the U.S. Court of Appeals.

Mayock v. Nelson
938 F2d 1006 (9th Cir. 1991)

Immigration attorney brought action against Immigration and Naturalization Service (INS), seeking to compel INS to timely respond to aliens' Freedom of Information Act (FOIA) requests. The United States District Court for the Northern District of California, Charles A. Legge, J., granted injunctive relief, 714 F. Supp. 1558, and INS appealed. The Court of Appeals, Beezer, Circuit Judge, held that fact issues as to whether increasing workload at INS offices created "exceptional circumstances" warranting its failure to timely respond to FOIA requests and whether INS demonstrated "due diligence" in responding to requests for information by aliens who had urgent need for information in pending deportation or exclusion proceedings precluded summary judgment.

Reversed and remanded.

BEEZER, Circuit Judge:
In this Freedom of Information Act (FOIA) case, the government appeals the district court's grant of summary judgment and injunctive relief. The court ordered the San Francisco District Office of the Immigration & Naturalization Service (INS) to respond to aliens' FOIA requests within statutory time-limits and ordered the INS (nationally) to give due consideration for priority to requests by aliens who have an urgent need for the information in pending deportation or exclusion proceedings.

The district court had jurisdiction under 5 U.S.C. §522(a)(4)(B). This court has jurisdiction under 28 U.S.C. §1291. Because material facts remain in dispute, we reverse.

I

James R. Mayock, an immigration attorney, originally brought suit on behalf of aliens he represented. The issues regarding those plaintiffs were resolved; Mayock then proceeded on his own behalf. He alleged the INS has a pattern and practice of (1) failing to produce certain categories of FOIA information and (2) failing to comply with FOIA requests within the statutory, ten-day period. Mayock claimed that this pattern and practice deprives his clients of information necessary to enable them to resist deportation before they are actually deported and their requests rendered moot. See *Mayock v. INS*, 714 F. Supp. 1558, 1559–60 (N.D. Cal. 1989).

Before the district court issued its final opinion, the government submitted declarations that set forth the volume of FOIA and Privacy Act requests handled by the San Francisco District Office for each of the past several years. The government also submitted evidence tending to show that in 1987, large employee turnover led to nine vacancies in the INS's FOIA/PA Program.

A. Exceptional Circumstances

The district court refused to conclude that a steadily increasing workload that creates a "normal" agency backlog is an exceptional circumstance, noting that "the INS has made no showing that it has sought more FOIA resources from Congress or attempted to redirect its existing resources." *Mayock*, 714 F. Supp. at 1565–66.

The government argued that the Immigration Reform and Control Act, enacted in 1986, led to a "surge" in requests for information and a loss of personnel. The facts established by the government reveal an increasingly large workload.

Year	Received
1981	285
1982	378
1983	512
1984	648
1985	798
1986	1271
1987	1607

B. Due Diligence

The district court determined that, even if exceptional circumstances existed, the INS had not demonstrated "due diligence" because it failed to give "due consideration for priority to the requests for information by aliens who have urgent need for the information in pending deportation or exclusion proceedings." *Mayock*, 714 F. Supp. at 1568. The government argues that the court improperly is attempting to create a class-wide priority for aliens seeking FOIA information relevant to immigration proceedings.

The district court found that the INS gives no special priority to requests needed in time for deportation or exclusion proceedings. *Mayock,*

714 F. Supp. at 1566. Yet, the government admits in its brief that a particular FOIA request accompanied by a showing of genuine urgency warrants priority over pending requests, at least as a matter of agency policy. Summary judgment also was improper on this issue.

We reverse and remand for further proceedings. Mayock's request for fees on appeal under 5 U.S.C. §552(a)(4)(E) is denied.

Reversed and Remanded.

CASE ABSTRACT

Please note when reading the case:
1. The court will determine whether the agency controls the records or not.
2. Exemption (6) of the FOIA is pertinent.
3. Privacy and inherent distress are viable objections to the release of records.
4. The case is in U.S. District Court, Washington, DC.

D. Mark Katz v. National Archives & Records Administration
862 F. Supp. 476 (DDC 1994)

FLANNERY, District Judge.

This is an action brought under the Freedom of Information Act ("FOIA"), 5 USC §552, by which plaintiff, author D. Mark Katz, seeks to challenge a decision of the National Archives and Records Administration ("the Archives") to withhold certain autopsy records of President John F. Kennedy.

I. *Procedural History*

By order dated December 16, 1992, Judge Revercomb converted the Archives' motion to dismiss for failure to state a claim into a motion for summary judgment. The Court ordered the parties to file supplemental briefs addressing the effect, if any, of the President John F. Kennedy Assassination Records Collection Act of 1992 ("ARCA"), Pub. L. No. 102–526, 106 Stat. 3443 (1992), on plaintiff's FOIA claim, as well as any other issues of importance to the case. The ARCA was signed into law on October 26, 1992. Subsequent to the Court's order, the parties filed cross-motions for summary judgment and oral argument was heard before Judge Revercomb. The case was reassigned to this Court following Judge Revercomb's death and is now before the Court on the parties' cross-motions for summary judgment.

II. *Factual Background*

On November 22, 1963, President John F. Kennedy was assassinated in Dallas, Texas. Later that day, an autopsy was performed on the President's body at the National Naval Medical Center in Bethesda, Maryland. The autopsy photographs and a number of x-rays of the deceased president were taken by Navy personnel during the autopsy and on the same night turned over to Secret Service Agent Kellerman. The photographs and x-rays remained in the custody of the Secret Service from November 22, 1963, until April 26, 1965.

**Does the family's right to privacy take precedence over
the public's right to know?**

On April 22, 1965, Senator Robert F. Kennedy wrote to Vice Admiral
George G. Burkley, personal physician to the president, the following letter:

> [t]his will authorize you to release to my custody all of the material of
> President Kennedy, of which you have personal knowledge, and now
> being held by the Secret Service.

I would appreciate it if you would accompany this material personally and turn it over for safekeeping to Mrs. Evelyn Lincoln at the National Archives. I am sending a copy of this letter to Mrs. Lincoln with instructions that this material is not to be released to *anyone* without my written permission and approval (emphasis in original).

On April 26, 1965, Admiral Burkley transferred the Kennedy materials to Mrs. Lincoln by letter which stated that the transfer was "in accordance with the instructions contained in Senator Kennedy's letter." . . .

By written instrument dated October 29, 1966 ("Deed of Gift"), the executors of the estate of President Kennedy, pursuant to provisions of the Presidential Libraries Act of 1955, 44 USC §397(e)(1), donated, as historical materials, the autopsy photographs, x-rays, and other material relating to the assassination of the president. . . .

On October 31, 1966, Professor Burke Marshall, representative of the Kennedy estate, delivered to the Archives the autopsy materials outlined in the Deed of Gift. . . .

The FOIA confers jurisdiction on district courts "to enjoin the agency from withholding agency records and to order the production of any agency records improperly withheld." . . .

As plaintiff asserts, the critical question in this case is whether the autopsy photographs are "agency records" under the FOIA. If the answer is no, then the plaintiff cannot prevail in this FOIA suit. If the photographs are agency records, then the question becomes whether the Archives must disclose them under the terms of the FOIA.

The Supreme Court has articulated a two-part test for determining when records are agency records. *Tax Analysts*, 492 US at 143, 109 S. Ct. at 2847. *Tax Analysts* held that in order for a record to be considered an agency record subject to the FOIA, the record must both have been created or obtained by an agency and the "agency must be in control of the requested materials at the time the FOIA request is made." . . .

The Archives argues that while the photographs were created by government personnel, once they were turned over to Mrs. Lincoln, they became either personal records or records of the Kennedy presidency. . . .

Once the records were turned over, rightfully or wrongfully, to a non-government employee, Mrs. Lincoln, the records left government possession and control. . . .

What plaintiff's argument ignores is the break in the chain of government custody when Admiral Burkley transferred the documents to Mrs. Lincoln, who was not a government employee. . . .

In the alternative, the Archives argues that even if the Court decides that the autopsy records are agency records subject to the FOIA, they are exempt from disclosure pursuant to Exemption 6, 5 USC §552(b)(6). . . .

. . . Exemption 6 exempts from mandatory disclosure "personnel and medical files and similar files the disclosure of which would constitute a clearly unwarranted invasion of personal privacy."

The Archives argues that because the x-rays convey information that "applies to an individual," they satisfy the threshold for Exemption 6. . . .

... plaintiff contends, that countervailing public interest in disclosure of the records is overwhelming, ...

In reviewing the evidence presented by the parties, the Court finds that the Kennedy family has a clear privacy interest in preventing the disclosure of both the x-rays and the optical photographs taken during President Kennedy's autopsy. ...

... Plaintiff is correct that access under the FOIA is not determined by whether the records sought will provide definitive answers to public debate, nor whether the records have been "judiciously" released to other requesters. However, there can be no mistaking that the Kennedy family has been traumatized by the prior publication of the unauthorized records and that further release of the autopsy materials will cause additional anguish. Moreover, while the Court, and not Congress, must perform the Exemption 6 balancing test, it is also relevant that the ARCA respected the Kennedy family's privacy interest in excluding the autopsy records from the scope of the act.

Therefore, in balancing the two interests, the Court finds that allowing access to the autopsy photographs would constitute a clearly unwarranted invasion of the Kennedy family's privacy. Thus, holding in the alternative, the Court finds that the Archives was justified in withholding the autopsy records under Exemption 6 of the FOIA.

In summary, the Court finds that the autopsy photographs are not agency records under the FOIA for the reasons stated above. Therefore, the Court does not have jurisdiction in this FOIA case and plaintiff's suit must be dismissed. Holding in the alternative, the Court finds that if the photographs are agency records, the Archives was justified in withholding them under Exemption 6 of the FOIA. An appropriate order is filed herewith.

ORDER

This matter came before the Court on the parties' cross-motions for summary judgment. Upon consideration of the parties' motions, the oppositions, and the replies thereto, and in accordance with the Memorandum Opinion filed herewith, it is this 2nd day of March, 1994, hereby

ORDERED that defendant's motion for summary judgment is granted and it is therefore

ORDERED that plaintiff's case is dismissed.

Katz was affirmed on appeal to U.S. Court of Appeals (68 F3d 1483).

Agencies constantly update and re-examine procedures as they interact with the public and the public's concerns. Previous circumstances at the Federal Bureau of Investigation (FBI) provide a good example of how agencies respond to the public. More than 400 files on certain individuals, many members of former Presidents' staffs, were turned over to the White House after form letters, bearing the heading White House Counsel, were sent to the FBI, requesting information and stating the request was for "routine use". Even though the requests were on pre-printed forms from the White House Counsel's office, they were actually submitted by other staff members.

"As long as the forms were facially valid, the FBI was legally entitled to assume that their author was acting within the scope of his or her authority," said FBI General Counsel, Howard Shapiro in a report released to news media.

The agency, the FBI, changed these procedures in June 1996, when the FBI refused form letters by people submitting them under the name of the White House Counsel as the person requesting the information. The new procedures state that the name of the person requesting the information must be on the form and the reason for the request. Also, the individual in the file must sanction the release of information, or a legitimate reason why that permission is not obtained must be supplied.

FBI Director, Louis Freeh said it "shows the FBI gave inadequate protection to the privacy interests of persons in FBI files."

The privacy of survivors and victims' families is often cited in FOIA cases.

Katz, and the privacy of surviving families victims — such as the surviving families of the Challenger astronauts and their tape recordings prior to the explosion — have often been cited in Freedom of Information cases.

In 2002, the FBI honored the request of the families of the victims on the plane that was hijacked and crashed in Pennsylvania (9/11/01), to listen to the cockpit tapes prior to the plane crash.

PARALEGAL PRACTICE EXAMPLE

One of your law firm's clients needs information, which has not been available to him, from an agency. Your lawyer asks you to look up the requirements and to draft a letter to the agency. You look up the Freedom of Information Act, 5 USC §552(A)(3), which gives the requirements for requesting information. You draft a letter that lists the proper agency, the proper cite of the Freedom of Information Act, the description of the record sought and the agency rules that you have followed, which include time limits and fees for copies of records.

1. Freedom of Information Act (1966)

. . . each agency shall make available to the public information . . .

The FOIA allows the public to view documents maintained by government agencies. The public may read agency information that is printed in the *Federal Register*. The following type of information might be printed:

1. description of the agency organization
2. general statement of formal and informal procedures available
3. actual procedural rules

4.   substantive agency rules
5.   description of agency forms
6.   general policy statements
7.   amendments to rules

The public may inspect and copy records at the agency; these include:

1.   final opinions of agency cases
2.   policy statements not printed in *Federal Register*
3.   staff manuals
4.   current indexes

The public may request other records and files by writing to the agency with:

1.   A reasonable description of the record requested, and
2.   Compliance with agency rules such as time limits, and fees.

After receipt of a request, the agency should within ten days:

1.   Comply with request, *or*
2.   Notify the person of the reason for denial and of the right to appeal.

If the denial is appealed, the agency should make a decision within twenty days. If still refused the information, an individual may file a complaint at a U.S. District Court. The court may order the records to be produced and may assess the agency attorney and litigation fees.

> . . . Upon any determination by an agency to comply with a request for records, the records shall be made promptly available to such person making such request . . .

The FOIA was amended in 1996 to allow electronic access (Internet) to agencies, such as requests and filings (EFOIA Amendments).

2.   Privacy Act (1974)

> No agency shall disclose any record . . . to any person, or to another agency, except pursuant to a written request by, or with the prior written consent of, the individual to whom the record pertains . . .

The Privacy Act protects certain documents from public viewing.
It does allow the disclosure of certain records in specific instances without the permission of the individual:

1.   For routine use — "the use of such records for a purpose which is compatible with the purpose for which it was collected; . . ."

2. To the Bureau of Census for survey.
3. To the person who requests, in writing, records for statistical research with identifying marks removed.
4. To another agency for civil or criminal enforcement.
5. To a person who needs an individual's last known address for health or safety reasons.
6. To the House or Senate.
7. By court order.

An individual may prevent the disclosure of records maintained on him or her by:

1. A written request to the agency to view the record.
2. A written request to the agency to keep that record from being released to others.

After receipt of the request, the agency should within ten days:

1. Agree with the request, *or*
2. Notify the person of the denial of the request and of the person's right to appeal for a review which will reach a decision in 30 days.

If the denial is appealed, the agency should review the denial and make a decision within thirty days. If a request is still rejected, the individual may file a complaint at the U.S. District Court. The Court may ask the agency to amend its decision and approve the individual's request. Damages may be assessed against the agency.

. . . the term "record" means any item, collection, or grouping of information about an individual that is maintained by an agency, including, but not limited to, his education, financial transactions, medical history, and criminal or employment history . . .

The following compiles the pertinent details of the FOIA and the Privacy Act:

Freedom of Information Act	**Privacy Act**
5 USC §551 (1966)	**5 USC §552a (1974)**
Disclosure	*Non-Disclosure*
records	records/files
policy	exemptions:
rules	written consent of individual
procedures	routine government use
decisions	court order
staff manuals	House/Senate
indexes	

Freedom of Information Act 5 USC §551 (1966)	Privacy Act 5 USC §552a (1974)
Requests	*Requests*
in writing	in writing
record description	record description
compliance with agency rules	compliance with agency rules
Remedy/Appeal	*Remedy/Appeal*
complaint in U.S. District Court	complaint in U.S. District Court

 PARALEGAL PRACTICE EXAMPLE

You work for the general counsel at the environmental agency. She has received a complaint that the agency is not following the proper procedures for open meetings. She tells you to find the basic federal sunshine statute. You copy 5 USC §552(b).

3. Sunshine Act (1976)

... the agency shall make public announcement, at least one week before the meeting, of the time, place, and subject matter of the meeting; whether it is to be open or closed to the public, and the name and phone number of the official designated by the agency to respond to requests for information about the meeting.

The Sunshine Act requires that all agency meetings be open to the public, with legally documented exceptions only. If a meeting is to be closed the chief legal officer of the agency must certify the reasons. The agency shall have transcripts and minutes of the closed meeting available for public viewing, except for those meetings that legally may be, kept private. Each federal agency must file a report to Congress stating the number of open and closed meetings held each year, with the reasons and statute exemptions for closed meetings.

An individual may file a complaint protesting the closed meeting prior to or within sixty days after the meeting in the U.S. District Courts. The court may grant equitable relief or injunctions.

The name "Sunshine" comes from a statement by U.S. Supreme Court Justice Louis Brandeis in 1933.

"Publicity is justly commended as a remedy for social and industrial disease. Sunlight is said to be the best disinfectant and electric light the most efficient policeman."

4. Trade Secrets Act (1976)

An agency meeting shall not "... disclose trade secrets and commercial or financial information obtained from a person and privileged or confidential; ..."

The Trade Secrets Act protects the disclosure of business secrets in agency actions including agency meetings. "Business secrets" may include statistics, profit or loss information, business costs, operations, or any other business matter that is confidential.

If the agency does not remedy a business secret "leak" to the satisfaction of the company, a company may file a complaint with the U.S. District Court and may be granted equitable relief.

STUDENT PRACTICE

Break into four teams. Answer as many questions as possible in three minutes. Do not look for answers in your books. The team with the most correct answers wins.

Quiz

Which Act?
1. 1976
2. 1966
3. 1974
4. 5 USC §552a
5. 5 USC §551
6. 5 USC §552b
7. Name two pieces of information printed in *Federal Register*.
8. Name two government organizations who have access to private information.
9. Which appellate court hears FOIA cases?
10. Where did term Sunshine Act come from?

E. Agency Liability for Violations

Administrative agencies, as part of the government, cannot be sued under the doctrine of sovereign immunity. "Sovereign immunity" is the barring of lawsuits against the government. There are practical reasons for this immunity: The government cannot function daily if its actions are constantly being halted by lawsuits; the government cannot afford to drain its budget fighting lawsuits and paying for alleged damages.

Yet, there are instances in which the government may be sued. For instance, if an administrative agency applies a rule in a discriminatory, unfair manner, it is liable for suit. An administrative judge who behaves unreasonably in the courtroom may be sued as an agency official, or possibly individually, but a judge who acts reasonably may not be sued for mistakes. Therefore, whenever a judge or agency officials are reasonably

Figure 4.3   **Sovereign Immunity**

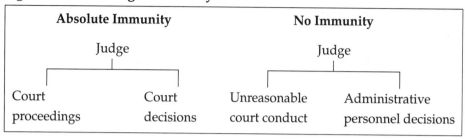

performing their duties they cannot be sued. An administrative agency cannot be sued:

1.   For any acts of discretion.
2.   For any reasonable actions of its employees.

This is absolute immunity and is often raised as a defense by the government when being sued.

Another type of immunity is limited immunity. For example, a judge may be liable for decisions on personnel matters in the courthouse. If an agency invokes absolute immunity, the lawsuit may be immediately dismissed. If an agency invokes qualified immunity, the lawsuit usually proceeds from the discovery process through to the trial. But even if sued, agency personnel have limited liability, unless their conduct was malicious. In that case they may have to pay damages for pain and reputational harm they caused the person or restraining orders may be issued against agency personnel.

Immunity for the federal government is waived often in judicial review actions. The Federal Administrative Procedure Act upheld this in 5 USC §702: "An action in a court of the United States seeking relief other than money damages . . . shall not be dismissed . . . on the ground that it is against the United States." The two major federal acts waiving government immunity are the Federal Tort Claims Act and the Tucker Act.

The Federal Tort Claims Act (FTCA), passed in 1946, 28 USCA §1346(b), waives government immunity for personal injuries caused by government negligence, but does not include agency officials making discretionary decisions. The FTCA limits the sueable actions to instances in which a private person would also be sueable. Suits are filed in the U.S. District Courts "for money damages, . . . for injury or loss of property, or personal injury or death caused by the negligent or wrongful act or omission of any employee of the Government . . . under circumstances where the United States, if a private person, would be liable. . . ."

The Tucker Act of 1887, 28 USC §1491, waives government immunity relating to businesses and contracts, and non-contract tax refund suits. Claims are filed in the U.S. Court of Federal Claims, which has "jurisdiction to render judgment upon any claim by or against, or dispute with, a contractor . . ."

F. Fair and Workable Procedures

Agency procedures have to work to be fair. An administrative agency's ability to develop standardized forms for claimants is part of fair and workable procedures; all claims are then handled according to set procedures. The jurisdiction of each claim is the office closest to the client in order to save the client physical and economic costs. There are appeals forms for an agency unemployment decision. Both the employee and the employer have access to appeals and both are supplied with proper forms.

PARALEGAL PRACTICE EXAMPLE

Your attorney tells you a client is planning to appeal an unemployment compensation denial. She gives you the Notice of Appeal form and the client's phone number. You call the client to set up an appointment, telling him which information and documents to bring to the office. You also check the agency's regulations for the time limit on appeals.

CHAPTER SUMMARY

Due process and equal and fair treatment are the basis of the rules and procedures that protect individuals and organizations interacting with administrative agencies. Due process rights of life, liberty, and property have expanded from the original concepts to include entitlement benefits, reputation, and others. Both federal and state agencies uphold these rights under the Fifth and Fourteenth Amendments. The Social Service agencies have made the most demands for the extension of due process as protection against undue hardship if people don't receive their benefits and aid. Yet, due process is not freely bestowed on all claims; the protection of the public and the costs to government are weighed against the injury to an individual. Individuals may obtain information and protect information shared with an agency through the Freedom of Information Act and the Privacy Act. Businesses may seek protection through the Trade Secrets Act. All persons may demand open government meetings through the Sunshine Act. Clients of agencies may appeal unfavorable decisions, but must be aware that their scope of appeal is limited by sovereign immunity.

Key Terms

due process
Fifth Amendment
Fourteenth Amendment
Freedom of Information Act
Privacy Act

procedural due process
substantive due process
Sunshine Act
Trade Secrets Act

Key Terms Crossword

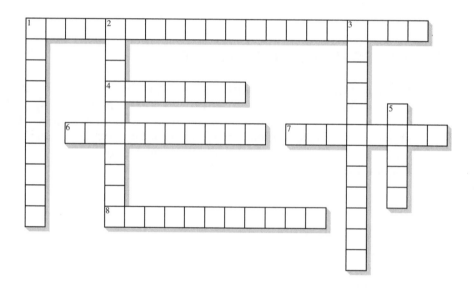

Across
1. Act—access to government records
4. Act—protect documents
6. _____ due process (methods)
7. Act—open government meetings
8. _____ due process (rights)

Down
1. Amendment—fair treatment
2. Constitutional protection
3. Act—protect business interests
5. Amendment—protect life, liberty, property

Statements

Student Study Time Hints: Look for answers under Chapter / Section

Chapter 4 / Section A. Protects life, liberty, and
property: _____

　　　　Person seeking agency services: _____

Section B.1. Notice of hearing: _____

Section C. Property includes: _____
and _____

Section C.2. Reputation destruction: _____
_____

　　　　Section D. The _____ protects privacy of information.

　　　　The _____ protects privacy of business
information.

　　　　The _____ protects access to information.

　　　　The _____ protects access to government
meetings.

No Hints:

Waives limited government immunity: _____
_____ _____ _____

Passed to eliminate racial discrimination: _____
_____

Web Resources

www.nara.gov   Freedom of Information Act and National Archives
www.uscis.gov   Immigration and Naturalization (Bureau of Homeland
　　　　　　　　Security)
www.cpsc.gov   Consumer Product Safety Commission

Advanced Studies

Due process protects life, liberty, and property and is intertwined within all the laws and regulations of the state and federal governments. Just as the legal theory in the due process amendments is interpreted in agency laws and regulations, so too is the legal theory within the freedom and privacy of information acts interpreted in agency rules.

The following documents used in this Advanced Studies will illustrate how agencies take statutes outside of the agency and inculcate them into agency regulations that outline agency procedures and actions. The two agencies discussed are the consumer protection and the immigration agencies. Although one might expect rules to protect immigrants within the immigration agency, some students might be surprised to see that the consumer protection agency also protects the rights of businesses and industries.

Document 1 — Consumer Product Safety Statute, 15 USCS §2051 — Purpose

Document 2 — Consumer Product Safety Statute, 15 USCS §2053 — Commission

Document 3 — Consumer Product Safety Statute, 15 USCS §2055 — Information

Document 3a — 5 USCS §552(b)(4) — Open Meeting

Document 3b — 18 USCS §1905 — Disclosure of Confidential Information

Document 4 — Consumer Product Safety Rule 16 CFR §1013 — Sunshine Act

Document 5 — Consumer Product Safety Rule 16 CFR §1014 — Privacy Act

Document 6 — Consumer Product Safety Rule 16 CFR §1015 — Freedom of Information Act

Document 7 — Consumer Product Safety Rule 16 CFR §1015.11 — Trade Secrets Act

Document 8 — Immigration and Naturalization 8 CFR §103.10 — Request for Information Rules

Document 8a — Excerpts from Freedom of Information Act, 5 USC §552

Outline and/or List

1. Justice Louis Brandeis commented on the need for public openness on page 124. List the parts of Document 4 (Sunshine Act) you think are applicable to Brandeis' statement. (pages 135–136)

2. Outline the similarities and dissimilarities in the Freedom of Information Act and the Privacy Act. (pages 121–122)

3. Outline the Trade Secrets Act. (page 124–125)

4. List the Fifth and Fourteenth Amendment protections. (page 124)

Analyzing Documents and Practices

1. Explain how agencies use cost analysis when giving notice. (page 110)

2. In Document 1, compare the findings in §2051(a) with the purposes in §2051(b). (page 133)

3. What type of information is protected in Document 3b? (page 135)

4. What type of agency is Consumer Product Safety and how are members appointed? (Document 2, page 134)

Take Home Exam

True/False 1. Notice informs clients of actions to take place.

True/False 2. Standardized claim forms are part of fair procedures.

True/False 3. Freedom of Information Act protects privacy of information.

True/False 4. Acts of discretion have absolute immunity for agencies.

True/False 5. The U.S. Constitution protects rights to welfare.

True/False 6. Due Process protects life, liberty, and property.

True/False 7. Trade Secrets Act protects access to government meetings.

True/False 8. FOIA does not allow appeals.

True/False   9.   The Privacy Act allows a person to keep records from being released.

True/False   10.   Both employer and employee have access to appeals.

Complete Diagrams

    1.   **Diagram** the three basic due process rights protected by the fifth amendment. (page 105)

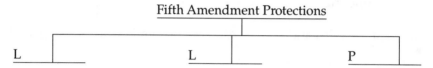

    2.   **Diagram** the requirements for a due process violation. (page 111)

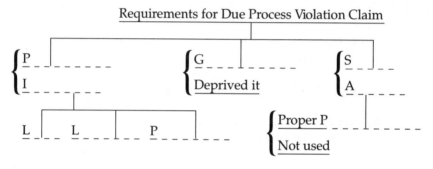

    3.   **Diagram** the Four Acts ensuring freedoms for agency clients. (page 112)

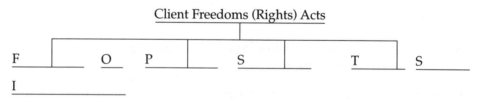

Three Venues of Research

    1. **In Book**   The Freedom of Information Act often balances the interest of two parties in agency action. (page 112) What are some of the opposing interests for information or privacy? (pages 117–121)

    2. **At Library**   (a) Read magazines and newspapers dated from November 2008 to June 2009. Choose two agencies mentioned concerning the national economy and tell what they are doing, what they did do, or what they are planning for the future.

(b) Research the information that the Consumer Product Safety Commission issues. What type of products do they address?

3. **On Internet** Check the USCIS website at *http://www.uscis.gov*. Research the USCIS as a part of the Bureau of Homeland Security, its mission, and other areas that interest you. Write up a report.

Internship

Your lawyer has a client charged with stealing air conditioners. She wants you to research some of the U.S. Citizenship and Immigration Services (USCIS) rules because the client believes he might be deported for not renewing his visitor papers. Key into *http://www.uscis.gov* for USCIS.

She wants you to write any information you find pertinent to his not renewing his papers in a memo. Your lawyer added that she wants you to also include the statute, the rules and regulations, and their U.S. Code and Code of Federal Regulations cites.

Documents

Document 1: Consumer Product Safety Statute, 15 USCS
§2051 — Purpose

§2051. Congressional findings and declaration of purpose

(a) The Congress finds that —
(1) an unacceptable number of consumer products which present unreasonable risks of injury are distributed in commerce;
(2) complexities of consumer products and the diverse nature and abilities of consumers using them frequently result in an inability of users to anticipate risks and to safeguard themselves adequately;
(3) the public should be protected against unreasonable risks of injury associated with consumer products;
(4) control by State and local governments of unreasonable risks of injury associated with consumer products is inadequate and may be burdensome to manufacturers;
(5) existing Federal authority to protect consumers from exposure to consumer products presenting unreasonable risks of injury is inadequate; and
(6) regulation of consumer products the distribution or use of which affects interstate or foreign commerce is necessary to carry out this Act.
(b) The purposes of this Chapter are —
(1) to protect the public against unreasonable risks of injury associated with consumer products;
(2) to assist consumers in evaluating the comparative safety of consumer products;
(3) to develop uniform safety standards for consumer products and to minimize conflicting State and local regulations; and

(4) to promote research and investigation into the causes and prevention of product-related deaths, illnesses, and injuries.

(Oct. 27, 1972, P.L. No. 92–573, §2, 86 Stat. 1207.)

Document 2: *Consumer Product Safety Statute, 15 USCS §2053 — Commission*

§2053. Consumer Product Safety Commission

(a) Establishment; Chairman. An independent regulatory commission is hereby established, to be known as the Consumer Product Safety Commission, consisting of five Commissioners who shall be appointed by the President, by and with the advice and consent of the Senate. In making such appointments, the President shall consider individuals who, by reason of their background and expertise in areas related to consumer products and protection of the public from risks to safety, are qualified to serve as members of the Commission. . . .

An individual may be appointed as a member of the Commission and as Chairman at the same time. Any member of the Commission may be removed by the President for neglect of duty or malfeasance in office but for no other cause.

Document 3: *Consumer Product Safety Statute, 15 USCS §2055 — Information*

§2055. Public disclosure of information

(a) Disclosure requirements for manufacturers or private labelers; procedures applicable. (1) Nothing contained in this Act shall be construed to require the release of any information described by subsection (b) of section 552 of title 5, United States Code [5 USCS §552(b) (Document 3a)], or which is otherwise protected by law from disclosure to the public.

(2) All information reported to or otherwise obtained by the Commission or its representative under this Act which information contains or relates to a trade secret or other matter referred to in section 1905 of title 18, United States Code [18 USCS §1905], or subject to section 552(b)(4) of title 5, United States Code [5 USCS §552(b)(4) (Document 3b)], shall be considered confidential and shall not be disclosed.

(3) The Commission shall, prior to the disclosure of any information which will permit the public to ascertain readily the identity of a manufacturer or private labeler of a consumer product, offer such manufacturer or private labeler an opportunity to mark such information as confidential and therefore barred from disclosure under paragraph (2).

Document 3a: 5 USCS §§552(b)(c) and (e)(4)

(b) Members shall not jointly conduct or dispose of agency business other than in accordance with this section. Except as provided in subsection (c), every portion of every meeting of an agency shall be open to public observation.

(c) Except in a case where the agency finds that the public interest requires otherwise, the second sentence of subsection (b) shall not apply to any portion of an agency meeting, . . .

. . . where the agency properly determines that such portion or portions of its meeting or the disclosure of such information is likely to — . . .

(4) disclose trade secrets and commercial or financial information obtained from a person and privileged or confidential; . . .

Document 3b: 18 USCS §1905

§1905. Disclosure of confidential information

Whoever, being an officer or employee of the United States or of any department or agency thereof, any person acting on behalf of the Office of Federal Housing Enterprise Oversight, or agent of the Department of Justice as defined in the Antitrust Civil Process Act (15 USC 1311–1314), publishes, divulges, discloses, or makes known in any manner or to any extent not authorized by law any information coming to him in the course of his employment or official duties or by reason of any examination or investigation made by, or return, report, or record made to or filed with, such department or agency or officer or employee thereof, which information concerns or relates to the trade secrets, processes, operations, style of work, or apparatus, or to the identity, confidential statistical data, amount or source of any income, profits, losses, or expenditures of any person, firm, partnership, corporation, or association; or permits any income return or copy thereof or any book containing any abstract or particulars thereof to be seen or examined by any person except as provided by law; shall be fined under this title, or imprisoned not more than one year, or both; and shall be removed from office or employment.

(As amended Oct. 28, 1992, P.L. No. 102–550, Title XIII, Subtitle A, Part 3, §1353, 106 Stat. 3970.)

Document 4: Consumer Product Safety Rule 16 CFR §1013 — Sunshine Act

PART 1013 — GOVERNMENT IN THE SUNSHINE ACT, RULES FOR COMMISSION MEETINGS

§1013.1 General policy considerations; scope.

(a) In enacting the Government in the Sunshine Act, 5 USC 552b, the Congress stated the policy that, to the fullest practicable extent, the public is entitled to information regarding the decision-making processes of the Federal Government. The purpose of the Government in the

Sunshine Act is to provide the public with such information while protecting both the rights of individuals and the ability of the Government to carry out its responsibilities.

§1013.3 Announcement of Commission meetings and changes after announcement.

(a) The Secretary of the Commission is responsible for preparing and making public the announcements and notices relating to Commission meetings that are required in this part.

(b) The Agency shall announce each Commission meeting in the Public Calendar or Master Calendar at least one week (seven calendar days) before the meeting. The Agency shall concurrently submit the announcement for publication in the FEDERAL REGISTER. The announcement and the FEDERAL REGISTER notice shall contain the following information:

(1) The date, time, and place of the meeting;

(2) The subject matter of the meeting;

(3) Whether the meeting will be open or closed to the public;

(4) The name and phone number of the official who responds to requests for information about the meeting.

§1013.4 Public attendance at Commission meetings.

(a) *Attendance by the public.* Every portion of every Commission meeting shall be open to public observation except as provided in paragraph (b) of this section.

(b) *Exemptions to the requirement of openness.* The requirement in paragraph (a) of this section that all Commission meetings be open to public observation shall not apply to any Commission meeting or portion thereof for which the Commission has determined in accordance with the procedures for closing meetings. . . .

Document 5: Consumer Product Safety Rule 16 CFR §1014—Privacy Act

PART 1014—POLICIES AND PROCEDURES IMPLEMENTING THE PRIVACY ACT OF 1974

§1014.1 Purpose and scope.

This part sets forth the regulations of the Consumer Product Safety Commission implementing the Privacy Act of 1974 (Pub. L. 93–579). The purpose of these regulations is to inform the public about records maintained by the Commission which contain personal information about individuals, and to inform the individuals how they may seek access to and correct records concerning themselves. These regulations do not apply to requests for information made pursuant to the Freedom of Information Act (except where such disclosures would constitute an invasion of privacy of an individual).

§1014.3 Procedures for requests pertaining to individual records.

(a) Any individual may request the Commission to inform him or her whether a particular record system named by the individual contains a record pertaining to him or her. The request may be made by mail or in person during business hours (8:30 a.m. to 5 p.m.).

§1014.6 Request for correction or amendment to a record.

(a) Any individual who has reviewed a record pertaining to himself or herself may request the Executive Director to correct or amend all or any part of the record.

(b) Each request for a correction or amendment of a record shall be in writing and shall contain the following information:

(1) The name of the individual requesting the correction or amendment;

(2) The name or other description of the system of records in which the record sought to be amended is maintained;

(3) The location of that record in the system of records to the extent that it is known;

(4) A copy of the record sought to be amended or a description of that record;

(5) A statement of the material in the record that should be corrected or amended;

(6) A statement of the specific wording of the correction or amendment sought. . . .

Document 6: Consumer Product Safety Rule 16 CFR §1015—Freedom of Information Act

PART 1015—PROCEDURES FOR DISCLOSURE OR PRODUCTION OF INFORMATION UNDER THE FREEDOM OF INFORMATION ACT

Subpart A—Production or Disclosure Under 5 USC §552(a)

§1015.1 Purpose and scope.

(a) The regulations of this subpart provide information concerning the procedures by which Consumer Product Safety Commission records may be made available for inspection and the procedures for obtaining copies of records from the Consumer Product Safety Commission.

(b) The Commission's policy with respect to requests for records is that disclosure is the rule and withholding is the exception. All records not exempt from disclosure will be made available. . . .

§1015.2 Public reference facilities.

(a) The Consumer Product Safety Commission will maintain in a public reference room or area the materials relating to the Consumer Product Safety Commission which are required by 5 USC 552(a)(2) and 552(a)(5) to be made available for public inspection and copying. The principal location will be in the Office of the Secretary of the Commission. The address of this office is:

Office of the Secretary, Consumer Product Safety Commission, Room 502, 4330 East West Highway, Bethesda, MD 20814.

§1015.3 Requests for records and copies.

(a) A request for access to records of the Commission shall be in writing addressed to the Secretary, Consumer Product Safety Commission. Washington, DC 20207. Any written request for records covered by this part shall be deemed to be a request for records pursuant to the Freedom of Information Act, whether or not the Freedom of Information Act is mentioned in the request. . . .

(b) A request for access to records must reasonably describe the records requested.

§1015.5 Time limitation on responses to requests for records and requests for expedited processing.

(a) The Secretary or delegate of the Secretary shall respond to all written requests for records within twenty (20) working days (excepting Saturdays, Sundays, and legal public holidays).

Document 7: Consumer Product Safety Rule 16 CFR §1015.11 — Trade Secrets Act

§1015.11 Disclosure of trade secrets to consultants and contractors; nondisclosure to advisory committees and other government agencies.

(a) In accordance with section 6(a)(2) of the CPSA, the Commission may disclose information which it has determined to be a trade secret under 5 USC 552(b)(4) to Commission consultants and contractors for use only in their work for the Commission. Such persons are subject to the same restrictions with respect to disclosure of such information as any Commission employee.

(b) In accordance with section 6(a)(2) of the CPSA, the Commission is prohibited from disclosing information which it has determined to be a trade secret under 5 USC 552(b)(4) to advisory committees, except when required in the official conduct of their business, or to other Federal agencies and state and local governments.

Document 8: Immigration and Naturalization 8 CFR §103.10—Request for Information Rules

Immigration and Naturalization Service

§103.10 Requests for records under the Freedom of Information Act.

(a) *Place and manner of requesting records*—(1) *Place.* Records should be requested from the office that maintains the records sought, if known, or from the Headquarters of the Immigration and Naturalization Service, 425 I Street, NW., Washington, DC 20536.

(2) *Manner of requesting records.* All Freedom of Information Act requests must be in writing. Requests may be submitted in person or by mail. If a request is made by mail, both the envelope and its contents must be clearly marked: "FREEDOM OF INFORMATION REQUEST" or "INFORMATION REQUEST."

Each request made under this section pertaining to the availability of a record must describe the record with sufficient specificity with respect to names, dates, subject matter, and location to permit it to be identified and located.

(c) *Prompt response*—(1) *Response within 10 days.* Within 10 days (excluding Saturdays, Sundays, and legal holidays) of the receipt of a request by the Service (or in the case of an improperly addressed request, of its receipt by the appropriate office as specified in paragraph (a) of this section), the authorized Service official shall either comply with or deny the request unless an extension of time is requested as required under 28 CFR §16.1(d).

Document 8a: Excerpts from Freedom of Information Act, 5 USC §552

§552. Public information; agency rules, opinions, orders, records, and proceedings

(a) Each agency shall make available to the public information. . . . upon any request for records which (i) reasonably describes such records and (ii) is made in accordance with published rules stating the time, place, fees (if any), and procedures to be followed, shall make the records promptly available to any person. . . .

(6)(A) Each agency, upon any request for records made under paragraph (1), (2), or (3) of this subsection, shall—

(i) determine within 20 days (excepting Saturdays, Sundays, and legal public holidays) after the receipt of any such request whether to comply with such request and shall immediately notify the person making such request of such determination and the reasons therefor, and of the right of such person to appeal to the head of the agency any adverse determination;

5

Agency Rules and Regulations

The Nation's News . . .

* *FCC CHIEF SAYS AGENCY FAILED CHILDREN*

* *STATE TO FREE 10,000 FIRMS FROM ENVIRONMENTAL PERMITS*

* *CITY GETS NEARLY $300M TO FIX SUBSIDIZED UNITS*

* *POLICE ENFORCE BAN ON WATERING*

—Newspaper Headlines

CHAPTER OBJECTIVES

This chapter answers the following questions:

- How are rules made?
- What is informal rulemaking?
- What is formal rulemaking?
- How do citizens participate in rulemaking?
- What information is in the *Federal Register*?
- What are the three major rules?
- What is a proposed rule?
- What is a final rule?

CHAPTER OVERVIEW

Agency rules and regulations implement broad legislative laws in a detailed manner. **Rulemaking** follows established procedures such as publication of notice of a proposed rule and also publication of a final rule. Interested parties are given the opportunity to comment on a proposed rule and to appeal a final rule. Some rulemaking procedures are **informal** allowing interested parties to mail comments on a proposed rule to an agency; other rulemaking procedures are quite **formal** allowing interested parties to present evidence and cross-examine witnesses at hearings on proposed rules. Because rules and regulations have been created by diverse government agencies over many years, there is a confusion in terminology. **Rule** and **regulation** are interchangeable terms; a rule is a regulation, a regulation is a rule. Some agencies use the term rule, when referring to a rule, yet, other agencies use the terms, **order** and **decision,** when referring to rules. For example, the Internal Revenue Service issues decisions, which are actually its rules. To add to this complexity, agencies call the judgment of an agency hearing officer, a decision. Both federal and state agencies make rules.

A. Definition and Purpose of Agency Rules and Regulations

The rules of the agency are the details the agency establishes to implement the enabling statute of the agency and the laws of the legislature. Agencies make rules to solve problems of public concern or to implement a policy or a requirement of the agency. Because agencies directly interact with citizens in their area of expertise, legislators believe agencies are in a better position to implement the practical, day-to-day practices of rulemaking, leaving legislatures free to concentrate on the broad aspects of law. However, without the authorization by the legislature in their enabling statutes, agencies do not have the legal permission to make rules.

A **rule** and a **regulation** are synonymous. The confusion between the words — rule, regulation, decision, and order — occurs because the agency enabling statutes interchange the terminology. Rules are a legislative function in an agency; they enforce legislative goals. Decisions are an adjudicatory function of an agency; they resolve disputes. Rules are applied to large groups or to the public; decisions are applicable to the specific parties concerned. Key factors in distinguishing a rule from a decision are time and general application: rules deal with the future and large groups.

The following is a comparison of the major differences between rules/regulations and decisions/orders.

Differences between Rules and Decisions

Rule	*Decision*
Implements laws	Solves conflicts
Directed toward future	Resolves past problem
Applicable to large group	Applicable to specific persons
An agency legislative function	An agency judicial function

The agency staff initiates the rulemaking process, although the idea for a rule may have originated with other government officials or agency clients. After the agency determines the need for a rule and follows rule-making procedures, the presiding officer of the agency issues the rule with a statement of the reasons for the rule.

The rules and regulations of the federal government are compiled in the **Code of Federal Regulations (CFR).** Like statutes, rules have cites. An example of a statute cite is 5 USC §701, and an example of a rule cite is 13 CFR §10. Similar to the federal government, state governments have codes of state statutes and codes of state rules.

B. Requirements of Rulemaking

Any rule made by a federal agency must be published in the *Federal Register* before it can be legally enforced. The *Federal Register* is a pamphlet of government actions published every day the federal government is officially working. In this way, the public gains knowledge of the rule and is held accountable. Agencies also publish proposed rules in the *Federal Register.*

Many colleges have the *Federal Register* in their libraries. For those students without access to a copy, a few pertinent pages are printed in this section from the *Federal Register* website, *http://www.archives.gov/federal-register/* and the Code of Federal Regulations website *http://www.gpoaccess.gov/cfr*. Exhibits 5.1 and 5.2 show the *Federal Register* main page and the main page for the Code of Federal Regulations.

Exhibit 5.3 shows Notice of a federal rule by the Environmental Protection Agency (EPA). There is a summary and a due date for comments; other pertinent information is also given. Exhibit 5.4 is the publication of a final rule and its due date. This final rule will be compiled and given a cite in the CFR.

1. Administrative Procedure Acts

a. *Federal*

The Administrative Procedure Act (5 USC §551) attempts to standardize federal agency functions. It begins by defining terminology. According

Exhibit 5.1   **Federal Register — Main Page**

Federal Register

FEDERAL REGISTER
Hot off the Presses
Find a Document
For Federal Agencies
Need More Information?
Contact Us

Print Page   E-mail Page   Bookmark Page

Federal Register

The Office of the Federal Register (OFR) provides access to the official text of:

- Federal Laws
- Presidential Documents
- Administrative Regulations and Notices
- **Learn more**

Learn about Public Laws

Within a couple of days after the President signs a bill into law:

The original, signed document is delivered to the OFR.

The OFR assigns a law number.

Learn more

View the Law Numbers

Current Session
Previous Sessions
Stay Updated

Search our Publications

PUBLIC WORKSHOPS

Upcoming Workshop:
Tuesday, April 14
(Washington, DC)

About our Free Workshops

Shortcuts to Federal Register Publications

On our Web Site:
Public Inspection List
Executive Orders
Public Laws

On GPO's Web Site:
Today's Federal Register
Electronic CFR
Search our Publications

Learn about Our Publications

Government Actions

Today's *Federal Register*

Tomorrow's *Federal Register*
See a preview of what will be printed in tomorrow's *Federal Register*.

Indexes & Tables of Contents

What is the *Federal Register*?

More Executive Branch Resources

U.S. Government Manual

A Federal Register Publication

Rules & Regulations

General and permanent rules published in the *Federal Register*.

Daily CFR
Annual CFR
Purchase Availability
Indexing Thesaurus

From the White House

The official publication of materials released by the White House Press Secretary.

Weekly Compilation of Presidential Documents
Public Papers of the Presidents
Executive Orders Disposition
Executive Orders Text

ELECTORAL COLLEGE

The Office of the Federal Register coordinates the functions of the **Electoral College** on behalf of the Archivist of the United States, the States, the Congress, and the American People.

Register to Vote

Archives.gov Home   Contact Us   Privacy Policy   Accessibility   Freedom of Information Act   No FEAR Act   Top of Page

The U.S. National Archives and Records Administration
8601 Adelphi Road, College Park, MD 20740-6001
Telephone: 1-86-NARA-NARA or 1-866-272-6272

http://www.archives.gov/federal-register/   4/15/2009

to the Act, a rule is an "agency statement of . . . future effect"; an order is "a final disposition . . . other than rulemaking"; rulemaking is an "agency process for formulating . . . a rule." The complete definitions are as follows:

(4) "rule" means the whole or a part of an agency statement of general or particular applicability and future effect designed to implement, interpret, or prescribe law or policy or describing the organization, procedure, or

Exhibit 5.2 **Code of Federal Regulations — Main Page**

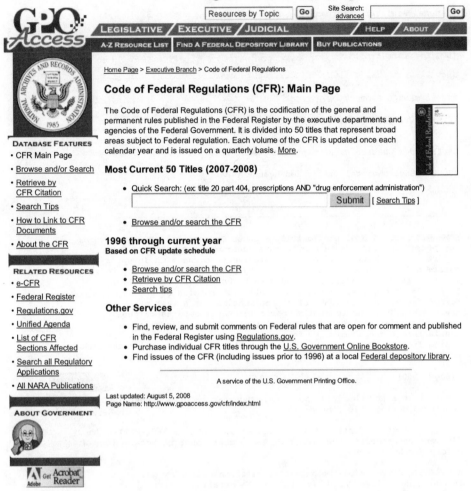

practice requirements of an agency and includes the approval or prescription for the future of rates, wages, corporate or financial structures or reorganization thereof, prices, facilities, appliances, services or allowances therefor or of valuations, costs, or accounting, or practices bearing on any of the foregoing;

(5) "rule making" means agency process for formulating, amending, or repealing a rule;

(6) "order" means the whole or a part of a final disposition, whether affirmative, negative, injunctive, or declaratory in form, of an agency in a matter other than rule making but including licensing.

Although the Administrative Procedure Act does standardize terms, it is not mandatory; agencies may still interchange the words such as rule,

Exhibit 5.3   Federal Register—Notice

```
[Federal Register: February 15, 2006 (Volume 71, Number 31)]
[Notices]
[Page 7959-7964]
From the Federal Register Online via GPO Access [wais.access.gpo.gov]
[DOCID:fr15fe06-65]
```

```
-------------------------------------------------------------------------
```

```
ENVIRONMENTAL PROTECTION AGENCY

[EPA-HQ-OPPT-2006-0106; FRL-7763-6]


Certain New Chemicals; Receipt and Status Information

AGENCY: Environmental Protection Agency (EPA).

ACTION: Notice.
```

```
-------------------------------------------------------------------------
```

```
SUMMARY: Section 5 of the Toxic Substances Control Act (TSCA) requires
any person who intends to manufacture (defined by statute to include
import) a new chemical (i.e., a chemical not on the TSCA Inventory) to
notify EPA and comply with the statutory provisions pertaining to the
manufacture of new chemicals. Under sections 5(d)(2) and 5(d)(3) of
TSCA, EPA is required to publish a notice of receipt of a
premanufacture notice (PMN) or an application for a test marketing
exemption (TME), and to publish periodic status reports on the
chemicals under review and the receipt of notices of commencement to
manufacture those chemicals. This status report, which covers the
period from January 16, 2006 to January 31, 2006, consists of the PMNs
pending or expired, and the notices of commencement to
```

```
[[Page 7960]]
```

```
manufacture a new chemical that the Agency has received under TSCA
section 5 during this time period.
```

```
DATES: Comments, identified by the docket ID number EPA-HQ-OPPT-2006-
0106 and the specific PMN number or TME number, must be received on or
before March 17, 2006.
```

```
ADDRESSES: Comments/may be submitted electronically, by mail, or
through hand delivery/courier. Follow the detailed instructions as
provided in Unit I. of the SUPPLEMENTARY INFORMATION.
```

```
FOR FURTHER INFORMATION CONTACT: Colby Lintner, Regulatory Coordinator,
Environmental Assistance Division, Office of Pollution Prevention and
Toxics (7408M), Environmental Protection Agency, 1200 Pennsylvania
Ave., NW., Washington, DC 20460-0001; telephone number: (202) 554-1404;
e-mail address: TSCA-Hotline@epa.gov.
```

```
SUPPLEMENTARY INFORMATION:

I. General Information

A. Does this Action Apply to Me?
```

Exhibit 5.4 Federal Register — Final Rule

```
[Federal Register: February 15, 2006 (Volume 71, Number 31)]
[Rules and Regulations]
[Page 7843-7845]
From the Federal Register Online via GPO Access [wais.access.gpo.gov]
[DOCID:fr15fe06-1]
```

```
=======================================================================

Rules and Regulations
                                                  Federal Register
```

This section of the FEDERAL REGISTER contains regulatory documents
having general applicability and legal effect, most of which are keyed
to and codified in the Code of Federal Regulations, which is published
under 50 titles pursuant to 44 U.S.C. 1510.

The Code of Federal Regulations is sold by the Superintendent of Documents.
Prices of new books are listed in the first FEDERAL REGISTER issue of each
week.

```
=======================================================================
```

```
[[Page 7843]]
```

DEPARTMENT OF TRANSPORTATION

Federal Aviation Administration

14 CFR Part 39

```
[Docket No. FAA-2005-22632; Directorate Identifier 2005-NM-158-AD;
Amendment 39-14486; AD 2006-04-05]
RIN 2120-AA64
```

Airworthiness Directives; Bombardier Model CL-600-2C10 (Regional
Jet Series 700, 701, & 702), CL-600-2D15 (Regional Jet Series 705), and
CL-600-2D24 (Regional Jet Series 900) Airplanes

AGENCY: Federal Aviation Administration (FAA), Department of
Transportation (DOT).

ACTION: Final rule.

SUMMARY: The FAA is adopting a new airworthiness directive (AD) for
certain Bombardier Model CL-600-2C10 (Regional Jet Series 700, 701, &
702), CL-600-2D15 (Regional Jet Series 705), and CL-600-2D24 (Regional
Jet Series 900) airplanes. This AD requires repetitive inspections for
cracking or fracturing of the output links of the power control unit
(PCU) for the ailerons, and related investigative and corrective
actions if necessary. This AD results from reports of fractured output
links of the aileron PCU. We are issuing this AD to prevent failure of

Exhibit 5.4 **Continued**

an output link of the aileron PCU, which, if both links on one aileron
fail, could result in reduced lateral control of the airplane.

DATES: This AD becomes effective March 22, 2006.
     The Director of the Federal Register approved the incorporation by
reference of a certain publication listed in the AD as of March 22,
2006.

ADDRESSES: You may examine the AD docket on the Internet at http://dms.dot.gov
     or in person at the Docket Management Facility, U.S.

Department of Transportation, 400 Seventh Street, SW., Nassif Building,
room PL-401, Washington, DC.
     Contact Bombardier, Inc., Canadair, Aerospace Group, P.O. Box 6087,
Station Centre-ville, Montreal, Quebec H3C 3G9, Canada, for service
information identified in this AD.

FOR FURTHER INFORMATION CONTACT: Daniel Parrillo, Aerospace Engineer,
Systems and Flight Test Branch, ANE-172, FAA, New York Aircraft
Certification Office, 1600 Stewart Avenue, suite 410, Westbury, New
York 11590; telephone (516) 228-7305; fax (516) 794-5531.

SUPPLEMENTARY INFORMATION:

Examining the Docket

     You may examine the airworthiness directive (AD) docket on the
Internet at http://dms.dot.gov or in person at the Docket Management

Facility office between 9 a.m. and 5 p.m., Monday through Friday,
except Federal holidays. The Docket Management Facility office
(telephone (800) 647-5227) is located on the plaza level of the Nassif
Building at the street address stated in the ADDRESSES section.

Discussion

     The FAA issued a notice of proposed rulemaking (NPRM) to amend 14
CFR part 39 to include an AD that would apply to certain Bombardier
Model CL-600-2C10 (Regional Jet Series 700, 701, & 702), CL-600-2D15
(Regional Jet Series 705), and CL-600-2D24 (Regional Jet Series 900)
airplanes. That NPRM was published in the Federal Register on October
7, 2005 (70 FR 58631). That NPRM proposed to require repetitive
inspections for cracking or fracturing of the output links of the power
control unit (PCU) for the ailerons, and related investigative and
corrective actions if necessary.

Comments

     We provided the public the opportunity to participate in the
development of this AD. We have considered the comments received.

Request for Method of Tracking Output Links of the Aileron PCUs

     The commenter, the National Transportation Safety Board (NTSB),
supports the proposed AD, except that the NTSB suggests that we require
the airplane manufacturer to develop and use a method for serializing
and tracking individual output links of the aileron PCUs. The commenter
observes that the output links do not have any identifying part number
or serial number markings. The commenter states that this makes

order, or decision. What the Treasury Department calls decisions are actually the Department's rules and regulations. Similarly, what the Environmental Protection Agency terms as orders are actually the rules and regulations of the agency. This confusion in terms exemplifies the need for the Act.

Rulemaking procedures and requirements are listed in Section 553 of the Administrative Procedure Act.

§553. *Rulemaking*

. . .

(b) General notice of proposed rulemaking shall be published in the Federal Register, unless persons subject thereto are named and either personally served or otherwise have actual notice thereof in accordance with law. The notice shall include—

(1)   a statement of the time, place, and nature of public rulemaking proceedings;

(2)   reference to the legal authority under which the rule is proposed; and

(3)   either the terms or substance of the proposed rule or a description of the subjects and issues involved.

Section (a) lists the exceptions to rulemaking; section (b) explains the notice required; section (c) relates to participation requirements; section (d) states the publication needed; and section (e) allows petition rights.

PARALEGAL PRACTICE EXAMPLE

You work as a legal instruments examiner in a federal agency. In this capacity you examine documents that are not claims, but do demand knowledge of certain laws and regulations. The document before you cites the Administrative Procedure Act, which your supervisor tells you to research for any recent amendments. Ironically, you realize your agency's copy of the APA still has the original 1946 cites, which you know have been changed and updated to 5 USC §551; you learned this in courses for your paralegal certificate. You request time to go down to the library for a more recent update.

b.   State

A paralegal may service clients who are affected by state rules and regulations, such as education rules, zoning regulations, and business or professional licensing rules. Many states have their own state administrative procedure acts. If the procedures in these state acts are not followed, the regulation or rule is not legal. Exhibit 5.5 is a rather concise example of a rulemaking section of a state administrative procedure act. In the cite,

10 State §101, the state's name would appear in a genuine state act or statute. Also, all of the sections would be lengthier in a genuine act. Much of the information in a state act is similar to the federal act. In §106 the economic impact is examined. In many rules and regulations, cost and budget are a major consideration.

Exhibit 5.5   A State Administrative Procedure Act
10 State §101 Rulemaking

§101
Definitions:

(1) "Agency" is a department, commission or any division of the state government.

(2) "Regulation" is a rule or standard having general application or future effect.

§102
Hearings:

(1) A public hearing is required if the enabling statute requires a public hearing or if violation of a regulation is punishable by imprisonment. Twenty-one (21) days prior to a public hearing, notice must be published. A copy of the notice must be filed with the state secretary and will state the statute under which the regulation is proposed, give the place and time of the hearing, and have a description of the proposed rule. If an emergency of public health, safety, or welfare exists, the requirements may be suspended; but the emergency regulation may remain in effect for ninety (90) days only.

(2) If no public hearing is required, the agency must give notice twenty-one (21) days prior to the anticipated agency action of adopting the regulation. This notice, with statutory authority for the rule, place and time of agency action, manner in which views or comments may be submitted to agency, description of the proposed regulation, shall be filed with the state secretary. The requirements for emergencies are the same as public hearing regulations.

§103
Notice:

Publication of notices in §102 shall be published by the state secretary at least a week before the hearings; if this requirement is not followed, the hearing and other actions shall be invalid.

§104
Petition:

Any interested person may petition an agency for the adoption, amendment or repeal of a regulation.

§105
Filing:

Two attested copies of a regulation shall be filed with the state secretary by the agency. The regulation will not become effective until the fiscal effect is estimated.

§106

The State Register:

The State Register shall be published biweekly with documents authorized to be published by the state secretary. Regulations shall become effective only after being published in the State Register. The state secretary shall send copies of the State Register to the clerk of the house of representatives, to the clerk of the senate, to the counsel of the house and senate, and to the state librarian.

§107

Code of State Regulations:

The state secretary shall supervise the collation and codification of state regulations, printed in the State Register, for publication in the Code of State Regulations.

c. Pros and Cons of Administrative Procedure Acts

There are many good reasons to have an administrative procedure act. Such an act generally requires the purpose for a rule or regulation be stated, along with the basis and authority for the rule. This brings reasonableness to the rulemaking process. The usual thirty day waiting period after a rule is published for it to become legal is an important time period for agencies to prepare for the rule. It also standardizes the enforcement of all agencies' rules. The required publication of all rules gives an opportunity to the public to participate.

Figure 5.1 **Pros and Cons of Administrative Procedure Acts**

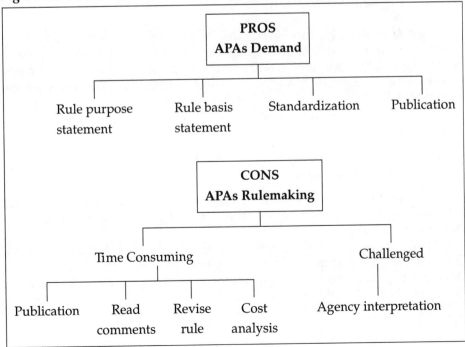

On the downside, rulemaking can be a time consuming process. For example, in 1974 guidelines for water pollution controls were issued, but the actual rulemaking didn't begin until 1977 and was not completed until 1979. Agencies must go through the following steps just to finalize a rule:

1. Write up the proposed rule.
2. Publish the rule in the *Federal Register*.
3. Send to any agencies involved for review.
4. Review any recent orders or guidelines.
5. Check with the budget office.
6. Read the views of those who responded to the *Federal Register*.
7. Revise the proposed rule accordingly.
8. Publish the revised proposed rule in the *Federal Register*.
9. Submit the revised rule to any interested agencies.
10. Make a cost analysis report for the budget department.
11. Approve final rule.
12. Publish final rule in the *Federal Register*.
13. Implement and enforce rule after thirty days by developing programs and hiring personnel.

After all that, the rule may be challenged in the courts because of the agency's interpretation of the statute.

2. Legislative Guidelines

Because the legislature enacts the statute that creates the agency and gives it the power to make rules, the legislature is the guiding force in rulemaking. This guidance results in three major types of agency rules: **substantive, interpretive**, and **procedural.** Substantive rules implement the statute, interpretive rules explain why the agency acted in implementing a substantive rule, and procedural rules govern the proceedings and practices within the agency.

a. *Substantive Rules*

Substantive rules (sometimes called legislative rules) have the force of law because they are carrying out the intent of the legislative statute in a detailed manner.

These rules are binding for two reasons: (1) They have been established through a formal, legislative type of process — rulemaking — and have usually changed an existing situation, and (2) They are carrying out the intent of the statute.

Example

Another Action—"Rulemaking"

Agencies and their rules are often challenged. In this case, the FDA rules to "reduce tobacco consumption among children . . ." were challenged.

FDA v. Brown & Williamson Tobacco Corp.
529 U.S. 120 (2000)

JUSTICE O'CONNOR delivered the opinion of the Court.

This case involves one of the most troubling public health problems facing our Nation today: the thousands of premature deaths that occur each year because of tobacco use. In 1996, the Food and Drug Administration (FDA), after having expressly disavowed any such authority since its inception, asserted jurisdiction to regulate tobacco products. See 61 Fed. Regs. 44,619–45,318. The FDA concluded that nicotine is a "drug" within the meaning of the Food, Drug, and Cosmetic Act (FDCA or Act), 52 Stat. 1040, as amended, 21 U.S.C. §301 et seq., and that cigarettes and smokeless tobacco are "combination products" that deliver nicotine to the body. 61 Fed. Reg. 44,397 (1996). Pursuant to this authority, it promulgated regulations intended to reduce tobacco consumption among children and adolescents. Id. at 44,615–44,618.

The FDA reasoned that its regulations fell within the authority granted by §360j(e) because they related to the sale or distribution of tobacco products and were necessary for providing a reasonable assurance of safety. 61 Fed. Regs. 44,405–44,407 (1996).

Respondents, a group of tobacco manufacturers, retailers, and advertisers, filed suit in United States District Court. . . . The District Court granted respondents' motion in part and denied it in part. 966 F. Supp. at 1400.

The Court of Appeals for the Fourth Circuit reversed, holding that Congress has not granted the FDA jurisdiction to regulate tobacco products. See 153 F.3d 155 (1998). . . .

It is therefore clear, based on the FDCA's overall regulatory scheme and the subsequent tobacco legislation, that Congress has directly spoken to the question at issue and precluded the FDA from regulating tobacco products. . . . For these reasons, the judgment of the Court of Appeals for the Fourth Circuit is affirmed.

It is so ordered.

Clients must comply with a substantive rule created by an agency. It has a direct impact on their lives by either creating a new obligation or changing an old obligation, and demands clients conform to the new rule or regulation. The rule is binding and enforceable.

b. Interpretive Rules

Interpretive rules explain an agency's action in implementing a statute and also explain the statute itself. Based on agency expertise, interpretive rules are the practical explanations of an agency action, providing guidelines to the public. Even though they do not have the full enforcement of law, interpretive rules are respected by the courts because of the agency's expertise.

c. Procedural Rules

Procedural rules establish the procedures necessary for the agency to function, such as rules of conduct for informal consultations and formal hearings. These rules are not as strict as court procedural rules because the agency is gathering information in a non-adversarial role. Agency procedural rules encourage participation. Procedural rules protect the rights of clients also.

d. Hybrid Rules

Agency rulemaking is a legislative function. An agency decision after a hearing is a judicial function. When an agency combines a legislative and a judicial function in its rulemaking, it is termed a **hybrid rule.** A cross examination of a witness in proceeding to gather information to make a new rule is a judicial function within the legislative function of rulemaking. This proceeding is in violation of the administrative procedure acts, which separate rulemaking from agency adjudicatory functions. The courts in recent years have frowned upon hybrid rules, but agencies do have them.

Figure 5.2 illustrates the primary rule categories.

Figure 5.2 **Primary Types of Rules**

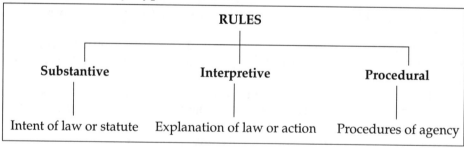

PARALEGAL PRACTICE EXAMPLE

You are a paralegal working for the Workers' Compensation agency. Your supervisor asks you to summarize some recent interpretations of some rules that have been made by hearing officers. Your office has received a memo that states some hearing officers' interpretations are being questioned.

C. Rulemaking Procedures

Agencies engage in rulemaking as legislatures engage in lawmaking. The administrative rules of procedure in agency rulemaking are termed informal and formal; their major components are listed as follows:

INFORMAL	FORMAL
An informal hearing/no hearing	Trial-type hearing
Notice of proposed rule	Notice of proposed rule
Comments of interested participants	Evidence, arguments, cross-examinations
Statement of basis and purpose of rule	Statement of findings and conclusions on each issue of rule presented at hearing
Publication of final rule	Publication of final rule

1. Informal Rulemaking

Informal rulemaking is the most common type of rulemaking. There are three processes to informal rulemaking:

1. Notice of the proposed rule published,
2. Participation by interested parties, and
3. A statement of the basis and purpose in the final rule.

If these requirements are followed, the final rule is published.

On the federal agency level, the notice of the proposed rule must be published in the *Federal Register* and must cite the proper statute or legal authority that the rule is implementing and from which it is deriving its rulemaking power. The participation of interested parties may include oral and/or written comments. The notice should include the time and place for oral comments, and/or the address to mail written comments with the closing date for comments.

In the statement of purpose, the issues should be presented in a concise and specific manner; vague statements have been thrown out by the courts. The publication must occur thirty days before the law becomes effective. Interested persons may petition to amend or repeal the rule. The purpose of informal rulemaking is to inform the agency of the various views and comments of interested participants; some of whom may have expertise in their fields.

2. Formal Rulemaking

Formal rulemaking demands that rules must be made "on the record after the opportunity for an agency hearing." Only the legislature has the power to order formal rulemaking in the enabling statute that creates the agency. These hearings must follow judicial procedures and be trial-like according to the adjudicatory procedures in the administrative procedure acts. The procedures to be satisfied are: (1) Publication of notice of the hearing date, (2) Conduct of a trial-type hearing, and (3) Publication of a final rule with "findings and conclusions."

The notice of the proposed rule must contain the same information as the informal notice, including the date of the hearing and the legal authority being implemented. Formal hearings require the production of evidence and the cross-examination of witnesses, although the rules of evidence are not as stringent as in court proceedings. Written testimony may be presented before the hearing, but parties have the right to cross-examine that partici-pant at the hearing. After the hearing, the hearing officer submits a "findings and conclusions, and the reasons or basis thereof, on all the material issues of fact, law, or discretion presented on the record." (Administrative Procedure Act, §557(c)(3)(A)) The final rule is published thirty days before it becomes effective. It may be appealed and interested parties have the right to petition for its repeal. Formal rulemaking is not preferred by most agencies and most industries; it involves tremendous costs and tremendous time. Actions under formal rulemaking, such as the hearings under the Food, Drug, and Cosmetic Act, usually take two years as a minimum to develop a rule. These hearings include thousands of pages of transcript.

3.   Policy Statements

Policy statements explain the objectives of agency actions. Some state-ments are distributed within the agency to encourage uniformity of deci-sions by the staff.

Other policy statements are public; these statements clarify conflicting situations. For example, severely ill people need medicine and drugs. Yet, the Federal Drug Administration (FDA) takes years to test new drugs. If the FDA alters its policy on a specific drug, it publishes a policy statement in the *Federal Register.*

Agency policy statements are not rules and are not subject to rulemak-ing provisions and procedures. Yet, if an agency veers too far from agency past practices in policy statements, the agency may be charged with making new or "covert" rules. In this situation, the U.S. Supreme Court has stated that these type of policy statements are subject to judicial review. Generally, however, policy statements are usually informal opinions of the agency.

CONCEPTS JOURNAL

Role Playing

You are a team of paralegals assigned to separate the various rules in a state agency into the following categories: substantive, interpretive, procedural, hybrid, decisions, orders, formal rules, informal rules, regulations, proposed rules, final rules.

As a Group:

1. Decide how you plan to define each kind of rule.
2. Decide which criteria you will need for each type of rule.
3. Decide which type of rules might appear in more than one category (ex. a rule may be procedural and proposed).

As a Group, decide if you should split into smaller teams to do the following:

1. Define each category.
2. List the criteria under each category.
3. Group categories that might be similar.
4. Choose any rules in this chapter that will fit under your categories.

Journal Notebook

Each member will take one of the rules and explain its category, the criteria for the category and similar categories.

Take notes and keep the definitions and concepts of each rule.

CHAPTER SUMMARY

Rulemaking follows requirements established by legislative guidelines; rules relate to the future conduct of a general population. Federal and state administrative procedure acts standardize the requirements of rulemaking in agencies in order to allow greater participation of interested parties and to garner information for agencies to create worthwhile rules and regulations. Substantive rules carry out the intent of the legislative statutes and are legally binding, being as enforceable as the statutes. Interpretive rules explain the basis for the substantive rules and the meaning of the statutes. Procedural rules establish procedures for agency proceedings. Most rulemaking is informal with requirements of notice, comment and publication; sometimes formal rulemaking is required with trial-type hearings presenting evidence, cross-examination of witnesses, and hearing of arguments.

Key Terms

Code of Federal Regulations
decision
Federal Register
hybrid rule
interpretive rule
order
procedural rule

regulation
rule
rulemaking
  formal
  informal
substantive rule

Key Terms Crossword

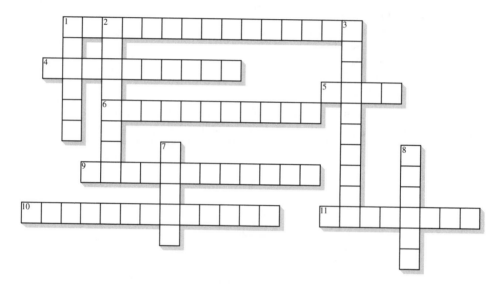

Across
1. Daily pamphlet of rules and regulations
4. Methods rule
5. A regulation
6. Statutory rule
9. Explanatory rule
10. Collection of rules—_____ _____ Regulations

Down
1. Hearings on record —_____ rulemaking
2. Conclusion reached
3. A rule
7. Agency decision
8. Legislative and judicial rule
11. Notice, comment—_____ rulemaking

Statements

Student Study Time Hints: Look for answers under Chapter / Section

Chapter 5 / Section A. A legislative function of agencies: _____

Adjudicatory function of agencies: _____

Rules are also called _____.

Section B.2. Rules with force of law: _____

Section C. No hearing: _____

No Hints:

Agency statements that are not rules: _____

To be enforced, a rule is published in the _____.

Web Resources

www.nara.gov   access to *Federal Register*
www.gpoaccess.gov/cfr/index.html/   access to *Federal Register*
www.epa.gov   Environmental Protection Agency
http://lcweb.loc.gov/   Library of Congress

Advanced Studies

Legal scholars and attorneys practicing within the administrative law field are knowledgeable of the major cases and their decisions in regard to rulemaking procedures for administrative agencies. Since the 1960s the U.S. Supreme Court has ruled in favor of the trend of rulemaking guiding the actions of agencies, instead of the former practice of the courts guiding agencies through individual case law. To equip the paralegal with the knowledge of these cases and their legal theories, which undoubtedly will be challenged during the paralegal's career, this Advanced Studies explores the pertinent rulemaking cases and the exception to APA Section 553 rulemaking. The documents used in this section are:

Document 1 — *Vermont Yankee Nuclear Power Corp. v. Natural Resources Defense Council*, 435 US 519 (1978)
Document 2 — *United States v. Florida East Coast Railway*, 410 US 224 (1973)
Document 3 — *Immigration and Naturalization Service v. Chadha*, 462 US 910 (1983)
Document 4 — President's statement citing *INS v. Chadha*
Document 5 — Rulemaking Impact List

Informal Rulemaking (Notice and Comment)

The *Vermont Yankee Nuclear Power Corp. v. Natural Resources Defense Council* case decided the question of informal rulemaking procedures by upholding the procedural requirements of the Administrative Procedure Act, which basically are notice, comments, and publication. In doing this, the U.S. Supreme Court deferred to the legislature's right to impose procedural requirements by having agencies follow legislative guidelines and not the court imposed decisions on guidelines.

Nuclear and environmental fields consistently have been regulated through agency informal rulemaking instead of the previous regulatory practice of trial-type hearings. Because of the complexity of the technology in these fields, the trial-type hearing is considered to be ineffective.

The issue in the case involves the rulemaking procedures and hearings. Vermont Yankee petitioned that the procedures were inadequate because cross-examination and discovery were not made available to them. These two procedures are found in formal (trial-type), not informal, rulemaking; the Atomic Energy Commission opted for informal rulemaking. The Court ruled that agencies have the right to decide their own rules of procedure as long as these procedures follow the minimum standards in the Administrative Procedure Act and the enabling act creating the agency.

Pertinent sections of the case are given in Document 1. Section 533 of the Administrative Procedure Act, referred to in the case, is printed earlier in the chapter.

Formal Rulemaking (Trial-Type Hearing)

The U.S. Supreme Court used the *United States v. Florida East Coast Railway* case (Document 2) as an example in *Vermont Yankee*. The *Florida East Coast Railway* decision stated that there is no requirement for a formal hearing in statutes that state rules must be made "after hearing;" this does not fulfill the APA's requirements for formal hearings. The U.S. Supreme Court again is frowning on formal rulemaking, yet does uphold formal rulemaking where it is correctly stated in statutes such as the Food, Drug, and Cosmetic Act, which regulates food standards.

The railroads in Florida objected to the incentives established by the Interstate Commerce Commission (ICC). The ICC created these incentives to relieve the freight car shortages across the nation. The railroads petitioned against the informal procedures of the ICC, claiming that the ICC statute demands formal rulemaking procedures "after hearing." (49 USC §1(14)(a)) The Court ruled that "after hearing" does not equal the APA's "on the record after opportunity for an agency hearing" (5 USC 553(c)) and further ruled that the informal rulemaking procedures satisfied the ICC and APA statutes.

Legislative Veto of Agency Rule

Immigration and Naturalization Service v. Chadha (Document 3) signaled a blockade of legislative attempts to influence agency rules after they had been mandated. Declaring the separation of powers doctrine inviolable, the U.S. Supreme Court invalidated legislative disapproval of agency actions by stating that the role of Congress is legislative and the role of reviewing agency rules is judicial. Justice White dissented and stated that this stringent interpretation of the separation of powers is unrealistic and impractical. Some states, such as Idaho (see *Mead v. Arnell*, 791 P2d 410 (Idaho 1990)), allow the legislature to review agency rules.

Chadha's deportation order had been suspended by the Immigration and Naturalization Service (INS). A resolution was passed in the House of Representatives to deport Chadha according to authority given in 8 USC §244(c)(2) of the Immigration and Naturalization Act. The constitutionality of this section was challenged and the U.S. Supreme Court declared that it was unconstitutional.

Exception from APA Section 553 Rulemaking

Interpretive rules are exceptions to the procedural requirements of notice and comment in the Administrative Procedure Act §553. An **interpretive rule** clarifies and explains the substantive rule that implements the legislative statute. Challenges to interpretive rules claim that some interpretive rules actually create new substantive rules because in their explanation of a rule, they are not strictly following the intent of the substantive rule and the statute. In these circumstances, petitioners request rulemaking procedures for substantive rules be utilized, invalidating the interpretive rule as an exception to §553.

Today, rules on abortion are being carefully scrutinized. This scrutiny is a result of *National Family Planning and Reproductive Health Association, Inc. v. Sullivan,* 979 F2d 227 (DC Cir. 1992). Sullivan is the Secretary of the U.S. Department of Health and Human Services (HHS). HHS, after notice and comment procedures, issued a rule in 1988 prohibiting abortion counseling in its programs (called a gag rule). The rule states that "title X projects may not provide counseling concerning the use of abortion as a method of family planning or provide referral for abortion as a method of family planning." This substantive rule implements the statute, Title X of Public Health Service Act, 42 USC §330a–6, "None of the funds appropriated under this subchapter shall be used in programs where abortion is a method of family planning."

By 1991 amid political uproar, President George Bush instructed Secretary Sullivan to apply the regulation only in a manner that does not interfere with the doctor-patient relationship, which was a complaint by the opposition of the rule. HHS issued a directive, an interpretive rule, that allowed doctors to discuss abortion with their patients. Challenges to this directive were made on procedural issues. This directive, challengers claimed, established a new substantive rule, which did not comply with notice and comment procedures in its creation, and was not an interpretive rule by the standards set by APA §553:

Except when notice or hearing is required by statute, this subsection does not apply—
(A) To interpretive rules, general statements of policy, or rules of agency organization, procedure, or practice, . . .

APA §553(b)(3)(A)

In the U.S. Supreme Court decision in this case, the Court stated:

... A rule that clarifies a statutory term is the classic example of an interpretive rule. ...
... a regulation that "merely tracked" the statutory requirements and thus "simply explained something the statute already required," has usually been deemed interpretive ...
Conversely, a legislative or substantive rule is one that does more than simply clarify or explain a regulatory term, or confirm a regulatory requirement, ...

One of the changes in the directive from the original regulation is the order that doctors, who could refuse to discuss abortion with patients in the original regulation, were ordered to discuss abortions with patients. If they refused to follow the regulation, the funding for their program would be lost.
The Court stated,

... the Directives do not simply explain or clarify the 1988 regulation or confirm requirements under that regulation. Instead, ... HHS is substantially amending and even repudiating part of its original regulation. ...

The Court ordered the new rule to be subject to notice and comment procedures before it may be enforced,

... when an agency adopts a new construction of an old rule that repudiates or substantially amends the effect of the previous rule on the public, ... the agency must adhere to the notice and comment requirements of §553 of the APA ...

Outline and/or List

1. Outline the final rule in the *Federal Register* on pages 147 and 148.

2. In Document 3 (*Chadha*), outline the actions of Congress and Justice White's dissent on §244(c)(2). (pages 169–171)

3. List the notice elements on page 146.

4. Outline the rule, rulemaking, and order on page 144–145.

Analyzing Documents and Practices

1. In Document 1 (*Vermont Yankee*), write the facts in the case. (page 165)

2. In Document 1, explain the Supreme Court's decision. (page 165)

3.   In Document 3, what did the Court state that the House of Representatives had no right to invalidate the deportation suspension in *Chadha*?

4.   In Document 5, choose one of the fields impacted that have a case in this Advanced Studies section. Explain the issue.

Take Home Exam

True/False   1.   Policy statements explain objectives of agencies.

True/False   2.   Proposed rules are published in the *Federal Reporter*.

True/False   3.   Proposed laws are published in the U.S. Code.

True/False   4.   A substantive rule is also a procedural rule.

True/False   5.   Informal rules are not written.

True/False   6.   Decisions of agencies resolve disputes.

True/False   7.   Agency rules are applicable to large groups.

True/False   8.   Notice includes time and place of rulemaking proceedings.

True/False   9.   Administrative procedural acts standardize requirements of rulemaking.

True/False   10. Rulemaking is a quick process.

Complete Diagrams

1.   **Diagram** the general notice of proposed rulemaking. (page 149)

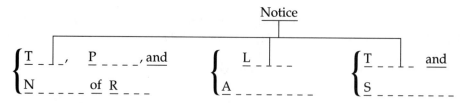

2.   **Diagram** informal rulemaking processes. (page 155)

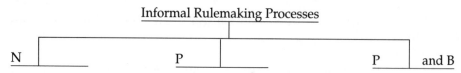

3. **Diagram** policy statements. (page 156)

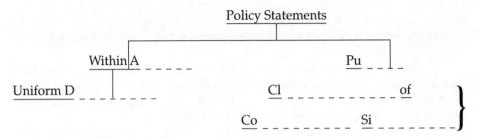

Three Venues for Research

1. **In Book** In Document 3, *Chadha*, the power of the Supreme Court was shown. Describe and explain this. (pages 169–171)

2. **At Library** Research *Federal Register*. Make up your own proposed rule.

3. **On Internet** Look up the *Federal Register* at *www.nara.gov*. Explain some topics that interest you.

Internship

You are trying to decide to which government agency you will apply for a position. You also want to have some background for an interview.

You like stocks and decide on the Securities and Exchange Commission. Look up its history and present actions (*www.sec.gov*).

Research the rules and statutes. Do the rules follow the statutes? Write your information in a report so that you will have background for the interview to show your interest.

Documents

Document 1: Vermont Yankee Nuclear Power Corp. v. Natural Resources Defense Council, *435 US 519 (1978)*

... Even apart from the Administrative Procedure Act this Court has for more than four decades emphasized that the formulation of procedures was basically to be left within the discretion of the agencies to which Congress had confided the responsibility for substantive judgments. ...

This case arises from two separate decisions of the Court of Appeals for the District of Columbia Circuit. In the first, the court remanded a decision of the Commission to grant a license to petitioner Vermont Yankee Nuclear Power Corporation to operate a nuclear power plant. ...

In December 1967, after the mandatory adjudicatory hearing and necessary review, the Commission granted petitioner Vermont Yankee a permit to build a nuclear power plant in Vernon, Vt. See 4 AEC. 36 (1967). Thereafter, Vermont Yankee applied for an operating license. Respondent Natural Resources Defense Council (NRDC) objected to the granting of a license, however, and therefore a hearing on the application commenced on August 10, 1971.

Excluded from consideration at the hearings, over NRDC's objection, was the issue of the environmental effects of operations to reprocess fuel or dispose of wastes resulting from the reprocessing operations. This ruling was affirmed by the Appeal Board in June 1972. . . .

After the hearing, the Commission's staff filed a supplemental document for the purpose of clarifying and revising the Environmental Survey. Then, the Hearing Board forwarded its report to the Commission without rendering any decision. The Hearing Board identified as the principal procedural question the propriety of declining to use full formal adjudicatory procedures. The major substantive issue was the technical adequacy of the Environmental Survey.

In April 1974, the Commission issued a rule which adopted the second of the two proposed alternatives. . . .

Respondents appealed from both the Commission's adoption of the rule and its decision to grant Vermont Yankee's license to the Court of Appeals for the District of Columbia Circuit. . . .

After a thorough examination of the opinion itself, we conclude that while the matter is not entirely free from doubt, the majority of the Court of Appeals struck down the rule because of the perceived inadequacies of the procedures employed in the rulemaking proceedings. . . .

. . . In short, all of this leaves little doubt that Congress intended that the discretion of the *agencies* and not that of the courts be exercised in determining when extra procedural devices should be employed.

But informal rulemaking need not be based solely on the transcript of a hearing held before an agency. Indeed, the agency need not even hold a formal hearing. See 5 USC §553(c). Thus, the adequacy of the "record" in this type of proceeding is not correlated directly to the type of procedural devices employed, but rather turns on whether the agency has followed the statutory mandate of the Administrative Procedure Act or other relevant statutes.

Reversed and remanded.

Document 2: **United States v. Florida East Coast Railway,**
410 US 224 (1973)

Mr. Justice Rehnquist delivered the opinion of the Court.

Appellees, two railroad companies, brought this action in the District Court for the Middle District of Florida to set aside the incentive per diem rates established by appellant Interstate Commerce Commission in a rulemaking proceeding. Incentive Per Diem Charges — 1968, Ex parte No. 252 (Sub-No. 1), 337 I.C.C. 217 (1970). They challenged the order of the Commission on both substantive and procedural grounds. The District Court sustained appellees' position that the Commission had failed to comply with the applicable provisions of the Administrative Procedure Act 5 USC §§551 et seq., and therefore set aside the order without dealing with the railways' other contentions. The District Court held that the language of §1(14)(a)[1] of the interstate Commerce Act, 49 USC §1(14)(a), required the Commission in a proceeding such as this to act in accordance with the Administrative Procedure Act, 5 USC §556(d), and that the Commission's determination to receive submissions from the appellees only in written form was a violation of that section because the appellees were "prejudiced" by that determination within the meaning of that section. . . .

1. Section 1(14)(a) provides:

The Commission may, after hearing, on a complaint or upon its own initiative without complaint, establish reasonable rules, regulations, and practices with respect to car service by common carriers by railroad subject to this chapter, including the compensation to be paid and other terms of any contract, agreement, or arrangement for the use of any locomotive, car, or other vehicle not owned by the carrier using it (and whether or not owned by another carrier), and the penalties or other sanctions for nonobservance of such rules, regulations, or practices. In fixing such compensation to be paid for the use of any type of freight car, the Commission shall give consideration to the national level of ownership of such type of freight car and to other factors affecting the adequacy of the national freight car supply, and shall, on the basis of such consideration, determine whether compensation should be computed solely on the basis of elements of ownership expense involved in owning and maintaining such type of freight car, including a fair return on value, or whether such compensation should be increased by such incentive element or elements or compensation as in the Commission's judgment will provide just and reasonable compensation to freight car owners, contribute to sound car service practices (including efficient utilization and distribution of cars), and encourage the acquisition and maintenance of a car supply adequate to meet the needs of commerce and the national defense. The Commission shall not make any incentive element applicable to any type of freight car the supply of which the Commission finds to be adequate and may exempt from the compensation to be paid by any group of carriers such incentive element or elements if the Commission finds it to be in the national interest.

I. *Background of Chronic Freight Car Shortages*

This case arises from the factual background of a chronic freight car shortage on the Nation's railroads. . . .

The Commission in 1966 commenced an investigation, Ex parte No. 252, Incentive Per Diem Charges, "to determine whether information presently available warranted the establishment of an incentive element increase, on an interim basis, to apply pending further study and investigation." 332 ICC 11, 12 (1967). Statements of position were received from the Commission staff and a number of railroads. Hearings were conducted at which witnesses were examined. In October 1967, the Commission rendered a decision discontinuing the earlier proceeding, but announcing a program of further investigation into the general subject.

In December 1967, the Commission initiated the rulemaking procedure giving rise to the order that appellees here challenge. It directed Class I
and Class II linehaul railroads to compile and report detailed information
with respect to freight car demand and supply at numerous sample stations
for selected days of the week during 12 four-week periods, beginning
January 29, 1968. . . .

The Commission, now apparently imbued with a new sense of mission, issued in December 1969 an interim report announcing its tentative
decision to adopt incentive per diem charges on standard boxcars based on
the information compiled by the railroads. . . .

Embodied in the report was a proposed rule adopting the Commission's tentative conclusions and a notice to the railroads to file statements of
position within 60 days. . . .

Both appellee railways filed statements objecting to the Commission's
proposal and requesting an oral hearing, as did numerous other railroads.
In April 1970, the Commission, without having held further "hearings,"
issued a supplemental report making some modifications in the tentative
conclusions earlier reached, but overruling in toto the requests of appellees
Seaboard and Florida East Coast.

The District Court held that in so doing the Commission violated
§556(d) of the Administrative Procedure Act, and it was on this basis
that it set aside the order of the Commission.

II. Applicability of Administrative Procedure Act

In *United States v. Allegheny-Ludlum Steel Corp.,* [406 US 742 (1972)] we held
that the language of §1(14)(a) of the Interstate Commerce Act authorizing
the Commission to act "after hearing" was not the equivalent of a requirement that a rule be made "on the record after opportunity for an agency
hearing" as the latter term is used in §553(c) of the Administrative Procedure Act. Since the 1966 amendment to §1(14)(a), under which the Commission was here proceeding, does not by its terms add to the hearing
requirement contained in the earlier language, the same result should
obtain here unless that amendment contains language that is tantamount
to such a requirement. . . .

. . . We recognized in *Allegheny-Ludlum* that the actual words "on the
record" and "after . . . hearing" used in §553 were not words of art, and that
other statutory language having the same meaning could trigger the provisions of §§556 and 557 in rulemaking proceedings. But we adhere to our
conclusion, expressed in that case, that the phrase "after hearing" in
§1(14)(a) of the Interstate Commerce Act does not have such an effect.

III. "Hearing" Requirement of §1(14)(a) of the Interstate Commerce Act

Inextricably intertwined with the hearing requirement of the Administrative Procedure Act in this case is the meaning to be given to the language
"after hearing" in §1(14)(a) of the Interstate Commerce Act. Appellees, both
here and in the court below, contend that the Commission procedure here

fell short of that mandated by the "hearing" requirement of §1(14)(a), even though it may have satisfied §553 of the Administrative Procedure Act.
. . . .

Here, the incentive payments proposed by the Commission in its tentative order, and later adopted in its final order, were applicable across the board to all of the common carriers by railroad subject to the Interstate Commerce Act. No effort was made to single out any particular railroad for special consideration based on its own peculiar circumstances. Indeed, one of the objections of appellee Florida East Coast was that it and other terminating carriers should have been treated differently from the generality of the railroads. But the fact that the order may in its effects have been thought more disadvantageous by some railroads than by others does not change its generalized nature. Though the Commission obviously relied on factual inferences as a basis for its order, the source of these factual inferences was apparent to anyone who read the order of December 1969. The factual inferences were used in the formulation of a basically legislative-type judgment, for prospective application only, rather than in adjudicating a particular set of disputed facts.

The Commission's procedure satisfied both the provisions of §1(14)(a) of the Interstate Commerce Act and of the Administrative Procedure Act, and were not inconsistent with prior decisions of this Court. We, therefore, reverse the judgment of the District Court, and remand the case so that it may consider those contentions of the parties that are not disposed of by this opinion.

The following case is cited in Document 4, President Bush's Statement.

Document 3: INS v. Chadha, 462 US 910 (1983)

CHIEF JUSTICE BURGER delivered the opinion of the Court. . . .

[This case] presents a challenge to the constitutionality of the provision in §244(c)(2) of the Immigration and Nationality Act, 8 USC §1254(c)(2), authorizing one House of Congress, by resolution, to invalidate the decision of the Executive Branch, pursuant to authority delegated by Congress to the Attorney General of the United States, to allow a particular deportable alien to remain in the United States.
. . .

Chadha is an East Indian who was born in Kenya and holds a British passport. He was lawfully admitted to the United States in 1966 on a non-immigrant student visa. His visa expired on June 30, 1972. On October 11, 1973, the District Director of the Immigration and Naturalization Service ordered Chadha to show cause why he should not be deported for having "remained in the United States for a longer time than permitted." . . . Chadha conceded that he was deportable for overstaying his visa and the [deportation] hearing was adjourned to enable him to file an application for suspension of deportation. . . .

Pursuant to §244(c)(1) of the Act, 8 USC §1254(c)(1), the immigration judge . . . suspended Chadha's deportation and a report of the suspension was transmitted to Congress. . . .

Once the Attorney General's recommendation for suspension of Chadha's deportation was conveyed to Congress, Congress had the power under §244(c)(2) of the Act, 8 USC §1254(c)(2), to veto the Attorney General's determination that Chadha should not be deported. Section 244(c)(2) provides:

> (2) In the case of an alien specified in paragraph (1) of subsection (a) of this subsection —
> if during the session of the Congress at which a case is reported, or prior to the close of the session of the Congress next following the session at which a case is reported, either the Senate or the House of Representatives passes a resolution stating in substance that it does not favor the suspension of such deportation, the Attorney General shall thereupon deport such alien. . . .

On December 12, 1975, Representative Eilberg, Chairman of the Judiciary Subcommittee on Immigration, Citizenship, and International Law, introduced a resolution opposing "the granting of permanent residence in the United States to [six] aliens," including Chadha. . . . The resolution was passed without debate or recorded vote. Since the House action was pursuant to §244(c)(2), the resolution was not treated as an Article I legislative act; it was not submitted to the Senate or presented to the President for his action. . . .

We turn now to the question whether action of one House of Congress under §244(c)(2) violates strictures of the Constitution.

Explicit and unambiguous provisions of the Constitution prescribe and define the respective functions of the Congress and of the Executive in the legislative process. Since the precise terms of those familiar provisions are critical to the resolution of this case, we set them out verbatim. Art. I. provides:

> All legislative Powers herein granted shall be vested in a Congress of the United States, which shall consist of a Senate *and* a House of Representatives Art. I, §1. (Emphasis added).

> Every Bill which shall have passed the House of Representatives *and* the Senate, *shall*, before it becomes a Law, be presented to the President of the United States. . . .
> Art. I, §7, cl. 3. (Emphasis added).
> These provisions of Art. I are integral parts of the constitutional design for the separation of powers. We have recently noted that "[t]he principle of separation of powers was not simply an abstract generalization in the minds of the Framers: it was woven into the documents that they drafted in Philadelphia in the summer of 1787." . . .
> The nature of the decision implemented by the one-House veto in this case further manifests its legislative character. After long experience with the clumsy, time-consuming private bill procedure, Congress made a deliberate

choice to delegate to the Executive Branch, and specifically to the Attorney General, the authority to allow deportable aliens to remain in this country in certain specified circumstances. . . .

The veto authorized by §244(c)(2) doubtless has been in many respects a convenient shortcut; the "sharing" with the Executive by Congress of its authority over aliens in this manner is, on its fact, an appealing compromise. In purely practical terms, it is obviously easier for action to be taken by one House without submission to the President; . . . .

. . . With all the obvious flaws of delay, untidiness, and potential for abuse, we have not yet found a better way to preserve freedom than by making the exercise of power subject to the carefully crafted restraints spelled out in the Constitution.

JUSTICE WHITE, dissenting.

Today the Court not only invalidates §244(c)(2) of the Immigration and Nationality Act, but also sounds the death knell for nearly 200 other statutory provisions in which Congress has reserved a "legislative veto." For this reason, the Court's decision is of surpassing importance. . . .

. . . Under the Court's analysis, the Executive Branch and the independent agencies may make rules with the effect of law while Congress, in whom the Framers confided the legislative power, Art. I, §1, may not exercise a veto which precludes such rules from having operative force.

Document 4: President's Statement citing INS v. Chadha

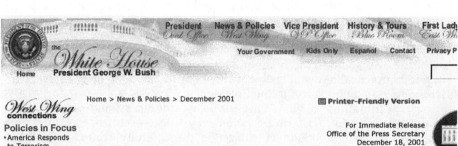

West Wing connections

Home > News & Policies > December 2001   🖶 Printer-Friendly Version

Policies in Focus
- America Responds to Terrorism
- Homeland Security
- Economy & Budget
- Education Reform
- Medicare
- Social Security
- More Issues
- En Español

News
- Current News
- Press Briefings
- Proclamations
- Nominations
- Executive Orders
- Radio Addresses
- Discurso Radial (en Español)

News by Date
- March 2002
- February 2002
- January 2002
- December 2001
- November 2001
- October 2001
- September 2001
- August 2001
- July 2001
- June 2001
- May 2001
- April 2001
- March 2001
- February 2001
- January 2001

Appointments
- Application

Photos

- Photo Essays
- State of the Union

Federal Facts
- Federal Statistics

West Wing
- History

For Immediate Release
Office of the Press Secretary
December 18, 2001

President Signs Transportation Appropriations Act
Statement by the President

Today I have signed into law H.R. 2299, the "Department of Transportation and Related Agencies Appropriations Act, 2002."

I appreciate the bipartisan effort that has gone into producing this Act. The bill abides by the agreed upon aggregate funding level for Fiscal Year 2002 of $686 billion and supports several of my Administration's key initiatives with:

— $140 million for border safety to ensure an open border for trade between the United States and Mexico through the establishment of an inspection and certification system that will ensure a high level of motor carrier safety;

— $5 billion for Coast Guard operations and capital expenses, including $243 million to support expanded drug interdiction efforts as authorized in the Western Hemisphere Drug Elimination Act;

— $1.2 billion for the newly created Transportation Security Administration to enhance airport and aircraft security;

— $32.8 billion for key highway infrastructure and safety initiatives in compliance with authorized levels;

— $10.2 billion for aviation operations and airport improvement grants to expand safety, security, and capacity; and

— $6.7 billion for mass transit grants and capital programs.

Several provisions in the bill purport to require congressional approval before executive branch execution of aspects of the bill. I will interpret such provisions to require notification only, since any other interpretation would contradict the Supreme Court ruling in INS v. Chadha.

GEORGE W. BUSH

THE WHITE HOUSE,

December 18, 2001.

Press I
- Press I
White
Secret
- Press I
Archiv

Radio
- Presid
Addres
Nation
- Discur
del Pre
Nacion
- Radio .
Archiv
- Archiv
Discur
del Pre

News
- March
- Februa
- Januar
- Decem
- Novem
- Octobe
- Septer
- Augus
- July 2(
- June 2
- May 2(
- April 2
- March
- Februa
- Januar

Procla
- Nation
Prever
Procla
- Procla
Archiv
- Execut

Federa
- Federa

West V
- History

Document 5: Rulemaking Impact List

Rulemaking decisions impact many individuals and industries. The following is a list of the activities and industries pressured by new rules, and a list of the rulemaking issues dealt with in these predominate cases.

Field Impacted	*Issue*	*Case*
Advertising	Participation/Comment	*Association of National Advertisers, Inc. v. Federal Trade Commission,* 627 F2d 1151 (DC Cir. 1979), *cert. denied* 447 US 921 (1980)
Airlines	General Applicability	*American Airlines v. CAB,* 359 F2d 624 (DC Cir. 1966)
Collective Bargaining/ Health	Substantive Rule	*American Hospital Assn. v. NLRB,* 111 S. Ct. 1539 (1991)
Commerce	Time Test	*Prentis v. Atlantic Coast Line Co.,* 211 US 210 (1908)
Employee Elections	Rule/Order	*NLRB v. Wyman-Gordon Co.,* 394 US 759 (1969)
Farm Insurance	Publication	*Federal Crop Insurance Corp. v. Merrill,* 332 US 380 (1947)
Immigrants	Legislative Veto	*INS v. Chadha,* 462 US 919 (1983)
Manufacturing	Notice	*Chocolate Manufacturers Association v. Block,* 755 F2d 1098 (4th Cir. 1985)
Mining Permits	Substantive Rule	*In re Permanent Surface Mining Regulation Litigation,* 653 F2d 514 (DC Cir. 1981)
Nuclear Power	Informal Rule	*Vermont Yankee Nuclear Power Corp. v. Natural Resources Defense Council,* 435 US 519 (1978)
Petroleum	Informal Rule	*Industrial Union Dept., AFL-CIO v. American Petroleum Institute,* 448 US 607 (1980)
Railroads	Formal Rule	*United States v. Florida East Coast Railway,* 410 US 224 (1973)
Small Power Production	Rule/Order	*American Paper Institute v. American Electric Power Corp.,* 461 US 402 (1983)
Sewage	Legislative Veto	*Mead v. Arnell,* 791 P2d 410 (Idaho 1990)

6

Investigations and Information Gathering

"... every employer ... shall make, keep and preserve such records ... and shall make such reports therefrom ..."

— Federal Fair Labor Standards Act
29 USC §211(c)

CHAPTER OBJECTIVES

Investigations and inspections are methods agencies use to gather information.

Questions answered in this chapter include:

- What are the requirements agencies must meet to investigate?
- What are records?
- What are reports?
- When may agencies attain search warrants?
- When may citizens refuse to supply information?
- What are inspections?
- Why do businesses comply with agencies?
- Which cases uphold agency powers to investigate?

CHAPTER OVERVIEW

Investigations are the process by which administrative agencies gather information for decision-making. In order to gather information from an individual or a business, the agency must have jurisdiction over the individual or business, employ a reasonable manner of collecting the information, and the information sought must be non-privileged information. Some of the information necessary is in records that the agencies may request and other information is sent regularly to agencies in reports. The agencies are restricted by the constitutional rights of the individuals and businesses they serve. Any search warrants the agencies may request must meet the standards of the Fourth amendment as must any subpoenas meet the standards of the Fifth amendment. Agencies may grant immunity to people testifying before the agency. In the majority of cases, however, clients and agencies share the information willingly. Most inspections are completed with the consent of businesses as the agency checks for compliance and/or violation of agency regulations.

A. Definition and Purpose of Agency Investigations

Investigations by an agency are a process of gathering information. Each agency develops its own unique methods of securing this information as well as utilizing common methods to all agencies, such as reports. For example, a business may supply reports of its compliance with agency rules directly to the agency on an annual basis. At other times, agency personnel may collect the information at the business site.

Agencies use the information gathered during investigations to make sound decisions concerning agency actions. For example, a rule may have to be created or amended, or a decision may have to be made on conflicting arguments between two businesses on agency requirements at a hearing. Without this information, agencies might make decisions that do not solve the problems for which agencies were created. The information supplied by the people and businesses the agency serves, helps the agency make better decisions for future actions.

B. Requirements for Gathering Information

Three conditions have been established for administrative agencies to gather information:

1. The business or person falls under the **jurisdiction** of the agency,
2. The means of collecting the information and sending it to the agency must be reasonable, and
3. The information qualifies as public interest.

Figure 6.1   **Information Gathering**

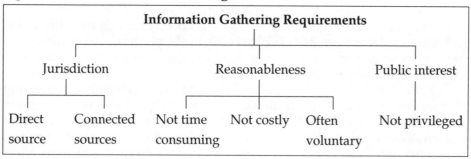

For a business to meet the statutory requirements of a regulatory agency, it must keep **records;** these records may be reviewed by the agency. If a business is ordered to send its records directly to the agency, the records are classified as **reports.** An agency may not request records that are not in its area of expertise. For example, the Workers' Compensation agency cannot review records on the zoning regulations of a business. Also, an agency may not request recordkeeping that is too costly or time-consuming for a business to maintain. If the information requested violates a trade secret, the business may object to supplying it. If the information requested is privileged, as in the reporting of information that could implicate the business employer in a criminal action, the employer may refuse to supply that information as a violation of Fifth Amendment privilege rights. In like manner, an agency cannot release information that might incriminate a person; the Environmental Protection Agency does not supply records for actions in murder trials.

1. Jurisdiction

The jurisdictional power of the agency is established by its enabling statute. The strict application of jurisdiction only to those industries under direct regulation of the agency has now been extended to include individuals and industries connected with the regulated industries. This expanded definition has been adopted in order to uncover violations and develop better regulations. The Court in *Sandsend Fin. Consultants v. Federal Home Loan Bank Board*, 878 F2d 875 (5th Cir. 1989), upheld this expanded jurisdiction. The Federal Home Loan Bank Board (FHLBB) regulates banks and therefore has the power to gather information from banks. While investigating a bank's loans, the FHLBB determined that it was necessary to gather information and records from a customer of the bank; the bank customer was not subject to the regulations of the FHLBB as was the bank. But, an agency is allowed to gather information from sources whose records are relevant to a legitimate examination of those industries being regulated; the loans of the customer were pertinent to the bank investigation being conducted by the FHLBB. The customer's own private records had to be produced so that the agency could intelligently examine the bank's records of transactions.

The question of agency jurisdiction has been ruled on over the years. In *Hammer v. Daqenhart*, 247 US 251 (1918), the Supreme Court struck down the authority of Congress to stop the interstate transportation of goods manufactured by child labor.

Even though Congress regulated interstate transportation, it could not tamper with the activities in the states which utilized that transportation system. In 1941, *United States v. Darby*, 312 US 100, upheld the extension of Congressional jurisdictional powers by stating, "The power of Congress over interstate commerce . . . extends to those activities which so affect interstate commerce . . ." Today agency jurisdiction may be limited to the immediate industry under regulation or may be vastly extended to connected persons for the legitimate exercise of agency information gathering and investigations.

2. Reasonable Means

Business and people voluntarily supply most of the information that agencies need. Without this voluntary cooperation, the millions of claims, complaints, and petitions that agencies receive each year would be impossible to process. To ensure that this information is collected in a reasonable manner, the U.S. Supreme Court stated in *Oklahoma Press Publishing Co. v. Walling*, 327 US 186 (1946), "Officious examination can be expensive, so much so that it eats up men's substance. It can be time consuming, clogging the processes of business. It can become persecution when carried beyond reason." The Fourth and Fifth Amendments protect against unreasonable collection of information from individuals and businesses.

Just as agencies are limited in their means of collecting information and in investigations, so is the Congress that authorizes the agency. In *Watkins v. United States*, 354 US 178 (1957), the U.S. Supreme Court stated, "The central theme was the application of the Bill of Rights as a restraint upon the assertion of government power. . . ." As Congress has shifted its emphasis to the stopping of "broad-scale intrusion into the lives and affairs of private citizens," agencies have limited their intrusion of inquiries to reasonable means.

 PARALEGAL PRACTICE EXAMPLE

You have just applied for a paralegal internship at the federal job information office. The information officer suggests that you fill out the forms, keeping in mind that the job requires understanding and applying laws and regulations, as well as agency procedures. You also will be involved in collecting and analyzing evidence for agency investigations.

3.   Non-Privileged Information

Agencies need substantial information to adequately perform rulemaking and decision-making, yet there is information that an agency may not request — protected or privileged information. Trade secrets and business secrets need not be disclosed, unless the agency insures the protection of that information from being released. Limitations on agency investigations are based on the limitations of legislative power. The Congress, like the state legislatures, is granted the power to legislate. In order to legislate, it needs information; thereby it acquires the power to investigate and gather information. However, this power to investigate may be utilized only when a need to legislate is demonstrated. In *Watkins,* the Court said,

> It is the responsibility of the Congress, in the first instance, to insure that compulsory process is used only in furtherance of the legislative purpose . . . "The Legislature is free to determine the kind of data that should be collected."

STUDENT PRACTICE

You are the staff of the Records Office for a university. Included in the records are:

- Income information of students' parents
- Alumni lists
- Criminal records of students
- Job listings
- Medical records of students and staff
- School year calendar
- Staff evaluations of other staff
- Class schedule times
- Student grades
- Course syllabi
- Student disciplinary actions at the university
- Future building proposals
- Staff salaries
- Future staffing projections by departments
- Student scholarship and loan funding amounts
- Plant maintenance costs
- Professional internship contacts

1. Develop a system for maintaining the records by categories and access to records.
2. Develop a request sheet for viewing records.

C. Recordkeeping

Figure 6.2 **Pertinent Data on Records**

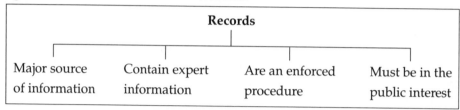

Records

| Major source of information | Contain expert information | Are an enforced procedure | Must be in the public interest |

1. Requirements

Those subject to the regulations of an agency fall under the agency's jurisdiction and recordkeeping requirements. Records have been the major information source for agencies since they were created in the late eighteenth century. Records and the filing of reports are an integral part of an agency's ability to make regulations based on sound knowledge by those most affected by the agency's rules and regulations. The U.S. Supreme Court has upheld enforced recordkeeping, "records required by law to be kept in order that there may be suitable information of transactions which are the appropriate subjects of governmental regulation and the enforcement of restrictions validly established . . ." (*Shapiro v. United States*, 335 US 1 (1948).

Legislative statutes have created the authority for agencies to demand record compliance; in the Federal Fair Labor Standards Act, 29 USC §211(c), Congress instructs employers to keep wage and hour records in the manner ordered by the agency that makes the regulations for the specific employer and business. The Internal Revenue Service requires taxpayers to keep records for tax deductions and requires wages earned statements as records.

Figure 6.3 **Need for Records**

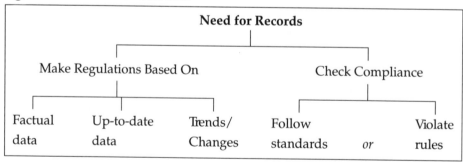

Need for Records

Make Regulations Based On

| Factual data | Up-to-date data | Trends/ Changes |

Check Compliance

| Follow standards | *or* | Violate rules |

When the Occupational Safety and Health Agency (OSHA) established standards for cancer exposure on the job, it provided that standards, and the records to prove compliance with agency standards, must be "technologically achievable at a cost that would not impair the viability of the industries subject to the regulations." *Industrial Union Dept., AFL-CIO v. American Petroleum Institute* (the Benzene Case), 448 US 607 (1981).

The legal basis for the requirement of recordkeeping emanated from the First Session of Congress in 1789, which required persons administering oaths to maintain records of the time and manner of the oath-taking. Also at that first Congress statutes were passed ordering importers to keep records of invoices so that duties and fees could be collected on the tonnage of vessels. The records were to be filed with the port collector.

The Fourth and Fifth Amendments may not be used as shields against the requirements of recordkeeping. As long as records are being sought for the public interest in a regulated activity, and are not sought to prove criminal involvement, the power to require records for compliance purposes predominates. In *United States v. Morton Salt Co.*, 338 US 632 (1950), Morton Salt Company appealed an order of the Federal Trade Commission to both cease and desist an activity, and also to file records of compliance. The company particularly objected to the need for specific records beyond the annual reports. The Court stated, "... agencies have a legitimate right to satisfy themselves that corporate behavior is consistent with the law and public interest."

PARALEGAL PRACTICE EXAMPLE

You are a paralegal in the Environmental Protection Agency. Besides keeping abreast of recent appellate court decisions, you have to review the records of field investigators to ascertain that the information necessary for a proper hearing has been gathered. In addition to reviewing these investigative reports, you also maintain the records of active cases.

2. Client Privilege Rights

Agencies have the power to seek and demand information, but clients have the right to protect certain information. The major protections originate in the Fourth and Fifth Amendments; the Fourth Amendment protects clients from improper searches and inspections and the Fifth Amendment protects clients from supplying information that could be self-incriminating. However, agency requests for records do not have to meet the stringent requirements of the criminal codes.

The Fifth Amendment privilege states:

No person shall be ... compelled in any criminal case to be a witness against himself, nor be deprived of life, liberty, or property, without due process of law. . . .

Figure 6.4 charts the records available to administrative agencies.

Figure 6.4   **Records Accessible to Agencies**

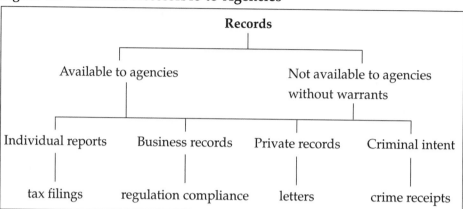

If an agency properly orders records to be kept and to be reported to the agency, those records are government property. In *Shapiro v. United States,* 335 US 1 (1948), the claim was made that the privilege against self-incrimination protected sales records of a fruit and produce wholesaler, because the records were private. The wholesaler, Mr. Shapiro, was prosecuted for violating regulations under the Emergency Price Control Act of 1942. To be in compliance with the Office of Price Administration, sales records had to be produced. Mr. Shapiro was charged with violations based on the records he produced. He then claimed the self-incrimination privilege of the Fifth Amendment. The U.S. Supreme Court stated, "The privilege which exists as to private papers cannot be maintained" if the private records are information needed to comply with government regulations.

The Fifth Amendment has been upheld in agency recordkeeping if the production of those records could lead to criminal prosecution. This was

Figure 6.5   **Application of Fifth Amendment**

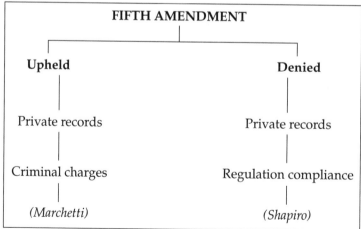

demonstrated in *Marchetti v. United States,* 390 US 39 (1968). The Internal Revenue Service (IRS) had ordered Marchetti, a gambler, to register with the IRS in relation to filing reports required for those participating in the practice of accepting wages as a business. If Marchetti filed, he would be subject to violating state and federal gambling laws and be prosecuted. The Court upheld Marchetti's Fifth Amendment privileges by commenting on the recordkeeping requirement, "Marchetti was not . . . obliged to keep and preserve records" but was actually being required to give information on "his wagering activities." The Court also stated that there were no "public aspects," and unlike *Shapiro,* Marchetti's case was not "an essentially non-criminal and regulatory area of inquiry" but was actually an order being directed at a "selective group inherently suspect of criminal activities."

CASE ABSTRACT

The following is a State of California case in which the Fifth Amendment shield for protection is to an employer that did not pay overtime wages. This excerpt is an example of the cases that appear in courts concerning records and government agencies.

The Division of Labor Standards Enforcement ordered wage records be produced in order to prove the failure of providing overtime wages. A lower court upheld the employer's refusal on the grounds of self-incrimination. The California Supreme Court overturned the lower court, stating, "The privilege does not apply where . . . the reporting requirement is intended to promote a legitimate regulatory aim. . . ."

Note the Fifth Amendment privilege reasoning and the discussion on *Shapiro.*

Craib v. Bulmash
777 P2d 1120 (Cal. 1989)

EAGLESON, Justice.

This case concerns the circumstances under which an employer may assert the Fourth and Fifth Amendments to the United States Constitution as defenses to judicial enforcement of an administrative agency's subpoena duces tecum for records of a kind which all employers are required by law to maintain.

We first reject the employer's claim that a court order compelling compliance with the agency's subpoena is an "unreasonable search and seizure" under the Fourth Amendment unless supported by "probable cause." Forty years of United States Supreme Court decisions establish that the subpoenaed records need only be relevant to an authorized regulatory purpose and described with reasonable specificity. While this approach traditionally has been applied in the context of subpoenaed corporate records, we see no reasoned basis for departing from precedent solely because the instant employer is an individual, rather than a corporation. Further, there is no reasonable expectation of privacy against judicially compelled disclosure of records required to be kept, and subject to administrative subpoena, under a lawful regulatory scheme.

Also, consistent with the traditional exemption of "required records" from the Fifth Amendment privilege against compulsory self-incrimination, an employer must unconditionally respond to a court order enforcing an agency's subpoena for wage and hour records which the employer is statutorily required to maintain. The privilege does not apply where, as here, the reporting requirement is intended to promote a legitimate regulatory aim, is not directed at activities or persons that are inherently "criminal," and only requires minimal disclosure of information of a kind customarily kept in the ordinary course of business.

The Court of Appeal therefore erred in relying on the Fourth and Fifth Amendments to reverse a court order compelling the employer to comply with the instant administrative subpoena. We will reverse the judgment of the Court of Appeal.

Background

Here, Jay S. Bulmash (Bulmash) was appointed trustee for his sister, Serena Gluck (Gluck), and employed attendants to care for her. In February 1986, Deputy Labor Commissioner Donald C. Craib (Commissioner) issued and served a subpoena duces tecum directing Bulmash to appear at the Division's Santa Barbara offices one month later and to produce time and wage records, and names and addresses, for all persons employed by the trust over the previous three-year period.

  . . .

After Bulmash failed to appear as requested, the Commissioner filed an unverified petition in the superior court seeking to enforce the subpoena. The petition alleged that the subpoena and investigation were authorized under the statutory provisions cited above. According to the petition, the investigation began after a "former employee" of the trust lodged a complaint against Bulmash for "failure to pay overtime wages as required by Industrial Welfare Commission Order 15-80."

  . . .

On appeal, . . . the court also addressed the question whether enforcement of the subpoena would violate Bulmash's Fifth Amendment privilege against compulsory self-incrimination. The court answered this question in the affirmative, apparently concluding that both the contents of the records and the compulsory act of production amounted to incriminating testimony of Bulmash's failure to pay the appropriate wage.

  . . .

Discussion

A. Fourth Amendment . . .

We agree with the Commissioner that no Fourth Amendment "privacy" claim can be asserted against an administrative subpoena limited to the production of records which the subpoenaed party is required to maintain, for the express purpose of agency inspection, under lawful statutes or regulations. . . .

Accordingly, we hold that the Fourth Amendment does not prohibit judicial enforcement of the instant administrative subpoena. The Court of Appeal erred in reversing the order compelling compliance on this ground. . . .

B. Fifth Amendment

Bulmash argues that, since the instant records could facially disclose noncompliance with wage and hour laws, the Fifth Amendment is a complete defense to court-ordered compliance with the subpoena.

The lower federal courts continue to apply the "required records doctrine" of *Shapiro, supra* [and] several cases have allowed the mandatory disclosure of information which, on its face, could implicate the reporter in criminal conduct. . . .

The same approach leads us to reject Bulmash's Fifth Amendment challenge to judicial enforcement of the commissioner's subpoena. As contemplated by *Shapiro, supra*, the information required by section 1174 is the "appropriate" subject of a lawful regulatory scheme. The reporting law is obviously intended to encourage voluntary compliance with minimum labor standards designed for the *mutual* benefit of employees *and* employers. . . .

Consistent with this statutory theme of statewide, uniform regulation is the significant number of "civil" enforcement techniques available to ensure employees receive the minimum wage under proper working conditions. These provisions, which seek to recover wages due and/or encourage continuing compliance with the law, would be rendered completely ineffectual were the state foreclosed from compelling the type of information sought here. Section 1174 requests the minimum amount of data necessary to implement the scheme's regulatory aim. . . .

The judgment of the Court of Appeal is reversed.

Figure 6.6 illustrates the major constitutional and statutory protections for clients in supplying records.

Figure 6.6   **Client Rights in Supplying Records**

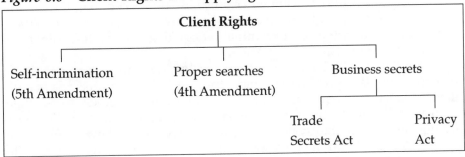

Exhibit 6.1 **Major Recordkeeping Cases**

INFORMATION GATHERING
   Oklahoma Press Publishing Co. v. Walling, 327 US 186 (1946)
   Watkins v. United States, 354 US 178 (1957)

JURISDICTION
   Sandsend Financial Consultants v. Federal Home Loan Bank Board, 878 F2d
      875 (5th Cir. 1989)
   United States v. Darby, 312 US 100 (1941)

RECORDKEEPING REQUIREMENTS
   Craib v. Bulmash, 777 P2d 1120 (Cal. 1989)
   ICC v. Goodrich Transit Co., 224 US 194 (1912)
   Industrial Union Dept., AFL-CIO v. American Petroleum Institute
      (the Benzene Case), 448 US 607 (1981)
   Marchetti v. United States, 390 US 39 (1968)
   Shapiro v. United States, 335 US 1 (1948)
   United States v. Morton Salt Co., 338 US 632 (1950)

PARALEGAL PRACTICE EXAMPLE

You work as a paralegal in a large engineering company where your job is to analyze legal compliance requirements for proposed projects on which the company has written bids. Your work involves knowledge of regulations from various states because your company has branches in many states. You have access to many of the company's confidential records for future proposals and are wary of releasing privileged information.

3. Exceptions to Recordkeeping Requirements

As a summary, the following are the major exceptions to the administrative agency requirements of recordkeeping.

SELF-INCRIMINATION. Under the Fifth Amendment a person is not required to supply information to an administrative agency that could lead to *criminal* prosecution. (Businesses cannot use this exception.) If the information is in records voluntarily kept, the individual must produce those records on request; the self-incrimination privilege only refers to mandatory information required by the agency.

REASONABLENESS. If a person or business proves the required recordkeeping is beyond a reasonable time and cost limit, records of compliance may not be required. If either an individual or business shows there is a reasonable opportunity of being harmed or injured, such as disclosure of a business secret, the agency may adjust the recordkeeping requirement.

JURISDICTION. If a person or business proves its actions are not under the agency's jurisdiction, the person or business is exempt from recordkeeping.

CONCEPTS JOURNAL

Role Playing

Each student is employed as a paralegal in a law firm that protects literary rights and intellectual property. You have been given this chapter as a document and record. Your firm is to protect the ideas in this chapter; your job is assisting the law firm in the following:

Individually
1. List the specific major ideas to be protected and define each idea.
2. List any connected ideas.
3. List any examples and illustrations.

As a Group
1. Take your specific lists and develop a generalized list that will appear in a legal document—don't give away any specific ideas. This legal document is going to be given as part of a records request for a government agency.
2. Make a specific list to correspond to the generalized list—one that is confidential and privileged—to be kept at the law firm and not released to the agency.

Journal Keeping

Keep both lists for your files. This should not only give you workable definitions but also generalized concepts.

Agencies investigate normal events and disasters.

D. Inspections

Administrative agency **inspections** are the investigations and examinations conducted on the actual physical premises owned by an individual or business. The purpose of an inspection is to discover any violations of agency rules and regulations. Inspections allow agencies to enforce laws such as public safety, health protections, and occupational safety. Some inspections include tests at the sites, but usually only are observations of the business plant and a review of records.

Most individuals and businesses voluntarily comply with regulations and agency inspections to secure licenses and show adherence to municipal codes; for example, building codes for safety and health. Strictly regulated businesses voluntarily comply with regulations and agency inspections in order to be allowed to operate in their industries. Legislation requires some businesses to agree to these inspections before beginning their enterprise; for example, railroads and utility companies.

1. Fourth Amendment Protection

The Fourth Amendment right of reasonable search is applicable to inspections, but is not applied as strictly as in criminal investigations. Although it is conceded that agencies need a certain amount of leeway in order to function and make informed decisions, the agencies are seeking violations of compliance, not criminal evidence. If an inspection could possibly result in a criminal prosecution, the stringent requirements of search and seizure laws are upheld.

Inspection is usually synonymous with entry and search of premises, be it reviewing the building or the records. Searches come under the protection of the Fourth Amendment privilege of the U.S. Constitution—

> The right of the people to be secure in their persons, houses, papers, and effects, against unreasonable searches and seizures, shall not be violated, and no warrants shall issue but upon probable cause, supported by oath or affirmation, and particularly describing the place to be searched, and the person or things to be seized.

 PARALEGAL PRACTICE EXAMPLE

You are working at a state agency that handles the state workers pension system. Although others process the pension claims, you assist an attorney evaluating information on various court decisions that are affecting retirement ages, and new reporting and disclosure laws. You have to list the current techniques for gathering reports and updating them for any new court rulings.

STUDENT PRACTICE

You have just discovered that a search warrant has been issued to search your belongings. Your lawyer tells you to comply with the warrant; it's legal and it's for drugs, but don't worry, you have nothing to conceal.

Unfortunately, your lawyer also tells you that many of your "personal things will be looked over." In this type of situation, what invasion of privacy occurs to you, the student, even if it is a legal search. List anything that qualifies (ex. bank book — to see if you are stashing earnings from drug sales).

Remember you are innocent but the search still takes place.

Do this exercise as a discussion group.

---

a. Private Premises

Inspections of private houses have been uniformly protected by the Fourth Amendment, although in a manner less stringent than the Fourth Amendment privileges in criminal cases. This limited protection theory abounds because private premises need services, such as sewerage and electricity, and these services must meet approval of building inspection codes. Unlike the specific search warrant with probable cause, administrative agency search warrants for homes are often generalized, area by area. For instance, towns often send notification that valuation of each property in the town will be ascertained and that the search warrant may be inspected at the town hall. Health inspectors use such generalized warrants.

The reasoning for this type of search arose from *Camara v. Municipal Court*, 387 US 523 (1967). In *Camara* a resident refused admittance to a housing inspector who had no search warrant to make a routine check of municipal housing code violations, a yearly routine. The U.S. Supreme Court upheld the request for a warrant but authorized the warrant to be generalized on a neighborhood, or other area, basis.

Forced inspections in private premises are prohibited unless the agency has a search warrant. This warrant may be of a general nature relating to a large area or neighborhood, if homes to be inspected are for health, safety, and legitimate public interest concerns; for example, updating the valuation of property.

b. Businesses

Unlike a private home, a place of business is public; the public enters and leaves the premises. Therefore, many inspections take place that are really observations of the public access areas of a business. On the state as well as federal level, the courts have found that "the owner or operator of commercial premises in a 'closely regulated' industry has a reduced expectancy of privacy." *New York v. Burger*, 482 US 691 at 702 (1987).

Most businesses, such as commercial companies, are protected from unreasonable inspections by the requirement of an agency search warrant. However, businesses that are strictly regulated (e.g. liquor and firearms businesses) do not have the right to demand a search warrant in agency inspections; but the warrantless inspection must be stated in legislation.

2. Pertinent Fourth Amendment Cases

The Fourth Amendment privilege has had its share of conflicts in administrative law. Conflicting decisions have occurred on both the federal and state levels. The Court in *Camara* required a warrant for the search of private premises, and in the inspection of a commercial business in *Marshall v. Barlow's, Inc.*, 436 US 307 (1978). But *Donovan v. Dewey*, 452 US 594 (1981), ruled a warrant was not required for *strictly* regulated businesses. The federal government upheld a warrantless search in *New York v. Burger*, but the state of New York took an opposite viewpoint in *People v. Scott*. The courts in these two cases took divergent views even though they concerned the same type of business — automobile junkyards.

In *Burger*, a junkyard was discovered to have stolen vehicles and parts on an inspection for licenses and records. The owner objected to the search, stating a warrant was necessary. The U.S. Supreme Court stated a warrantless search was satisfactory because the junkyard came under the description of a "closely regulated" business.

In *Scott*, a totally different ruling is delivered by the State of New York. Individual rights and the right to a search warrant under the Fourth Amendment for businesses were upheld, stating that "... the administrative search exception should remain a narrow and carefully circumscribed one."

E. Investigatory Procedures

Agencies have investigatory procedures to more forcefully compel the gathering of information: search warrants, subpoenas, and testimony grants of immunity.

1. Search Warrants

Search warrants have been discussed in the prior section on the Fourth Amendment and inspections. That discussion focused on the client's need

Figure 6.7   **Agency Information Gathering**

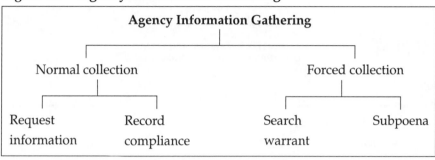

for a search warrant. This section focuses on the agency's view of search warrants.

The agency has the right to provide a search warrant for its searches and inspections. There is no need for a warrant, if the business desires to comply with the rules and regulations of the agency, and essentially invites the agency onto the property. When there is a refusal to allow an agency to conduct a search, the search warrant is used. To obtain the search warrant, the agency must show probable cause that a violation of an agency regulation exists. The warrant is issued by a magistrate who will accept less stringent evidence for probable cause in administrative matters than in criminal matters. The agency follows the general rules for court system warrants: The agency shows a potential violation; the warrant is limited to specific areas. In the search, if an agency extends its search beyond the specifications in the warrant, it is in violation of the warrant and in contempt of court. If the business refuses to allow the agency onto its premises, the business is in contempt of court.

2. Subpoenas

Agencies have subpoena powers. A subpoena is an order for a person to appear at a hearing to testify or to appear at the agency with specific records; the subpoena compels a business or an individual to provide information. If a statute authorizes the agency to have subpoena power, the subpoena is issued by the agency; otherwise, it must be issued by a court.

A party requests the agency to authorize the subpoena; the agency decides if the request is relevant and reasonable before it issues or denies a subpoena request. If the business or person refuses to comply with an agency subpoena, the agency may file a suit in a court to enforce the subpoena. The court then issues an order; if this order is not followed, the person is in contempt of court. In some instances, a person or business may decide to file an objection with the agency over its subpoena. When that happens, the agency reviews the issuance. The person or business may

Exhibit 6.2 **Subpoena Form**

SUBPOENA
_____

UNITED STATES OF AMERICA
NATIONAL LABOR RELATIONS BOARD

To _____

_____

As requested by :_____

_____

whose address is _____
                    (Street)   (City)   (State)   (ZIP)

YOU ARE HEREBY REQUIRED AND DIRECTED TO APPEAR BEFORE _____

_____ of the National Labor Relations Board

at _____

in the City of _____

on the _____ day of _____ 20 _____ at _____ (a.m.) (p.m.) to testify in

_____
                              (Case Name and Number)

_____

_____

_____

_____

_____

Under the seal of the National Labor Relations Board, and authorized by
the undersigned Member of the Board, this Subpoena is

Issued at

this   day of   20

NOTICE TO WITNESS. Witness fees for attendance, subsistence, and mileage under this subpoena are payable by the party at whose request the witness is subpoenaed. A witness appearing at the request of the General Counsel of the National Labor Relations Board shall submit this subpoena with the voucher when claiming reimbursement.

_____

raise constitutional issues as objections if the agency brings the refusal to obey the subpoena to a court. The validity of administrative subpoenas are based on reasonableness and relevancy of the information sought for the agency investigation.

The agency cannot compel the subpoena to be obeyed. A court may hold a person in contempt who refuses to comply with a subpoena, but agencies do not have this authority of enforcement. The agency must seek a court order. Agencies that have attempted to provide criminal sanctions for failure to answer a subpoena have been in violation of the Fourth Amendment. It is considered to be a protection to the individual subpoenaed that he is first allowed to present his reasons and justifications to a court for refusing to answer a subpoena before any punishment may be inflicted.

When an agency issues a subpoena, it is assumed by the court that the agency has jurisdiction. The court rarely hears the issue of jurisdiction. One reason for this is that it probably would be a common complaint in each case, taking too much valuable court time. Another reason is that if the agency does not have jurisdiction, then logically the agency cannot bring the case to court, which would mean that the person contesting the case could not be heard. This was explained by Justice Murphy in his dissent in *Endicott Johnson Corp. v. Perkins*, 317 US 501 (1943).

> If petitioner is not subject to the Act as to the plants in question, the Secretary has no right to start proceedings or to require production of records with regard to those plants. In other words, there would be no lawful subject of inquiry, and under present statutes giving the courts jurisdiction to enforce administrative subpoenas, petitioner is entitled to a judicial determination of this issue before its privacy is invaded.

CASE ABSTRACT

The following case illustrates the problem of jurisdiction and subpoenas.

EEOC v. Kloster Cruise Ltd.
939 F2d 921 (11th Cir. 1991)

ANDERSON, Circuit Judge:

The Equal Employment Opportunity Commission ("EEOC") appeals from the district court's order denying enforcement of its administrative subpoenae deuces tecum. The EEOC sought to subpoena documents relating to its investigation of alleged instances of employment discrimination by appellee Kloster Cruise Ltd. ("Kloster"). We reverse; and we order Kloster to produce the subpoenaed documents.

1. The Proceedings Below

This case began when two charges of employment discrimination against Kloster were filed with the EEOC. Kloster, a Bermudian corporation, owns and operates Bahamian registered cruise ships from its offices in Miami, Florida. Judy B. Corbeille, an assistant cruise director, alleged that she was fired as a result of her pregnancy. Fernando Watson, bar manager, charged that he had been forced to resign because of discrimination based on his race and national origin. Pursuant to its statutory duty under Title VII of the Civil Rights Act of 1964, 42 USC §2000e, et seq., the EEOC commenced an investigation of these charges. To aid its investigation, the EEOC issued two administrative subpoenae duces tecum under 42 USC §§2000e-8 and 9, seeking to discover evidence relating to Kloster's corporate structure and employment practices. After Kloster refused to comply with the subpoenae, the EEOC sought judicial enforcement in the district court pursuant to 42 USC §2000e-9.

The district court declined to enforce the subpoena. EEOC v. Kloster Cruise Ltd., 743 F. Supp. 856 (S.D. Fla. 1990). Although finding that the employees worked both in the United States and elsewhere, and that Kloster had its principal executive offices in Miami, the court held that the application of Title VII to foreign flagged vessels owned by a foreign corporation, without clear congressional authorization, would "undermine the sovereignty of another country" and violate principles of international law. Id., 743 F. Supp. at 858. Having concluded that Title VII did not apply to Kloster's activities with respect to its cruise ship employees, the court refused to enforce the subpoenae. Although we do not decide the issue of the jurisdictional reach of Title VII with respect to owners of foreign flagged cruise ships, we reverse the district court's ruling because it was prematurely made in this subpoena enforcement action.

The Supreme Court has not indicated that the "law of the flag" is dispositive in a case such as this. Thus, we cannot conclude that there is a clear absence of jurisdiction. . . .

. . . Rather, we conclude only that the jurisdictional issue was prematurely resolved by the district court in this subpoena enforcement action and that the EEOC must be allowed to investigate the facts, including the facts relevant to jurisdiction, as an initial matter. "To do otherwise would be to 'not only place the cart before the horse, but to substitute a different driver for the one appointed by Congress.'" . . . Accordingly, we reverse the district court, and we order Kloster to comply with the EEOC's administrative subpoenae duces tecum.

REVERSED.

3. Grants of Immunity

In order to acquire information, people supplying that information may be given immunity from liability and prosecution. This immunity is given by approval of the Attorney General after the agency proves that the information is necessary for the public interest. Immunity stops any prosecution against a witness for the information that is supplied to the agency; it is only the evidence approved for immunity that is excepted from future liability or prosecution.

PARALEGAL PRACTICE EXAMPLE

Your lawyer has just received a subpoena issued to one of his clients; your lawyer leaves it on your desk and tells you to look up the zoning board rules on subpoenas. Also you should start preparing the documents listed in the subpoena request; list which documents are in this office and which are at the clients.

 PARALEGAL PRACTICE EXAMPLE

You, a paralegal, are called into the Human Resources office where the Director tells you that the records for the bio-medical trial you are working on have been found. Last week the client told the lawyer that not all the records had been returned; the law firm this week looked at the diary schedule you filed for that week. They contacted the other client whose case you had been collecting reports on and returning records. The missing documents of the first client were sent in the returned records to the second client. Your initials were on the mailing slip. The Director tells you the law firm will no longer need your services.

CHAPTER SUMMARY

Information gathering is a vital function of agencies that encompasses recordkeeping, inspections, and use of investigatory procedures. Investigation procedures include search warrants, subpoenas and testimony with a grant of immunity. Recordkeeping requests must meet the requirements of reasonableness, jurisdiction and non-privileged information. The protections for clients include the Fourth Amendment privilege against unreasonable search and the Fifth Amendment privilege against self-incrimination. Searches without warrants in strictly regulated industries are considered to be a viable means of gathering information. When ignored, the agency subpoena needs to be enforced by court orders.

Key Terms

immunity	jurisdiction	search warrant
inspection	record	subpoena
investigation	report	testimony

Key Terms Crossword

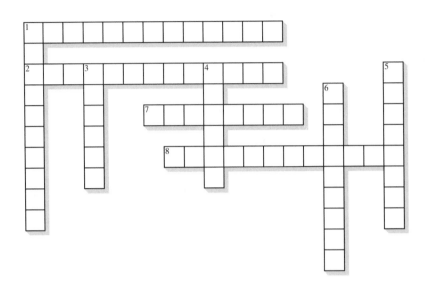

Across
1. An inquiry
2. Written order to search
7. An order to appear in person
8. Area under agency authority

Down
1. An examination
3. Written document
4. Written explanation
5. Protection from liability
6. Information under oath

Statements

Student Study Time Hints: Look for answers under Chapter / Section.

Chapter 6 / Section A.   Agencies make d_____
after information is gathered during agency investigations.

Section B.   Businesses regulated by agencies must keep
r_____.

Section B.1.   The basis of an agency's jurisdiction is established
in its _____ _____.

Section B.2.   Businesses are protected from unreasonable collection
of information by the _____ and _____
Amendments.

Section C.2.   The Fourth Amendment protects clients from improper _____ and _____.

Section C./Figure 6.6   The Trade Secrets Act protects _____ _____.

Section D.   _____ are the examinations conducted on the physical premises of a business or person.

Section E.1.   An agency must show _____ _____ to obtain a search warrant.

Section E.2.   A subpoena is an _____ for a person to appear at the agency with specific _____.

Web Resources

www.nlrb.gov   National Labor Relations Board
www.uscourts.gov   United States Courts
www.ftc.gov   Federal Trade Commission

Advanced Studies

This section provides the opportunity to read and analyze the opposition to today's thinking about gathering of information. Two of the major cases on recordkeeping are discussed in the chapter: *Shapiro v. United States,* 335 US 1 (1948) and *Craib v. Bulmash,* 777 P2d 1120 (Cal. 1989). These cases are also noteworthy for the dissents written by some of the justices. Excerpts from those dissents are given in Document 1.

In 1924, *FTC v. American Tobacco Co.* upheld probable cause as a necessity for administrative subpoenas. The ruling, strongly expressed by Justice Holmes, has been changed in cases like *Craib* and *Morton Salt.* Document 2 includes excerpts from *FTC* and *Morton Salt.*

> Document 1 — Dissents (Fifth Amendment) *Shapiro v. United States,* 335 US 1 (1948), *Craib v. Bulmash,* 777 P2d 1120 (Cal. 1989)
>
> Document 2 — Subpoenas (Probable Cause) *FTC v. American Tobacco,* 264 US 298 (1924), *United States v. Morton Salt Co.,* 338 US 632 (1950)

Outline and/or List

1. List the pertinent facts in the National Labor Relations Board subpoena. (page 192)

2. Outline the limited protection of private premises. (page 189)

3. Outline the statement of Justices Frankfurter and Jackson in Document 1. (page 201)

4. Outline the exceptions to recordkeeping requirements. (page 184)

Analyzing Documents and Practices

1. Discuss the Fourth Amendment, reasonable search and inspections. (page 188)

2. In Document 1, analyze Justice Frankfurter's view of the Fifth Amendment. (page 201)

3. Explain "fishing" in *Morton Salt*—quote from the document. (page 203)

4. In Document 2, explain Justice Holmes' opinion of "not to all documents. . . ." (page 202)

Take Home Exam

True/False 1. Agency investigations are a process of gathering information.

True/False 2. An agency does not need jurisdiction to seek information.

True/False 3. Privileged information is between two judges.

True/False 4. The enabling act establishes the agency's jurisdiction.

True/False 5. A regulatory agency may review business records.

True/False 6. The Atomic Energy Commission decides which businesses should keep wage and hour records.

True/False 7. The Fourth Amendment protects against self-incrimination.

True/False 8. Agencies limit inquiry intrusions to reasonable means.

True/False 9. A subpoena orders a person to testify at a hearing.

True/False 10. With a search warrant, an agency has unlimited search powers.

Complete Diagrams

1. **Diagram** the Gathering of Information of *FTC* and *Morton Salt*. (pages 202–203)

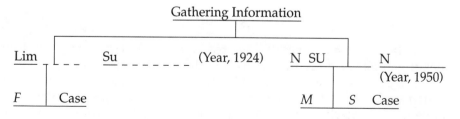

2. **Diagram** the definition and purpose of inspections. (page 188)

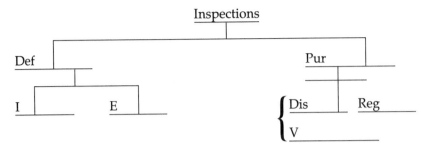

3. **Diagram** the two major amendment protections. (pages 184–185)

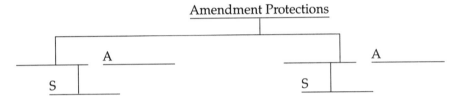

Three Venues of Research

1. **In Book** Research the Fourth Amendment. Include *Camara, Burger,* and *Scott.* (pages 188–190)

2. **At Library** (a) The Equal Employment Opportunity Commission (EEOC) is the focus of *EEOC v. Kloster.* Look up EEOC's rules for information gathering in the Code of Federal Regulations. Then look up the full case, *EEOC v. Kloster,* and write a report of any insights you gained, *or*
(b) *United States v. Morton Salt* (1950) changes the view of agency access to information from the time of *FTC v. American Tobacco* (1924). Research the nation's lifestyle and thinking in 1924 and in 1950.

3. **On Internet** Look up the U.S. Supreme Court. Write a biographical report on a justice. (*www.uscourts.gov*)

Internship

The law firm has a small business as a client. The lawyers will be appearing at a hearing with the client at the U.S. Department of Labor.
Your assignment is to research the U.S. Codes and the Code of Federal Regulations for any information on the Labor Department's ability to issue subpoenas and search warrants. Write a memo covering any pertinent facts and cites. (*www.dol.gov*)

Documents

Document 1: Dissents (Fifth Amendment) Shapiro v. United States, 335 US 1 (1948)

Justice Frankfurter dissented with the intrusion on Fifth Amendment rights and the extension of exemptions from the Fifth Amendment privilege.

The Justice stated:

> Virtually every major public law enactment — to say nothing of State and local legislation — has record keeping requirements. In addition to record keeping requirements is the network of provisions for filing reports. Exhaustive efforts would be needed to track down all the statutory authority, let alone the administrative regulations, for record keeping and reporting requirements. Unquestionably they are enormous in volume.
>
> The Congress began its history with such legislation. Chapter 1 of the Laws of the First Session of the First Congress — "An Act to regulate the Time and Manner of administering certain Oaths" — contained a provision requiring the maintenance of records by persons administering oaths to State officials. 1 Stat. 23, 24. Chapter V — "An Act to regulate the Collection of the Duties imposed by law on the tonnage of ships or vessels, and on goods, wares and merchandise imported into the United States" — contained a provision requiring an importer to produce the original invoice and to make a return concerning the consigned goods with the collector of the port of arrival. 1 Stat. 29, 39–40.
>
> Every Congress since 1789 has added record keeping and reporting requirements. . . .

He then discussed the recent legal thinking.

> . . . The notion that whenever Congress requires an individual to keep in a particular form his own books dealing with his own affairs his records cease to be his when he is accused of crime, is indeed startling.

Justice Frankfurter made his famous glass house comment in this dissent: "If records merely because required to be kept by law ipso facto become public records, we are indeed living in glass houses."

Justice Jackson also dissented in *Shapiro*: "It would, no doubt, simplify enforcement of all criminal laws if each citizen were required to keep a diary that would show where he was at all times, with whom he was, and what he was up to."

Each of the justices develops the present thinking on recordkeeping into the travesties that could occur if agency power is allowed to eat away at Fifth Amendment rights. These are the dissents. The decision did not agree with them.

In *Craib v. Bulmash*, 777 P2d 1120 (Cal. 1989), Justice Kaufman tackles the Fifth Amendment problem and comments on *Shapiro* as well.

KAUFMAN, Associate Justice, concurring and dissenting. . . .

I respectfully dissent from the holding of the majority as to defendant's Fifth Amendment claim. Although the United States Supreme Court has held that the Fifth Amendment to the Constitution of the United States does not apply when a regulatory agency subpoenas an individual's records which may provide self-incriminating evidence (*Shapiro v. United States* (1948) 335 US 1.), I am not persuaded that the analysis and reasoning of that decision is sound. Thus, in my view we should invoke the authority of article I, section 15 of our state Constitution and provide greater protection against self-incrimination than that provided by the wartime influenced, result-oriented *Shapiro* case.

While I recognize the state's need to verify compliance with valid police power regulations, I am troubled that, in many cases, the *Shapiro* rule gives regulatory agencies virtually the unchallengeable power to enforce its regulations by criminal prosecution based on compelled disclosure. It is wholly contrary to the state and federal guaranties against compelled self-incrimination to allow government the unbridled authority to compel an individual to provide self-incriminating testimonial evidence without at the same time preventing its use as evidence in the prosecution of that individual for any crimes disclosed therein.

Document 2: Subpoenas (Probable Cause)

FTC v. American Tobacco Co.
264 US 298 (1924)

[The FTC petitioned the district court to require the defendant company to produce "all letters and telegrams received by the Company from, or sent by it to all of its jobber customers, between January 1, 1921 to December 31, 1921, inclusive." The commission claimed the documents were needed in connection with an investigation of the tobacco industry called for by a Senate resolution. The district court denied the petition.]

MR. JUSTICE HOLMES delivered the opinion of the Court.

The mere facts of carrying on a commerce not confined within State lines and of being organized as a corporation do not make men's affairs public, as those of a railroad company now may be. . . . Anyone who respects the spirit as well as the letter of the Fourth Amendment would be loath to believe that Congress intended to authorize one of its subordinate agencies to sweep all our traditions into the fire (*Interstate Commerce Commission v. Brimson*, 154 US 447, 479) and to direct fishing expeditions into private papers on the possibility that they may disclose evidence of crime.

The interruption of business, the possible revelation of trade secrets, and the expense that compliance with the Commission's wholesale demand would cause are the least considerations. It is contrary to the first principles of justice to allow a search through all the respondents' records, relevant or irrelevant, in the hope that something will turn up. . . .

The right of access given by the statute is to documentary evidence — not to all documents, but to such documents as are evidence. The analogies of the law do not allow the party wanting evidence to call for all documents in order to see if they do not contain it. Some ground must be shown for supposing that the documents called for do contain it.

... [t]he demand must be reasonable. ... A general subpoena in the form of these petitions would be bad. Some evidence of the materiality of the papers demanded must be produced. ...

We have considered this case on the general claim of authority put forward by the Commission. The argument for the Government attaches some force to the investigations and proceedings upon which the Commission had entered. The investigations and complaints seem to have been only on hearsay or suspicion—but even if they were induced by substantial evidence under oath the rudimentary principles of justice that we have laid down would apply. We cannot attribute to Congress an intent to defy the Fourth Amendment or even to come so near to doing so as to raise a serious question of constitutional law.

Judgments affirmed.

United States v. Morton Salt Co.
338 US 632 (1950)

We must not disguise the fact that sometimes, especially early in the history of the federal administrative tribunal, the courts were persuaded to engraft judicial limitations upon the administrative process. The courts could not go fishing, and so it followed neither could anyone else. Administrative investigations fell before the colorful and nostalgic slogan "no fishing expeditions."

The only power that is involved here is the power to get information from those who best can give it and who are most interested in not doing so. Because judicial power is reluctant if not unable to summon evidence until it is shown to be relevant to issues in litigation, it does not follow that an administrative agency charged with seeing that the laws are enforced may not have and exercise powers of original inquiry. It has a power of inquisition, if one chooses to call it that, which is not derived from the judicial function. It is more analogous to the Grand Jury, which does not depend on a case or controversy for power to get evidence but can investigate merely on suspicion that the law is being violated, or even just because it wants assurance that it is not. When investigative and accusatory duties are delegated by statute to an administrative body, it too, may take steps to inform itself as to whether there is probable violation of the law.

7

Informal Proceedings

"[T]he development of standards governing the agency's use of informal methods ... is an issue. ..."

Ricci v. Chicago Mercantile Exchange
409 US 289 (1973)

CHAPTER OBJECTIVES

Informal proceedings facilitate the work of the agency because decisions are based on accepted standards from past practices.
This chapter discusses:

- The rules for issuing licenses
- How a claim is filed
- Why citizens file claims
- How standards are set
- Arbitration
- Negotiation
- Mediation
- The cost savings of informal actions

CHAPTER OVERVIEW

Most agency actions are informal proceedings with discretionary decisions by agency personnel rather than the stringent procedural decisions of formal hearings and rulemaking. License applications, claims for benefits, employer/employee arbitration are informal proceedings. In informal proceedings clients demonstrate compliance with agency standards and regulations; often this compliance is simply filling out the applicable forms truthfully and in a timely manner. Many informal proceedings authorize requested actions, such as approving licenses for motor vehicle drivers after proper testing.

A. What Are Informal Proceedings and How Do They Work?

Informal proceedings are the majority of agency proceedings, which depend on discretionary agency decisions. Clients initiate informal proceedings by filing a claim for a government service or benefit, such as Social Security employment or applying for a license. After claims are mailed to the agency, a decision is rendered by agency personnel, and the decision is mailed to the client. The agency employee who is trained and is a specialist in a certain task participates in the decision-making of informal proceedings. Even if an application is rejected, the client may still stay within informal proceedings by supplying pertinent information to support their claim.

Informal proceedings take place during applications for licenses, claims processing, arbitration, and mediation. The informal proceedings are non-adversarial. The agency's role is to solve a problem and facilitate a needed service.

Many actions and problems resolved by agencies are similar to previous agency decisions, and are routinely followed. By adhering to past decisions, clients can anticipate the outcome of an agency action. These standard decisions stop any lengthy, expensive formal actions. Rarely do agencies veer from an acceptable action that has been successful in past decisions.

B. Licenses

Licenses are a familiar part of our culture: automobile drivers are licensed, real estate brokers are licensed, attorneys are licensed. A license is an authorization or permission granted by an administrative agency to engage in an activity that would be illegal without such permission. Licensees all comply with the standards and regulations of the agency licensing them; if they violate the agency rules and regulations, licensees may lose or temporarily surrender their licenses.

 PARALEGAL PRACTICE EXAMPLE

You are a paralegal working for a lawyer representing a client charged with drunk driving; her license has been revoked. You interview the client to discover the facts of this charge. During the interview you learn the client has had prior drunk driving charges. You make a notation to look up the usual amount of time allowed for this type of situation before the agency will reinstate a license.

Licenses may be required by some businesses, as well as by individuals. For example the communications industry requires licenses for television and radio stations, telephone services, satellites, and computers. Because of the diversity of the industry (private and public participation) this section will discuss licenses using illustrations from the agency that regulates communications, the Federal Communications Commission (FCC), established by the Communications Act of 1934.

1. Standards

The standards for issuing licenses are published in the agency's rules and regulations. These rules and regulations are codified in the *Code of Federal Regulations* (CFR); summaries of recent rules are published in the *Federal Register*. The FCC rules and regulations are published in Title 47 of the CFR in a listing similar to the six bureaus that comprise the operating functions of the FCC:

(1) The Mass Media Bureau regulates radio and television broadcast stations; besides licensing, the Bureau assigns frequency bands, reviews station practices, and sanctions any violations of FCC standards.

(2) The Cable Services Bureau protects cable rates and regulates the cable industry.

(3) Telegraph and radio communications are regulated at the Common Carrier Bureau.

(4) The Compliance and Information Bureau monitors and authorizes the radio spectrum that aids aircraft and ships, analyzes and resolves interference with communication lines, and answers public inquiries.

(5) The Wireless Telecommunications Bureau serves the telecommunications needs of cellular/mobile phones, private marine, aviation and amateur radio, and operates the radio operator examination program.

(6) The International Bureau handles the satellite programs and international telecommunications.

Figure 7.1 depicts the FCC's departments and their corresponding published statutes.

The FCC bureaus set the standards and rules in their areas of expertise and licensees comply with the standards. A major criterion of the FCC in setting standards is, "if public convenience, interest, or necessity will be served thereby." (47 USC §303) This criterion is the measure for many of the standards of the FCC. Even though it authorizes extraordinarily broad powers, this standard has been upheld by the United States Supreme Court since 1943 in *National Broadcasting Co. v. United States*, 319 US 190. At that time the technology of communications was developing so rapidly in varied fields, Congress authorized these vast powers. Today, with

Figure 7.1   **FCC Statutes and Departments**

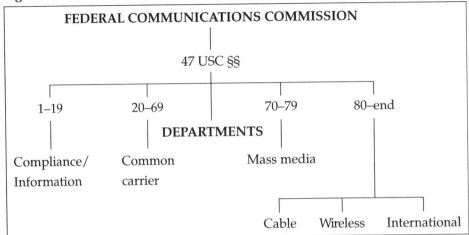

satellites, computers, and other swiftly transforming technology, the same underlying presumption allows the FCC such a vast standard in a complex and intricate communications industry. To some legal scholars, this standard — "public convenience, interest, or necessity" — is too vast in permitting discretion and powers to the agency. To others, it is a necessity dictated by the technology of the communications industry.

2. Procedures

The application for and granting of licenses is an informal agency proceeding. At the FCC, licenses are granted after an application form has been submitted; the FCC allows television licenses for seven years and radio licenses for five years. Fees are charged for both new licenses and for renewal of licenses. This procedure for granting licenses is typical of most agencies. Exhibit 7.2 is a typical application for renewing a license.

PARALEGAL PRACTICE EXAMPLE

You are a paralegal trying to find information on a new client's intention of starting a cellular-mobile phone business. You check out the FCC's organization chart, which you find in an information flyer. You find the phone numbers for the cellular-mobile division and request rules from them.

Exhibit 7.1 Website of FCC/Wireless Telecommunications Bureau

Wireless Telecommunications Bureau

FCC

Search the FCC:

[   ] GO

Help - Advanced

WTB Home
  About the WTB
  Accessibility
  Databases
  Releases
  Rules and Regulations
Licensee & Consumer Information
Forms & Fees
Towers & Antennas
Wireless Services
WTB Site Map

Related Sites

3G
Third Generation Wireless
911 Services
Basic and Enhanced
CALEA
Communications Assistance for Law Enforcement Act
CMRS Competition Reports
Commercial Mobile Radio Services
Geographic Data Extracts
Public Safety & Homeland Security Bureau
Secondary Markets Initiative
Small Entity Compliance Guide Program
Spectrum Cap
Spectrum Policy Task Force
Proceedings and Initiatives
Wireless Facilities Siting Issues
Wireless Local Number Portability

Translate

Select a language:
[   ]

Translation Survey

The Wireless Telecommunications Bureau (WTB) handles nearly all FCC domestic wireless telecommunications programs, policies, and outreach initiatives.

All Services | About the WTB

Wireless Headlines

4/10/2009
LETTER (DA 09-788)
Alan S. Tilles, Esq. Request for Waiver and Extension of 800 MHz Construction Requirements, File No. 0003507658

Granted the Request for Waiver and Extension of the 800 Construction Requirements with conditions for the two frequencies (861.1125 MHz and 862.1125 MHz) associated with call sign WPYD855.

pdf - Word

4/8/2009
LETTER (DA 09-782)
Marjorie K. Conner, Esq.

Granted a modified version of the Petition for Reconsideration.

pdf - Word

4/8/2009
ORDER (DA 09-789)
Farm Credit Building & Garage LLC Station WPXB508, Omaha, Nebraska Request for Cancellation of License

Granted the request and will modify the Commission's licensing records to reflect the cancellation of the license.

pdf - Word

4/8/2009
LETTER (DA 09-797)
Mr. William K. Keane, Esq. Re: Spectrum Tracking Systems, Inc. - Request for Extension of Time Industrial/Business Pool, Conventional Station WPNV955

Denied the request, but provide STS a period of sixty days from the date of this letter to terminate its Puerto Rico operations or make other arrangements.

pdf - Word

4/8/2009
LETTER (DA 09-793)
Dennis C. Brown, Esq. Re: Request by Maritime Communications/Land Mobile, LLC for Clarification of Sections 80.385 and 80.215 of the Commission's Rules

Granted in part and denied in part the request filed by Maritime Communications/Land Mobile, LLC on December 18, 2008.

pdf - Word

4/8/2009
ORDER ON RECONSIDERATION (DA 09-798)
Amendment of the Commission's Rules Concerning Maritime Communications/Petition for Rule Making Filed by Regionet Wireless License, LLC

Dismissed the instant petition for reconsideration as repetitious. By Second Order on Further Reconsideration.

pdf - Word

Headline Archive

Last reviewed/updated on 4/14/2009.

Exhibit 7.2   Application for Renewal of Radio Station License

FCC 405   FCC WIRELESS TELECOMMUNICATIONS BUREAU   Approved by OMB
                                                                                         3060-0093
                         APPLICATION FOR RENEWAL OF RADIO STATION LICENSE
                              FOR SPECIFIED SERVICES (47 CFR Parts 5 & 21)

	File Number (FCC USE ONLY)

1. Name Of Applicant (must be identical with that shown on current authorization)

Mailing Street Address Or P. O. Box, City, State and ZIP Code of Applicant

E-Mail address	(Area Code) Telephone Number

Call Sign or Other FCC Identifier	FCC Registration Number (FRN)	Identify Rule/subpart under which filing is made

2. FEE DATA (Refer to 47 CFR 1.1104 or the WTB Fee Filing Guide for Information for Multipoint Distribution Service)

If this application has been submitted without a fee, indicate reason for fee exemption (see 47 C.F.R. § 1.1114).

☐ Governmental Entity   ☐ Noncommercial Educational License   ☐ Other _____

3. Application is for renewal of license in exact conformity with the existing license as specified below:

(a) File Number	(b) Date Issued	(c) Call Sign	(d) Location
(e) Nature of Service	(f) Class of Station		(g) Expiration Date

4. Note any changes which have been made since the last application covering this station was filed (i.e., discontinuance of use of a frequency, type of emission, transmitter, etc.)

5(a) Has there been a removal of equipment or alteration of facilities so as to render the station not operational? If YES, indicate when: _____   YES ☐ NO ☐

(b) Is there an ownership interest in, control by, affiliation with, or leasing agreement with a cable television company?   YES ☐ NO ☐

6. Applicant represents that there has been no change in applicant's organization and no transfer of control or changes in the applicant's relation to the station or financial responsibility; that the applicant's most recent application or report embodying this information, as identified below, is to be considered as part of this application, and the truth statement therein contained is hereby affirmed. Note here any further exceptions not already covered in questions 4 and 5.

File Number: _____   Date: _____

7. **CERTIFICATION**

--Neither the applicant nor any other party to the application is subject to a denial of Federal benefits that includes FCC benefits pursuant to Section 5301 of the Anti-Drug Abuse Act of 1988, 21 U.S.C. Section 862, because of a conviction for possession or distribution of a controlled substance.

--The applicant hereby waives any claim to the use of any particular frequency or electromagnetic spectrum as against the regulatory power of the United States because of the previous use of same, whether by license or otherwise, and requests authorization in accordance with this application. (See Section 304 of the Communications Act of 1934, as amended.)

--The applicant acknowledges that all statements made in the application and attached exhibits are considered material representations; and that all the exhibits are a material part hereof and are incorporated herein as if set out in full in this application, undersigned certifies that all statements in this application are true, complete and correct to the best of his/her knowledge and belief and are made in good faith.

--Applicant certifies that construction of the station would NOT be an action which is likely to have a significant environmental effect. See the Commission's Rules, 47 CFR 1.1301-1.1319.

WILLFUL FALSE STATEMENTS MADE ON THIS FORM OR ANY ATTACHMENTS ARE PUNISHABLE BY FINE AND/OR IMPRISONMENT (U.S. Code, Title 18, § 1001) AND/OR REVOCATION OF ANY STATION LICENSE OR CONSTRUCTION PERMIT (U.S. Code, Title 47, § 312(a)(1)), AND/OR FORFEITURE (U.S. Code, Title 47, § 503).

Type or Print Name of Person Signing	Title of Person Signing
Signature	Date

Designate appropriate classification

☐ Individual   ☐ Member of Partnership   ☐ Officer & Member of Applicant's Association   ☐ Authorized Rep. of Corporation   ☐ Official of Government Entity

FCC 405 - April 2005

Exhibit 7.2 **Continued**

FCC 405   **FEDERAL COMMUNICATIONS COMMISSION**

Approved by OMB
3060 -0093
Est. Avg. Burden
Per Response:
2 Hrs 15 Min.

APPLICATION FOR RENEWAL OF RADIO STATION LICENSE
FOR SPECIFIED SERVICES

NOTICE TO INDIVIDUALS REQUIRED BY THE PRIVACY ACT OF 1974 AND
THE PAPERWORK REDUCTION ACT OF 1995

Public reporting burden for this collection of information is estimated to range from 30 minutes to 4 hours per response, with an average of 2 hours and 15 minutes per response, including the time for reviewing instructions, searching existing data sources, gathering and maintaining the data needed, and completing and reviewing the collection of information. Send comments regarding this burden estimate, or any other aspect of this collection of information, including suggestions for reducing the burden to Federal Communications Commission, AMD-PERM, Washington, DC 20554, Paperwork Reduction Project (3060-0093), or via the Internet to Judith-B.Herman@fcc.gov. DO NOT SEND COMPLETED APPLICATION FORMS TO THIS ADDRESS.

Individuals are not required to respond to a collection of information unless it displays a currently valid OMB control number. This collection has been assigned OMB control number 3060-0093.

The solicitation of personal information requested in this form is authorized by the Communications Act of 1934, as amended. The Commission will use the information provided in this form to determine whether grant of this application is in the public interest. If we believe there may be a violation or potential violation of a statute, regulation, rule or order, your application may be referred to the appropriate Federal, state, or local agency responsible for investigating, prosecuting, enforcing or implementing the statute, rule, regulation or order. In certain cases, the information in your application may be disclosed to the Department of Justice or a court or adjudicative body when (a) the FCC; or (b) any employee of the FCC; or (c) the United States Government, is a party to a proceeding before the body or has an interest in the proceeding.

As of December 3, 2001, all parties and entities doing business with the Commission must obtain a unique identifying number called the FCC Registration Number (FRN) and supply it when doing business with the Commission. Failure to provide the FRN may delay the processing of the application. This requirement is to facilitate compliance with the Debt Collection Improvement Act of 1996 (DCIA). The FRN can be obtained electronically through the FCC webpage at https://svartifoss2.fcc.gov/cores/CoresHome.html or by manually submitting FCC Form 160. FCC Form 160 is available from the FCC's web site at http://www.fcc.gov/formpage.html, by calling the FCC's Forms Distribution Center 800-418-FORM (3676), or from FCC's Fax Information System by dialing (202) 418-0177.

If you owe a past debt to the Federal Government, any information you provide may also be disclosed to the Department of Treasury Financial Management Service, other federal agencies and/or your employer to offset your salary, IRS tax refund or other payments to collect that debt. The FCC may also provide this information to these agencies through the matching of computer records when authorized. In addition, all information provided in this form will be available for public inspection. If information requested on the form is not provided, processing of the application may be delayed or the application may be returned without action.

This notice is required by the Privacy Act of 1974, Public Law 93-579, December 31, 1974, 5 U.S.C. Section 552a(e)(3) and the Paperwork Reduction Act of 1995, Public Law 104-13, October 1, 1995, 44 U.S.C. 3507.

http://www.fcc.gov/forms/405/405

FCC 405 – INSTRUCTIONS
April 2005 – PAGE 1

STUDENT PRACTICE

Separate into three groups. Each group will analyze three different topics. You will not have all of the information you need to fully understand the topics. Often in law firms a paralegal's initial examination of a document is sketchy. If it is decided the document is pertinent, you would then have to contact the source of the document for information about symbols, etc. This exercise is an initial examination of a document in which you try to dig out as much information as possible without having to take the time and money to further search. It is quite possible the information your lawyer wants is apparent and clear.

Your assignment is to analyze the documents and list any facts you are able to gain knowledge of in this examination.

Group 1 — In Exhibit 7.1, What types of information and documents do you think you can receive on the FCC website?

Group 2 — Analyze the Health Hazards report in Exhibit 7.3. Then check out the website on Exhibit 7.4 for any information if the hazard were related to the construction industry.

Group 3 — Analyze and explain the application for renewal of the radio station license in Exhibit 7.2.

Join together and discuss what facts you learned from the analysis.

List what information you would seek from the source of each document if your attorney sought further information.

C.   Claims

1.   Right to Make a Claim

A claim is a complaint, a petition, and a request for assistance from an administrative agency. The people seeking assistance direct their complaints, petitions, and requests to the agency. Claimants generally petition to have their rights be restored or that relief be supplied. Some claimants request monetary benefits, such as workers' compensation; others seek relief from threatening situations, such as hazards.

The basis of a person's right to make a claim is the Fourth Amendment's right to "life, liberty, and property." A claim is a benefit a person is entitled to under the "property" section of the amendment; because most government benefits are financial, they are classified under property and ownership concepts. Although individuals don't "own" government benefits because they have to first qualify for them, they do have procedural protections in securing and keeping benefits.

In *Goldberg v. Kelly*, 397 US 254 (1970), the U.S. Supreme Court allowed due process rights to any citizen receiving government benefits. In *Board of Regents v. Roth*, 408 US 564 (1972), the U.S. Supreme Court defined benefits as "property," thus definitively qualifying claims as Fourth Amendment rights. This was a reversal from the Court's ruling in a 1960s case in which the Court stated that the legislature may reduce or terminate benefits, emphasizing that an individual does not own the benefits. "To engraft upon the Social Security system a concept of 'accrued property rights' would deprive it of the flexibility and boldness in adjustment to everchanging conditions which it demands." *Flemming v. Nestor*, 363 US 602 (1960). Yet twelve years later the court reversed itself in *Roth* stating, "It is a purpose of the ancient institution of property to protect those claims upon which people rely in their daily lives, reliance that must not be arbitrarily undermined," 408 US 564 at 577 (1972). In this way, claims for benefits became protected entitlements under the concept of property requiring due process. Of course, claims are subject to agency regulations. To clarify this, the U.S. Supreme Court stated, "the welfare recipients in *Goldberg v. Kelly* . . . had a claim of entitlement to welfare payments that was grounded in the statute defining eligibility for them." *Roth*.

2.   Filing a Claim

The Occupational Safety and Health Agency (OSHA) in the Department of Labor is well-known to most people. OSHA is the agency developed by the Occupational Safety and Health Act in 1970 ". . . to assure so far as possible every working man and woman in the Nation safe and healthful working conditions and to preserve our human resources." 29 USC 651. The Act is applicable to all United States workers except the self-employed and family farm workers.

Protecting anonymity, a worker may simply telephone an OSHA office and report the threatening hazard or physical harm. In other instances, the worker may choose to formally, in writing, file a claim or complaint such as the form, "Notice of Alleged Safety or Health Hazards" in Exhibit 7.3. The cover sheet to the form states, "This form is provided for the assistance of any complainant and is not intended to constitute the exclusive means by which a complaint may be registered with the U.S. Department of Labor." The forms are also on the OSHA website.

On the cover sheet to this form OSHA states two sections of the Act to aid the person filing a claim or complaint, which are partially as follows:

> Sec. 8(f)(1) . . . provides as follows: Any employees or representative of employees who believe that a violation of a safety or health standard exists that threatens physical harm, or that an imminent danger exists, may request an inspection by giving notice . . .
>
> NOTE: Section 11(c) of the Act provides explicit protection for employees exercising their rights, including making safety and health complaints.

Exhibit 7.3   OSHA Claim/Complaint Form

U. S. Department of Labor
Occupational Safety and Health Administration

Notice of Alleged Safety or Health Hazards

For the General Public:

This form is provided for the assistance of any complainant and is not intended to constitute the exclusive means by which a complaint may be registered with the U.S. Department of Labor.

Sec 8(f)(1) of the Williams-Steiger Occupational Safety and Health Act, 29 U.S.C. 651, provides as follows: Any employees or representative of employees who believe that a violation of a safety or health standard exists that threatens physical harm, or that an imminent danger exists, may request an inspection by giving notice to the Secretary or his authorized representative of such violation or danger. Any such notice shall be reduced to writing, shall set forth with reasonable particularity the grounds for the notice, and shall be signed by the employee or representative of employees, and a copy shall be provided the employer or his agent no later than at the time of inspection, except that, upon request of the person giving such notice, his name and the names of individual employees referred to therein shall not appear in such copy or on any record published, released, or made available pursuant to subsection (g) of this section. If upon receipt of such notification the Secretary determines there are reasonable grounds to believe that such violation or danger exists, he shall make a special inspection in accordance with the provisions of this section as soon as practicable to determine if such violation or danger exists. If the Secretary determines there are no reasonable grounds to believe that a violation or danger exists, he shall notify the employees or representative of the employees in writing of such determination.

NOTE: Section 11(c) of the Act provides explicit protection for employees exercising their rights, including making safety and health complaints.

For Federal Employees:

This report format is provided to assist Federal employees or authorized representatives in registering a report of unsafe or unhealthful working conditions with the U.S.Department of Labor.

The Secretary of Labor may conduct unannounced inspection of agency workplaces when deemed necessary if an agency does not have occupational safety and health committees established in accordance with Subpart F, 29 CFR 1960; or in response to the reports of unsafe or unhealthful working conditions upon request of such agency committees under Sec. 1-3, Executive Order 12196; or in the case of a report of imminent danger when such a committee has not responded to the report as required in Sec. 1-201(h).

INSTRUCTIONS:

Open the form and complete the front page as accurately and completely as possible. Describe each hazard you think exists in as much detail as you can. If the hazards described in your complaint are not all in the same area, please identify where each hazard can be found at the worksite. If there is any particular evidence that supports your suspicion that a hazard exists (for instance, a recent accident or physical symptoms of employees at your site) include the information in your description. If you need more space than is provided on the form, continue on any other sheet of paper.

After you have completed the form, return it to your local OSHA office.

NOTE: It is unlawful to make any false statement, representation or certification in any document filed pursuant to the Occupational Safety and Health Act of 1970. Violations can be punished by a fine of not more than $10,000. or by imprisonment of not more than six months, or by both. (Section 17(g))

Public reporting burden for this voluntary collection of information is estimated to vary from 15 to 25 minutes per response with an average of 17 minutes per response, including the time for reviewing instructions, searching existing data sources, gathering and maintaining the data needed, and completing and reviewing the collection of information. An Agency may not conduct or sponsor, and persons are not required to respond to the collection of information unless it displays a valid OMB Control Number. Send comment regarding this burden estimate or any other aspect of this collection of information, including suggestions for reducing this burden to the Directorate of Enforcement Programs, Department of Labor, Room N-3119, 200 Constitution Ave., NW, Washington, DC; 20210.

OMB Approval# 1218-0064; Expires: 2-29-2008

Do not send the completed form to this Office.

OSHA-7(Rev. 9/93)

Exhibit 7.3 **Continued**

U. S. Department of Labor
Occupational Safety and Health Administration

Notice of Alleged Safety or Health Hazards

	Complaint Number	
Establishment Name		
Site Address		
	Site Phone	Site FAX
Mailing Address		
	Mail Phone	Mail FAX
Management Official		Telephone
Type of Business		

HAZARD DESCRIPTION/LOCATION. Describe briefly the hazard(s) which you believe exist. Include the approximate number of employees exposed to or threatened by each hazard. Specify the particular building or worksite where the alleged violation exists.

Has this condition been brought to the attention of:	☐ Employer ☐ Other Government Agency(specify)
Please Indicate Your Desire:	☐ Do NOT reveal my name to my Employer ☐ My name may be revealed to the Employer
The Undersigned believes that a violation of an Occupational Safety or Health standard exists which is a job safety or health hazard at the establishment named on this form.	(Mark "X" in ONE box) ☐ Employee ☐ Federal Safety and Health Committee ☐ Representative of Employees ☐ Other (specify)

Complainant Name		Telephone	
Address(Street,City,State,Zip)			
Signature		Date	

If you are an authorized representative of employees affected by this complaint, please state the name of the organization that you represent and your title:

Organization Name: Your Title:

2

As a priority, OSHA determines whether the hazard in the complaint violates a standard. OSHA standards are based on the purpose of the Act: "Encourage employers and employees to reduce workplace hazards and to implement new or existing safety and health programs; . . . Develop mandatory job safety and health standards and enforce them through worksite inspections, employer assistance, and sometimes, by imposing citations or penalties or both." *All About OSHA,* U.S. Department of Labor, Occupational Safety and Health Administration, 2000 (Revised).

STUDENT PRACTICE

Class divides into two groups.

The document used in this exercise is the OSHA complaint form, Exhibit 7.3

Group 1 — Complainants. Develop a hazard and a company. Fill out the complaint form.

Group 2 — OSHA investigators. Question and evaluate Group 1 by analyzing their complaint and talking to them directly. Then fill out the complaint evaluation section.

Both groups rejoin. Group 2 inform Group 1 of your decision. Then check to see if any section of the complaint and agency evaluation has to be revised.

D. Negotiations and Arbitration

Negotiation is the bargaining and consequent resolution of differences between disputing sides in order to arrive at a satisfactory mutual agreement or compromise. Arbitration is the submission of the dispute to a third party, an arbiter, with both parties agreeing to follow the arbiter's decision. In a somewhat similar manner as arbitration, mediation is the assistance of a third party in reconciling the disputants so that they can voluntarily make their decisions in reaching an agreement. Disputes often involve the employer/employee situation and these conflicts come under the shields of various government agencies.

When parties cannot negotiate an agreement they enter into voluntary or mandatory arbitration. In voluntary arbitration, the parties agree on arbitration procedures that may be formal or informal discussions/negotiations, hearings, or the options of trial-like discovery and sworn witnesses. In madatory arbitration, the agency imposes the procedures on the parties and the resultant resolution.

Arbitration's goal is to reach a final decision in an expeditious manner. The U.S. Arbitration Act, 9 USCA §103 (1980) allows judicial review of arbitration resolutions only if there are procedural problems such as arbitrator misconduct or criminal misdeeds. Generally, arbitration is the

Exhibit 7.4 OSHA Home Page

UNITED STATES DEPARTMENT OF LABOR
OCCUPATIONAL SAFETY & HEALTH ADMINISTRATION

Search OSHA [GO]

| Topics | Inspection Data | Regulations | Publications | Training | News |

What's New

RSS Feeds

Subscribe: Email Address [GO]
Twice Monthly E-News
E-News Privacy Notice

OSHA News

- U.S. Labor Department's OSHA orders Southern Air Inc. to withdraw retaliatory lawsuit and pay more than $7.9 million to 9 whistleblowers
- OSHA's new guidance document focuses on mandatory respirator selection provisions added to existing Respiratory Protection standard
- U.S. Department of Labor's OSHA revises Field Operations Manual to enhance enforcement and compliance assistance
- Stimulus package tops agenda for OSHA's Advisory Committee on Construction Safety and Health meeting
- Secretary of Labor takes action to prevent workers' exposure to food flavorings chemical

More News...

Audiences:

En Español
Hispanic Employers & Workers
Small Business
Workers
Teen Workers

Offices

OSHA and State Plan Offices

Select a State [GO]

How do I?

Report possible hazards in the workplace
Find hazards by industry or operation
Find a regulation and related information
Order publications

Contact OSHA
Submit comments on draft rulemaking
Apply for a training grant
Download the recordkeeping forms (300, 300A, 301)
Subscribe to RSS feeds

In Focus

Proposed Cranes and Derricks Standard in Construction - Transcripts from March Hearings
March 17   March 18   March 19   March 20

Keeping Workers Safe in Response to Flooding and Tornadoes

Programs & Resources

Compliance Assistance
eTools, Grants, Quick Start, Small Business, Hispanic employers & workers, more...

Newsroom
News Releases, Speeches, Statements, Testimonies, more...

Safety & Health Topics
Biological Agents, Construction, Ergonomics, Maritime, Hazard Communication, more...

Statistics
Inspection Data, SIC/NAICS Search, more...

Laws & Regulations
Standards, Interpretations, Directives, Federal Registers, Docket, more...

Enforcement
Federal Agency Programs, Local Emphasis Programs, Whistleblower Protection, more...

Cooperative Programs
Alliances, Consultation, SHARP, VPP, Strategic Partnerships, more...

State Programs
State Plan Information, State Offices

International
China, Europe, NAFTA, more...

Find It in DOL
About OSHA
Compliance Assistance
Recordkeeping
Laws & Regulations
Enforcement
Construction
Cooperative Programs
State Programs
Newsroom
Safety/Health Topics
Statistics
International
Freedom of Information Act (FOIA)

More Resources

DOL.gov
The White House
USA.gov
GovBenefits.gov
DisabilityInfo.gov
HireVetsFirst.gov
Career Voyages
Business.gov
Regulations.gov
PandemicFlu.gov
USA Freedom Corps
No Fear Act

Back to Top   http://osha.gov/index.html   http://www.dol.gov/

Contact Us | Freedom of Information Act | Customer Survey
Privacy and Security Statement | Disclaimers

Occupational Safety & Health Administration
200 Constitution Avenue, NW
Washington, DC 20210

Page last updated: 04/09/2009

final step. Arbitration follows agency precedents; this is encouraged by the U.S. Supreme Court. In deciding whether the Merit Systems Protection Board (MSPB), the arbitrator for government employee disputes, should practice its normal procedures for dispute resolution or practice the arbitration procedures in the Civil Reform Act of 1978, the court stated, "Congress did not wish that choice to be made on the basis of a predictable difference in substantive outcome." *Devine v. Pastore,* 732 F2d 213 at 216 (DC Cir. 1984) The court further stated that arbitration laws should "promote consistency . . . and . . . avoid forum shopping."

Arbitration has been challenged as a violation of Article III (the judicial powers). In *Thomas v. Union Carbide Agr. Products Co.,* 473 US 568 (1985), binding arbitration by the Environmental Protection Agency was challenged by manufacturers who refused to supply research data to EPA in order to register a pesticide. The U.S. Supreme Court stated that Congress had the right to facilitate the effectiveness of a public program by limiting judicial review as long as a limited judicial review was included (this was provided for in the EPA pesiticide act, Federal Insecticide, Fungicide and Rodenticide Act (FIFRA)).

Figure 7.2 illustrates negotiation and arbitration.

Figure 7.2   Negotiation and Arbitration

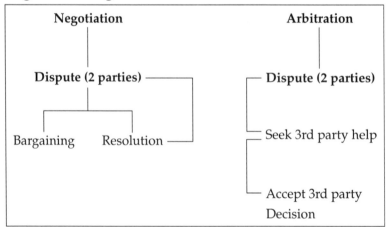

1.   Voluntary and Involuntary Resolutions

Employers and employees are expected to bargain in good faith to settle disputes. In contract situations, particularly with a union, bargaining in good faith is written into the contract. Whatever the employment situation, good faith bargaining is a federal regulation under the National Labor Relations Act (NLRA). Section 8(a)(5) of the NLRA states it is illegal for an employer to refuse to bargain in good faith and §8(b)(3) states it is illegal for a labor organization to refuse to bargain in good faith. The regulations are enforced by the federal agency, the National Labor

Relations Board (NLRB); the NLRB follows the purpose of the NLRA, which is to avoid and reduce strife in industry. It attempts to promote voluntary resolution of disputes, but has the power to order involuntary compliance with its decisions.

The NLRA places obligations on the employer and the labor organization to meet at reasonable times in good faith to discuss conditions, and then to write out any agreement arrived at between the parties if so requested by one of the parties.

To seek the assistance of the NLRB, a petition or charge must be filed at an office of the NLRB by either the employee, the employer, the labor organization, or others. The office will investigate the complaint. If the NLRB suspects that there are unfair labor practices, it will attempt to bring about a voluntary resolution. If this fails, the NLRB will issue a complaint and send notification of a hearing to be held before an administrative law judge at the NLRB. After this hearing, a decision will be written — an involuntary resolution to the situation. The NLRB estimates that 90 percent of the cases are resolved within forty-five days without an appearance before an administrative law judge. Even though the NLRB is mandated to enforce all violations in commerce, it limits its jurisdictional standards to certain sized businesses involved in the conflict.

PARALEGAL PRACTICE EXAMPLE

You are a paralegal working with the National Labor Relations Board. You are to develop an outline for an intern coming to the agency to work with you. A few of the topics you decide to teach the intern are:

1. some labor laws, NLRB decisions, regulations, procedures, and policies;
2. analytical and investigative skills; and
3. negotiation techniques.

2. Mediation

Mediation attempts to resolve a dispute through conciliation. The third party, the mediator, is neutral and cannot impose a resolution on the disputing parties. Mediation is used in family courts, environmental disputes, and employer-employee relations that are at an impasse. The mediator's role is difficult; the mediator must not only be perceptive, but must also be diplomatic. In some instances, the mediator holds confidential meetings with each disputant to gain insight into sensitive areas and to then propose realistic options for agreement acceptable to both sides. The Federal Mediation and Conciliation Service (FMCS) was established in 1947 by the Labor Management Relations Act, 29 USC §172. The FMCS enters into disputes that are disturbing interstate commerce and have not been settled after thirty days of conflict. Section 8(d) of the act requires both the unions and employers to file with the FMCS a notice of such a dispute. Involvement of the FMCS in the dispute is generally considered a final step in the attempt to promote mutual accord between employer and labor. Its decisions are not mandatory or binding, but FMCS can supply qualified arbitrators if requested. FMCS may enter a dispute at the request of a disputant or by its own volition.

 PARALEGAL PRACTICE EXAMPLE

You are a paralegal intern in a federal mediation agency office. You help to draft revised collective bargaining agreements. The skills you bring to the position include your knowledge of labor laws. Since working with the agency, you read and research economic trends in business and labor.

E.   Settlements

Settlements are agreements that resolve disputes; settlements occur during and after hearing actions. An administrative agency settlement may result in: an arrangement to schedule compliance with regulations, financial adjustments and payments, or accommodations in working conditions.

Section 554(c) of the Administrative Procedure Act requires agencies to consider settlements:

> The agency shall give all interested parties opportunity for —
> (1) The submission and consideration of facts, arguments, offers of settlement or proposals of adjustment when time, the nature of the proceeding, and the public interest permit;

Settlement offers do not have to be accepted, just considered. If they are accepted, the settlement is the same as a final agreement or decision. Agencies allow for settlement techniques in their regulations. The Federal Energy Regulatory Commission (FERC) eases its caseload by advocating settlements. ". . . the agency has a strong policy favoring the disposition of cases through settlements." 44 Fed. Reg. 34, 936 (1979)

1.   Standards

The standards on which settlements are based are the rules and regulations of an agency. For example, settlements in the Internal Revenue Service (IRS) center on standards that regulate earned income credit, tax tables, and deductions. A tax examiner reviews the various standards as they apply to a taxpayer's tax return; if the taxpayer disagrees with the examiner's decisions, a process toward settlement begins.

Some of the steps toward settlement are:

1. Requesting a meeting with the examiner's supervisor. At this meeting the facts and findings are discussed; this meeting could result in an agreement or settlement of the issue. If not, the taxpayer may appeal to the Internal Revenue Service or the courts.
2. Appealing to the Internal Revenue Service. Appeals are made to the regional Appeals Office. If requested in writing, a conference will be held to attempt to settle the issues in dispute. The IRS states that most disputes reach settlement at this level. At the conference, the taxpayer may bring witnesses, accountants or legal representatives, if desired.
3. Making a compromise offer. The taxpayer has the right to offer a compromise on the liability of the amount requested or the ability to make full payment. The Commissioner of the IRS has the authority to consider and accept a compromise from the taxpayer.
4. Contacting the IRS Problem Resolution Program. This service is offered to taxpayers who have used all normal channels and still have not resolved their problems. A Problem Resolution Officer can discuss any significant matters in hope of reaching a settlement.

If none of the above appeals are satisfactory in reaching a settlement with the IRS, appeals may be made to the U.S. District Court, the U.S. Claims Court or the U.S. Tax Court.

2.   Cost Savings

The administrative agency tries to save costs by encouraging settlements. The IRS states that its appeal system through the IRS is less expensive and less time-consuming for the taxpayer than appeals to the court system. It is less expensive also for the IRS, because the IRS may be liable for administrative and litigation costs if the taxpayer wins the court case after having proceeded through the administrative remedies of the IRS before appealing.

F.   Advisory Protections and Opinions

An advisory opinion of an agency is a clarification of a rule or procedure that implements an administrative agency policy. Agencies distribute advisory opinions on their policies and regulations, particularly when there is a rule change. These advisory opinions help the public to properly follow the regulations. In order to update procedures in keeping with the changing conditions in its area of expertise, agencies amend and alter policies and rules, then issue advisory opinions to explain the changes. This process protects people dealing with the agency as they file documents with the agency; if the advisory opinion is followed, time-consuming and expensive redoing of documents to qualify under the amended rules is eliminated.

Advisory protections (often called agency summary actions) are upheld by statutes. The Consumer Product Safety Act, 15 USCA §2061 (1988), allows the seizure of hazardous products; the seizure of tainted food, drugs, or cosmetics comes under the Federal Food, Drug, and Cosmetic Act, 21 USCA §334. To offset any harm to individuals involved in advisory opinions, agencies such as the Justice Department control publicizing matters by agency regulations.

1. Public Pronouncements

Some advisory opinions are released to the general public. The Immigration and Naturalization Service (INS) changed one of its previous policies for people filing applications to become United States citizens. Instead of demanding orginal documents or certified copies of documents, the INS' new policy allowed photocopies of documents to be submitted. In 2003, the INS became a bureau of the Department of Homeland Security (DHS). The immigration segment is now called the United States Citizenship and Immigration Services (USCIS). On a 2004 Fact Sheet, USCIS explains that background and security checks are processed on "all persons seeking immigration benefits." The Fact Sheet was published on the USCIS website, *www.uscis.gov.*

2. Private Advisory Opinions

A business may ask for a private advisory opinion on a rule that impacts that business as it attempts to comply with the rule. The agency directs its advisory opinion to that specific business and to the specific agency rule or standard being questioned by the business. Advisory opinions are not binding. They usually stipulate that if a particular situation occurs, the proper compliance would be whatever relates to the specific business or person. For example, the IRS gives advisory opinions to people who seek advice on unusual tax situations. The EPA may give a private advisory opinion to a business in regard to disposal of hazardous waste.

G. Public Information

All agencies supply the public with information about agency activities. Some agencies have publications describing their agencies; all publish their rules in the *Federal Register;* many issue advisory opinions. Agencies are aware of funding and budget concerns, so they use their public information capacities to present their work favorably. Information regarding administrative agency activities usually is quite valuable to the public, such as announcements of potential hazards. For example, severe weather warnings from the U.S. Weather Bureau or tainted food or drugs that are often "red-flagged" by various agencies which issue warnings and/or recalls of the items with the brand names and identification numbers published so that the public may remove the dangers from their homes, as well as be alert when shopping.

Agencies also assist the public by publishing "how to" information. Students wishing to further their education usually need money; the U.S. Department of Education offers "how to" information for students seeking federal aid.

CONCEPTS JOURNAL

Individually

You are a paralegal student who needs to present an analysis of a case in order to secure an internship at a general practice law firm that handles drunk driving cases, labor cases, workers' compensation claims, etc. The lawyers suggest the following:

1. Write a memo summarizing the major aspects of informal agency actions.
2. Brief the *Goldberg v. Kelly* case — keep the brief to two pages.

Join with the Class

Swap papers with a fellow student and criticize each other's work; then return the papers.

Journal

As the class discusses the important points in the memo and brief, take notes.
    Decide which comments to record in your journal.

CASE ABSTRACT

Goldberg is an often quoted benefits claim case.

Goldberg v. Kelly
397 US 254 (1980)

Mr. Justice Brennan delivered the opinion of the Court.
    The question for decision is whether a State which terminates public assistance payments to a particular recipient without affording him the

opportunity for an evidentiary hearing prior to termination denies the recipient procedural due process in violation of the Due Process Clause of the Fourteenth Amendment.

This action was brought in the District Court for the Southern District of New York by residents of New York City receiving financial aid under the federally assisted program of Aid to Families with Dependent Children (AFDC) or under New York State's general Home Relief program. Their complaint alleged that the New York State and New York City officials administering these programs terminated, or were about to terminate, such aid without prior notice and hearing, thereby denying them due process of law. At the time the suits were filed there was no requirement of prior notice or hearing of any kind before termination of financial aid. However, the State and city adopted procedures for notice and hearing after the suits were brought, and the plaintiffs, appellees here, then challenged the constitutional adequacy of those procedures. . . .

[T]he New York City Department of Social Services promulgated Procedure No. 68-18. A caseworker who has doubts about the recipient's continued eligibility must first discuss them with the recipient. If the caseworker concludes that the recipient is no longer eligible, he recommends termination of aid to a unit supervisor. If the latter concurs, he sends the recipient a letter stating the reasons for proposing to terminate aid and notifying him that within seven days he may request that a higher official review the record, and may support the request with a written statement prepared personally or with the aid of an attorney or other person. If the reviewing official affirms the determination of ineligibility, aid is stopped immediately and the recipient is informed by letter of the reasons for the action. Appellees' challenge to this procedure emphasized the absence of any provisions for the personal appearance of the recipient before the reviewing official, for oral presentation of evidence, and for confrontation and cross-examination of adverse witnesses. However, the letter does inform the recipient that he may request a post-termination "fair hearing." This is a proceeding before an independent state hearing officer at which the recipient may appear personally, offer oral evidence, confront and cross-examine the witnesses against him, and have a record made of the hearing. If the recipient prevails at the "fair hearing" he is paid full funds erroneously withheld. . . . A recipient whose aid is not restored by a "fair hearing" decision may have judicial review. . . .

It is true, of course, that some governmental benefits may be administratively terminated without affording the recipient a pre-termination evidentiary hearing. But we agree with the District Court that when welfare is discontinued, only a pre-termination evidentiary hearing provides the recipient with procedural due process. . . . For qualified recipients, welfare provides the means to obtain essential food, clothing, housing, and medical care. . . . Thus the crucial factor in this context — is that termination of aid pending resolution of a controversy over eligibility may deprive an *eligible* recipient of the very means by which to live while he waits. Since he lacks independent resources, his situation becomes immediately desperate.

His need to concentrate upon finding the means for daily subsistence, in turn, adversely affects his ability to seek redress from the welfare bureaucracy.

Moreover, important governmental interests are promoted by affording recipients a pre-termination evidentiary hearing. From its founding, the Nation's basic commitment has been to foster the dignity and well-being of all persons within its borders. We have come to recognize that forces not within the control of the poor contribute to their poverty. . . .

Thus, the interest of the eligible recipient in uninterrupted receipt of public assistance, coupled with the State's interest that his payments not be erroneously terminated, clearly outweighs the State's competing concern to prevent any increase in its fiscal and administrative burdens. As the District Court correctly concluded, "[t]he stakes are simply too high for the welfare recipient, and the possibility for honest error or irritable misjudgment too great, to allow termination of aid without giving the recipient a chance, if he so desires, to be fully informed of the case against him so that he may contest its basis and produce evidence in rebuttal." 294 F. Supp. at 904–905. . . .

Affirmed.

CHAPTER SUMMARY

The majority of agency activities are conducted by informal proceedings using discretionary decisions adhering to the pattern of previous, similar agency proceedings. Issuing licenses and processing claims are daily occurrences at most agencies. When disputing parties are unable to reach a solution, agencies offer arbitration, mediation, and settlement options. When a question arises over an agency policy, the agency may issue an advisory opinion. Agencies also inform the public of possible health and safety hazards, and supply information on the many services available through the agency.

Key Terms

advisory opinion   license
arbitration   mediation
claim   settlement
hearing

Key Terms Crossword

Across

4. Issuance of agency's interpretation of policy
5. Demand of a right
6. Third party reconciles dispute
7. Agreement between disputants

Down

1. Proceeding where evidence is presented
2. Permission to practice
3. A dispute heard by a third party

Statements

Student Study Time Hints: Look for answers under Chapter / Section.

Chapter 7 / Section A.   Agency's role in informal proceedings is: _____.

Section B.1.   Regulates T.V. broadcasting: _____.

Section C.1.   Right to make a claim: _____.

Section D.2.   Disputes settled by conciliation: _____.

These decisions by the FMCS are not: _____ or _____.

Section F.   Settlements save _____ _____.

No Hints:

License applications: _____ agency procedures.

Settlements are _____ that resolve disputes.

Web Resources

www.fcc.gov   Federal Communications Commission
www.osha.gov   Occupational Safety and Health Administration
www.dol.gov   Department of Labor

Advanced Studies

This Advanced Studies section discusses two cases that challenged informal agency actions. In one, appellants felt that the agency's actions were threatening; in the other, expert decisions on the informal level were questioned as to self-interest and bias. A typical form for compiling information for claims in informal actions is also presented. The documents used in this Advanced Studies are:

> Document 1—*Writers Guild of America, West, Inc. v. American Broadcasting Cos.*, 609 F2d 355 (9th. Cir), cert. denied, 449 US 824 (1980)
> Document 2—*Gibson v. Berryhill*, 411 US 564 (1973)
> Document 3—Log and Summary of Occupational Injuries and Illnesses, Bureau of Labor Statistics

In closely regulated agencies, such as the FCC, there is often much contact between agency regulators and the regulated parties. This informal communication becomes a means of informally regulating the industry by circumventing rulemaking and hearings that are governed by stringent procedural laws. The benefit to the regulated parties of this type of informal action is the ability to voluntarily establish standards that may be easily modified. Both the agency and the regulated share in the cost savings benefit in this approach.

However, the legality of these discretionary decisions have been questioned by some of the regulated parties from time-to-time. This was the case over the use of violence during prime time television. The prime time hour between 8 and 9 p.m. is considered family-oriented entertainment time. In order to avoid new regulations and to avoid the threat of censorship, the FCC and the public networks met to create a television family time code. At issue in *Writers Guild* is the questionable imposing of the non-violent family time by the FCC: (1) by using pressure tactics such as public statements, or (2) by using tactics that could be considered leadership quality. While reading the case (Document 1) decide if pressure tactics restrict First Amendment rights by limiting violence and sex?

One of the major reasons that agencies are granted vast discretionary power is the belief that agencies have the expertise to clearly observe facts and make good, analytical decisions based on that expertise. This reasoning extends to the appointment to agency positions of individuals in the occupations that an agency is licensing and regulating. At times, this practice has been challenged. One such challenge happened when expert members of an agency had a financial interest in the outcome of their decisions. As seen in the *Gibson* Case (Document 2) that interest does not have to be immediate to raise questions about an expert's bias in decision-making. The possibility of self-interested bias has to be weighed against the benefit of having such expert knowledge in the agency and the opportunity of having expert contacts in gaining cooperation of those being regulated in the industry. *Gibson* illustrates how the informal agency decision-making by experts can lead to difficult, formal problems.

Outline and/or List

1. List the items requested on an OSHA form. (pages 214–215)

2. Outline licenses and standards. (pages 206–207)

3. List the differences in voluntary and mandatory arbitration. (page 216)

4. List the steps toward settlement. (page 220)

Analyzing Documents and Practices

1. What were the proposals of ABC, CBS, and NBC in Document 1? (pages 232, fourth and fifth paragraphs)

2. What is the issue in *Writers Guild*? (page 230)

3. In Document 2, what was the basis of the suit against the Board of Optometry? (page 235)

4. In Document 3, what is requested in OSHA (A)(B)(C)(D)(E)(F)? (page 236)

Take Home Exam

True/False 1. Agencies release both private and public opinion announcements.

True/False 2. The Fifth Amendment protects the right to make a claim.

True/False 3. Negotiation and mandatory arbitration are the same.

True/False 4. All OSHA claims must be signed.

True/False 5. Administrative agencies grant licenses.

True/False 6. IRS settlements must be accepted by the taxpayer.

True/False 7. Standards for licenses are published in agency's rules and regulations.

True/False 8. Negotiation is submission of disputes to a third party.

True/False 9. Arbitration is submission of disputes to a third party.

True/False 10. Internal Revenue Service handles only banking concerns.

Complete Diagrams

1. **Diagram** the proceedings to solve disputes. (pages 216, 219)

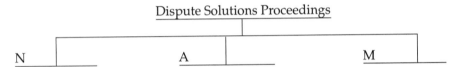

2. **Diagram** settlement offers. (page 220)

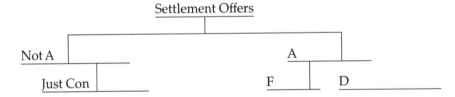

Three Venues of Research

1. **In Book** Explain what a claim is and the basis for making a claim. (pages 212–213)

2. **At Library** Look up FEMA. Explain both its positive and negative roles in New Orleans Hurricane Tragedy in early 21st Century.

3. **On Internet** Search to see if there are any new topics or rules since September 11, 2001, that came about because of the events of 9/11.

Internship

Your lawyer has a job injury case. He wants you to find information about OSHA from their public information office. Also, look up the rules for job injuries in OSHA's Code of Federal Regulations cites. Then look up the same information on the OSHA website (*http://www.OSHA.gov*). Which is faster? More thorough?

Documents

Document 1: Writers Guild of America, West, Inc. v. American Broadcasting Cos., *609 F2d 355 (9th Cir.), cert. denied, 449 US 824 (1980)*

Before SNEED AND HUG, Circuit Judges, and ENRIGHT, District Judge.

SNEED, J.: Plaintiffs Writers Guild of America, West, Inc. (Writers Guild) ... and Tandem Productions, Inc. (Tandem) instituted these consolidated actions against the Federal Communications Commission (FCC) and its Commissioners Wiley, Hooks, Lee, Quello, Reid, Robinson, and Washburn, the three major television networks (ABC, CBS, and NBC), and the National Association of Broadcasters (NAB) to challenge the adoption of the so-called "family viewing policy" as an amendment to the NAB Television Code. ... The actions were consolidated and tried before the district court. The court, in a lengthy and closely reasoned published opinion, concluded that:

(1) threats, influence, and pressure by the Chairman of the FCC caused the networks and the NAB to adopt the family viewing policy;

(2) the FCC committed a per se violation of the First Amendment by exerting improper pressure on the networks;

(3) the FCC violated the Administrative Procedure Act (APA) by implementing public policy by informal pressure instead of by complying with the Act's procedural requirements;

(4) the action of the networks and the NAB constituted "government action" for purposes of the First Amendment both because adoption of the family viewing policy had been caused substantially by FCC pressure and because the networks, the NAB, and the FCC participated in an "unprecedented joint venture" in an effort to compromise the independent judgments of other broadcast licensees; and

(5) the networks and the NAB violated the First Amendment by "fail[ing] to exercise independent program judgments and instead becom[ing] surrogates in the enforcement of government policy" and by agreeing to compromise the independent programming judgments of individual broadcast licensees.

Writers Guild of America, West, Inc. v. FCC, 423 F. Supp. 1064 (C.D. Cal. 1976). All parties have appealed. ...

I. Factual Background — Promulgation of the Family Viewing Policy

The impact of violent and sexually-oriented television programming was the subject of intense public and congressional concern throughout the two decades preceding the adoption of the family viewing policy as an amendment to the NAB Television Code. The specific events giving rise to this lawsuit, however, commenced in June 1974 when the House Appropriations Committee directed the Federal Communications Commission "to submit a report to the Committee by December 31, 1974, outlining the specific positive actions taken or planned by the Commission to protect children from excessive violence and obscenity." H.R. Rep. No. 1139, 93d Cong., 2d Sess. 15 (1974). On August 1, 1974, the Senate Appropriations Committee followed suit, "urging the Commission to proceed as vigorously and as rapidly as possible — within Constitutional limitations — to determine what is its power in the area of program violence and obscenity, particularly as to their effect on children." S. Rep. No. 1056, 93d Cong., 2d Sess. 19 (1974).

After soliciting suggestions from his staff concerning how best to respond to the congressional directive, the Chairman of the FCC, Richard Wiley, embarked on a course of what is described by the press as "jawboning," to have the networks adopt a system of self-regulation that would reduce the amount of sex and violence in television programming without the need for any "formal" Commission action. . . .

Chairman Wiley's campaign ultimately involved: (1) five meetings between himself and/or members of the Commission staff and industry representatives at which various proposals for dealing with the problem of televised sex and violence were discussed; (2) three public speeches by Chairman Wiley in which he exhorted the industry to undertake its own action but indicated that unless some action were taken, the government might well be forced to become formally involved with the problem; (3) several telephone conversations between Chairman Wiley and various network executives; and (4) suggestions by Chairman Wiley to various NAB representatives that the NAB expedite its consideration of a proposal for a Code amendment incorporating the family viewing policy. . . .

On December 30, 1974, Arthur Taylor, president of CBS, sent a letter to Wayne Kearl, chairman of the NAB Television Code Review Board, in which CBS proposed that the NAB Code be amended to reflect the principle that "[p]rogramming in the first hour of the network prime-time schedule should be suitable for family viewing." On the same day, the CBS proposal was released publicly and NBC issued a press release stating that its current schedule "reflects the policy of" opening its prime time programming with series suitable for family viewing. . . .

On January 8, 1975, ABC announced that "the first hour of each night of its prime time network entertainment schedule will be devoted to programming suitable for general family audiences starting with the new television season in the fall of 1975." . . .

On February 19, 1975, the FCC submitted its Report to Congress. *See* Report on the Broadcast of Violent, Indecent, and Obscene Material, 51 F.C.C.2d 418 (1975). The Report recounted the longstanding public and congressional concern with the effects of television on young people, mentioned the growing number of complaints about violent and sexually-oriented programs filed with the Commission, and noted the receipt of various petitions to deny broadcast license renewals as well as petitions for rulemaking in the area of televised violence. . . .

On April 8, 1975, the NAB Television Board of Directors formally adopted the family viewing policy as an amendment to the Television Code.

II. The District Court Decision

[T]he district court . . . concluded that government pressure substantially caused the adoption of the family viewing policy which deprived the individual licensees of their right and duty to make independent decisions. . . . This deprivation violated the First Amendment.

III. Primary Jurisdiction

. . . At issue in this case is whether a family viewing hour imposed by the FCC would contravene the First Amendment. This is a considerably more narrow and precise issue than is the district court's bedrock principle and with respect to which the FCC's expertise and procedures could provide enormous assistance to the judiciary.

The . . . assertion on which [the district court] rested its rejection of the primary jurisdiction doctrine falls of its own weight once the district court's findings regarding liability are put in doubt. The FCC and its Chairman engaged in "serious misconduct" only if the law is as the district court found it. Weaken that foundation and what appeared as "serious misconduct" looks more like, at worst, jawboning of the type often praised as effective leadership by those satisfied with its results and condemned as unprincipled administration by those who disapprove of those results. . . .

We acknowledge that informal procedures permit the FCC to exercise "wide-ranging and largely uncontrolled administrative discretion in the review of telecommunications programming" which can be used to apply "sub silentio pressure" on broadcast licensees. Bazelon, FCC Regulation of the Telecommunications Press, 1975 Duke L.J. 213, 215. Regulation through "raised eyebrow" techniques or through forceful jawboning is commonplace in the administrative context, and in some instances may fairly be characterized, as it was by the district court in this case, as official action by the agency. . . .

While we agree that the use of these techniques by the FCC presents serious issues involving the Constitution, the Communications Act, and the APA, we nevertheless believe that the district court should not have thrust itself so hastily into the delicately balanced system of broadcast regulation. Because the "line between permissible regulatory activity and impermissible 'raised eyebrow' harassment of vulnerable licensees" is so exceedingly vague, Bazelon, *supra*, 1975 Duke L.J. at 217, it is important that judicial attempts to control these techniques be sensitive to "the particular regulatory context in which it occurs, the interests affected by it, and the potential for abuse." *Consolidated Edison Co. v. FPC*, 168 US App. D.C. 92, 101, 512 F2d 1332, 1341 (D.C. Cir. 1975) (footnote omitted). The development of standards governing the agency's use of informal methods to influence broadcast industry policy is an issue "that should be dealt with in the first instance by those especially familiar with the customs and practices of the industry." *Ricci v. Chicago Mercantile Exchange*, 409 U.S. 289, 305 (1973). . . .

Vacated and remanded.

Document 2: **Gibson v. Berryhill, *411 US 564 (1973)***

MR. JUSTICE WHITE delivered the opinion of the Court.

Prior to 1965, the laws of Alabama relating to the practice of optometry permitted any person, including a business firm or corporation, to maintain a department in which "eyes are examined or glasses fitted," provided that such department was in the charge of a duly licensed optometrist. This permission was expressly conferred by §210 of Title 46 of the Alabama Code of 1940, and also inferentially by §211 of the Code which regulates the advertising practices of optometrists, and which, until 1965, appeared to contemplate the existence of commercial stores with optical departments. In 1965, §210 was repealed in its entirety by the Alabama Legislature, and §211 was amended so as to eliminate any direct reference to optical departments maintained by corporations or other business establishments under the direction of employee optometrists.

Soon after these statutory changes, the Alabama Optometric Association, a professional organization whose membership is limited to independent practitioners of optometry *not* employed by others, filed charges against various named optometrists, all of whom were duly licensed under Alabama law but were the salaried employees of Lee Optical Co. . . .

It was apparently the Association's position that, following the repeal of §210 and the amendment of §211, the practice of optometry by individuals as employees of business corporations was no longer permissible in Alabama, and that, by accepting such employment, the named optometrists had violated the ethics of their profession. It was prayed that the Board revoke the licenses of the individuals charged following due notice and a proper hearing.

Two days after these charges were filed by the Association in October 1965, the Board filed a suit of its own in state court against Lee Optical, seeking to enjoin the company from engaging in the "unlawful practice of optometry." . . . on March 17, 1971, the state trial court rendered judgment for the Board, and enjoined Lee Optical both from practicing optometry without a license and from employing licensed optometrists. The company appealed this judgment.

Meanwhile, following its victory in the trial court, the Board reactivated the proceedings pending before it since 1965 against the individual optometrists employed by Lee, noticing them for hearings to be held on May 26 and 27, 1971. Those individuals countered on May 14, 1971, by filing a complaint in the United States District Court naming as defendants the Board of Optometry and its individual members, as well as the

Alabama Optometric Association and other individuals. The suit, brought under the Civil Rights Act of 1871, 42 USC §1983.

The thrust of the complaint was that the Board was biased and could not provide the plaintiffs with a fair and impartial hearing in conformity with due process of law.

A three-judge court was convened in August 1971, and shortly thereafter entered judgment for plaintiffs, enjoining members of the State Board and their successors "from conducting a hearing on the charges heretofore preferred against the Plaintiffs" and from revoking their licenses to practice optometry in the State of Alabama. . . .

The District Court apparently considered either source of possible bias — prejudgment of the facts or personal interest — sufficient to disqualify the members of the Board. Arguably, the District Court was right on both scores, but we need reach, and we affirm, only the latter ground of possible personal interest.

It is sufficiently clear from our cases that those with substantial pecuniary interest in legal proceedings should not adjudicate these disputes. *Tumey v. Ohio*, 273 US 510 (1927). And *Ward v. Village of Monroeville*, 409 US 57 (1972), indicates that the financial stake need not be as direct or positive as it appeared to be in *Tumey*. It has also come to be the prevailing view that "[m]ost of the law concerning disqualification because of interest applies with equal force to . . . administrative adjudicators." K. Davis, Administrative Law Text §12.04, p.250 (1972), and cases cited. The District Court proceeded on this basis and, applying the standards taken from our cases, concluded that the pecuniary interest of the members of the Board of Optometry had sufficient substance to disqualify them, given the context in which this case arose. As remote as we are from the local realities underlying this case and it being very likely that the District Court has a firmer grasp of the facts and of their significance to the issues presented, we have no good reason on this record to overturn its conclusion and we affirm it. . . .

Gibson was limited by the Court to a particular proceeding in *Friedman v. Rogers* (440 US 1) 1979.

Document 3: Log and Summary of Occupational Injuries and Illnesses, Bureau of Labor Statistics

OSHA's Form 300

Log of Work-Related Injuries and Illnesses

You must record information about every work-related death and about every work-related injury or illness that involves loss of consciousness, restricted work activity or job transfer, days away from work, or medical treatment beyond first aid. You must also record significant work-related injuries and illnesses that are diagnosed by a physician or licensed health care professional. You must also record work-related injuries and illnesses that meet any of the specific recording criteria listed in 29 CFR Part 1904.8 through 1904.12. Feel free to use two lines for a single case if you need to. You must complete an injury and illness incident Report (OSHA Form 301) or equivalent form for each injury or illness recorded on this form. If you're not sure whether a case is recordable, call your local OSHA office for help.

Attention: This form contains information relating to employee health and must be used in a manner that protects the confidentiality of employees to the extent possible while the information is being used for occupational safety and health purposes.

Year 20 _____

U.S. Department of Labor
Occupational Safety and Health Administration

Form approved OMB no. 1218-0176

Establishment name _____

City _____   State _____

Identify the person

(A) Case no.	(B) Employee's name

Describe the case

(C) Job title (e.g., Welder)

(D) Date of injury or onset of illness

(E) Where the event occurred (e.g., Loading dock north end)

(F) Describe injury or illness, parts of body affected, and object/substance that directly injured or made person ill (e.g., Second degree burns on right forearm from acetylene torch)

Classify the case

Using these four categories, check ONLY the most serious result for each case:

(G) Death
(H) Days away from work
(I) Remained at work — Job transfer or restriction
(J) Remained at work — Other record-able cases

Enter the number of days the injured or ill worker was:

(K) On job transfer or restriction _____ days
(L) Away from work _____ days

Check the "Injury" column or choose one type of illness:

(M)
(1) Injury
(2) Skin disorder
(3) Respiratory condition
(4) Poisoning
(5) All other illnesses

Page totals ▶

Be sure to transfer these totals to the Summary page (Form 300A) before you post it.

Page _____ of _____

Public reporting burden for this collection of information is estimated to average 14 minutes per response, including time to review the instructions, search and gather the data needed, and complete and review the collection of information. Persons are not required to respond to the collection of information unless it displays a currently valid OMB control number. If you have any comments about these estimates or any other aspects of this data collection, contact: US Department of Labor, OSHA Office of Statistics, Room N-3644, 200 Constitution Avenue, NW, Washington, DC 20210. Do not send the completed forms to this office.

8

Administrative Agency Hearings

A Hearing . . . "investigates, declares and enforces . . ."

Justice Oliver Wendell Holmes
Prentis v. Atlantic Coastline Co.
211 US 236 (1908)

CHAPTER OBJECTIVES

Hearings are agency proceedings at which disputants present evidence to support their arguments and receive a decision. You will learn in this chapter:

- When a hearing may be requested.
- How agencies determine valid reasons for hearings.
- How agency decisions may be appealed.
- What procedures are enforced.
- The duties of administrative law judges.
- Which pre-hearing steps are encouraged.
- How decisions are rendered.

CHAPTER OVERVIEW

When an individual or a business does not comply with agency regulations, a hearing to determine facts and laws may be requested. The need for the hearing is ascertained by the agency after an applicant files a complaint. Procedures of notice, discovery, and the fundamental rights of due process prevail during the hearing process. Paralegals assist in all facets of the hearing process. During the pre-hearing stages, law firm paralegals interview parties and witnesses. At the agencies, paralegals assume duties in the administrative law judge's office. Throughout the hearings, paralegals prepare evidence for presentation and examination, review documents, and aid in assessing any settlement offers.

A. What Is a Hearing and When Is It Needed?

Hearings, or adjudications, in administrative agencies are on a level similar to civil or criminal court trials. The procedures for administrative agency hearings are formulated in agency statutes and administrative procedure acts. The proceedings may ensue when there is a violation of a regulation, when there is a suspension or revocation of a license or permit, when employees lose their jobs, and other instances in which decisions of the agency are contested. Justice Oliver Wendell Holmes defined a hearing as a proceeding "that investigates, declares, and enforces liabilities as they stand on present or past facts and under laws supposed to already exist. That is the purpose and end." *Prentis v. Atlantic Coastline Co.,* 211 US 210 at 236 (1908).

Hearings are held after all the other processes offered by the agency to reach agreement have been exhausted. Often there is a loss to a claimant, such as a job loss or a license revocation. Claimants believe there is a violation of their rights or that they have been wronged and contest the agency decision on their claims at hearings. If a party believes the agency decision that revokes a license is incorrect, the parties appeal. The agency reconsiders the facts in light of the evidence presented.

Hearings are held at the administrative agencies. The parties, witnesses and hearing officers, along with pertinent agency personnel, attend the hearing. Attorneys and paralegals for both sides prepare the documents and evidence to be presented at the hearings. Witnesses may be cross-examined at administrative agency hearings.

Figure 8.1 illustrates situations in which a hearing may be needed.

Figure 8.1 **When Hearings Are Needed**

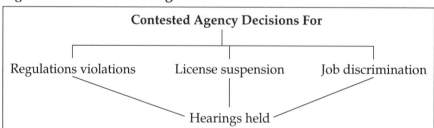

CASE ABSTRACT

The U.S. Supreme Court has upheld agency rights to decide hearing methods.

Louisiana Association of Independent Producers and Royalty Owners v. Federal Energy Regulatory Commission
958 F2d 1101 (DC Cir. 1992)

Federal Energy Regulatory Commission (FERC) issued certificate of need for 370-mile pipeline extending from Canadian border in upstate New York to Long Island. Coalition of upstate New Yorkers concerned about environmental effects of pipeline and fuel oil dealers from New England and Louisiana challenged certification as did domestic oil and natural gas producers. The Court of Appeals held that: (1) ex parte discussions between FERC and proponents of projects did not render proceedings unfair; (2) proceedings did not violate due process rights of opponents; (3) substantial evidence supported FERC's decision; (4) FERC's environmental impact statement fulfilled purpose of Natural Environmental Policy Act; (5) FERC was not required to adjust rates of proposed pipeline to offset alleged competitive advantage that would otherwise accrue to Canadian gas carried on pipeline due to differences between Canadian and domestic rate design policies; and (6) American pipeline company which agreed to perform exchange services was not entitled to case-specific certificate of need.

Petitions denied. . . .

Before MIKVA, Chief Judge, SILBERMAN and RANDOLPH, Circuit Judges.

Opinion for the court filed per curiam.

Per curiam:

The Iroquois/Tennessee Project is part of a billion dollar plan to ship natural gas from Alberta across the Canadian prairie to the Northeastern United States. Participants in the plan have sought licenses, certifications, and authorizations before numerous state, federal, and Canadian regulatory bodies. In this case, three groups of petitioners challenge the Federal Energy Regulatory Commission's certification of the American transportation component, a 370-mile pipeline extending from the Canadian border in upstate New York to Long Island. The first group consists of a coalition of upstate New Yorkers concerned about the environmental effects of the pipeline and fuel oil dealers from New England and Louisiana (the "Coalition"). They challenge the certification on the ground that the Commission reached its decision unfairly, improperly, and in violation of due process. The second group of petitioners are domestic oil and natural gas producers led by the State of Louisiana (the "domestic producers"). They argue that the Commission should have adjusted the rates of the proposed pipeline to compensate for what they allege to be the anticompetitive effects of Canadian rate designs. The final petitioner, the Texas Eastern

Transmission Company, is one of the domestic pipelines involved in the project. It seeks review of FERC's refusal to grant it a case-specific certificate. Finding none of these petitions persuasive, we deny them. . . .

The hearing before the ALJ lasted for ten days, with opponents of the Project first offering evidence to rebut the Commission's current views. After reviewing proposed findings of fact, the ALJ found a need for the Project, primarily because the market projections credited by the Commission remained the most reasonable ones before him. . . .

A

[1] The Coalition begins its litany of procedural complaints by accusing the Commission of engaging in *ex parte* meetings with the Iroquois proponents during both the Northeast open season and the Iroquois/Tennessee certification proceedings. However, as both the Commission and Iroquois observe, the Coalition never actually argues that these meetings were improper or that they tainted the proceedings below. . . .

According to the Commission, due process did not require the August hearing or indeed any additional proceedings. Opponents of the Project had ample opportunity to oppose the Project in written submissions and oral argument. In the Commission's view, the only thing they lacked was a trial-type evidentiary hearing, but, given the nature of the facts in dispute, there was no need for such a hearing. Trial-type proceedings, the Commission reasoned, are necessary only when "a witness' motive, intent, or credibility needs to be considered" or "where the issue involves a dispute over a past occurrence." Preliminary Order at 61,368. That was not the situation here. . . .

In addition to questioning the manner in which the Commission conducted private meetings, the manner in which it conducted public hearings, the manner in which it discussed options, and the manner in which it analyzed the evidence before it, the Coalition petitioners also criticize the manner in which the Commission applied its own policies.

B. Steps to Obtaining a Hearing

1. Determination of Need

In order to fully illustrate the various procedures of the hearing process in administrative agencies we will follow the process through the U.S. Department of Housing and Urban Development (HUD). The rules and procedures to be followed for all agencies are in the Code of Federal Regulation (CFR), those specific to HUD are at 24 CFR §§20.10–24.18. A HUD hearing takes place at the HUD Board of Contract Appeals (HUD BCA). Similar to other agencies, the hearing is held after an agency decision has been authorized, usually (HUD's) termination of a contract, but found to be unsatisfactory by the recipient. The recipient decides to appeal the decision and request a hearing. Before any hearing commences, the agency makes the determination that there is a valid need for a hearing. First the person contesting the agency decision files a notice of appeal, stating the intention to appeal and the decision in dispute. It might be an appeal of HUD terminating a contract for services, including: cleaning HUD property, construction, and demolition of buildings.

Second, the appeal is given a docket number and a file is opened. A notice of docketing is sent to the person filing the appeal (appellant). Next, the appellant must file a complaint within thirty days after receiving notice of docketing.

Third, the respondent (HUD) has thirty days to answer the complaint. The answer must adhere to specific requirements; in this case Rule 8(b), 24 CFR Section 20.10.

Fourth, after receiving the respondent's answer, the appellant then informs the HUD BCA if a hearing is requested or if the record of the case will be submitted to without a hearing. A request for a HUD hearing must be in writing and follow Rules 10, 13, 14, & 24 CFR Section 20.10. An appellant may request an accelerated procedure if the appeal involves $25,000 or less.

STUDENT PRACTICE

Separate into two groups.

Group 1 — You are the contractor planning to appeal HUD's decision. Develop and write questions that you will want to ask the paralegal you will work with initially at the law firm.

Group 2 — You are the paralegal in the law firm. Prepare a written memo for your file that explains:

1.   The sections of the CFR on which you will rely
2.   Summarizes the pertinent CFR sections (use Exhibit 8.1)

Both Groups Meet

Group 1 presents its questions and Group 2 answers the questions while one member of each group takes notes.

Decide which questions you are unable to answer at this time due to a lack of (1) sufficient factual information or (2) a legal opinion by the attorney.

Make copies of both groups' notes for a later class exercise.

Exhibit 8.1 reprints the pertinent sections of the CFR for appealing a HUD decision and proceeding to a hearing.

Exhibit 8.1   **24 CFR Part 20**

PART 20—BOARD OF CONTRACT APPEALS

Subpart A—Development of Housing and Urban Development Board of Contract Appeals

Sec.
20.1 Scope of part.
20.2 Establishment of Board.
20.3 Organization and location of the Board.
20.4 Jurisdiction of the Board.
20.5 Board powers.

Subpart B—Rules of the Department of Housing and Urban Development Board of Contract Appeals

20.10 Rules.

PRELIMINARY PROCEDURES

Rule
1. Appeals, how taken.
2. Notice of appeal, contents of.
3. Docketing of appeals.
4. Preparation, content, organization, forwarding, and status of appeal file.
5. Dismissal for lack of jurisdiction.
6. Pleadings.
7. Amendments of pleadings or record.
8. Hearing election and motions.
9. Prehearing briefs.
10. Prehearing of presubmission conference.
11. Submission without a hearing.
12. Optional small claims (expedited) and accelerated procedures. (These procedures are available solely at the election of the appellant.)
12.1 Elections to utilize small claims (expedited) and accelerated procedure.
12.2 The small claims (expedited) procedure.
12.3 The accelerated procedure.
12.4 Motions for reconsideration in Rule 12 cases.
13. Settling the record.
14. Discovery—depositions.
15. Interrogatories to parties, admission of facts, and production and inspection of documents.
16. Filing and service of papers other than subpoenas.

HEARINGS

17. Where and when held.
18. Notice of hearings.
19. Unexcused absence of a party.

Subpart A — Department of Housing and Urban Development Board of Contract Appeals

SOURCE: 50 FR 45911, Nov. 5, 1985, last updated July 21, 2005, unless otherwise noted.

§20.4   Jurisdiction of the Board.

(a) *Contract appeals.* The Board shall consider and determine appeals from decisions of contracting officers under the Contract Disputes Act of 1978 (41 USC 601–613) relating to contracts entered into by (1) the Department of Housing and Urban Development or (2) any other executive agency when that agency or the Administrator for Federal Procurement Policy has designated the Board to decide the appeal.

(b) *Other matters.* The Board or its individual members shall have jurisdiction over other matters assigned to it by the Secretary or designee. Determinations in other matters shall have the finality provided by the applicable statute, regulation or agreement.

. . .

§20.10   Rules.

These rules govern the procedure in all matters before the Department of Housing and Urban Development Board of Contract Appeals, unless otherwise provided by applicable law or regulation. The Federal Rules of Civil Procedure may be applied where procedures are not otherwise provided in these rules. For applications and proceedings involving award of attorney fees and other expenses, the rules set forth in 24 CFR part 14 shall apply.

PRELIMINARY PROCEDURES

Rule 1. Appeals, how taken.

(a) *General.* Notice of an appeal shall be in writing and mailed or otherwise furnished to the Board within 90 days from the date of receipt of a final written decision of the contracting officer.

(b) *Contracting officer's failure to act—claim of $100,000 or less.* Where the contractor has submitted a claim of $100,000 or less to the contracting officer and has requested a written decision within 60 days from receipt of the request, and the contracting officer has not issued the decision, the contractor may file a notice of appeal as provided in paragraph (a) of this section, citing the failure of the contracting officer to issue a decision.

(c) *Contracting officer's failure to act—claim in excess of $100,000.* Where the contractor has submitted a claim in excess of $100,000 to the contracting officer and the contracting officer has failed, within 60 days of submission of the claim, to issue a final written decision, or to advise the contractor of a date when the final written decision will be issued, the contractor may file a notice of appeal as provided in paragraph (a) of this section, citing the failure to issue a decision.

(d) *Unreasonable delay by contracting officer.* A contractor may request the Board to direct a contracting officer to issue a final written decision within a specified period of time, as determined by the Board, in the event of an unreasonable delay on the part of the contracting officer.

(e) *Stay of proceedings.* Upon docketing of appeals filed under paragraph (b) or (c) of this section, the Board may stay further proceedings pending issuance of a final decision by the contracting officer within the period of time determined by the Board.

Rule 2. Notice of appeal, contents of.

A notice of appeal shall indicate that an appeal is being taken and shall identify the contract (by number), the department and agency involved in the dispute, the final written decision from which the appeal is taken, and the amount in dispute, if known. The notice of appeal shall be signed by the appellant (the contractor making the appeal), or by the appellant's duly authorized representative or attorney. The complaint referred to in Rule 6 may be filed with the notice of appeal, or the appellant may designate the notice of appeal as a complaint, if it otherwise fulfills the requirements of a complaint. A notice of appeal from a final written decision of a contracting officer involving a claim in excess of $100,000 shall state that certification has been made as required under section 6(c)(1) of the Contract Disputes Act of 1978 [41 USC §606(c)(1)].

Rule 3. Docketing of appeals.

When a notice of appeal in any form has been received by the Board, it shall be docketed promptly. A written notice of docketing shall be transmitted to the appellant with a copy of these rules, to the contracting officer, and to HUD's Office of General Counsel.

. . .

Rule 6. Pleadings.

(a) *Appellant.* Within 30 days after receipt of notice of docketing of the appeal, the appellant shall file a complaint with the Board. The complaint shall set forth simple, concise and direct statements of each of the appellant's claims.

. . .

Rule 8. Hearing election and motions.

(a) *Hearing election.* After the filing of the Government's answer or notice from the Board that it has entered a general denial on behalf of the Government, each party shall advise whether it desires a hearing as prescribed in Rules 17 through 25, or whether it elects to submit its case on the record without a hearing, as prescribed in Rule 11.

. . .

Rule 10. Prehearing or presubmission conference.

(a) *Conference.* Whether the case is to be submitted under Rule 11, or heard under Rules 17 through 25, the Board may upon its own initiative, or upon the application of either party, arrange a telephone conference or call upon the parties to appear before an Administrative Judge for a conference to consider:

(1) Simplification, clarification, or severing of the issues;

(2) The possibility of obtaining stipulations, admissions, agreements and rulings on admissibility of documents, understandings on matters already on record, or similar agreements that will avoid unnecessary proof;

(3) Agreements and rulings to facilitate discovery;

(4) Limitation of the number of expert witnesses or avoidance of cumulative evidence;

(5) The possibility of agreement disposing of any or all of the issues in dispute; and

(6) Such other matters as may aid in the dispositon of the appeal.

(b) *Results of conference.* The Administrative Judge shall make such rulings and orders as may be appropriate to achieve settlement by agreement of the parties or to aid in the disposition of the appeal. The results of the conference, including any rulings and orders, shall be reduced to writing by the Administrative Judge or the conference shall be transcribed. The writing or the transcript shall constitute a part of the record.

. . .

HEARINGS

Rule 17. Where and when held.

Hearings will be held at places determined by the Board to best serve the interest of the parties and the Board. Hearings will be scheduled at the discretion of the Board with due consideration to the regular order of appeals, Rule 12 requirements, the convenience of the parties, the requirement for just and inexpensive determination of appeals without necessary delay, and other pertinent factors. On request or motion by either party and for good cause, the Board may adjust the date of a hearing.

Rule 18. Notice of hearings.

Parties shall be given not less than 20 days notice of the time and place for hearing, unless otherwise agreed. The notice of hearing shall be sent by certified mail (return receipt requested).

Rule 19. Unexcused absence of a party.

The unexcused absence of a party at the time and place set for hearing will not be occasion for delay. Notwithstanding the provisions of Rule 31, in the event of an unexcused absence: (a) The appeal will be dismissed with prejudice for want of prosecution; or (b) the hearing will proceed and the case will be regarded as submitted on the record by the absent party.

Rule 20. Hearings: conduct; examination of witnesses.

(a) *Conduct of hearings.* Hearings shall be as informal as may be reasonable and appropriate under the circumstances. Appellant and the Government may offer such evidence as would be admissible under the Federal Rules of Evidence or as otherwise determined to be reliable and relevant by the presiding Administrative Judge. Stipulations of fact agreed upon by the parties may be regarded and used as evidence at the hearing. The parties may stipulate the testimony that would be given by a witness if the witness were present. The Board may require evidence in addition to that offered by the parties.

(b) *Examination of witnesses.* Oral testimony before the Board shall generally be given under oath or affirmation. However, if the testimony of a witness is not given under oath or affirmation, the Board shall advise the witness that his statements may be subject to the provisions of title 18 USC, sections 287 and 1001, and any other provision of law imposing penalties for knowingly making false representations in connection with claims against the United States or in any matter within the jurisdiction of any department or agency.

Rule 21. Subpoenas.

(a) *General.* Upon written request of either party filed with the Board or on the Administrative Judge's initiative, the Administrative Judge to whom a case is assigned or who is otherwise designated by the Chairman may issue a subpoena requiring:

(1) Testimony at a deposition—the deposing of a witness in the city or county where he or she resides, is employed or transacts business in person, or at another location convenient for the witness that is specifically determined by the Board;

(2) Testimony at a hearing—the attendance of a witness for the purpose of taking testimony at a hearing; and

(3) Production of books and papers—the production by the witness at the deposition or hearing of books and papers designated in the subpoena.

. . .

REPRESENTATION

Rule 26. Appellant.

An individual appellant may appear before the Board in person; a corporation by one of its duly authorized officers; and a partnership or joint venture by one of its duly authorized members; or any of these by an attorney at law duly licensed in any State, commonwealth, territory, the District of Columbia, or in a foreign country. An attorney representing an appellant shall file a written notice of appearance with the Board.

Rule 27. Government.

Government counsel may, in accordance with their authority, represent the interest of the Government before the Board. They shall file notices of appearance with the Board. This notice of appearance will be given appellant or appellant's attorney in the form specified by the Board from time to time. Whenever an appellant and the Government are in agreement as to dispositon of the controversy, the Board may suspend further processing of the appeal. However, if the Board is advised by either party that the controversy has not been disposed of by agreement, the case shall be restored to the Board's calendar without loss of position.

DECISIONS

Rule 28. Decisions.

Decisions of the Board shall be made in writing. Copies of the decision shall be forwarded simultaneously to both parties. The rules of the Board and all final orders and decisions (except those required for good cause to be held confidential and not cited as precedents) shall be open for public inspection at the offices of the Board in Washington, DC. Decisions of the Board shall be made solely upon the record, as described in Rule 13. Oral decisions shall be rendered in accordance with Rules 12.2(c) and 12.3(c).

STUDENT PRACTICE

Split the class into the same groups as Student Practice beginning on page 241 **BUT** this time reverse the roles.
Group 1 — paralegal
Group 2 — contractor

Meeting with Client

Bring your notes to the meeting.
Group 1 — Explain HUD's answer to the client and the CFR rule cited.
Group 2 — Request answers from questions at prior meeting (Student Practice page 241).
Meeting is rescheduled allowing paralegal time to get answers (create some plausible answers).

Followup Meeting

Group 1 — Give answers in a professional manner because the client has been overheard asking the legal secretary if rates are cut for meetings at which people are unprepared.
Group 2 — Ask Group 1 to explain the CFRs for requesting a hearing. You will decide whether to request a hearing later.

Figure 8.2 provides an overview of the steps that must be followed in order to appeal on agency decision and make the determination of whether to hold a hearing.

Figure 8.2   **Contesting an Agency Decision**

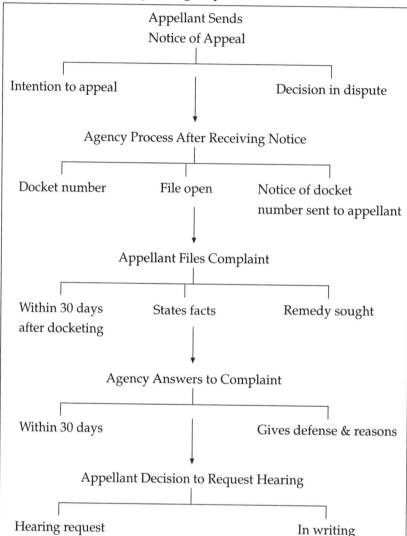

2. Pre-Hearing Procedures

In the pre-hearing stage, agencies, like the courts, follow certain procedures that protect the clients of the agency and that allow the government to function.

Pre-hearing procedures generally include notice, parties, discovery, and conferences. Agencies make specific rules regarding these procedures, such as allowing depositions be taken during discovery, the submission of briefs, setting time limits, and amending pleadings. These agency rules regarding hearing procedures are found in the Code of Federal Regulations (CFR).

a. Notice

All parties must receive notice of an impending hearing. This notice informs the parties of the time of the hearing, the type of hearing, the place of the hearing, and the laws that relate to the hearing. A notice may be challenged if a party states that there is insufficient time for preparation of the case. In order for a party to properly prepare for the hearing, the notice should explain the factual and legal issues that are the basis for the agency's action, particularly if an agency is charging a violation of a regulation.

In *Memphis Light, Gas and Water Div. v. Craft,* 436 US 1 (1978), the U.S. Supreme Court upheld the right to notice of a hearing for utility customers. When the utility company informs customers that service will be terminated, the utility company must include notice of a hearing that is available for customers protesting the termination of service. The Court also insisted that the particulars of the termination causes be outlined in the notice.

When a license may be revoked, the U.S. Supreme Court ordered that the licensee must be informed in the notice of the specific rules that he is being accused of violating. *Wolfenbarger v. Hennessee,* 520 F2d 809 (Okl. 1974)

The Administrative Procedure Act, 5 USCS §554(b), states that notice should include:

(1) the time, place, and nature of the hearing;
(2) the legal authority and jurisdiction . . .
(3) the matters of fact and law . . .

b. Parties

Those named as participants in the hearing, usually the appellant and the respondent, are the parties. Parties may also include: the person filing the claim, others who have a strong interest, such as those who could be economically harmed by an agency action, and those qualified by the agency as parties for non-economic reasons. Because each party has the right to participate in the hearing, the agency carefully screens and decides which are qualified; each added party adds time and cost factors to the process. All parties must receive copies of all written documents pertaining to the hearing filed with the Agency.

c. Discovery

Discovery is the gathering and exchange of information in order to prepare for the hearing. As each side becomes aware of the other side's case through discovery, the knowledge of the factual and legal issues often encourages settlement of the case before a hearing. Unlike court cases,

How are administrative hearings similar to trials?

discovery is not a guaranteed right; each agency administers its own rules for discovery. If discovery is allowed, depositions, interrogatories, production of documents, and stipulations are common procedures. For example, the National Labor Relations Board determines the use of discovery on each individual case. Much of discovery in administrative agencies takes place at the pre-hearing conference.

d. Pre-Hearing Conferences

The pre-hearing conference serves to clarify issues. Stipulations to certain facts also may be made. This streamlines the process, because these facts will not have to be presented and argued over at the formal hearing. Both sides receive witness lists, the evidence to be presented, and exhibits at the conference; similar to discovery in the courts. At this time, both sides may agree to settle, if not, the hearing officer will discuss the plans for the hearing. The agency decides when a conference will be held; some are held days before a hearing, others months before a hearing.

C. Hearings

Administrative hearings have procedures that appear to be similar to court hearings—opening statements, witness examination and court examination, presentation of evidence, closing statements; but agency requirements in these categories are often different than court requirements. An administrative law judge (ALJ) (also called a hearing officer or hearing examiner) presides at administrative hearings, rendering a decision on the record presented. This decision is based on the law and findings of fact.

The procedural requirements and rules that the ALJs enforce are in the Administrative Procedure Act's §§554, 556, and 557. These APA rules are followed when the statute that created the agency demands a "hearing on record." If such a hearing is not required, an agency has the discretion to allow less stringently ruled hearings and other proceedings; this usually is the practice when a party does not fulfill the time limits request for a hearing, the facts in the case are not in dispute, or the agency decides a hearing is unnecessary. In *Weinberger v. Hyman, Westcott & Dunning, Inc.*, 412 US 609 (1973), the U.S. Supreme Court stated, "We cannot impute Congress the design of requiring, nor does due process demand, a hearing when it appears conclusively from the applicant's pleadings that the application cannot succeed."

1.   Participants in a Hearing

Logically, the claimant contesting the agency decision will be involved in the hearing. Also included are the interested parties as determined by the agency during the pre-hearing stage. But equally important are the attorneys, paralegals, the judge, and the witnesses.

a.   Judges

The ALJ conducts the hearing; other titles they maybe referred to as are hearing, examining, or presiding officer. The ALJ is not the independent judge that is found in the court system. The administrative law judge is an employee of the administrative agency, which empowers the judge to:

1. conduct the hearing and preside at the hearing,
2. make decisions on evidence, procedural requests, and findings,
3. make the decision at the conclusion of the hearing, and
4. perform other actions authorized by the agency.

Various measures are taken to ensure the ALJ maintains some independence from the agency, for instance ALJs are usually assigned cases in rotation to avoid being assigned cases in which the judge is sympathetic with the agency's viewpoint. Many judges' salary and tenure decisions are made by civil service agencies and not the agency in which they are employed and ALJ staff functions are separate from agency staff functions. Usually, a government personnel agency keeps a list of qualified candidates and does the selection, not the agency in which the judge is to be employed. Judges cannot hear cases in which they have a bias or personal interest and must remove themselves from these cases. They cannot be arbitrarily removed from a case without a just reason. Finally, judges may not discuss the case to be heard with agency employees or opposing parties.

The Administrative Procedures Act §554(d) states that "an employee or agent engaged in the investigative or prosecuting functions" may not discuss any of the case with the administrative law judge. In 1976, the APA separated ALJ tenure (5 USCS §5362) and ALJ salary decisions (5 USCS §4301) from the agency. ALJs may only be removed after a hearing before the Merit Systems Protection Board. The tenure and salary decision steps are to promote the impartiality of the judge. In *Marshall v. Jerrico, Inc.*, 446 US 228 (1980), the U.S. Supreme Court stated that impartiality "serves as the ultimate guarantee of a fair and meaningful proceeding." It also said, "This requirement of neutrality in adjudicative proceedings safeguards the two central concerns of procedural due process, the prevention of unjustified or mistaken deprivations, and the promotion of participation and dialogue by affected individuals in the decision-making process." If an instance occurs when this neutrality or impartiality may have been broken by a contact with a member of the case, §557(d)(1)(C) of the APA requires that this contact be placed in the public record of the hearing.

b. Paralegals

Paralegals assist in all procedures and stages of hearings whether working for the appellant's attorneys, the respondent's attorneys, or the agency. Any functions that they perform may be assisted by experienced paralegals.

c. Attorneys

At most administrative agency hearings, each party has the right to be represented by an attorney; in fact many of the hearing proceedings demand the expertise of attorneys. The complexities of the legal issues are often beyond the understanding of the non-legal educated person, and the findings of fact often necessitate the skill of an attorney to properly scrutinize and present only the pertinent facts. The attorney becomes the combatant for its client against the opposing party after explaining the facts and laws. Section 555(b) of the Administrative Procedure Act encourages representation by an attorney: "A party is entitled to appear in person or by or with counsel or other duly qualified representative in an agency proceeding." HUD Rule 27, 24 CFR §20.10 delineates attorney representation.

d. Expert Witnesses

Much of the subject matter that comes before an administrative agency is technical, needing expert information; sometimes this expertise is supplied by the agency itself. In litigation, expert witnesses explain evidence or refute evidence. All are under oath, and are subject to examination and cross-examination. There is a procedure called "official notice" in which the administrative law judge may declare certain facts as true, thus not needing proof to substantiate that the fact is true; this is accomplished through the expertise of the judge and agency. For instance, an agency may have compiled many studies and statistics on injuries caused by leakage of a certain element in steel producing factories. That fact is part of official notice as long as it is relevant to the litigation, but is not a fact that is necessary to the in-depth structure of the litigation. Official notice may be approved by the parties in the case.

e. Other Witnesses

Witnesses are sworn in and must answer truthfully, if they are untruthful, they are liable for perjury and subject to criminal prosecution. Both parties may call witnesses.

Unlike court trials, cross-examination is not automatically allowed at hearings. There must be demonstrated a need for cross-examination. The Administrative Procedure Act §556 demands a need be shown "for a full and true disclosure of the facts." (5 USCA §556(d)). In *Cellular Mobile Systems of PA, Inc. v. FCC*, 782 F2d 183 at 198, the U.S. Supreme Court stated that cross-examination's "necessity must be established under specific circumstances by the party seeking it." The party seeking cross-examination must "point to any specific weaknesses in the proof which might have been explored or developed more fully by that technique" (cross-examination) than by other procedures offered by the agency.

2. Stages of a Hearing

a. Presentation of Evidence

The rules governing permissible evidence are different in administrative hearings than in court trials. Unlike many court trials, hearsay is often admissible at administrative hearings. For example, an employee may testify that another employee told her that a third employee had taken off unwarranted days. In a court trial this testimony would be considered hearsay and not allowed, but in an administrative hearing it would be admitted as evidence whose trustworthiness must be determined by the judge. Agencies do not always follow the exclusionary rule either and may allow some illegally obtained evidence.

Figure 8.3 **Evidence**

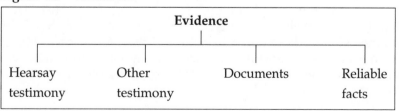

But like the courts, the administrative agency does recognize certain privileges such as a husband not being allowed to testify against his wife and vice versa, or a doctor not being allowed to give private, medical information on a patient. Not all evidence that would be excluded in a court is excluded in an administrative agency. Generally, ALJs admit all the evidence presented, and then sift through the evidence, determining which evidence is more important and more trustworthy than other evidence. One of the reasons this is allowed is because ALJs are perceived as being experts in the subject matter presented, thus able to apply the correct amount of weight to different evidence. As a check, the judge must demonstrate on what the decision was based; reliable, competent evidence must support the judge's decision.

The view that because agencies are considered to be experts in their field and are the "triers of fact", the rules of evidence may be less stringent in an administrative hearing than for jury or other court actions has been upheld by the courts since 1937 in *Ohio Bell Tel. Co. v. Public Utilities Comm'n of Ohio*, 301 US 292. The U.S. Supreme Court stated, "Regulatory commissions have been invested with broad powers within the sphere of duty assigned to them by law. Even in quasi-judicial proceedings their informed and expert judgment enacts and receives a proper deference from courts when it has been reached with due submission to constitutional restraints." The right of agencies to admit hearsay evidence was upheld in *Richardson v. Perales*, 401 US 389 (1971), in which the court stated, "We conclude that a written report by a licensed physician who has examined the claimant and who sets forth in his report his medical finding in his area of competence may be received as evidence in a disability hearing, and, despite its hearsay character and an absence of cross-examination." The court upheld trustworthy hearsay as a basis for an agency decision.

b. Proof

Proof is established by a party producing the evidence and persuading the judge that the party's argument is the correct one. Producing evidence and persuading the judge is called the burden of proof. The burden of proof is usually on the party who has initiated the action. Usually a preponderance of the evidence (51 percent or greater) is the standard by which the judge decides if there is enough evidence to prove a party's case. Some agencies demand clear and convincing evidence when a civil right is being debated. Rarely is the criminal standard, beyond a reasonable doubt, used in administrative hearing decisions.

In *Steadman v. SEC*, 450 US 91 (1981), the preponderance of evidence standard of proof was upheld by the U.S. Supreme Court. The court rejected the need for the clear and convincing standard of proof. This preponderance standard was also upheld in *Vance v. Terrazas*, 444 US 252 (1980). In §556(d) of the APA, the party who must assume the burden of proof is the "proponent of a rule or order"; the only exception being when a statute states otherwise.

PARALEGAL PRACTICE EXAMPLE

You, a paralegal, have been asked to sit down with a client who is frustrated because she knows she is right in her claim and doesn't know why she has to spend all this time preparing evidence for a hearing. You explain that a preponderance of evidence is necessary; and because she is bringing the complaint, the burden of proof is on her.

c. Findings

Findings are the results and conclusions arrived at after the evidence as been presented. An administrative hearing has two types of findings: (1) proposed findings by the parties after the hearing and before the decision; (2) findings presented by the judge to back up the decision.

The ALJ's findings and conclusions are put in a written decision. Any relevant fact that influenced the case must by analyzed in the judge's findings. It is from this analysis that the judge makes conclusions and eventually reaches a decision. These findings give an accountability of the judge's position; they demonstrate an analysis of the case and allow future cases a background and possible precedent. By reviewing the findings, future parties and attorneys can ascertain the agency's manner of enforcing its rules and regulations. Costly future litigation is reduced when attorneys and parties understand their viewpoints may not be sustained by hearing action. Also judicial review is aided to by understanding the reasoning behind the decision that is being reviewed.

3. Hearing Decisions

Decisions are different in administrative hearings than in court cases. The ALJ makes a decision after considering the facts and legal issues presented at the hearing, but the agency then issues the final decision.

Figure 8.4 illustrates administrative agency decisions.

Figure 8.4 **Administrative Hearing or Agency Decisions**

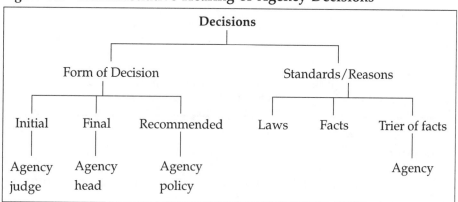

a. Form of Decision

The decisions issued by the ALJ are either initial decisions or recommended decisions. If it is a routine case, the agency allows the ALJ to issue an initial decision. This decision is upheld by the agency and becomes final if it is not contested or appealed. If an initial decision is appealed, the head officer reviews all parts of the case. The agency then issues its decision, which still may be appealed in the courts.

A recommended decision by an ALJ is usually a decision of law or policy. This decision is given to the agency head. The agency reviews the decision and decides which action the agency will take.

b. Standards and Reasons for Decisions

All ALJ decisions have to state the reasons upon which they are based; these reasons must support all fact, law, and discretionary aspects that arose during the hearing. The agency is the trier of fact. It must explain how the facts influenced the decision that was made. What conclusions were made based on the facts and laws? What part did discretion play in the decision? In answering these questions, the ALJ relates the decision to specific reasons.

A hearing at HUD includes all of the parties and procedures discussed.

1. The contractor is afforded a right to be heard at the hearing, with an attorney and with the opportunity to present evidence and witnesses.
2. After the ALJ or hearing officer makes an initial or recommended decision, a written decision is presented to the Secretary, or designee, of HUD; the decision is then finalized, modified, or reversed.
3. The secretary signs the final decision and it is sent to all parties by registered or certified mail.

CONCEPTS JOURNAL

You are a paralegal working for a lawyer. Using your notes from the two Student Practice sections in this chapter, write a memo to your lawyer summarizing your view of the meeting with the client.

Journal

Keep the two Student Practice exercises and this memo in your journal to aid in your understanding of hearings.

CASE ABSTRACT

Gonzalez is an actual case on debarment; note the discussion on required procedures.

Gonzalez v. Freeman
334 F2d 570 (DC Cir. 1964)

Burger, J. . . . In January 1960, Thos. P. Gonzalez Corporation, which had a record of contractual relations with Commodity Credit [Corporation, a federal corporate instrumentality] for a number of years, received notice by telegram that the Gonzalez Corporation and its officers and affiliates . . . were temporarily debarred from doing business with Commodity Credit pending investigation into possible misuse of official inspection certificates relating to commodities exported to Brazil by Gonzalez Corporation. . . .

. . . On May 24, 1962, after consideration of information and arguments submitted by appellants, Commodity Credit informed appellants by letter that they were suspended for five years from the date of the original temporary suspension on January 13, 1960. The letter stated no reasons or grounds for the final debarment action. . . .

Appellants sought review by the Secretary of Agriculture, who declined to reconsider, stating: "We feel that further discussions would serve no useful purpose unless you are in a position to present new facts concerning this matter which heretofore have not been considered." Appellants offered none.

Thereafter, appellants instituted the declaratory judgment action from which this appeal arises. Since January 1960, appellants have been ineligible to participate in any programs of Commodity Credit or to purchase surplus government commodities for resale. Their complaint in the District Court alleged that in appellants' course of dealings with Commodity Credit they had purchased for export under license an aggregate of more than $7,000,000 in surplus commodities, that this was a large part of their business, and that loss of this business has deprived them of more than $100,000 in profits. . . .

The issues that emerge from the opposing contentions can be restated as follows:

(1) Does debarment of a government contractor from eligibility for purchase of surplus commodities give rise to a justiciable controversy if it is alleged that debarment was imposed without due process?
(2) Did Congress provide for judicial review of the debarment process conducted by Commodity Credit?
(3) May debarment of a government contractor be imposed without express statutory authority?
(4) If Commodity Credit has legal authority to debar, can appellants be debarred:
   (a) in the absence of regulations establishing standards and procedures, and
   (b) in the absence of written notice of charges, evidentiary hearing and findings on charges of misconduct?

(1) Justiciability and Standing
. . . Interruption of an existing relationship between the government and a contractor places the latter in a different posture from one initially

seeking government contracts and can carry with it grave economic consequences.

The consequences of administrative termination of all right to bid or contract, colloquially called "blacklisting" and formally called suspension or debarment, will vary, depending upon multiple factors: the size and prominence of the contractor; the ratio of his government business to non-government business; the length of his contractual relationship with government; his dependence on that business; his ability to secure other business as a substitute for government business. These are some of the basic factors involved. The impact of debarment on a contractor may be a sudden contraction of bank credit, adverse impact on market price of shares of listed stock, if any, and critical uneasiness of creditors generally, to say nothing of "loss of face" in the business community. These consequences are in addition to the loss of specific profits from the business denied as a result of debarment. . . .

Thus to say that there is no "right" to government contracts does not resolve the question of justiciability. Of course there is no such *right;*. . . .

. . . . The injury to appellants alleged in their complaint gives them standing to challenge the debarment processes by which such injury was imposed. See *Copper Plumbing & Heating Co. v. Campbell,* 100 U.S. App. D.C. 177, 179–180, 290 F.2d 368, 370–371 (1961). . . .

(4) Debarment Procedures

. . . Disqualification from bidding or contracting for five years directs the power and prestige of government at a particular person and, as we have shown, may have a serious economic impact on that person. Such debarment cannot be left to administrative improvisation on a case-by-case basis. The governmental power must be exercised in accordance with accepted basic legal norms. Considerations of basic fairness require administrative regulations establishing standards for debarment and procedures which will include notice of specific charges, opportunity to present evidence and to cross-examine adverse witnesses, all culminating in administrative findings and conclusions based upon the records so made. . . . we conclude that although the Act vests Commodity Credit with power to impose debarment for misuse of official inspection certificates, we cannot agree that Congress intended to authorize such consequences without regulations establishing standards and procedures and without notice of cha[r]ges, hearings, and findings pursuant thereto. Absent such procedural regulations and absent notice, hearing, and findings in this case, the debarment is invalid; to reach any other conclusion would give rise to serious constitutional issues. . . .

Accordingly, we remand with directions to enter summary judgment in favor of Thomas P. Gonzalez and Thos. P. Gonzalez Corporation, whose debarment was invalid because it was imposed without observance of procedural requirements and hence in excess of statutory jurisdiction and authority; and to enter summary judgment in favor of Carmen Gonzalez, whose debarment was invalid for the same reasons and because arbitrary and capricious, and hence an abuse of discretion.

Reversed and remanded.

CHAPTER SUMMARY

Hearings are proceedings in which the facts and laws in dispute are examined by an impartial hearing officer, or administrative law judge, who makes an initial decision or recommendation. The agency determines if a hearing is necessary by reviewing the application and complaint sent to the agency by a person or business contesting an agency action. Complaints requesting a hearing are often filed after an agency acts on violations of its regulations. When a need for a hearing is sanctioned, the agency gives notice to the parties with the time, place, and nature of the hearing. Prior to the hearing, parties may seek information through discovery and pre-conferences, if granted in agency regulations. At the hearing, parties present evidence and witnesses to establish a preponderance of evidence on which the hearing officer may base a decision.

Key Terms

complaint	findings	notice
discovery	hearing	proof
dispute		

Key Terms Crossword

Across
2. Disagreement
4. Petition for relief
6. Validity of evidence
7. Process where evidence is presented

Down
1. Exchange of information
3. Results
5. Document stating an initiation of an action

Statements

Student Study Time Hints: Look for answers under Chapter / Section.

Chapter 8 / Section A.   Hearings are similar to: _____

Decisions of an agency may be: _____

Section C.1.   Paralegals work with _____
or _____

Section C.2.   Findings are: _____
and _____

Section C.3.   Two types of decisions are: _____
or _____

No hints:

Hearing held after a decision is _____

Web Resources

www.hud.gov   HUD—U.S. Department of Housing and Urban Development

www.ssa.gov   Social Security Administration

Advanced Studies

This Advanced Studies takes an in-depth look at cases that have impacted administrative hearings. In these cases the lawyers and paralegals dealt with situations similar to what you will encounter when trying to understand and explain the difficulties of the formal hearing process. Over the years, such cases have played a vital part in the evolution of the administrative agency hearing and the role of the administrative law judge. The documents are:

Document 1— *Maher Terminals v. Director, Office of Workers' Compensation Programs*, 992 F2d 1277 (3d Cir. 1993)
Document 2— *Salling v. Bowen*, 641 F. Supp. 1046 (WD Va. 1986)
Document 3— *Rosa v. Bowen*, 677 F. Supp. 782 (D. NJ 1988)
Document 4— *NLRB v. Baldwin Locomotive Works*, 128 F2d 39 (3d Cir. 1942)

Burden of Proof

The burden of proof is on the moving party in an agency hearing. Administrative Procedure Act 5 USC §556(d) states, "except as otherwise provided by statute, the proponent of a rule or order has the burden of proof." In this way, every fact that is presented at the hearing is to be established as evidence in order to satisfy the burden of proof. If an agency is the proponent, the agency must establish those facts that are evidence supporting the agency action. The standard for burden of proof in most agencies is "a preponderance of the evidence." However, if the hearing has great impact on a person, such as deportation, the standard for burden of proof is "clear and convincing evidence." (*Woodby v. INS*, 385 US 276 (1966)).

Workers' Compensation Cases

Workers' Compensation provides benefits to workers for work- or job-related injuries or diseases. It is part of a system developed to aid the injured workers, protect the employer, and ease society from the costs of supporting workers through charity or welfare. Run by the individual states with state laws and statutes, the states spread the cost of the programs among the employers in the state by compulsory participation. Because the programs are mandatorily funded by employers, the costs are passed on to the consumer in the price of the products of the companies. State statutes dictate the eligibility requirements for benefits and the amount of compensation. Employees must show a causal connection between the injury and the workplace. The burden of proof is on the employee seeking an order, or ruling, from the compensation program for benefits for the work-related injury.

There are also federal Workers' Compensation acts to protect employees in interstate commerce and allow remedy for injury (Federal Employers Liability Act). Other federal labor acts addressing workers' compensation include: the Federal Employees Compensation Act, the Jones Act, the Merchant Marine Act, and the Longshoremen's and Harbor Workers' Compensation Act.

Workers' Compensation hearings use the preponderance of the evidence standard for burden of proof. This is illustrated by a major workers' compensation case, *Maher Terminals v. Director, Office of Workers' Compensation Programs*, 992 F2d 1277 (3d Cir 1993), which was filed under the Longshoreman's Act. (Document 1) Because the claimant in this case sought a ruling for compensation, the claimant bears the burden of proof under the Longshoremen's Act Section 19(d), which states that hearings will be conducted according to the Administrative Procedure Act's policy of burden of proof "except otherwise provided by statute, the proponent of a rule or order has the burden of proof." (§556(d)).

In the *Maher* case, the claimant had the burden of proof but the ALJ found that the claimant's and the employer's evidence were equal in supporting factual evidence. The claimant did not prove with a preponderance of the evidence her request for benefits under the Act, but the ALJ found in the claimant's favor relying on the "true doubt" rule instead of a preponderance of the evidence. The Court sent this case back to the ALJ, after an appeal by the employer, and ordered the ALJ to rule on a preponderance of the evidence for burden of proof and not the "true doubt" rule.

Social Security Cases

Social Security hearings generally place the burden of proof on the claimant initially, but the final burden of proof often shifts to the agency. The claimant has the burden to show a disability that is keeping him or her from work, but the agency has the burden to show there is no other work available for the claimant. The reasoning behind this shift in burden of proof is theory and reality. In theory the claimant bears the burden, but in reality the Social Security Agency understands that the claimant is often unrepresented by counsel and technically doesn't have the skills to prove burden of proof, even if a claimant has a true, justifiable claim.

At a Social Security hearing, the ALJ acts impartially to develop the facts; this is not an adversary role. The proceeding is informal with the ALJ reviewing medical reports and questioning the claimant and witnesses to obtain evidence that the claimant has met the two major criteria of disability—impairment and inability to work. The U.S. Supreme Court and other courts have consistently upheld the non-adversarial approach, saying that the Social Security system is "designed to function throughout with a high degree of informality and solicitude for the claimant." *Walters v. National Assn. of Radiation Survivors*, 472 US 305 (1985).

Attempts to alter the ALJ's position of assuming the burden of proof in the final stages of the hearing have been thwarted by the courts, such as in the *Salling v. Bowen* case. (Document 2)

A demonstration program to improve the hearing process of disability cases was appealed in Virginia. The court ruled that the program only encumbered the ALJ's "who are the only people in the entire system who are oriented toward the main goal which should be the seeking of truth and ultimate triumph of justice."

Administrative Law Judges

Prior to the passage of the Administrative Procedure Act in 1946, agency heads realized the impossibility of presiding over hearings to gather evidence as well as functioning as agency administrators with the voluminous daily work schedules. To compensate, the agency heads delegated the position of hearing evidence to hearing or trial examiners. These examiners filed written reports stating findings of fact and recommendations for agency actions. Parties could object to the decisions and file arguments with the agency head who made the final decision. Objections were raised that these examiners were too closely run by the agencies. By 1939 Congress considered revamping the examiner's role. After World War II, the Administrative Procedure Act was passed; the examiners were given more independence by having their tenure come under the Civil Service Commission instead of the individual agencies. Their titles were changed from hearing examiner to administrative law judge in 1978.

The ALJ's under the Civil Service Commission (now the Office of Personnel Management (OPM)) are initially examined and certified by OPM; their pay is determined by OPM and any termination action must be authorized by OPM. The ALJ's do not have to be lawyers, nor do they have to reflect the racial character of the surrounding population.

The role of the administrative law judge has been challenged in the courts. In *Guerrero v. New Jersey*, 643 F2d 148 (3d Cir. 1981), Dr. Floro A. Guerrero raised the issue in his malpractice case that an agency head, and not an ALJ, must hear the case to ensure due process. The ALJ had heard the case at hearing and sent a written decision with findings and conclusions of law to the New Jersey Board of Medical Examiners; the Board accepted the guilty decision. Dr. Guerrero claimed the Board itself should have taken evidence and heard testimony to provide him with due process protections of the right to be heard. Although the U.S. Supreme Court has stated that "the one who decides must actually hear" in *Morgan v. United*

States, 298 US 468 (1936), the Court added that "evidence may be taken by an examiner. . . . The officers which make the determination must consider and appraise the evidence which justifies them." This supports the practice of having an ALJ supply a written record on which an agency board or head relies for final decision.

Not all agencies have ALJ's. The major federal agencies not utilizing ALJ's are: U.S. Citizenship and Immigration Services (formerly INS), at which immigration judges conduct deportation hearings and are subordinate to USCIS for tenure; the Veterans Administration; General Services Administration; the Nuclear Regulatory Commission; and the Railway Retirement Board.

Only a dozen states have independent hearing officers. In California ALJ's are appointed by the State Office of Administrative Hearings for five years and are maintained in a central pool. A similar type of central ALJ pool has been suggested for the federal government with ALJ's being assigned to various agencies according to the workload. This is seen as a control on bias or the appearance of bias.

The courts have objected to bias and improper behavior in ALJ's performances. In the notable *Rosa v. Bowen* case, (Document 3) the U.S. District Court judge states, "This court can do nothing to highlight the wrongfulness and offensiveness of the ALJ's behavior; his conduct speaks for itself."

The present ALJ position has evolved as the agencies themselves have evolved. An historical footnote is the view of hearing officers as stated in a 1942 National Labor Relations Board case, *NLRB v. Baldwin Locomotive Works.* (Document 4)

Outline and/or List

1.   List the people at a hearing. (pages 238, 251)

2.   Outline the pre-hearing conference. (page 250)

3.   Outline three possible standards of proof. (page 254)

4.   Outline the forms of decision an ALJ makes. (page 256)

Analyzing Documents and Practices

1.   State the facts in *Gonzalez.* (page 257)

2.   In Document 3, what was offensive in the ALJ's behavior? (page 270)

3.   In *Gonzalez,* compare the issue of debarment (#1) with justiciability (#1). (page 257)

4. In Document 1, explain preponderance of evidence versus true doubt. (page 269)

Take Home Exam

True/False 1. Hearings are held in District Courts.

True/False 2. A claim is a request for assistance.

True/False 3. All arbitration is mandatory.

True/False 4. The mediator is a neutral third party.

True/False 5. Settlements are agreements that resolve disputes.

True/False 6. Findings of Fact is a criteria in hearing decisions.

True/False 7. Hearings are held at administrative offices.

True/False 8. Hearings are held at Superior Courts.

True/False 9. The Burden of Proof Standard is guilty or not guilty.

True/False 10. Administrative agencies do not have to give notice.

Complete Diagrams

1. **Diagram** the parties in a hearing. (page 249)

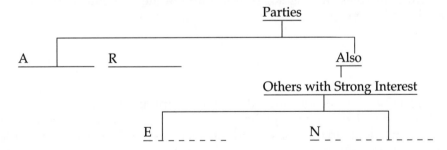

2. **Diagram** a comparison of court hearings and agency hearings. (pages 251, 253, and 254)

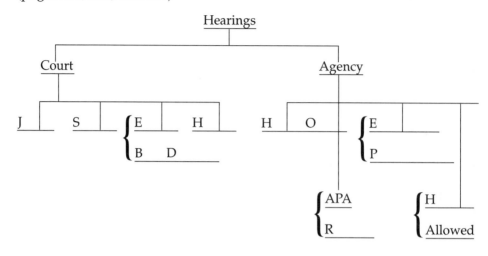

Three Venues of Research

1. **In Book**   Explain the standards used in settlements.

2. **At Library**   (a) Choose an agency. Research and write a memo on its rules for hearings. Cite the Code of Federal Regulations, *or*
(b) Look up the history of disability cases before the Social Security statute was enacted. How did the disabled support themselves?

3. **On Internet**   Research Consumer Safety Protection. Choose an age group (babies, teenagers, seniors) and write a memo summarizing your information.

Internship

Your lawyer tells you she's thinking of applying for an administrative law judge position in either a labor, welfare, or transportation agency. She wants you to look up the rules of federal agencies in those fields as the rules apply to administrative law judges. She wants you to include compensation, tenure, and the requirements necessary, such as education and experience. She'd like that information in a memo.

Also, search for any information through periodicals, books, or the Internet about administrative law judges. Just give her the cites. She'll look up the entire piece if she's interested.

Documents

Document 1: Maher Terminals v. Director, Office of Workers' Compensation Programs, *992 F2d 1277 (3d Cir. 1993)*

Mrs. Pasqualina Santoro filed a claim for temporary total disability benefits and for death benefits on her husband, Michael Santoro, at the Office of Workers' Compensation Programs, under the Longshoremen's Act. The employer, Maher Terminals, contested Michael Santoro's disability and death as being work related. The ALJ ruled in favor of the claimant, as did the appeal board—Benefits Review Board of the U.S. Department of Labor; the ALJ's reasoning being the "true doubt" rule, which favors the claimant if both sides present evidence that is equally balanced. In the Longshoremen's Act, the standard for the burden of proof is not "true doubt" but is a preponderance of the evidence. Maher Terminal appealed to the court on the issue that the Administrative Procedure Act upholds the preponderance of evidence standard as burden of proof. In bringing a claim pursuant to the Act, the Claimant bears the initial burden of production. . . .

The problem in many cases, as in this proceeding, is that the factfinder finds the evidence so close that he or she is beset by grave doubt as to the critical issue. Some courts have held that, when considering the evidence on the record as a whole, the judge may resort to the true doubt rule. . . .

In the instant case, . . . the ALJ ultimately did apply the true doubt rule. He found that the evidence was in equipoise and then summarily resolved the doubt in favor of the claimant: "In view of this record, acceptance of the employer's position would be inconsistent with the purposes and policy of the Act. The issue of causality is still deemed to be debatable, but the doubt is resolved in favor of the Claimant."

. . .

Section 19(d) of the Longshoremen's and Harbor Workers' Compensation Act, 33 U.S.C. §919(d), requires that any hearing under the Act be conducted in accordance with the provisions of section 554 of the APA. . . .

Addressing the claimant's ultimate burden of persuasion under the Act involved in the case sub judice, the first sentence of section 7(c) of the APA provides: "Except as otherwise provided by statute, the proponent of a rule or order has the burden of proof." 5 USC §556(d).

The third sentence of that section continues: "A sanction may not be imposed or rule or order issued except on consideration of the whole record or those parts thereof cited by a party and supported by and in accordance with the reliable, probative, and substantial evidence." Id.

. . . [T]he Supreme Court [has] stated, "The language of [section 7(c) of the APA] itself implies the enactment of a standard of proof, and that standard of proof is the preponderance of the evidence standard." *Steadman v. SEC,* 450 US 91, 98, 102 (1981).

. . . [I]n *Steadman,* the Court specifically addressed the third sentence of section 7(c). The Court there stated that the third sentence of section 7(c) means that the standard of proof necessary to carry the burden of persuasion under the APA is the preponderance of the evidence standard.

... Where there is evidence pro and con, the agency must weigh it and decide in accordance with the preponderance. As noted earlier, the party initiating the case has the general burden of coming forward with a prima facie case; we now see that this party, if it meets both its burden of production (prima facie) and the burden of persuasion (where "substantial" is construed as standing for the preponderance standard), it will succeed, unless its evidence is unconvincing.

In sum, the first sentence of section 7(c) places the burden of production on the proponent of the order or rule, i.e., the proponent must go forward with evidence or the case will come to an end. The third sentence of that section establishes the standard for the burden of persuasion, i.e., a preponderance of the evidence, and also allocates the burden.... the burden of production and persuasion both rest upon the claimant, Mrs. Santoro....

The ALJ found that the evidence was in equipoise, which, by definition, means that the claimant did not carry her burden of proof by a preponderance of evidence. The finding in her favor, therefore, was error.... The APA is the polestar which guides our course and is the fundament upon which we strike down the ALJ's use of the true doubt rule in this case.

. . .

In sum, we hold that the APA prohibits application of the true doubt rule to cases involving benefits under the Longshoremen's Harbor Workers' Compensation Act because: (1) under the APA, the claimant bears the ultimate burden of persuasion by a preponderance of the evidence; and (2) the true doubt rule allows a claimant to prevail despite a failure to prove entitlement by a preponderance of evidence. This contravenes the APA. Because there is no express provision in the Act which overrides the APA, the claimant must prove that her husband's death was related to his work injury by a preponderance of evidence.

It is not clear, however, if the ALJ in this case ever considered whether the claimant's evidence satisfied the preponderance of evidence standard. It is possible that, upon reaching the point of equipoise, and believing the true doubt rule to be valid, the ALJ halted his inquiry short of deciding whether Mrs. Santoro's evidence preponderated.

Accordingly, the order of the Benefits Review Board will be vacated with directions to remand the case to the ALJ to make this determination. If the ALJ again concludes that the evidence is in equipoise, then Maher must prevail.

Document 2: Salling v. Bowen, 641 F. Supp. 1046 (WD Va. 1986)

WILLIAMS, D.J. This complaint was filed on November 12, 1982, by seven applicants for Social Security benefits, seeking injunctive and declaratory relief and challenging a proposed experiment whereby a government advocate appeared at their Social Security and Supplemental Security Income (SSI) disability hearings.

The challenged program began operations October 12, 1982, and was considered a demonstration project under the supervision of the Office of Hearings and Appeals (OHA) called SSA Representation Project (SSARP). . . .

Court Exhibit 1 is 20 CFR Parts 404 and 416 entitled "Project to Improve the Hearing Process through the Involvement of SSA Representatives." . . . This is called a project the purpose of which is to determine whether SSA representatives in disability cases at the administrative hearing level can contribute toward improving the quality and timeliness of hearing dispositions. . . .

[SSARP was restructured in April 1986.] The most significant change in the restructuring of the SSARP is the separation of SSARP offices from the participating OHAs offices, both physically and organizationally. This also results in a revision of the case processing procedures for SSARP cases, makes the SSARP offices entirely independent of the ALJs and OHAs.

. . . Instead of going to the OHA in Kingsport, the claim file goes directly to the SSARP office and remains under its control until such time as the case is ready for hearing. Only then will the ALJ see the file and have anything to do with the case. The SSARP offices do all the pre-hearing screening, case docketing, control, selection of documents to be included in the hearing exhibit, preparation of the exhibit list, preparation and release of development requests, contact with the attorney if there is one, and contact with the claimant where there is no attorney and direct intervention on the part of an SSAR where the person is not represented, by communication with the claimant. Indeed, the ALJ who will eventually try the case will not know that he is assigned to the case until the case has been received in the OHA for hearing. The SSARP . . . will have complete control of the file without the ALJ even seeing it until the time of the hearing. This again acts as a halter on the independence of the ALJs in the handling of cases, and places the file not in the hands of an independent person but in the hands of an advocate of the government. Once the ALJ receives the file, assuming that he should decide that additional evidence is needed for development of the case, the SSAR again will be given the opportunity to review the file, including additional development prior to the case being scheduled for hearing. No such provision is made for the representative of the claimant. The SSAR, in addition to appearing, will submit written proposed findings of fact and conclusions of law to the ALJ after the case has been heard. . . .

This court notes that when this program began . . . the court was of the opinion that the program might be needed to help develop the cases, because many cases came before the court poorly developed. The court must note, however, that there has been no improvement in the development of cases; indeed, the opposite effect has occurred.

(6) This case has been represented as one in which there is an experimental project going on in which there is no adversary proceeding involved; that it is simply a situation in which the SSAR is there to assist the ALJ. The latest action which removes the SSAR offices from the OHAs and establishes them at a different location where they can handle the cases

as they see fit without supervision by ALJs shows that this program has moved at a rapid pace to become a full-fledged adversary proceeding. Let us compare a normal lawsuit which is filed in a clerk's office, an independent office. In this experimental Social Security program, the suit is brought and the file remains in the hands of one attorney (an adversary) and the other one does not have possession of the file until such time as the ALJ gets to hear it and the ALJ does not have the file until such time as he gets ready to hear the case. The ALJ is required to develop the case but is prevented from doing so because it is in the hands of an SSAR who is representing one side of the case.

The situation exemplified here shows jurisprudence at its worst. An ALJ can only conduct an informal hearing; he is not set up to conduct a court trial. He has no power of contempt. He has no way of maintaining order. How is he expected to carry out his function as a judge charged with developing the evidence when the file is in the possession of a person representing the government?

The greatest lack of fundamental fairness . . . is that the proceedings which have heretofore been deemed to have been informal and nonadversial are now formal, stiff, strict and adversarial. . . .

SSARP is in violation of the fundamental principles of procedural due process as prescribed by the Fifth Amendment and as determined by the courts to be applicable in social security cases.

For the reasons stated herein, a permanent injunction shall be granted enjoining any further proceedings using the SSARP. . . . An appropriate order will be entered this day.

Document 3: Rosa v. Bowen, 677 F. Supp. 782 (DNJ 1988)

SAROKIN, District Judge.

On December 5, 1985, this court remanded plaintiff's social security disability case to the Secretary of the Department of Health and Human Services ("the Secretary") for further administrative proceedings. The Appeals Council of the Department of Health and Human Services, in turn, vacated its prior denial of plaintiff's request for review and remanded the case to an administrative law judge ("ALJ") for a hearing. That hearing was an offense to the Social Security Act. The court therefore vacates the Secretary's decision a second time and remands the case for a fair hearing.

. . .

Plaintiff is a fifty-year-old woman who was born in Puerto Rico and moved to New Jersey in 1958. Until August 12, 1982, she held a steady job. At that time, however, she entered the hospital with rectal bleeding, abdominal cramps, and weakness. She was diagnosed as suffering from ulcerative colitis and uncontrolled diabetes mellitus. Since her hospitalization in 1982, plaintiff has not returned to work.

She filed for disability insurance benefits and supplemental security income on December 20, 1982. The Secretary denied her application, but this court remanded the case for further administrative action on

December 5, 1985. The Appeals Council of the Department of Health and Human Services, which had earlier denied plaintiff's request for review, then vacated that denial and remanded the case to an ALJ for a hearing.

The ALJ convened the hearing on the morning of September 5, 1986. Plaintiff was represented by an attorney at that hearing, and also had a Spanish language interpreter. The hearing lasted slightly less than one hour.

On October 27, 1986, the ALJ issued a recommended decision in which he found plaintiff not disabled and recommended that she be denied disability insurance benefits as well as supplemental security income. The Appeals Council adopted the findings and conclusions of the ALJ in a decision dated January 30, 1987.

On her appeal from the adverse decision of the Secretary, plaintiff contends that the Secretary's decision was not supported by substantial evidence as 42 USC §405(g) requires. Defendant, in response, argues that his decision was in fact so supported. Plaintiff, however, also argues that defendant denied her due process and her statutory right to a hearing. Because the transcript so vividly demonstrates an abject violation of plaintiff's statutory rights, the court does not reach the merits of plaintiff's disability claim.

. . .

Although a district court's most frequent task in disability cases is to determine whether the Secretary's decisions are supported by substantial evidence, *see* 42 USC §405(g), a court may also ascertain whether a claimant was accorded a full and fair hearing. . . .

When the Secretary fails or refuses to provide a disability claimant with the fair procedures to which the claimant is entitled, a court may remand the case to the Secretary with instructions to afford the claimant fair treatment. In the case before the court, plaintiff's entitlement to a fair hearing flowed from the Social Security Act itself, 42 USC §405(b)(1) . . .

The hearing that the Secretary actually provided for the plaintiff was shameful in its atmosphere of alternating indifference, personal musings, impatience and condescension. The court is confident that the hearing was not the sort of procedure which Congress intended in enacting 42 USC §405(b)(1).

As the transcript of the hearing speaks largely for itself, the court here recounts only the most offensive and egregious improprieties:

The ALJ's most pressing concern at the hearing was expedience. His denials of all of the claimant's attorney's procedural requests were not merely perfunctory; they were impatient and irritated. Plaintiff's attorney began the hearing by requesting a subpoena for plaintiff's treating physician (Tr. 251). The ALJ ruled that "the motion is denied as usual, you know" (Tr. 252). The lawyer then asked for permission to make an opening statement (Tr. 252). The ALJ refused the request, asking rhetorically, "what are you going to say that won't come out in the hearing? . . . I'd prefer you to have a closing statement after we're fully aware of all of the facts, and you can put that in writing" (Tr. 254).

Nor did the ALJ confine his impatience to his rulings on the claimant's procedural requests. He continually harassed the claimant's attorney and ordered him to accelerate his presentation of the case. . . .

When the attorney attempted to dispute the ALJ's time limitation, the judge revealed the true motivation for his hurry: "Joel, we got three cases together this morning. Don't you want to go to lunch at all?" (Tr. 276).

During the few moments that the ALJ actually devoted to the substance of the hearing, his focus was wholly improper. He measured the gravity of plaintiff's condition against his own mother's illnesses.

Most importantly, the ALJ demonstrated genuine contempt for the statute he was administering. After hearing plaintiff testify for a few minutes, the ALJ became convinced that plaintiff was not entitled to benefits for the first year or two of her claimed period of disability. He used this conclusion to attempt to turn the hearing into a cheap bargaining session, in which the ALJ would agree to make a finding of disability in exchange for plaintiff's choosing a later disability onset date and ending the hearing:

This court can do nothing to highlight the wrongfulness and offensiveness of the ALJ's behavior, his conduct speaks for itself . . .

Even where no one error, standing alone, would suffice to set aside an administrator's determination, a large number of errors can have the combined effect of rendering a hearing unfair and inadequate. . . .

The court has no difficulty in concluding that the ALJ's errors combined to create an unfair hearing in this case.

This court has previously criticized this agency's heartlessness in the repeated and unfounded rejection of a multitude of clearly valid claims. However, even in those cases, the unjust results followed seemingly adequate procedures. In this matter there was not even the pretense of a full and fair hearing. Once we foresake fairness and due process because of the pressure of heavy caseloads, then our system of justice will end. Although administrative hearings are not formal trials, nor should they be so informal or limited that their fairness is destroyed.

The hearing conducted in this matter fell far below the standards of the Social Security Act, 42 USC §405(b)(1). Accordingly, the court vacates the decision of the Secretary and remands the case for a full and fair hearing.

Document 4: NLRB v. Baldwin Locomotive Works, 128 F2d 39 (3d Cir. 1942)

. . . The Labor Board Examiner seems somewhat of a legal hermaphrodite. Judicial, like other human bodies, suffer from limitations of time and space. To overcome them they early resorted to what might be termed the tentacle system. Its earliest emanation appears to have eventuated from the method of taking testimony in Chancery. As the judge, unlike the jury, was supposed to be able to read, the advantages of observation of demeanor were felt outweighed by the opportunity for quiet study of the written page. So evidence was by interrogatory and their answering was supervised by Examiners either standing or appointed pro hac vice. At first the task was one of collection and collation, and the subordinate court officer had only the power and discretion necessary to the accomplishment of that more or less ministerial task. That it was not and could not be quite color-less is disclosed in the ancient rules for the guidance of Examiners.

Once having intrusted discretion it was easy to expand its limits and make the deputization more actual. So we find the ancient office of Master in Chancery. His duty was not only to collect and collate but also to report and recommend. With the growth of the centralized and centrally placed quasi-judicial body, the time-space factor compelled an increased resort to both kinds of assistant. So nearly everyone of the Federal Boards employs some kind of field hearer. The Labor Board Examiner at first blush seems to fall into the more important and elevated category. He may be called on, as here, to file an intermediate report with recommendations. As he need not be required to do so and as even his unexcepted-to recommendations are not always treated with much respect by the parent board, his position is, as the writer has said, somewhat hybrid. But whether more strictly an exam-iner or, a fortiori, a master, he has not the automatic character of the slot machine or the stenographer.

Reread the Court's views in *Louisiana Ass'n of Indep. Producers v. F.E.R.C.* (this chapter).

9

Judicial Review

"... the impact of the regulations upon the petitioners is sufficiently direct and immediate to render the issue appropriate for Judicial Review. ..."

Justice Harlan
Abbott Laboratories v. Gardner
387 US 136 (1967)

CHAPTER OBJECTIVES

Judicial Review is the examination of an agency decision by the courts. This chapter answers the following questions:

- What is judicial review?
- What are the requirements for appeal?
- What is a silent statute?
- What is preclusion?
- What are the four judicial review procedures?
- What is scope of review?
- When is judicial review denied?

CHAPTER OVERVIEW

In judicial review the courts examine agency decisions that have been appealed after all of the administrative agency processes discussed in previous chapters have been utilized. The access to judicial review, the procedural requirements, such as standing, the legal barriers, and the extent or scope of judicial review are explored. In judicial review cases, the paralegal researches statutes, helps determine if the client qualifies for the appeal system, drafts petitions, processes documents for discovery and other procedures, and sometimes assists at the court proceedings.

A.   What Is Judicial Review?

Judicial review is the power of the courts to examine and review agency decisions based on the rules, regulations, and orders of an administrative agency. Both the law and the findings of fact (the factual conclusions made by the agency founded on the evidence presented) may be judicially reviewed. People, or entities (businesses, corporations, and the like), seek judicial review to obtain a remedy from an agency decision if they feel they have been injured by the agency decision. A remedy is the enforcement of the rights of a person, persons, or entity, and the prevention of the violation of these rights. Sometimes a remedy includes compensation.

The agency decision must directly injure the person or entity seeking judicial review. In other words, an intellectual concern of an observer is not acceptable as a right to be granted judicial review.

Before seeking judicial review the party must complete any appeal process within the agency, allowing the agency the opportunity to correct itself. Judicial review is only available after all agency remedies and all agency processes have been completed.

The court jurisdiction stated in the enabling statute that the agency will have judicial review of agency decisions. State agencies commonly have review in the state courts; federal agencies have review in the federal courts. The Social Security statute selects the federal district courts for review, but other federal agencies have review in the courts of appeal.

Figure 9.1 illustrates the agency/court process for judicial review.

B.   Access to Judicial Review

Judicial review is applicable to administrative agencies on all government levels — municipal, county, state and federal. However, it is not automatically available to everyone displeased with an administrative agency decision. Standards and requirements established by laws and precedents govern access to judicial review of an agency decision. These also guide the courts in their judgments to affirm and approve of an agency decision, or to remand (send back the case to the agency for further agency processing, e.g., more findings of fact) the decision back to the agency with instructions for the agency to reassess and correct its decision according to the appellate opinion.

Figure 9.1   **Judicial Review**

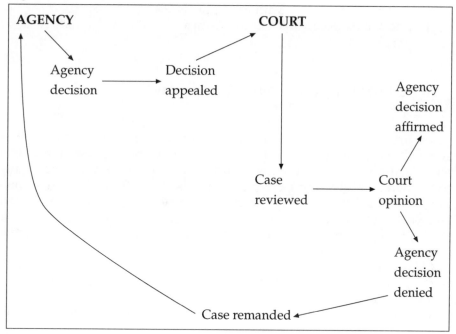

The persons or entities seeking judicial review may operate outside of an agency or may be employed inside an agency, for example: a group of thirty-seven pharmaceutical manufacturers were granted judicial review when they objected to the Federal Food and Drug Administration's (FDA) regulations on the labeling of prescription drugs in *Abbott Laboratories v. Gardner*, 387 US 136 (1967); a Central Intelligence Agency (CIA) employee was granted judicial review of a CIA regulation upon which his termination for homosexuality was based in *Webster v. Doe*, 486 US 592 (1988).

An appellant may seek judicial review as a means of temporarily delaying an agency action. For instance, the pharmaceutical drug companies in *Abbott Laboratories* may delay the retooling of machinery to comply with the new FDA regulations.

Judicial review not only resolves the complaint of the injured party seeking judicial review, it also may result in the eventual change of a regulation. For example the labeling requirements in *Abbott Laboratories* may be amended and the discriminatory regulation against homosexuality in the CIA may be eliminated, helping others in the future.

The following is a list of the federal courts:

The Supreme Court of the United States
United States Courts of Appeals
United States District Courts
United States Court of Federal Claims
United States Court of Appeals for the Federal Circuit
United States Court of International Trade

Territorial Courts
United States Court of Military Appeals
United States Court of Veterans Appeals

C. The Power of the Courts to Review

Courts are granted the power and authority to review administrative
agency decisions in two ways: (1) the statute creating the agency provides
for judicial review, (2) the federal and state constitutions or federal and
state general statutes (for example, Administrative Procedure Acts) provide for judicial review if the specific agency statute does not. In rare
instances, some statutes creating agencies refuse (or preclude) judicial
review. Even in these agencies, legal manuevers are often utilized to
allow for judicial review.

Many federal agencies use the statute creating the Federal Trade Commission, as a model in providing judicial review. Enacted in 1914, this
federal statute provides for judicial review, directs the method of (or application for requesting) review, the timing of review, and the place of review:

> Any person, partnership, or corporation required by an order of the Com-
> mission to cease and desist from using any method of competition or act or
> practice may obtain a review of such order in the court of appeals of the
> United States, "by filing in the court, within sixty days from the date of the
> service of such order, a written petition praying that the order of the Com-
> mission be set aside." 15 USC §45

By stating that the court of appeals has the authority to review the
orders of the agency, the statute implements appeals of agency decisions.
It is important that the exact words of the statute be read before filing an
appeal. The method of (or application for requesting) review is "a written
petition." The timing is "sixty days." Provisions for time limits are followed
precisely; many federal statutes have a sixty-day time limit, but some may
be as short as thirty days. If the time limit for review has expired, any
appeal for judicial review will be dismissed. The place of filing the written
petition is "in the court" (court of appeals). To be accepted for judicial
review, the appeal must follow the procedures and methods designated
in the statute. The provision for place, or jurisdiction, of court review is
specified in the statute. Most federal statutes follow the model of the
Federal Trade Commission statute and specify review in the courts of
appeal, but the Social Security statute provides for review in federal district
courts.

Figure 9.2 illustrates judicial review of an agency decision up to
the U.S. Supreme Court. The appeal of an action by the Social Security
Administration, the Federal Trade Commission, and a state agency is
depicted.

Exhibit 9.1   **Website of the Federal Judiciary**

Figure 9.2   **Routes to Judicial Review**

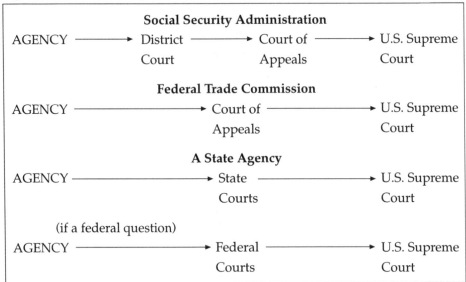

 PARALEGAL PRACTICE EXAMPLE

You are a paralegal working in the Social Security Administration claims division. Your supervisor informs you that an agency decision is being appealed to the courts. She instructs you to find and review the file. You should check that all the proper documents are in the file, examine the decision and reasons for the decision for any discrepancies or errors, and ascertain that all proper procedures have been followed.

D.   Impact of a Judicial Review Statute

It is important to remember that judicial review not only effects the person seeking the appeal, but it effects the agency making the decision; judicial review may create a more time consuming and more intricate processing within the agency. Judicial review may also create repercussions in the day to day operation of agencies.

The impact of a statute granting judicial review is perhaps best understood by studying the effects of an actual statute that not only provided for judicial review, but even created a new court of appeal. The statute is the Veterans Judicial Review Act passed in 1988. Before this act, judicial review was denied in most Veterans Agency decisions. Now regulations of the Veterans Agency and decisions of the Board of Veterans Appeals are being contested in the courts. This act provides veterans with a system to resolve disputes and to have claims adjudicated (a court decision). A problem experienced by the agency as a result of the act is the substantial length of time needed for the newer, more intricate proceedings.

Along with judicial review, the statute created the United States Court of Veterans Appeals, which is establishing its own precedents for the various cases that come under its jurisdiction. With its chief judge and associate judges appointed for fifteen years, the court hears appeals filed on final decisions of the Board of Veterans Appeals within the agency.

The statute limits the subject matter of the court's jurisdiction to: (1) a final decision of the agency, (2) the filing of a notice of disagreement with the agency, and (3) the filing of notice of appeal with the court within 120 days of the mailing date of the agency decision. Like the Federal Trade Commission statute, this veterans statute states the method (filing of a notice of appeal), the time limit (within 120 days of the mailing date) and the jurisdiction (the United States Court of Veterans Appeals).

STUDENT PRACTICE

Exercise

Divide the class in two groups: Group 1 is the paralegals for the law firm. Group 2 is the paralegals for the agency and court.

1. List the sections of the illustration that apply to your group.
2. Divide your list into agency pre-hearing, agency hearing, and court actions.
3. Develop a list of skills and duties a paralegal needs for each of the three stages. *For example* — "file a complaint," skill: research (statutes); duty: drafting (complaint)
4. Both groups join together to exchange ideas on the skills and duties they listed.

Illustration — Steps to Judicial Review for the Massachusetts Commission Against Discrimination

1. File a complaint
   a. Six month statute of limitations for filing
   b. Statute of limitations tolls if grievance filed
   c. Utilize Rule of Procedure, 804 Mass. Reg. 1.000
2. Case assigned to Investigating Commissioner
3. Investigating Commissioner assigns case to Compliance Officer
   a. Position statements
   b. Fact-finding conferences
   c. Subpoenas
   d. Interrogatories
4. Officer makes recommendations
   a. Probable cause finding
   b. Sufficient evidence
   c. 804 CMR 1.137

5. Case assigned to legal division
   a. Attempt at conciliation
   b. Certified to public hearing
6. Hearing Commissioner
   a. Discovery
   b. Pre-hearing conference
   c. Hearing (c. 30A)
7. Decision
   a. Findings of fact
   b. Conclusion of law
8. Appeal to full commission (3 commissioners)
9. Appeal to Massachusetts Superior Court
   a. Punitive damages
   b. Substantial evidence
   c. Errors of law committed by hearing commissioner

E.   Barriers to Judicial Review

1.   The Statute Does Not Provide for Judicial Review

If judicial review is not provided for in the enabling statute, the statute is referred to as "silent." In the case of a silent statute, the parties must seek other established legal precedents in order to appeal an agency decision. Those affected by silent statutes may lay the foundation for their right to appeal through constitutional provisions or through rights in general statutes such as federal and state Administrative Procedure Acts. (For example, Article III of the U.S. Constitution allows courts to hear illegal wrongs against individuals.)

A silent statute is often enacted during a time of national crisis when decisions need to be quickly implemented; judicial review may delay implementation of agency decisions. The banking statute of 1991, (Federal Deposit Insurance Corporation Improvement Act, Pub. L. No. 102-242, 105 Stat. 2236, 1991, amending FDI Act, 12 USC §1811, 1988) enacted to resolve the national economic banking crisis of the late 1980s and early 1990s, is silent. During the banking crisis, the Federal Deposit Insurance Corporation (FDIC) was given the power to dismiss bank employees. According to the statute, bank employees have the right to appeal to the FDIC, but not the right to appeal outside of the agency to a court. When a statute is silent, it does not mean the legislature intends to stop judicial review, but judicial review must be sought through other means. The bank employees will have to rely on rights to appeal of government actions that have been developed outside of specific agency statutes.

Figure 9.4 on page 291 charts the various barriers to judicial review. Note the references under silent statute.

a.   Presumption of Review

The United States courts often presume the right to judicial review. In 1943, the U.S. Supreme Court stated, "the silence of Congress as to judicial review is, at any rate in the absence of an administrative remedy, not to be construed as a denial of authority to the aggrieved person to seek appropriate relief in the federal courts in the exercise of their general jurisdiction." (*Stark v. Wickard,* 321 US 288 (1944)) In *Stark,* milk producers claimed an order by the Secretary of Agriculture setting milk market prices and requiring deductions to a fund run by the agency was illegal. An injunction against the Secretary of Agriculture was sought. A district court and court of appeals dismissed the suit by the milk producers, stating that the Secretary had violated no legal right of the milk producers. Reversing the lower courts, the U.S. Supreme Court stated the milk producers did have a legal right of judicial review. "It is because every dollar of deduction comes from the producer that he may challenge the use of the fund." (*Stark* at 308) The court further stated "it is not to be lightly assumed that the silence of the statute bars from the courts an otherwise justiciable issue." (*Stark* at 308) The court referred to the lack of appeal in the statute by saying, "Here, there is no forum, other than the ordinary courts, to hear this complaint." (*Stark* at 309). The Court did not consider the actual allegations of the petitioners; it is for the lower courts to hear the case and decide. The issue before the Supreme Court was the lower courts refusal of judicial review. "We merely determine the petitioners have shown a right to a judicial examination of their complaint." (*Stark* at 311)

In *Stark,* the court stated, "There is no direct judicial review granted by this statute for these proceedings. The authority for a judicial examination of the validity of the Secretary's action is found in the existence of courts and the intent of Congress as deduced from the statutes and precedents as hereinafter considered." (*Stark* at 307, 308). In the absence of a statute that provides for appeal, an appellant must first establish the right to appeal the agency decision. *Stark* recognized both statutory and non-statutory judicial review.

STATUTORY	NON-STATUTORY
agency statute	silent statute
judicial review process	constitutional rights

b.   General Statutory Review

Instead of invoking constitutional issues, the appellant's right to appeal a decision of an agency whose statute is silent may be based on general statutes available in the federal and state governments. On the federal level, the Administrative Procedure Act (5 USC §§701–706) (APA) is the general statute for appeals of federal agency decisions. It has been used as a model for many state statutes. The APA was enacted in 1946 as a result of the many abuses by agencies established to resolve the national

economic crisis that ravaged the nation during the 1930s. Although the
need for the APA had been proposed in the thirties, Congress awaited
the end of World War II before signing it into power. The APA has been
amended since it was passed.

The availability of a general statute such as the APA has an effect even
on the agencies whose statutes are silent on judicial review. Significant
agency decisions are made with the knowledge that the courts may review
the decisions and actually stop the implementation of the decisions temporarily or permanently.

Section 702 of the APA gives the right of review to "a person suffering
legal wrong because of an agency action. . . ." This is the party in the
appeal. Section 704 provides that "agency action made reviewable by statute and final agency action for which there is no other adequate remedy in a
court are subject to judicial review. . . ." This basically says that review can
be only of final agency actions after all of the agency appeals and remedies
have been exhausted.

The courts have broad powers of review and examination of agency
decisions under Section 706. "To the extent necessary to decision and when
presented, the reviewing court shall decide all relevant questions of law,
interpret constitutional and statutory provisions, and determine the meaning and applicability of the terms of an agency action."

Figure 9.3 sets out the bases for a right to appeal as well as the denial
of the right to appeal discussed in the next section of the chapter. The
pertinent sections of the APA relating to judicial review are set out in
Example 9.1.

 PARALEGAL PRACTICE EXAMPLE

Your firm is reviewing the case of a bank employee who was
fired during the bank crisis of the early 1990s. During the intake
interview, your client tells you that she was told she hadn't the right
to appeal, but now discovered others did appeal. In a discussion
with your attorney, you learn that the banking emergency statute
did not provide for appeal originally. Your attorney asks you to look
up the statute to see if it was amended, adding an appeal process.
Your attorney also wants you to start a file folder—dating time of
client's work situation with time of any changes in the statute; also
time of other bank employees' appeals noting the basis of their
appeals.

2. Denial of Power to Review Agency Decisions

Judicial review of agency decisions is denied in the following
instances: (1) the statute precludes (forbids) judicial review and (2) agency
discretion prevents judicial review. In both instances, the courts are

Figure 9.3   **Right to Appeal and Denial of Right**

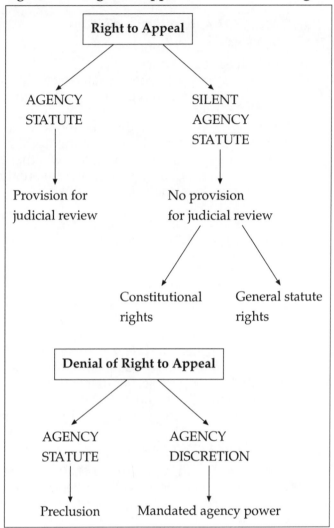

prohibited from examining agency decisions. (See the Denial branch of Figure 9.4.)

a.   *Statute Precludes Judicial Review*

If a provision in a statute states that judicial review is not allowed, this is preclusion. Preclusion is the prohibiting of an action; in this case, the action prohibited is the court examination or review of an agency decision. If the intent of the statute is to preclude judicial review and the statute distinctly states this, it is called expressed preclusion. If the intent of the statute is to preclude judicial review and the statute does not express this, it is called implied preclusion.

Example 9.1

5 USC §701 Application; definitions

(a) This chapter applies; according to the provisions thereof, except to the extent that —
(1) statutes preclude judicial review; or
(2) agency action is committed to agency discretion by law.
(b) For the purpose of this chapter —
(1) "agency" means each authority of the Government of the United States, whether or not it is within or subject to review by another agency, but does not include —
(A) the Congress;
(B) the courts of the United States;
(C) the governments of the territories or possessions of the United States;
(D) the government of the District of Columbia;
(E) agencies composed of representatives of the parties or of representatives of organizations of parties to the disputes determined by them;
(F) courts martial and military commissions;
(G) military authority exercised in the field in time of war or in occupied territory; or
(2) "person," "rule," "order," "license," "sanction," "relief," and "agency action" have the meanings given them by section 551 of this title.

5 USC §702 Right of Review

A person suffering legal wrong because of agency action, or adversely affected or aggrieved by agency action within the meaning of a relevant statute, is entitled to judicial review thereof. An action in a court of the United States seeking relief other than money damages and stating a claim that an agency or an officer or employee thereof acted or failed to act in an official capacity or under color of legal authority shall not be dismissed nor relief therein be denied on the ground that it is against the United States or that the United States is an indispensable party. The United States may be named as a defendant in any such action, and a judgment or decree may be entered against the United States: Provided, that any mandatory or injunctive decree shall specify the Federal officer or officers (by name or by title), and their successors in office, personally responsible for compliance. Nothing herein (1) affects other limitations on judicial review or the power or duty of the court to dismiss any action or deny relief on any other appropriate legal or equitable ground; or (2) confers authority to grant relief if any other statute that grants consent to suit expressly or impliedly forbids the relief which is sought.

5 USC §703 Form and Venue of Proceeding

The form of proceeding for judicial review is the special statutory review proceeding relevant to the subject matter in a court specified by statute or, in the absence or inadequacy thereof, any applicable form of legal action, including actions for declaratory judgments or writs of prohibitory or mandatory injunction or habeas corpus, in a court of competent jurisdiction. If no special statutory review proceeding is applicable, the action for judicial review may be brought against the United States, the agency by its official title, or the appropriate officer. Except to the extent that prior, adequate, and exclusive opportunity for judicial review is provided by law, agency action is subject to judicial review in civil or criminal proceedings for judicial enforcement.

5 USC §704 Actions Reviewable

Agency action made reviewable by statute and final agency action for which there is no other adequate remedy in a court are subject to judicial review. A preliminary, procedural, or intermediate agency action or ruling not directly reviewable is subject to review on the review of the final agency action. Except as otherwise expressly required by statute, agency action otherwise final is final for the purposes of this section whether or not there has been presented or determined in application for a declaratory order, for any form of reconsideration, or, unless the agency otherwise requires by rule and provides that the action meanwhile is inoperative, for an appeal to superior agency authority.

5 USC §705 Relief Pending Review

When an agency finds that justice so requires, it may postpone the effective date of action taken by it, pending judicial review. On such conditions as may be required and to the extent necessary to prevent irreparable injury, the reviewing court, including the court to which a case may be taken on appeal from or on application for certiorari or other writ to a reviewing court, may issue all necessary and appropriate process to postpone the effective date of an agency action or to preserve status or rights pending conclusion of the review proceedings.

5 USC §706 Scope of Review

To the extent necessary to decision and when presented, the reviewing court shall decide all relevant questions of law, interpret constitutional and statutory provisions, and determine the meaning or applicability of the terms of an agency action. The reviewing court shall —

(1) compel agency action unlawfully withheld or unreasonably delayed; and
(2) hold unlawful and set aside agency action, findings, and conclusions found to be —
(A) arbitrary, capricious, and abuse of discretion, or otherwise not in accordance with law;
(B) contrary to constitutional right, power, privilege, or immunity;
(C) in excess of statutory jurisdiction, authority, or limitations, or short of statutory right;
(D) without observance of procedure required by law;
(E) unsupported by substantial evidence in a case subject to sections 556 and 557 of this title or otherwise reviewed on the record of an agency hearing provided by statute; or
(F) unwarranted by the facts to the extent that the facts are subject to trial de novo by the reviewing court.

In making the foregoing determinations, the court shall review the whole record or those parts of it cited by a party, and due account shall be taken of the rule of prejudicial error.

Expressed preclusion became an issue in *McNary v. Haitian Refugee Center, Inc.*, 488 US 479 (1991). Seventeen non-U.S. citizen (or alien) farmworkers were denied judicial review of the practices of the Special Workers' Amnesty Program under the Immigration and Nationality Agency. Under the program, farmworkers with temporary residence in the United States could apply to have their status changed to legal permanent residence. If denied, an applicant could not seek judicial review unless deportation proceedings were initiated. The seventeen farmworkers filed a class action, stating they were not seeking judicial review as individual applicants who were denied legal permanent residence, which was precluded by statute, but were a group protesting the entire program and its procedures. Some of the objectionable procedures included: not keeping verbatim records of all applicants' interviews, not allowing challenges to adverse evidence, and conducting the program in an arbitrary manner.

The District Court and the Court of Appeals upheld the farmworkers. The U.S. Supreme Court dealt only with the question: If the individual agency decisions are precluded and not appealable, is the class action challenge appealable? The Supreme Court upheld the general appeal to program policies and procedures. But even though it granted this class action judicial review, it still upheld the express preclusion on individual applications as stated in the statute. The individual has no right to judicial review on the denial of an application unless deportation proceedings are initiated.

Refer to Figure 9.4, Statute Preclusion, under Denial of Judicial Review.

Generally, expressed preclusion is upheld by the courts. Yet, the courts will allow judicial review of agency decisions if the appellant cites proper constitutional or statutory issues. This is even true of security agencies as in *Webster* (p. 277) in which an appeal of an employee of the CIA was granted judicial review on constitutional issues. One of the most notable examples of expressed preclusion was the Veterans Agency before the 1988 Act, which provided judicial review.

Implied preclusion is rarely upheld; the exception being labor relations cases. The Supreme Court has stated that labor relations controversies should be settled quickly and not dragged into the courts. When the National Labor Mediation Board certified the results of a labor election, the action was appealed. The court upheld the certification of election results as being binding. It was upheld in the interest of ending the controversy and in the interest of time in *Switchmen's Union v. Board*, 320 US 297 (1943).

b.   Agency Discretion Prevents Judicial Review

Administrative statutes allow agencies the discretion to choose among alternative courses of action in making agency decisions. The agency, guided by the objectives in the statute, bases its decision on the facts involved. While some facts are straightforward, many facts must be interpreted in the context of the case. Findings of fact fall within agency discretion. The statute may limit this discretion by delineating the agency jurisdiction and control. This legislative mandate allows the agencies to more quickly and more fairly serve the person or business that enters the agency environment. The expertise and ability of the agency solves many problems so that the bulk of agency decisions are not appealed. Although agency discretion is respected by the courts, it is not considered to be inviolate. The courts have been narrowing the view that agency discretion is not subject to court review; while upholding certain types of agency discretion as not subject to judicial review.

It is important to remember that administrative agencies are vested with power because legislatures have deemed the agency the best way to serve the citizenry. Discretion is part of the agency authority to exercise that power, but discretion must have its foundation in reason and rationality. If an appellant thinks an agency has abused its discretionary powers, the decision is appealable. The courts determine if the official of the agency acted reasonably in using discretionary powers. Generally, the courts defer to the agency's expertise in handling certain problems and adherence to certain regulations that have been consistently part of the agency decisions over the years. A party expects a decision to follow precedents of prior agency decisions. If a discretionary act abuses this consistency of decisions precedent, judicial review may be granted. If an agency violates a constitutional right, judicial review will be granted.

Two notable cases on agency discretion preventing judicial review are *Chaney* and *Overton*. In *Heckler v. Chaney*, 470 US 821 (1985), several prisoners appealed the use of certain lethal drugs for executions claiming the drugs were not safe for human execution, thus violating the Federal Food, Drug, and Cosmetic Act. The Federal Food and Drug Administration (FDA) refused to initiate the investigations and enforcement policies which the prisoners requested. The U.S. Supreme Court stated, "This Court has recognized on several occasions over many years that an agency's decision not to prosecute, or enforce, whether through civil or criminal process, is a decision generally committed to an agency's absolute discretion." Thus, the FDA's decision not to become involved in the prisoners' action was part of its discretionary power — not to enforce the authority it had to control the use of drugs; the "agency decision not to institute proceedings" was upheld. The court further stated, "No colorable claim is made in this case that the agency's refusal to institute proceedings violated any constitutional rights of respondents, and we do not address the issue that would be raised in such a case."

In *Citizens to Preserve Overton Park, Inc. v. Volpe*, 401 US 402 (1971), the Secretary of Transportation funded a highway through a public park. The Secretary claimed he had the discretionary power to decide if there were better alternative routes; he decided there were none. The citizens appealed. The Court stated, "A threshold question — whether petitioners are entitled to any judicial review — is easily answered. Section 701 of the Administrative Procedure Act provides that the action of 'each authority of the Government of the United States,' which includes the Department of Transportation, is subject to judicial review except where there is a statutory prohibition on review or where 'agency action is committed to agency discretion by law.' . . . The Secretary's decision here does not fall within the exception for action 'committed to agency discretion.' This is a very narrow exception." Although the courts do uphold discretion, the courts continue to narrow the extent to which agency discretionary power may not be reviewable.

Figure 9.4 is the complete chart analyzing the barriers to judicial review.

STUDENT PRACTICE

"Courthouse Bee"
In order to bring your appeal to court you will need to be familiar with the language of the agency and courts.

1. Separate into two groups.
2. The definitions of pertinent legal words will be given. You have ten seconds to answer with the correct word. If you answer incorrectly you must sit down.
3. The group with the least members sitting down is the winner.

Figure 9.4 **Barriers to Judicial Review**

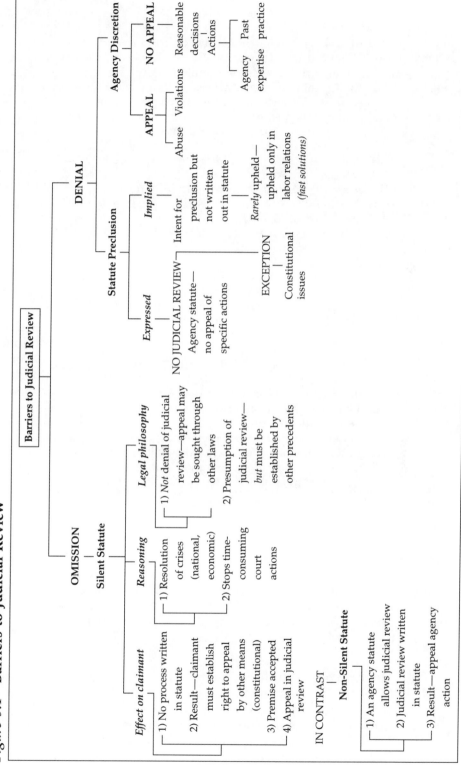

What is . . .

1. An agency conclusion reached by considering issues?
2. The word used to indicate the court's agreement with a prior court's or agency's ruling?
3. An appeal of an agency decision in the courts?
4. A court's decision with reasons for the decision?
5. A person named on record in a legal action?
6. The word used to send back a case for more action?
7. A method used to enforce a violated right?
8. A federal statute that codifies agency procedures?
9. A federal division of court systems?
10. A court that reviews prior courts' rulings?
11. A federal court with jurisdiction over a specific land territory that includes many states?
12. The authorization to make a law?
13. The authority to hear legal cases?
14. A written request?
15. A law enacted by a legislature?
16. The power given by a legislature?
17. The right to make reasonable actions?
18. Quality experience or knowledge?
19. The portion of the law being disputed?
20. A party in a lawsuit?
21. A past case decision cited as the legal foundation for the present case?
22. The method followed by all in an agency?
23. Unreasonable behavior or decision?
24. A schedule of dates for trials?
25. A new hearing by a reviewing court?
26. A written history of a case from claim to decision?
27. The extent and limitation of judicial examination?
28. The protection of life, liberty, and property?

CASE ABSTRACT

Shaughnessy v. Pedreiro is a U.S. Supreme Court case related to the Immigration Act; a relatively short opinion, it is printed in its entirety. The ruling in this case had an effect on changing agency procedures.

Please note when reading the case:

1. The case began in the Immigration and Naturalization Services (INS) agency, then Pedreiro appeals the unfavorable INS decision to the Federal District Court in New York.
2. Pedreiro is claiming due process violations.
3. The INS claims preclusion by stating that the words "final" in the Immigration Act preclude (or do not allow for) judicial review.

4. The District Court dismisses the case; the Court of Appeals reverses this decision and states judicial review is applicable.
5. The U.S. Supreme Court accepts the case to clarify different rulings that have come out of the lower courts on these same issues.
6. The Supreme Court supports its decision with the Administrative Procedure Act and the Immigration Act.
7. The Court rejects the belief that only heads of agencies may hear appeals of immigrants, and orders INS to delegate authority to other employees. This struck down the habeas corpus claim of the INS which would require an immigrant to travel to Washington, D.C. to "bodily present himself" (habeas corpus) to the INS Director.

Shaughnessy, District Director of Immigration and Naturalization v. Pedreiro
349 US 48 (1954)

CERTIORARI TO THE UNITED STATES COURT OF APPEALS
FOR THE SECOND CIRCUIT.

No. 374. Argued March 31, 1955. — Decided April 25, 1955.

1. Under §10 of the Administrative Procedure Act, an alien whose deportation has been ordered administratively under the Immigration and Nationality Act of 1952 may obtain a judicial review of such order by an action in a federal district court for a declaratory judgment and injunctive relief. Pp. 49–52.
    (a) *Heikkila v. Barber,* 345 US 229, distinguished. P. 50.
    (b) The provision of §242(b) of the Immigration and Nationality Act of 1952 which makes deportation orders of the Attorney General "final" does not "expressly" supersede or modify the provisions of the Administrative Procedure Act, within the meaning of §12 thereof, and does not make §10 of the latter Act inapplicable to deportation proceedings. Pp. 50–52.
    (c) A habeas corpus proceeding is not the sole means of obtaining judicial review of a deportation order issued under the 1952 Act. An action in a federal district court to declare the order void and enjoin its execution is an appropriate remedy. P. 52.
2. In an action in a federal district court against a District Director of Immigration and Naturalization to review a deportation order, declare it void and enjoin its execution, the Commissioner of Immigration and Naturalization is not an indispensable party. Pp. 52–54.

213 F2d 768, affirmed.

Oscar H. Davis argued the cause for petitioner. On the brief were *Solicitor General Sobeloff, Assistant Attorney General Olney, John F. Davis, Beatrice Rosenberg* and *Edward S. Szukelewicz.*

Aaron L. Danzig argued the cause and filed a brief for respondent.

Mr. Justice Black delivered the opinion of the Court.

After administrative hearings, the respondent Pedreiro, an alien, was ordered deported under the Immigration and Nationality Act of 1952.[1] He petitioned the District Court for the Southern District of New York to review the deportation order, declare it void and issue a temporary injunction restraining its execution pending final district court action. In part he contended that there was no legal evidence to support the order and that in violation of due process he had been compelled to incriminate himself in the hearings. Relief was sought only against the District Director of Immigration and Naturalization for the District of New York. The District Court dismissed the petition on the ground that either the Attorney General or the Commissioner of Immigration and Naturalization was an indispensable party and should have been joined. This holding made it unnecessary for the District Court to pass on another ground urged for dismissal, that the Immigration and Nationality Act of 1952 precluded judicial review of deportation orders by any method except habeas corpus. The Court of Appeals reversed, rejecting both contentions of the Government. 213 F2d 768. In doing so it followed the Court of Appeals for the District of Columbia Circuit which had held that deportation orders entered under the 1952 Immigration Act can be judicially reviewed in actions for declaratory relief under §10 of the Administrative Procedure Act.[2] *Rubinstein v. Brownell*, 92 US App. D. C. 328, 206 F2d 449, affirmed by an equally divided Court, 346 US 929. But the Court of Appeals for the First Circuit has held that habeas corpus is the only way such deportation orders can be attacked. *Batista v. Nicolls*, 213 F2d 20. Because of this conflict among the circuits and the contention that allowing judicial review of deportation orders other than by habeas corpus conflicts with *Heikkila v. Barber*, 345 US 229, we granted certiorari, 348 US 882.

The *Heikkila* case, unlike this one, dealt with a deportation order under the Immigration Act of 1917. That Act provided that deportation orders of the Attorney General should be "final"[3] and had long been interpreted as precluding any type of judicial review except by habeas corpus. Heikkila contended that this narrow right of review of deportation orders under the 1917 Act had been broadened by §10 of the 1946 Administrative Procedure Act which authorizes review of agency action by any appropriate method "except so far as (1) statutes preclude judicial review. . . ." Because this Court had construed the word "final" in the 1917 Act as precluding any review except by habeas corpus, it held that the Administrative Procedure Act gave no additional remedy since §10 excepted statutes that precluded judicial review. The Court carefully pointed out, however, that it did not consider whether the same result should be reached under the 1952

---

[1] 66 Stat. 163, 8 USC §1101 *et seq.*
[2] 60 Stat. 243, 5 USC §1009.
[3] 39 Stat. 889, as amended, 54 Stat. 1238.

Immigration and Nationality Act "which took effect after Heikkila's complaint was filed."[4] Consequently *Heikkila* does not control this case and we must consider the effect of the 1952 Immigration and Nationality Act on the right to judicial review under the Administrative Procedure Act.

Section 10 of the Administrative Procedure Act provides that "Any person suffering legal wrong because of any agency action, or adversely affected or aggrieved by such action within the meaning of any relevant statute, shall be entitled to judicial review thereof." And §12 of the Act provides that "No subsequent legislation shall be held to supersede or modify the provisions of this Act except to the extent that such legislation shall do so expressly." In the subsequent 1952 Immigration and Nationality Act there is no language which "expressly" supersedes or modifies the expanded right of review granted by §10 of the Administrative Procedure Act. But the 1952 Immigration Act does provide, as did the 1917 Act, that deportation orders of the Attorney General shall be "final." The Government contends that we should read this as expressing a congressional purpose to give the word "final" in the 1952 Act precisely the same meaning *Heikkila* gave "final" in the 1917 Act and thereby continue to deprive deportees of all right of judicial review except by habeas corpus. We cannot accept this contention.

Such a restrictive construction of the finality provision of the present Immigration Act would run counter to §10 and §12 of the Administrative Procedure Act. Their purpose was to remove obstacles to judicial review of agency action under subsequently enacted statutes like the 1952 Immigration Act. And as the Court said in the *Heikkila* case, the Procedure Act is to be given a "hospitable" interpretation. In that case the Court also referred to ambiguity in the provision making deportation orders of the Attorney General "final." It is more in harmony with the generous review provisions of the Administrative Procedure Act to construe the ambiguous word "final" in the 1952 Immigration Act as referring to finality in administrative procedure rather than as cutting off the right of judicial review in whole or in part. And it would certainly not be in keeping with either of these Acts to require a person ordered deported to go to jail in order to obtain review by a court.

The legislative history of both the Administrative Procedure Act and the 1952 Immigration Act supports respondent's right to full judicial review of this deportation order. The sponsors of the Administrative Procedure Act were Representative Walter in the House and Senator McCarran in the Senate. They were also the sponsors of the 1952 Immigration Act. While the latter Act was under consideration in the House, an amendment was proposed which provided for liberal judicial review of deportation orders. Representative Walter assured the House that the proposed amendment was not needed. He said: "Now, we come to this question of the finality of the decision of the Attorney General. That language means that it is a final decision as far as the administrative branch of the Government is concerned, but it is not final in that it is not the last remedy

---

[4]*Heikkila v. Barber*, 345 US 229, 232, note 4.

that the alien has. Section 10 of the Administrative Procedures Act is applicable."[5] With reference to the same problem Senator McCarran assured the Senate that "the Administrative Procedure Act is made applicable to the bill."[6] It is argued that these assurances by the chairmen of the committees in charge of the bills were but isolated statements and that other legislative history is sufficient to refute them. We cannot agree. Our holding is that there is a right of judicial review of deportation orders other than by habeas corpus and that the remedy sought here is an appropriate one.

We also reject the Government's contention that the Commissioner of Immigration and Naturalization is an indispensable party to an action for declaratory relief of this kind.[7] District Directors are authorized by regulation to issue warrants of deportation, to designate the country to which an alien shall be deported, and to determine when his mental or physical condition requires the employment of a person to accompany him. The regulations purport to make these decisions of the District Director final.[8] It seems highly appropriate, therefore, that the District Director charged with enforcement of a deportation order should represent the Government's interest. Otherwise in order to try his case an alien might be compelled to go to the District of Columbia to obtain jurisdiction over the Commissioner. To impose this burden on an alien about to be deported would be completely inconsistent with the basic policy of the Administrative Procedure Act to facilitate court review of such administrative action. We know of no necessity for such a harsh rule. Undoubtedly the Government's defense can be adequately presented by the District Director who is under the supervision of the Commissioner.

It is argued, however, that the Commissioner should be an indispensable party because a judgment against a District Director alone would not be final and binding in other immigration districts. But we need not decide the effect of such a judgment. We cannot assume that a decision on the merits in a court of appeals on a question of this kind, subject to review by this Court, would be lightly disregarded by the immigration authorities. Nor is it to be assumed that a second effort to have the same issue decided in a habeas corpus proceeding would do any serious harm to the Government. In habeas corpus proceedings district courts would have the duty to consider previous court decisions on the same matter. And even though in extraordinary circumstances new matters not previously adjudicated may arise in habeas corpus proceedings, this is no adequate reason for subjecting an alien to the great burden of having to go with his witnesses to the District of Columbia, which may be far distant from his home, in order to contest his deportation. Our former cases have established a policy under which indispensability of parties is determined on practical considerations. See, e.g., *Williams v. Fanning*, 332 US 490. That policy followed here causes

[5]98 Cong. Rec. 4416.
[6]98 Cong. Rec. 5778.
[7]Compare *Paolo v. Garfinkel*, 200 F2d 280; *Rodriguez v. London*, 212 F2d 508.
[8]8 CFR §§243.1, 243.2.

us to conclude that the Commissioner of Immigration and Naturalization is not an indispensable party.

Affirmed.

Mr. Justice Minton, with whom Mr. Justice Reed and Mr. Justice Burton join, dissenting.

In *Heikkila v. Barber*, 345 US 229, this Court held that §19(a) of the Immigration Act of 1917, making decisions of the Attorney General "final," was a statute which precluded judicial review within the meaning of the first exception to §10 of the Administrative Procedure Act. Now, slightly more than two years later, the Court holds that judicial review of deportation orders is available under §10 even though §242(b) of the 1952 Act is a re-enactment, almost verbatim, of the "final" clause of the 1917 Act. The decision is based on three considerations. First, §12 of the Administrative Procedure Act provides that, "No subsequent legislation shall be held to supersede or modify the provisions of this Act except to the extent that such legislation shall do so expressly," and, in the opinion of the majority, there is no language in the 1952 Act which "expressly" establishes a more limited review. Second, it is believed more consistent with the liberal review provisions of the Administrative Procedure Act to construe "final" as referring to finality in the administrative process. And third, isolated statements in the congressional debates indicate that Congress actually intended to permit review under the Administrative Procedure Act.

Section 12 of the Administrative Procedure Act, however, as I read it, applies only where subsequently enacted legislation, in the words of the Court, "supersedes or modifies the expanded right of review granted by §10 of the Administrative Procedure Act," and this Court held in the *Heikkila* case that the rights of aliens subject to deportation were not enlarged by the Administrative Procedure Act. Moreover, notwithstanding significant substantive changes in the immigration laws in the 1952 Act, I hesitate to consider the re-enactment of a provision, with minor changes in language, "subsequently enacted legislation." The issue then is much like the one the Court faced in *Heikkila*: whether, in the context of the liberal review provisions of the Administrative Procedure Act, Congress intended, by §242(b), to preclude application of §10 of the Administrative Procedure Act. As this Court pointed out in *Heikkila*, the word "final," though ambiguous in other contexts, as used in immigration legislation since the Immigration Act of 1891, has precluded judicial review except by habeas corpus. In view of this long history and the re-enactment of §242 with only minor textual changes, I hesitate to impute to Congress an intention to change the method of review absent a clear showing. The Court found in examining the legislative history that Representative Walter, one of the sponsors of the 1952 Act as well as of the Administrative Procedure Act, believed that §10 of the Administrative Procedure Act applied to deportation orders. The statement by Senator McCarran, however, that "the Administrative Procedure Act is made applicable to the bill," in context, may merely refer to the administrative procedures aspect of an amendment proposed by Senator Moody. 98 Cong. Rec. 5778, 5779. In any event, the statements of Congressman Walter and Senator McCarran, in the course of debate on the floor, are less persuasive than the more carefully prepared and authoritative committee report, and the report of the Senate Committee in charge of the bill would seem to indicate that no change in the law was intended.

The Immigration and Nationality Act of 1952 was preceded by extensive studies of the structure and operation of the immigration law. These studies culminated in a report by the Senate Committee on the Judiciary entitled, The Immigration and Naturalization Systems of the United States, S. Rep. No. 1515, 81st Cong., 2d Sess. It contains the following statement, at page 629:

> *Judicial review*
>
> Once the order and warrant of deportation are issued, the administrative process is complete. Under the fifth amendment to the Constitution, the "due process" provision, the alien may, however, petition for a writ of habeas corpus. In a habeas corpus proceeding, based on a deportation case, the court determines whether or not there has been a fair hearing, whether or not the law has been interpreted correctly, and whether or not there is substantial evidence to support the order of deportation. Habeas corpus is the proper remedy to determine the legality of the detention of an alien in the custody of the Immigration and Naturalization Service. The dismissal of an application for a writ of habeas corpus is not a bar to the filing of another application before another judge.

Although this report was dated April 1950, it serves to clarify any ambiguity in the statement in the Senate report accompanying the bill in final form that judicial review in immigration cases was not expanded "beyond that under existing law." S. Rep. No. 1137, 82d Cong., 2d Sess. 28. The Committee, in using the phrase "existing law," particularly in light of the long history of exclusive habeas corpus review, was necessarily referring to the law as understood and expressed in its prior report. Moreover, the report also states, at page 30, that "The bill declares that the prescribed deportation proceedings shall be the sole and exclusive procedure for determining the deportability of any alien, notwithstanding the provisions of any other law." The legislative history, therefore, would seem to make it unmistakably clear that Congress, aware that the word "final" as used in immigration legislation was not ambiguous, intended to preserve habeas corpus as the only escape from a deportation order. It was error to give relief under the Administrative Procedure Act.

PARALEGAL PRACTICE EXAMPLE

Before cases reach the U.S. Supreme Court, they start in the agencies and pass through the lower court systems. The following is a conversation you might have with your attorney.

Attorney: I received a phone call from a client. She has decided to appeal a decision of the Federal Trade Commission that she thinks will hurt her business. As a recently graduated paralegal, you should be able to research the judicial review process. I need to know filing information.

You: What specifically do you need to know?

Attorney: In which court, when, and where to start an appeal.

Because the Federal Trade Commission is a federal government agency, you search the United States Code and find Title 15 references the Federal Trade Commission. In Section 45 you find the information requested. You write this memo:

RE: Federal Trade Commission Appeal — Client No. #3174

DT: January 15, 1998

As you requested, I researched the filing information. A written petition must be filed at the Court of Appeals within sixty days from service of the order or decision.

15 USC §45

You copy the statute paragraph and staple it to the memo.

Exhibit 9.2 is a case on standing — a judicial review procedure.

F. Judicial Review Procedures

If the court does have the proper authority to review an agency decision, the court then determines if the appellant has satisfied the procedures necessary for judicial review. Procedures are the methods or processes necessary to follow in order for a case to be heard. These procedures are: standing, ripeness, exhaustion, and primary jurisdiction.

1. Standing

Standing requires that the party questioning the legality of the agency action have a personal interest, and an injury associated with the agency decision. Being an interested observer is not enough. Personal interest is shown by the party being affected by the decision; an injury is demonstrated by a harm, economic or otherwise directly as a result of the agency decision.

The standing doctrine has been established by three major cases: (1) *City of Los Angeles v. Lyons,* 461 US 95 (1983) (defining direct injury for standing) (Case excerpt is given in the Advanced Studies section of the Chapter.); (2) *Association of Data Processing Service Organization v. Camp,* 197 US 150 (1970) (exhibiting the legitimacy of protected interests); and (3) *Flast v. Cohen,* 397 US 150 (1970) (explaining a dispute "capable of judicial resolution").

Exhibit 9.2   Another Action — "Standing"

One must establish an injury associated with an agency decision.

Branton v. FCC
993 F.2d 906 (D.C. Cir. 1993)

D. H. Ginsburg, Circuit Judge:

This is a petition for review of a letter ruling of the Federal Communications Commission refusing to take action against National Public Radio for allegedly broadcasting "obscene, indecent, or profane" language in violation of 18 U.S.C. §1464. We hold that the petitioner lacks standing under Article III of the Constitution to challenge the FCC's decision.

I. Background

In the early evening of February 28, 1989, NPR's news show "All Things Considered" ran a report on the trial of John Gotti, the alleged leader of an organized crime syndicate in New York. The report featured a tape recording of a wiretapped phone conversation between Gotti and an associate. In the 110-word passage that NPR excerpted from the tape recording for broadcast, Gotti used variations of "the f-word" ten times. . . . NPR made no effort, such as substituting beeps for any or all of these references, to render the passage less offensive to persons of ordinary sensibility.

Peter Branton, who heard the broadcast and was offended, filed a complaint with the Mass Media Bureau of the FCC. The Bureau concluded that the broadcast material in question was "not actionably indecent" and did not provide "the necessary legal basis for further Commission action" pursuant to 18 U.S.C. §1464. Mr. Branton then wrote to the Commission asking how he could appeal the Bureau's decision. The Commission treated his letter as an Application for Review, and in a brief letter ruling (over one dissent), affirmed the Bureau's decision. The Commission explained that the Gotti tape was part of a "bona fide" news story; indeed, it had been introduced as evidence in the criminal trial that was the subject of that story. The Commission also noted its longstanding reluctance "to intervene in the editorial judgments of broadcast licensees on how best to present serious public affairs programming to their listeners." Letter Ruling, 6 FCCRcd. 610 (1991).

Mr. Branton now petitions for judicial review of the agency's decision not to proceed against NPR.

III. Conclusion

This dispute between the petitioner and the FCC falls outside the constitutional domain of the federal courts. The petitioner fails to establish a justiciable case or controversy because his asserted injury is too attenuated and improbable and because this injury neither resulted from the challenged Government decision nor would be remedied by a reversal of that decision. Accordingly, the petition for review is dismissed.

Figure 9.5   **Judicial Review Procedures**

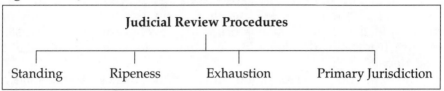

Questions asked in determining standing are: (1) Did the party suffer actual harm? (2) Are the interests stated within the area protected by constitution or statute? (3) Will the harm be redressed by a favorable opinion? It is possible for a statute to alter the requirements of standing, for example, the Communications Act allows private individuals the right to appeal government actions in the communications arena. These private individuals act as representatives of the public interest. According to this statute, the individuals do not have to show a direct personal or economic interest in the Communications agency's decision in order to represent the public interest.

2. Ripeness

Ripeness determines if the controversy has matured enough to permit judicial review. The major requirement of ripeness is that the hardship or injury must be demonstrated as actual and real, not abstract. To be considered for judicial review, present issues must be visible in the case. Hypothetical possibilities will not be accepted by the courts.

One of the major cases clarifying the ripeness issue is *Abbott Laboratories v. Gardner*, 387 US 136 (1967). The drug laboratories challenged the FDA regulation requiring certain information be placed on drug labels by drug manufacturers. The Supreme Court considered the case "ripe" even though the actual damage hadn't occurred; there would be significant harm if the regulations were followed, and the issues were fully and legally developed. The procedural issue of ripeness demands that the case reach maturity before it will be considered for judicial review. The ripeness procedure stops the courts from being entangled in hypothetical and time-consuming controversies.

3. Exhaustion

Exhaustion requires that a party use all administrative processes and remedies before seeking judicial review in a court. In this way, there is no premature intrusion by the courts into an administrative agency function.

No petition for review will be considered until the administrative agency has had the opportunity to review its own procedures and decisions and develop all the remedies under its domain. Exhaustion not only prevents the judicial branch from entering into an agency function; it also stops the courts from being flooded with cases that could have been settled at the agency level.

The steps and processes of the administrative agency must be followed to establish the record of the case with facts determined by experts in the area of dispute. As an example, consider a typical labor relations case. First, there is a grievance meeting with the immediate supervisor; second, a meeting with a local manager; if there are third and fourth steps, they are usually on the regional and national level of the union/management spectrum. The steps and processes that must be exhausted are enumerated in the contract between the employer and the employee. After all of these processes have been utilized, the controversy is brought before the appropriate labor relations board/agency. Within agency, steps are followed that lead to a final decision. After the agency final decision, then, and only then, can judicial review be considered. In this way, the agency autonomy is upheld, the facts in the case are established for the record, and there is no unnecessary repetition.

4. Primary Jurisdiction

Primary jurisdiction is the concept that the court will refrain from acting on a case brought before it until the agency renders decisions on issues requiring its expertise.

The court passes the case before it to the agency that has been established by statute with the expertise in certain matters. After the agency has made its decision, judicial review may continue in the court.

As an example, a private party may be suing another party over a transportation matter. The court may decide to turn the case over to the Interstate Commerce Commission for expert handling of the matter. If the matter isn't successfully resolved to the satisfaction of both parties by the agency, the court will then hear the case. A court may decide to turn a case over to an agency for findings by an expert in the matter. If the agency decision is accepted, the court has been saved time and money. If the decision is not accepted, the court benefits by receiving a record developed by experts. Usually primary jurisdiction involves closely regulated industries such as airlines, railroads, and other transportation industries. By allowing the agency primary jurisdiction, the court aids in keeping the decisions in the industry uniform.

Exhibit 9.3 lists the questions to be answered in determining procedural requirements for judicial review.

Exhibit 9.3 **Procedural Questions**

Standing

1. Who may seek judicial review?
2. Did the party suffer an actual injury or a threat of an injury?
3. Will the injury be redressed by a favorable judicial opinion?
4. Are the interests within the rights protected by statute or constitution?

Ripeness

1. Has the controversy reached maturity?

Exhaustion

1. Have all administrative agency procedures been utilized?
2. Have all administrative remedies been addressed?

Primary Jurisdiction

1. Does the administrative agency have the needed expertise in the field?
2. Does jurisdiction lie within the agency?

CONCEPTS JOURNAL

Role Playing

You are the legal team for a tobacco company defending a lawsuit by the family of an individual who died from a rare form of lung cancer, which is considered to be much more painful than other forms of lung cancer. Your client believes this case could lead to many class action suits. To complicate matters, the deceased began this case when alive as an Occupational Safety and Hazard Agency (OSHA) complaint while working for the tobacco company. OSHA had ruled favorably for the tobacco company and against the deceased family. This case is being appealed to the district court; the case documents are due to arrive tomorrow.

The first defense your firm is formulating is on the judicial review procedural level; looking to have the case thrown out for not meeting procedural requirements.

Divide your team into four sections: standing, exhaustion, ripeness, and primary jurisdiction.

1. Each team should define their topic and develop a list that determines which requirements to challenge.
2. Each team should develop a possible example for each item on the list to look for when the case documents arrive.

G. The Scope of Judicial Review

After the court is satisfied that the procedural requirements for judicial review have been met, the court determines if the case fits within the court's scope of review. The scope of review is the range and limits to which court examination of an agency decision is bound. If review is too broad, the agencies lose their power. Yet, the courts want enough leeway to look fully into the questionable issues. The scope of review is affected by agency expertise and the court calendar. Because of the need for agency expertise in certain technical areas, the court usually yields to administrative experts. Unfortunately the court calendar only allows time to review a limited number of cases. Attorneys learn that they have to have a clear presentation for the court to consider their cases for review. Despite time limitations, a judge may assign any amount of court time to a particular case if it is warranted.

Section 706 of the federal Administrative Procedure Act presents a clear explanation of the extent of the scope of judicial review.

> [T]he reviewing court shall decide all relevant questions of law, ...
> The reviewing court shall-
>   (2) hold unlawful and set aside agency action, findings, and conclusions found to be- . . . . [§706(2)]
>   (D) without observance of procedure required by law; . . . .
>   In making the foregoing determinations, the court shall review the whole record or those part of it cited by a party, ... [§706(2)(D)]

1. Limitations on the Scope of Review

a. Agency Record

Judicial review is an appellate proceeding, therefore, the review is restricted to the agency record. The court reviews the decision of the agency and the evidence. Only evidence heard by the agency (on the record) will be reviewed by the courts. If new evidence or evidence incorrectly omitted from the agency record is presented, the court will remand the case back to the agency and order the agency to hear that evidence. The court can not review that evidence until the agency has exercised its authority in hearing the evidence.

b. Issues Raised

The court will not hear any issue (the matter in controversy) that was not presented before the agency. In other words, objections and arguments have to be raised during the agency proceedings. This ensures the agency has the chance to remedy the situation.

Exhibit 9.4 **Attorney's Appearance for U.S. Court of Appeals**

**UNITED STATES COURT OF APPEALS
FOR THE FIRST CIRCUIT**

_____

APPEARANCE FORM
(Please type or print all answers)

Case No.:
Case Name (short):

**FAILURE TO FILL OUT COMPLETELY MAY RESULT IN THE REJECTION
OF THIS FORM AND COULD AFFECT THE PROGRESS OF THE APPEAL**

THE CLERK WILL ENTER MY APPEARANCE AS COUNSEL ON BEHALF OF:

_____ as the
(Specify name of person or entity represented.)

If you represent a litigant who was a party below, but who is not a party on appeal, do not designate yourself as counsel for the appellant or the appellee.

[   ] appellant(s)   [   ] appellee(s)   [   ] amicus curiae

[   ] petitioner(s)   [   ] respondent(s)   [   ] intervenor(s)

                            [   ] not a party on appeal

_____
           (Signature)
Name & Address:
_____
_____
_____
_____

Telephone:_____   **Court of Appeals Bar Number**:_____

Fax: _____   E-Mail: _____

Has this case or any related case previously been on appeal?

Yes _____   Court of Appeals No. _____
No _____

c. Reasons for Agency Decisions

The court's review is limited to reasons on which the agency states it based its decision. The court may only uphold an agency decision based on the reasons stated by the agency. If that reasoning is questioned and is not supported by the agency record, the decision will not stand. The court will remand the case back to the agency for further consideration.

2. Law/Fact Standards in Scope of Review

Although the court is allowed to review both questions of law and fact, basically, it is the court's role to interpret the law and the agency's role to determine the facts. The agency is the expert on finding the facts in the case presented before it. Then the court reviews the agency's decision. For questions of law, the courts are the experts and the standards used by the courts are more strenuous and demanding in reviewing questions of law than in reviewing questions of fact. Often, the court does defer to the agency's familiarity with statutes that have been consistently interpreted by the agency.

a. Arbitrary or Capricious

The court reviews the work of the agency; the record the agency compiled during the proceedings. It reviews the record to see if the agency exceeded jurisdictional boundaries, if the agency followed procedures, if the agency made clear and reasonable decisions. The court reviews whether the agency abused its discretionary powers by not upholding the arbitrary or capricious standard (no reasons given for the decision). This standard is applicable to informal agency actions such as rulemaking.

Agency discretion is questioned when a finding of fact is in issue. At one time, a national maritime union in the United States protested the shipping of military cargo to Vietnam in foreign-owned vessels. The union believed their rights to be employed for shipping in domestic vessels were being violated. The Department of Defense stated it had the right to make the decision under its discretionary powers. In this case, the Court decided that the agency did have a right to make that decision under its discretionary powers.

b. Substantial Evidence and Reasonableness

"Substantial evidence" requires that a reasonable person, after viewing the evidence, may arrive at the same decision as the agency. This is applicable to formal adjudications. Courts use the standard of substantial evidence in reviewing agency decisions. The reasonable person would not have had to make the same decision, but could have made that decision based on the evidence that was presented. Courts use reasonableness and substantial evidence standards often in a judicial review of facts.

3. Exception to Scope of Review — De Novo Review

In judicial review, the courts only review the record of the agency. In rare cases, the court does have the power to hear new evidence. This is called **de novo** review. The case may be tried as though no agency action had taken place, or the record of the agency may be reviewed with the new evidence also presented to the court. **De novo** review of factual issues and agency discretion takes place only when provided for in the statutes. Decisions under the Freedom of Information Act are subject to **de novo** review.

Exhibit 9.5 outlines the scope of judicial review.

Exhibit **9.5 Scope of Review**

1. Limitations

   - Agency Record
   - Issues Raised
   - Reasons for Agency Decisions

2. Extent

   - Relevant Questions of Law
   - Procedures
   - Entire Agency Record

3. Law/Fact

   - Rightness/Correctness
   - Substantial Evidence
   - Reasonableness

PARALEGAL PRACTICE EXAMPLE

You, a paralegal for a solo lawyer who handles discrimination appeals, have just taken home some documents to work on over the weekend. You have two duties:

1. You need to develop a simple filing system for the lawyer to use in the court room. Because the client, a black professor suing a college for tenure discrimination, is taking on a large university with a mega law firm representation, there are numerous documents generated by the firm that will have to be indexed. Your lawyer will need to quickly identify and find them in the appeal trial.

2. You must read the documents to prepare a court exhibit. The exhibit will take quotes from the five faculty members who voted not to allow permanent tenure. You should quote discriminatory words and phrases to illustrate the client's claim. The exhibit will be shown to the jury from an easel.

CHAPTER SUMMARY

Judicial review is the appeal process for decisions, rules, regulations, and orders of an administrative agency. The statute creating the administrative agency often provides the manner in which judicial review is granted. If the agency statute does not provide for judicial review, the appellant may appeal on federal and state constitutional issues or through federal and state administrative procedure acts. Some enabling statutes prohibit judicial review, this is rare, but appellants still may seek review of constitutional and other legal issues. Sometimes, there is no review of discretionary decisions based on the expertise of the agency, but this lack of review is limited. If agencies abuse that discretionary power, judicial review is available under the Administrative Procedure Act. Certain procedures must be followed in judicial review. These procedures of standing, exhaustion, ripeness, and primary jurisdiction delineate the extent and limitations of judicial review.

Key Terms

Administrative Procedure Act	issue
affirm	judicial review
arbitrary, capricious	jurisdiction
authority	litigant
circuit	opinion
court calendar	party
court of appeals	petition
decision	precedent
de novo	procedures
discretion	record
district court	remand
enact	remedy
expertise	scope of review
finding of fact	

Key Terms Crossword

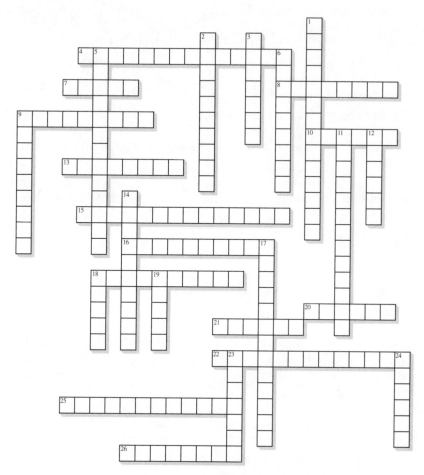

Across

4. _____ Procedure Act
7. Disputed question
8. Written request
9. Legislative power given to agency
10. Upholds a decision
13. Party in a lawsuit
15. Appeal of agency decision to court
16. Arbitrary
18. Decisions for future cases
20. Written document
21. New hearing by review court
22. Trial date schedules
25. Area under agency authority
26. A conclusion

Down

1. Court that reviews prior decisions
2. Agency methods
3. Court divisions
5. A federal court
6. Quality experience
9. Unreasonable
11. Decision on evidence
12. Methods to enforce a right
14. Right to take reasonable action
17. Extent/limit of judicial review
18. Litigant
19. Make a law
23. Court's decision
24. Send case back

Statements

Student Study Time Hints: Look for answers under Chapter / Section.

Chapter 9 / Section A.   In judicial review, courts
e_____ and r_____ agency decisions.

Both the laws and the f_____ c_____
made by the agency may be reviewed.

Section B.   To receive a judicial review, an appellant must follow
s_____ and r_____ .

Section C.   The agency s_____ creating the agency
and the A_____
        P_____ A_____ provide for judicial
review of a decision.

Section D.   Judicial review affects both the person seeking the
appeal and the a_____ itself.

Section E.   If an agency statute does not allow for judicial review,
a client may appeal through A_____
        P_____ A_____ .

Section F.   The procedures or methods of judicial review are:
_____ , _____ , _____ ,
and _____ _____ .

Section G.1.a.   Judicial review is restricted to
the _____ _____ .

Web Resources

www.uscourts.gov   United States Courts
www.cia.gov   Central Intelligence Agency
www.fda.gov   Federal Food and Drug Administration

Advanced Studies

Basis and Authority of Judicial Review

Judicial Review is a natural form of government logic in nations where there are either federal/local governments or branches of government with checks and balances. Throughout the world, governments such as Brazil, Canada, and Japan sanction judicial review. Nations not practicing judicial review, such as Great Britain, often permit their courts to interpret statutes, an action quite similar to judicial review.

Burgeoning Philosophy of Court Review of Administrative Actions

In the United States, the American Revolution was an outgrowth of challenging the validity of government actions. Even in the colonies, people questioned local statutes by appealing to a higher authority in England. This challenging of statutes continued after the Revolution and became the basis of judicial review in the United States. Alexander Hamilton endorsed judicial review in *The Federalist Papers No. 78*. A majority of members of the 1787 Constitutional Convention approved of judicial review.

Court Decides to Review an Administrative Action

The doctrine of judicial review was enunciated by the U.S. Supreme Court for the first time in 1803. Chief Justice John Marshall ruled an act of Congress unconstitutional in *Marbury v. Madison,* 5 US (1 Cranch) 137 1803. Marshall stated that when a statute conflicts with the U.S. Constitution, the supreme law of the land must prevail.

The Court had decided that decisions of other government agencies and branches could be reviewed. Despite this decision, court review was not often utilized in the early era of the country. In fact, in 1840, the court refused judicial review, ruling that resolution of a dispute was an administrative function in *Decatur v. Paulding,* 39 US 497 (1840). The widow of War of 1812 hero, Stephen Decatur, filed a mandamus action (an order from a court to a public official to compel the performance of an administrative act or a mandatory duty) requesting both of her late husband's pensions awarded by Congress. One pension was awarded to Decatur individually in recognition of meritorious service; the other pension was part of the general enactment of pensions for all veterans. The Secretary of the Navy ordered Mrs. Decatur to choose one of the pensions. The Supreme Court ruled that the case was not subject to judicial review and was a legitimate administrative function of the Navy Department.

At the turn of the twentieth century, changes erupted in the area of judicial review. The courts initiated judicial review to protect the rights of individuals. Use of agency power was questioned as to its correctness.

If Individual Rights Violated, a Court Review

In 1902, the Postmaster General attempted to cease fraud via the mails by an order demanding a prohibition of the mails for fraudulent usage. This seemingly simple action resulted in the *American School of Magnetic Healing v. McAnnulty*, 187 US 94 (1902) case. The Postmaster was charged with exceeding his authority given by statute. The Postmaster rejoined that the order was an administrative function of government and not reviewable by the courts. The U.S. Supreme Court's position differed with the government's. The Court stated that if an individual's rights were violated, the Court may review that administrative decision. When an administrative agency action is not sanctioned by law, judicial review is not restricted or precluded.

JOHN MARSHALL,
Chief Justice of the U.S. 1801.

Individual Rights with Court Control of Administrative Actions

Right to Judicial Review Under the Constitution

The U.S. Supreme Court in 1944 established the position that there is a presumption in favor of judicial review. This presumption is based on Article III, Section 1, U.S. Constitution.

Outline and/or List

1. Outline 5 USC §702 Right of Review. (page 286)

2. List judicial review procedures. (page 299)

3. Outline implied and expressed preclusion. (pages 288 and 289)

4. Outline the requirements of primary jurisdiction. (page 302)

Analyzing Documents and Practices

1. Analyze what the Court did and did not consider in *Stark*. (page 322)

2. What are the facts to be reviewed in *Abbott*? (pages 313–314)

3. Explain the history of judicial review. (pages 311–313)

Complete Diagrams

1. **Diagram** the FTC and Judicial Review on page 278.

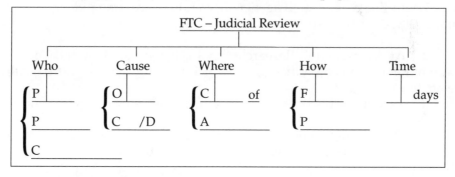

2. **Diagram** Judicial Review in *Heckler* and *Overton*. (pages 317–320)

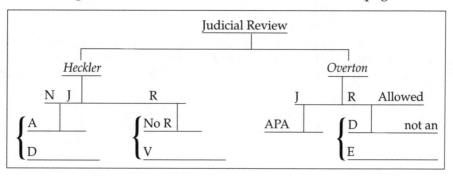

Take Home Exam

True/False   1. When a statute precludes judicial review, the statute forbids it.

True/False   2. Implied preclusion is written in the statute.

True/False   3. Most agency decisions are appealed.

True/False   4. The scope of review is the limit of court examination.

True/False   5. An agency record is a limitation in judicial review.

True/False   6. Findings of fact are within the agency's discretion.

True/False   7. Court review is limited to the agency's reason for its decision.

True/False   8. It is rare for a court to hear new evidence in review.

True/False   9. Substantial evidence requires an expert decision.

True/False   10. In ripeness, the hardship may be abstract.

Three Venues of Research

1. **In Book**   Research agency discretion preventing judicial review. (pages 289, 290, 317–320)

2. **At Library**   (a) Research the FTC statute, then its Code of Federal Regulations on judicial review. How do the statute and the rules relate to each other?, *or*
(b) Look up the history of the FTC and its relevancy to modern society.

3. **On Internet**   Look up the U.S. courts website, *www.uscourts.gov*. (a) What is available for paralegals to examine? (b) Key into "Educational Access" on the website.

Internship

1. You are an intern in a law firm where your attorney, new to the firm, is handling appeals from administrative agencies to the courts. She instructs you to prepare a memo explaining how you would approach the following:
    a. Keeping a filing system for clients and cases
    b. Keeping a schedule of cases and preparation time needed for each case

c.   Keeping copies and a briefing file of the following cases, and shepherdizing them:

Abbott Laboratories v. Gardner
Citizens to Preserve Overton Park v. Volpe
Heckler v. Chaney
City of Los Angeles v. Lyons
Stark v. Wickard

She tells you that she is very busy, so if you are not familiar with any of these areas, please look them up in the law library in paralegal/lawyer textbooks and periodicals.

2.   Your lawyer reviews your memo and asks you to prepare an example for each of the three sections in order that she may be certain you are both discussing the same thing.

3.   She also wants examples for item "c" from each of the five cases.

CASE ABSTRACTS

Abbott Laboratories et al. v. Gardner, Secretary of Health, Education, and Welfare, et al.
387 US 136 (3d Cir. 1967)

Mr. Justice Harlan delivered the opinion of the Court.

In 1962 Congress amended the Federal Food, Drug, and Cosmetic Act (52 Stat. 1040, as amended by the Drug Amendments of 1962, 76 Stat. 780, 21 USC §301 *et seq.*), to require manufacturers of prescription drugs to print the "established name" of the drug "prominently and in type at least half as large as that used thereon for any proprietary name or designation for such drug," on labels and other printed material, §502(e)(1)(B), 21 USC §352(e)(1)(B). The "established name" is one designated by the Secretary of Health, Education, and Welfare pursuant to §502(e)(2) of the Act, 21 USC §352(e)(2); the "proprietary name" is usually a trade name under which a particular drug is marketed. The underlying purpose of the 1962 amendment was to bring to the attention of doctors and patients the fact that many of the drugs sold under familiar trade names are actually identical to drugs sold under their "established" or less familiar trade names at significantly lower prices. The Commissioner of Food and Drugs, exercising authority delegated to him by the Secretary, 22 Fed. Reg. 1051, 25 Fed. Reg. 8625, published proposed regulations designed to implement the statute, 28 Fed. Reg. 1448. After inviting and considering comments submitted by interested parties the Commissioner promulgated the following regulation for the "efficient enforcement" of the Act, §701(a), 21 USC §371(a):

If the label or labeling of a prescription drug bears a proprietary name or designation for the drug or any ingredient thereof, the established name, if such there be, corresponding to such proprietary name or designation, shall accompany each appearance of such proprietary name or designation. 21 CFR §1.104 (g)(1).

A similar rule was made applicable to advertisements for prescription drugs, 21 CFR §1.105(b)(1).

The present action was brought by a group of 37 individual drug manufacturers and by the Pharmaceutical Manufacturers Association, of which all the petitioner companies are members, and which includes manufacturers of more than 90% of the Nation's supply of prescription drugs. They challenged the regulations on the ground that the Commissioner exceeded his authority under the statute by promulgating an order requiring labels, advertisements, and other printed matter relating to prescription drugs to designate the established name of the particular drug involved every time its trade name is used anywhere in such material.

The District Court, on cross motions for summary judgment, granted the declaratory and injunctive relief sought, finding that the statute did not sweep so broadly as to permit the Commissioner's "every time" interpretation. 228 F. Supp. 855. The Court of Appeals for the Third Circuit reversed without reaching the merits of the case. 352 F2d 286. It held first that under the statutory scheme provided by the Federal Food, Drug, and Cosmetic Act pre-enforcement review of these regulations was unauthorized and therefore beyond the jurisdiction of the District Court. Second, the Court of Appeals held that no "actual case or controversy" existed and, for that reason, that no relief under the Administrative Procedure Act. 5 USC §§701-704 (1964 ed., Supp. II), or under the Declaratory Judgment Act, 28 USC §2201, was in any event available. Because of the general importance of the question, and the apparent conflict with the decision of the Court of Appeals for the Second Circuit in *Toilet Goods Assn. v. Gardner,* 360 F2d 677, which we also review today, *post,* p. 158, we granted certiorari. 383 US 924.

. . . the agency does have direct authority to enforce this regulation in the context of passing upon applications for clearance of new drugs, §505, 21 USC §355, or certification of certain antibiotics, §507, 21 USC §357.

This is also a case in which the impact of the regulations upon the petitioners is sufficiently direct and immediate as to render the issue appropriate for judicial review at this stage. These regulations purport to give an authoritative interpretation of a statutory provision that has a direct effect on the day-to-day business of all prescription drug companies; its promulgation puts petitioners in a dilemma that it was the very purpose of the Declaratory Judgment Act to ameliorate. As the District Court found on the basis of uncontested allegations, "Either they must comply with the every time requirement and incur the costs of changing over their promotional material and labeling or they must follow their present course and risk prosecution." 228 F. Supp. 855, 861. The regulations are clear-cut, and were made effective immediately upon publication; as noted earlier the agency's counsel represented to the District Court that immediate compliance with their terms was expected. If petitioners wish to comply they must change all their labels, advertisements, and promotional materials; they must destroy stocks of printed matter; and they must invest heavily in new printing type and new supplies.

The alternative to compliance — continued use of material which they believe in good faith meets the statutory requirements, but which clearly does not meet the regulation of the Commissioner — may be even more costly. That course would risk serious criminal and civil penalties for the unlawful distribution of "misbranded" drugs.

It is relevant at this juncture to recognize that petitioners deal in a sensitive industry, in which public confidence in their drug products is especially important. To require them to challenge these regulations only as a defense to an action brought by the Government might harm them severely and unnecessarily. Where the legal issue presented is fit for judicial resolution, and where a regulation requires an immediate and significant change in the plaintiffs' conduct of their affairs with serious penalties attached to noncompliance, access to the courts under the Administrative Procedure Act and the Declaratory Judgment Act must be permitted, absent a statutory bar or some other unusual circumstance, neither of which appears here.

The Government does not dispute the very real dilemma in which petitioners are placed by the regulation, but contends that "mere financial expense" is not a justification for pre-enforcement judicial review. It is of course true that cases in this Court dealing with the standing of particular parties to bring an action have held that a possible financial loss is not by itself a sufficient interest to sustain a judicial challenge to governmental action.

. . . If the agency believes that a suit of this type will significantly impede enforcement or will harm the public interest, it need not postpone enforcement of the regulation and may oppose any motion for a judicial stay on the part of those challenging the regulation. *Ibid.* It is scarcely to be doubted that a court would refuse to postpone the effective date of an agency action if the Government could show, as it made no effort to do here, that delay would be detrimental to the public health or safety. See *Associated Securities Corp. v. SEC,* 283 F2d 773, 775, where a stay was denied because "the petitioners . . . [had] not sustained the burden of establishing that the requested stays will not be harmful to the public interest . . ."; see *Eastern Air Lines v. CAB,* 261 F2d 830; cf. *Scripps-Howard Radio v. FCC,* 316 US 4, 10–11; 5 USC §705.

Lastly, although the Government presses us to reach the merits of the challenge to the regulation in the event we find the District Court properly entertained this action, we believe the better practice is to remand the case to the Court of Appeals for the Third Circuit to review the District Court's decision that the regulation was beyond the power of the Commissioner.

Reversed and remanded.

Citizens to Preserve Overton Park v. Volpe
401 US 402 (6th Cir. 1971)

. . .

These statutes prohibit the Secretary of Transportation from authorizing the use of federal funds to finance the construction of highways through public parks if a "feasible and prudent" alternative route exists. If no such route is available, the statutes allow him to approve construction through parks only if there has been "all possible planning to minimize harm" to the park.

Petitioners, private citizens as well as local and national conservation organizations, contend that the Secretary has violated these statutes by authorizing the expenditure of federal funds for the construction of a six-lane interstate highway through a public park in Memphis, Tennessee. Their claim was rejected by the District Court, which granted the Secretary's motion for summary judgment, and the Court of Appeals for the Sixth Circuit affirmed. After oral argument, this Court granted a stay that halted construction and treating the application for the stay as a petition for certiorari, granted review. 400 US 939, 91 S.Ct. 246 L.Ed.2d. 262. We now reverse the judgment below and remand for further proceedings in the District Court.

Overton Park is a 342-acre city park located near the center of Memphis. The park contains a zoo, a nine-hole municipal golf course, an outdoor theater, nature trails, a bridle path, an art academy picnic areas, and 170 acres of forest. The proposed highway, which is to be a six-lane, high-speed, expressway, will sever the zoo from the rest of the park. Although the roadway will be depressed below ground level except where it crosses a small creek, 26 acres of the park will be destroyed.

. . .

[3] A threshold question — whether petitioners are entitled to any judicial review — is easily answered. Section 701 of the Administrative Procedure Act 5 USC §701 (1964 ed., Supp. V), provides that the action of "each authority" of the Government of the United States which includes the Department of Transportation, is subject to judicial review except where there is a statutory prohibition on review or where "agency action is committed to agency discretion by law." In this case, there is no indication that Congress sought to prohibit judicial review and there is most certainly no "showing of 'clear and convincing evidence' of a * * * legislative, intent to restrict access to judicial review." *Abbott Laboratories v. Gardner*, 387 US 136, 141, 87 S.Ct. 1507, 1511, 18 L.Ed.2d 681 (1967). *Brownell v. We Shung*, 352 US 180, 185, 77 S.Ct. 242, 255–256, 1 L.Ed.2d 225 (1956).

Similarly, the Secretary's decision here does not fall within the exception for action "committed to agency discretion". This is a very narrow exception. Berger, Administrative Arbitrariness and Judicial Review, 65 Col. L. Rev. 55 (1965).

. . .

Plainly, there is "law to apply" and thus the exemption for action "committed to agency discretion" is inapplicable. But the existence of judicial review is only the start: the standard for review must also be determined. For that we must look to §706 of the Administrative Procedure Act, 5 USC §706 (1964 ed., Supp. V), which provides that a "reviewing court shall *** hold unlawful and set aside agency action, findings, and conclusions found" not to meet six separate standards. In all cases agency action must be set aside if the action was "arbitrary, capricious, an abuse of discretion, or otherwise not in accordance with law" or if the action failed to meet statutory, procedural, or constitutional requirements. 5 USC §§706(2).

· · ·

"Similarly, the Secretary's decision here does not fall within the exception for action 'committed to agency discretion.' This is a very narrow exception. . . . The legislative history of the Administrative Procedure Act indicates that it is applicable in those rare instances where 'statutes are drawn in such broad terms that in a given case there is no law to apply.' S.Rep. No. 752, 79th Cong., 1st Sess., 26 (1945)." *Overton Park, supra,* 401 US, at 410, 91 S.Ct., at 820–821 (footnote omitted).

[2] The above quote answers several of the questions raised by the language of §701(a), although it raises others. First, it clearly separates the exception provided by §(a)(1) from the §(a)(2) exception. The former applies when Congress has expressed an intent to preclude judicial review. The latter applies in different circumstances; even where Congress has not affirmatively precluded review, review is not to be had if the statute is drawn so that a court would have no meaningful standard against which to judge the agency's exercise of discretion. In such a case, the statute ("law") can be taken to have "committed" the decision-making to the agency's judgment absolutely. This construction avoids conflict with the "abuse of discretion" standard of review in §706 — if no judicially manageable standards are available for judging how and when an agency should exercise its discretion, then it is impossible to evaluate agency action, for "abuse of discretion." In addition, this construction satisfies the principle of statutory construction mentioned earlier, by identifying a separate class of cases to which §701(a)(2) applies.

· · ·

Overton Park did not involve an agency's refusal to take requested enforcement action. It involved an affirmative act of approval under a statute that set clear guidelines for determining when such approval should be given. Refusals to take enforcement steps generally involve precisely the opposite situation, and in that situation we think the presumption is that judicial review is not available.

Heckler v. Chaney
470 US 821 (DC Cir. 1985)

Justice Rehnquist delivered the opinion of the Court.

This case presents the question of the extent to which a decision of an administrative agency to exercise its "discretion" not to undertake certain enforcement actions is subject to judicial review under the Administrative Procedure Act, 5 USC §501 *et seq.* (APA). Respondents are several prison inmates convicted of capital offenses and sentenced to death by lethal injection of drugs. They petitioned the Food and Drug Administration (FDA), alleging that under the circumstances the use of these drugs for capital punishment violated the Federal Food, Drug, and Cosmetic Act, 52 Stat. 1040, as amended, 21 USC §301 *et seq.* (FDCA), and requesting that the FDA take various enforcement actions to prevent these violations. The FDA refused their request. We review here a decision of the Court of Appeals for the District of Columbia Circuit, which held the FDA's refusal to take, enforcement actions both reviewable and an abuse of discretion, and remanded the case with directions that the agency be required "to fulfill its statutory function." 231 US App. DC 136, 153, 718 F2d 1174, 1191 (1983).

. . . This Court first addressed the "threshold question" of whether the agency's action was at all reviewable. After setting out the language of §701(a), the Court stated:

> In this case, there is no indication that Congress sought to prohibit judicial review and there is most certainly no "showing of 'clear and convincing evidence' of a . . . legislative intent" to restrict access to judicial review. *Abbott Laboratories v. Gardner,* 387 US 136, 141 [87 S.Ct. 1507, 1511, 18 L.Ed.2d 681] (1967).

and the Court has recognized on several occasions over many years that an agency's decision not to prosecute or enforce, whether through civil or criminal process, is a decision generally committed to an agency's absolute discretion.

. . .

[9] We therefore conclude that the presumption that agency decisions not to institute proceedings are unreviewable under 5 USC §701(a)(2) is not overcome by the enforcement provisions of the FDCA. The FDA's decision not to take the enforcement actions requested by respondents is therefore not subject to judicial review under the APA. The general exception to reviewability provided by §701(a)(2) for action "committed to agency discretion" remains a narrow one, see *Citizens to Preserve Overton Park v. Volpe,* 401 US 402, 91 S.Ct. 814, 28 L.Ed.2d 136 (1971), but within that exception are included agency refusals to institute investigative or enforcement proceedings, "unless Congress has indicated otherwise. In so holding, we essentially leave to Congress, and not to the courts, the decision as to whether an agency's refusal to institute proceedings should be judicially reviewable. No colorable claim is made in this case that the agency's refusal to institute proceedings violated any constitutional rights of respondents, and we do not address the issue that would be raised in such a case." Cf. *Johnson v. Robison,* 415 US 361, 366, 94 S.Ct. 1160, 1165, 89 L.Ed.2d 389 (1974); *Yick Wo v. Hopkins,* 118 US 356, 372–374, 6 S.Ct. 1064, 1072-1073, 30 L.Ed. 220 (1886). The fact that the drugs involved in this case are ultimately to be used in imposing the death penalty must not lead this Court or other courts to import profound differences of opinion over the meaning of the Eighth Amendment to the United States Constitution into the domain of administrative law.

The judgment of the Court of Appeals is *Reversed.*

City of Los Angeles v. Lyons
461 US 95 (1983)

JUSTICE WHITE delivered the opinion of the Court.

The issue here is whether respondent Lyons satisfied the prerequisites for seeking injunctive relief in the Federal District Court.

This case began on February 7, 1977, when respondent, Adolph Lyons, filed a complaint for damages, injunction, and declaratory relief in the United States District Court for the Central District of California. The defendants were the City of Los Angeles and four of its police officers. The complaint alleged that on October 6, 1976, at 2 a.m., Lyons was stopped by the defendant officers for a traffic or vehicle code violation and that although Lyons offered no resistance or threat whatsoever, the officers, without provocation or justification, seized Lyons and applied a "chokehold" — either the "bar arm control" hold or the "carotid-artery control."

... A preliminary injunction was entered enjoining "the use of both the carotid artery and bar arm holds under circumstances which do not threaten death or serious bodily injury." The Court of Appeals affirmed in a brief per curiam opinion stating that the District Court had not abused its discretion in entering a preliminary injunction, 656 F2d 417 (1981). We granted certiorari, 455 US 937 (1982), and now reverse. ...

It goes without saying that those who seek to invoke the jurisdiction of the federal courts must satisfy the threshold requirement imposed by Art. III of the Constitution by alleging an actual case or controversy. *Flast v. Cohen*, 392 US 83, 94–101 (1968); *Jenkins v. McKeithen*, 395 US 411, 421-425 (1969) (opinion of Marshall, J.) Plaintiffs must demonstrate a "personal stake in the outcome" in order to "assure that concrete adverseness which sharpens the presentation of issues" is necessary for the proper resolution of constitutional questions. *Baker v. Carr*, 369 US 186, 204 (1962). Abstract injury is not enough. The plaintiff must show that he "has sustained or is immediately in danger of sustaining some direct injury" as the result of the challenged official conduct and the injury or threat of injury must be both "real and immediate," not "conjectural" or "hypothetical." See, e.g. *Golden v. Zwickler*, 394 US 103, 109–110 (1969); *United Public Workers v. Mitchell*, 330 US 75, 89–91 (1947); *Maryland Casualty Co. v. Pacific Coal & Oil Co.*, 312 US 270, 273 (1941); ...

In order to establish an actual controversy in this case, Lyons would have had not only to allege that he would have another encounter with the police but also to make the incredible assertion either, (1) that *all* police officers in Los Angeles *always* choke any citizen with whom they happen to have an encounter, whether for the purpose of arrest, issuing a citation, or for questioning, or (2) that the City ordered or authorized police officers to act in such manner. Although Count V alleged that the City authorized the use of the control holds in situations where deadly force was not threatened, it did not indicate why Lyons might be realistically threatened by police officers who acted within the strictures of the City's policy. If, for example, chokeholds were authorized to be used only to counter resistance to an arrest by a suspect, or to thwart an effort to escape, any future threat to Lyons from the City's policy or from the conduct of police officers would be no more real than the possibility that he would again have an encounter with the police and that either he would illegally resist arrest or detention or the officers would disobey their instructions and again render him unconscious without any provocation.

. . .

Lyons fares no better if it be assumed that his pending damages suit affords him Art. III standing to seek an injunction as a remedy for the claim arising out of the October 1976 events. The equitable remedy is unavailable absent a showing of irreparable injury, a requirement that cannot be met where there is no showing of any real or immediate threat that the plaintiff will be wronged again — a "likelihood of substantial and immediate irreparable injury." *O'Shea v. Littleton*, 414 US, at 502. The speculative nature of Lyons' claim of future injury requires a finding that this prerequisite of equitable relief has not been fulfilled.

Nor will the injury that Lyons allegedly suffered in 1976 go unrecompensed; for that injury, he has an adequate remedy at law. Contrary to the view of the Court of Appeals, it is not at all "difficult" under our holding "to see how anyone can ever challenge police or similar administrative practices." 615 F2d, at 1250. The legality of the violence to which Lyons claims he was once subjected is at issue in his suit for damages and can be determined there.

Absent a sufficient likelihood that he will again be wronged in a similar way, Lyons is no more entitled to an injunction than any other citizen of Los Angeles; and a federal court may not entertain a claim by any or all citizens who no more than assert that certain practices of law are unconstitutional.

As we noted in *O'Shea*, 414 US, at 503, withholding injunctive relief does not mean that the "federal law will exercise no deterrent effect in these circumstances." If Lyons has suffered an injury barred by the Federal Constitution, he has a remedy for damages under §1983. Furthermore, those who deliberately deprive a citizen of his constitutional rights risk conviction under the federal criminal laws. *Ibid.*

Beyond these considerations the state courts need not impose the same standing or remedial requirements that govern federal-court proceedings. The individual States may permit their courts to use injunctions to oversee the conduct of law enforcement authorities on a continuing basis. But this is not the role of a federal court, absent far more justification than Lyons has proffered in this case.

The judgment of the Court of Appeals is accordingly reversed.

Justice Marshall, with whom Justice Brennan, Justice Blackmun, and Justice Stevens join, dissenting.

Stark v. Wickard
321 US 288 (DC Cir. 1944)

. . .

Without considering whether or not Congress could create such a definite personal statutory right in an individual against a fund handled by a federal agency, as we have here, and yet limit its enforceability to administrative determination, despite the existence of federal courts of general jurisdiction established under Article III of the Constitution, the Congressional grant of jurisdiction of this proceeding appears plain. There is no direct judicial review granted by this statute for these proceedings. The authority for a judicial examination of the validity of the Secretary's action is found in the existence of courts and the intent of Congress as deduced from the statutes and precedents as hereinafter considered.

. . .

With this recognition by Congress of the applicability of judicial review in this field, it is not to be lightly assumed that the silence of the statute bars from the courts an otherwise justiciable issue, *United States v. Griffin,* 303 US 226, 238; *Shields v. Utah Idaho R. Co.,* 305 US 177, 182; cf. *A.F. of L. v. Labor Board,* 308 US 401, 404, 412. The ruling in *Texas & Pacific Ry. Co. v. Abilene Cotton Oil Co.,* 204 US 426, is not authority to the contrary. It was there held that the statute placed the power in the Interstate Commerce Commission to hear the complaint stated, not in the state court where it was brought. The Commission award was then to be enforced in court. P. 438. Here, there is no forum, other than the ordinary courts, to hear this complaint. When, as we have previously concluded in this opinion, definite personal rights are created by federal statute, similar in kind to those customarily treated in courts of law, the silence of Congress as to judicial review is, at any rate in the absence of an administrative remedy, not to be construed as a denial of authority to the aggrieved person to seek appropriate relief in the federal courts in the exercise of their general jurisdiction. When Congress passes an Act empowering administrative agencies to carry on governmental activities, the power of those agencies is circumscribed by the authority granted. This permits the courts to participate in law enforcement entrusted to administrative bodies only to the extent necessary to protect justiciable individual rights against administrative action fairly beyond the granted powers. The responsibility of determining the limits of statutory grants of authority in such instances is a judicial function entrusted to the courts by Congress by the statutes establishing courts and marking their jurisdiction. Cf. *United States v. Morgan,* 307 US 183, 190–91. This is very far from assuming that the courts are charged more than administrators or legislators with the protection of the rights of the people. Congress and the Executive supervise the acts of administrative agents. The powers of departments, boards, and administrative agencies are subject to expansion, contraction, or abolition at the will of the legislative and executive branches of the government. These branches have the resources and personnel to examine into the working of the various establishments to determine the necessary changes of function or management. But under Article III, Congress established courts to adjudicate cases and controversies as to claims of infringement of individual rights whether by unlawful action of private persons or by the exertion of unauthorized administrative power.

It is suggested that such a ruling puts the agency at the mercy of objectors, since any provisions of the Order may be attacked as unauthorized by each producer. To this objection there are adequate answers. The terms of the Order are largely matters of administrative discretion as to which there is no justiciable right or are clearly authorized by a valid act. *United States v. Rock Royal Co-op.*, 307 US 533. Technical details of the milk business are left to the Secretary and his aides. The expenses of litigation deter frivolous contentions. If numerous parallel cases are filed, the courts have ample authority to stay useless litigation until the determination of a test case. Cf. *Landis v. North American Co.*, 299 US 248. Should some provisions of an order be held to exceed the statutory power of the Secretary, it is well within the power of a court of equity to so mold a decree as to preserve in the public interest the operation of the portion of the order which is not attacked pending amendment.

It hardly need be added that we have not considered the soundness of the allegations made by the petitioners in their complaint. The trial court is free to consider whether the statutory authority given the Secretary is a valid answer to the petitioners' contention. We merely determine the petitioners have shown a right to a judicial examination of their complaint.

Reversed.

10

Paralegalism in Administrative Law

PARALEGALS...

* International Law
* Jury Research
* ProBono
* Mediation
* Foreclosures
* Employment Law
* Litigation
* Environmental Law

* Social Security
* Constitutional Law
* Trial Work
* Research
* Probate
* Securities
* Immigration Law

A. The Paralegal Profession

Paralegals work in government for administrative agencies, in law firms that work with administrative agencies and appear before them for their clients.

One agency that is looking for workers in 2009 is the *U.S. Census Bureau*, preparing for the 2010 Census.

Salary: $17.50 per hour; a forty hour week
Pay for 3 or 4 hours of training
Five to ten weeks work at minimum

Sign up for the test: Names, numbers, plans, details — all skills paralegals have been trained at that need clear focus, a paralegal trait.

Look into the Department even when the Census isn't imminent.

Medical firms that handle drugs, hospitals, rules and regulations: These firms all need detail oriented people who can work on their own. They need people who can write and edit.

The **Labor Department** is always collecting, reviewing, and sorting facts.

The **National Labor Relations Board** handles cases from businesses and labor unions. Be a union representative or steward. I filed with the NLRB when I was a steward, representing some members. As a steward, you are always gathering information to handle problems between the company people and the union people. You have to speak and write clearly, definite paralegal assets. You have to keep written records. You must interact with different personalities.

Law firms. Patent law firms represent clients who have new ideas they want protected. I know a paralegal who on a Friday sent the new proposed patent back to the wrong company for review before being filed at the **U.S. Patent Bureau.** She was spastic the whole weekend wondering if she would have a job when she went to work Monday. But somehow they were able to retrieve the patent before any harm was done. Secrecy is a major factor in law firms.

Criminal law firms work with clients who have been charged with white collar crime, with murder, robbery, etc.

Paralegals have to be flexible enough to research information in various agencies. Some businesses may be involved in food, others in automobiles, etc.

Key in the websites on pages 333-334. Most agencies list a job section. Take a look. Even if it's not the job you want, it may give you ideas about what skills are needed in the work force.

Of Current Interest

As the stock market rises and falls, paralegals in the securities field handle registration and liability problems as they pertain to the Securities and Exchange Act.

Some interesting websites for securities paralegals are:

www.sec.gov — This is the Home Page of the Securities and Exchange Commission. Click on jobs to see a video and other listings of possible occupations.

http://aolsearch.aol.com — This is the America Online search page. In the Search box, key in "securities paralegal." There is information about paralegal topics, and also the Securities Exchange world itself.

Immigration paralegals are in a field under quite a bit of pressure these days. They are involved in the immigration process from visas, to removal, to hearings and appeals.

There are many websites for immigration paralegals:

www.uscis.gov — The Immigration and Naturalization Service (now U.S. Citizenship and Immigration Services) can be found at this site. In 2003, INS (now USCIS) became a Bureau of the Homeland Security Department. Click on some of the job-related links.

http://aolsearch.com — This is the America Online search page. In the Search box, key in "immigration paralegal." There are information sites listed.

For all careers, look up the National Federation of Paralegals.

www.paralegals.org — You can access the most recent monthly magazine.

If you are interested in research, records, and archives, check out *www.nara.gov* or *www.archives.gov*. (See Exhibit 10.1)

Guidelines for Using Paralegals

The American Bar Association has proposed some model guidelines to assist lawyers in utilizing the legal assistant in an effective manner. These guidelines address professional conduct, delegation of work, legal opinions, client confidences, and conflict of interest.

The lawyer is responsible for the professional conduct of the paralegal while at the law firm or administrative agency. The lawyer must inform the paralegal as to the professional expectations of the firm and following this, the attorney must supervise the paralegal in that regard.

B. Skills Development and Practical Experience

Administrative law paralegals require the same general skills of all paralegals, but particularly should concentrate on communication, research, and document drafting. These skills are most desirable for work in administrative agencies and law firms.

At the agencies paralegals need good communication skills for gathering information from individuals and answering their questions. Paralegals are involved in the processing of claims and complaints, so they must be able to access the rules and regulations and perform other research. In some agencies paralegals draft documents and prepare for hearings.

Paralegals working at law firms practicing administrative law also must be familiar with the many sources of administrative laws and rules on both the state and federal levels. The paralegal juxtaposes communicating with experienced attorneys in the field and relating to uninformed clients where clarifying the violations of regulations is paramount.

In administrative law cases such as workers' compensation, a paralegal's skills must excel in the proper intake of client and witness information, the gathering of evidence such as medical reports, the coordination of documents, and the drafting of pleadings.

Exhibit 10.1   **NARA Website**

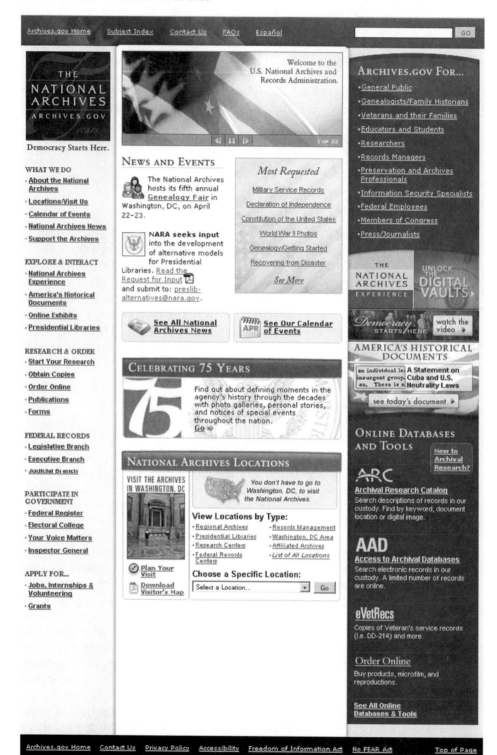

1. Computer and Internet Skills

Paralegals need to be well versed in the technology of today's computer for it is a vital tool in legal pursuits. Programs to assist the computer illiterate are established in the legal field and in the schools and colleges.

They include the databases, Westlaw, and Lexis-Nexis.

Much of the legal documentation that paralegals need from laws to cases is now available on Internet sites. The *http://www.fedworld.gov* website offers a master list of government websites. The *www.nara.gov* website gives access to the National Archives and documents like the *Federal Register*.

An interesting study for computer/Internet users is the burgeoning of protective and privacy issues on the Internet, particularly the Internet Child Protection Acts being sponsored by legislators.

2. Pro Bono Work

Pro bono work can prepare paralegal students for the real legal world as well as help paralegals establish future business contacts. Many paralegals gain experience by doing pro bono work before they graduate, which is an asset on their resumes. It also helps some students define their interests and goals. Many students have been hired by lawyers they met during their pro bono work and continue the pro bono work after they graduate.

3. Paralegals at Hearings

Paralegals and others may appear at Social Security hearings. They are the representatives of the claimant and may aid in the claimants' case presentation. Paralegals and others may also practice before the Federal Patent and Trademark Office.

C. The Working Paralegal

Paralegals in different areas of the legal field have specific duties related to those areas. Some of these positions include: corporate legal assistant/paralegal, litigation paralegal, probate paralegal, real estate paralegal, lay advocate, and federal government paralegal. Anywhere there is a profession, there are usually paralegals, including the expanding nurse-health fields and animal care.

Corporate paralegals are responsible for the corporate docket and scheduling of meetings for the board of directors and the shareholders. They draft notices, keep minutes of meetings, and prepare documents to be presented at corporate meetings.

The litigation paralegal may interview clients, view on-site investigations, and draft documents pertinent to the claim. During pre-trial the paralegal prepares evidence summaries, exhibit books, and witnesses for court appearances.

The probate paralegal prepares all the documents required to begin a probate. The documents are reviewed by the firm's attorney before filing. This paralegal must be well versed in the rules of inheritance and federal taxation.

Real estate paralegals are able to prepare legal descriptions on deeds and mortgages. They become very familiar with registry proceedings at the county courthouse. Using their office computer, they are able to advance themselves professionally by doing legal research on substantive real estate law.

The law advocate is commonly called the "public paralegal." This paralegal serves the poor and represents clients before agencies in welfare cases or matters of social security.

The federal government paralegal is a civil service classification in a group known as the "Paralegal Series." This paralegal may work for attorneys, general counsel, and solicitors of various agencies.

The above positions demonstrate the wide variety of opportunities in the paralegal profession.

1. Private Sector

Paralegals working in the private sector face a diverse employment field. They may choose to specialize in jury research, employment law, foreclosure issues, litigation, corporate law, probate, and environmental law. Moreover paralegals may decide to participate as full-time in-house staff, or as freelancers.

Paralegals must keep up with the skills of the professional business world as law firms interact with many diverse companies and other institutions. The following are some of the areas in which paralegals in the private sector may work.

a. Jury Research

Jury research is a relatively new field for the paralegal. There are many internship programs to educate the paralegal in the psychology and evidence factors of trials. Jury research programs are expensive for law firm clients but for certain trials are worth the time, money, and research. The research is conducted by professional jury consultants.

The litigation paralegal assists the jury consultants in evaluating the case, planning tactical approaches, and developing demonstrative evidence. Consultant firms train the paralegal on how to organize juror information, make demographic evaluations of juries, assess witnesses through interviews, and prepare juror notebooks. These skills, along with interpreting the non-verbal communication of jurors, may eliminate unexpected negative surprises from the jury and result in a favorable outcome.

b. *Employment Law*

Paralegals undertaking employment law need diverse training in evaluating documents, interviewing clients, and the law of torts. These paralegals must develop good oral, written, and analytical skills. Often, paralegals attend lectures on employment issues to keep abreast of the field. Paralegals sometimes draft employment contracts for businesses, which demands an understanding of the levels of compensation, non-competition clauses, and terms of dismissal such as poor performance, insubordination, and other acts. Paralegals may be involved in torts for wrongful discharge, fraud, defamation, and invasion of privacy. Another intriguing aspect of this field is the legal protection afforded the paralegal and law firm if clients are unethical and supply incorrect information on which the law firm acts. When does unethical become illegal? The paralegal has to be aware of this question and discover the answer.

c. *Foreclosures*

Paralegals who decided to work in the field of real estate foreclosure must be very detail oriented. Precise timing, schedules, and documentation are essential in this field.

Paralegals collect information during and after a lender's first call. During this time copies of demand letters sent to the borrower, the original note, the deed of trust, the rents report, the copy of the mortgagee's title policy, payment history, the principal balance, and the address of the borrower are sent to the law firm. With this information, the paralegal drafts the foreclosure documents, including a public trustee's sale document. Timing is critical and the deadlines for serving notices must be met or the foreclosure may fail.

The paralegal must prepare for a hearing, if there is one, and then must prepare for the actual sale of the property after the hearing. Again, all the parties involved have to receive notice or the foreclosure is in jeopardy. The paralegal also is involved in setting the price of the bid for the property. This usually occurs two weeks before the sale when the paralegal meets with the lender and attorney to calculate the price of the bid, which should be at least 70 percent of the property's value.

After the sale of the property, the paralegal prepares a trustee's deed and assures the delivery of the certificate of purchase. As you can imagine, the paralegal is a terrific economic asset to both the firm and the client.

d. *Litigation*

Litigation paralegals have a very demanding job. Much of their work is before trial. It is best to develop a checklist of tasks and not to rely on memory.

A file for each witness must be established. Updated requests as well as prior interviews and affidavits must be in the file. All depositions must be summarized.

A list of trial exhibits should be prepared. This may include depositions, statements, affidavits, and charts. Copies should be made for each lawyer, for the witnesses, the judge, and for the witness file folder. Another file on pre-trial motions, objections to exhibits, jury instructions, etc. should be prepared.

In addition, litigation paralegals often check hotel availability for out-of-state witnesses, who are not required to pay their own hotel bills. On the hearing or trial days, the paralegal must be sure that the witness is escorted to the agency or the courthouse.

During a trial, the attorneys will expect the paralegal to quickly locate any information they may need at that moment.

2.   Government Sector

Paralegals in government not only serve as paralegals but also use their skills in other capacities. This has been particularly true since the 1990s. The Department of Labor, in its "Social Scientists and Legal Occupations" brochure, states:

"The duties of paralegals who work in government vary depending on the type of agency that employs them. Generally, paralegals in government analyze legal material for internal use, maintain reference files, conduct research for attorneys, collect and analyze evidence for agency hearings, and prepare informative or explanatory material on the law, agency regulations, and agency policy for general use by the agency and public."

Most federal agencies employ paralegals. Many are found in these departments: Justice, Health and Human Services, and the Treasury. Comparative state and municipal governments employ paralegals.

The Labor Department predicts, "Job opportunities for paralegals will expand even in the public sector. Community legal service programs — which provide assistance to the poor, the aged, minorities, and the middle-income families — operate on limited budgets and will employ more paralegals to keep expenses down and serve the most people. Federal, state and local government agencies, consumer organizations, and the courts also should continue to hire paralegals in increasing numbers."

Exhibit 10.2 lists federal agencies' website addresses.

The following are federal agencies listed in descending order by the number of paralegals they currently employ. Although these are federal agencies, states have similar agency positions.

1. Department of Justice
2. Department of Health and Human Services
3. U.S. Court System Nationwide
4. Department of Treasury
5. Department of the Army
6. Department of Transportation
7. Department of the Navy
8. Department of Labor

9. Department of State
10. Department of Energy
11. Department of the Interior
12. U.S. Office of Personnel Management
13. Small Business Administration
14. Department of Veterans Affairs
15. Environmental Protection Agency
16. Equal Employment Opportunity Commission
17. Department of Education
18. Department of the Air Force
19. Department of Housing and Urban Development
20. Department of Commerce

Exhibit 10.2   **Agency Websites**

Central Intelligence Agency (CIA)	*www.cia.gov*
Child Protection	*www.safekids.com*
Code of Federal Regulations	*www.gpoaccess.gov*
Congress/House of Representatives	*www.house.gov*
Congress/Administrative Agencies	*http://thomas.loc.gov*
Consumer Product Safety Commission	*www.cpsc.gov*
Constitution, U.S.	*www.uscourts.gov*
Dust Bowl (1930s)	*www.pbs.org/wgbh/pages/amex/ dustbowl*
Environmental Protection Agency (EPA)	*www.epa.gov*
Federal Communications Commission (FCC)	*www.fcc.gov*
Federal Government web pages access	*www.whitehouse.gov*
Federal Register access	*www.nara.gov*
Federal Trade Commission (FTC)	*www.ftc.gov*
Freedom of Information Act	*www.nara.gov*
Government websites	*www.fedworld.gov*
Housing and Urban Development (HUD)	*www.hud.gov*
Labor Department	*www.dol.gov*
Library of Congress	*http://lcweb.loc.gov*
National Archives	*www.nara.gov*
National Labor Relations Board	*www.nlrb.gov*
New Deal (1930s)	*http://newdeal.feri.org*
Occupational Safety and Health Administration (OSHA)	*www.osha.gov*

Paralegals — National Association of Legal Assistants	*www.nala.org*
Paralegals — National Paralegal Association	*www.nationalparalegal.org*
Securities and Exchange Commission	*www.sec.gov*
Social Security Administration	*www.ssa.gov*
U.S. Citizenship and Immigration Services (USCIS)	*www.uscis.gov*
Veterans' Affairs	*www.va.gov*
White House	*www.whitehouse.gov*

a. Environmental Law

Since the National Environmental Policy Act of 1970 was passed creating the Environmental Protection Agency (EPA) environmental law has become very big business.

Paralegals at the EPA interact with the private sector and need to be aware of the following areas this law affects: transfer of corporation real estate, tax returns involving contaminated property, and disclosures of contamination to administrative agencies such as the Securities and Exchange Commission.

The EPA paralegals need not only to be well-versed on federal regulations, but also state and even local ordinances. There may be multi-state and multi-site transactions. By keeping knowledgeable, paralegals assist the agency attorneys with careful examinations of documents as well as the drafting of any necessary agency documents.

b. International Law

What does a paralegal do in agencies dealing with international law? Work that is very similar to other agency paralegals but with the additional requirement of dealing with foreign languages and foreign customs. International law is a rather new field for paralegals. Courses are offered at universities to develop expertise, but most of the knowledge is acquired through practical experience at the agencies.

In order to perform this type of work, paralegals should be prepared to learn how the United States regulates international trade, contracts, and documents; how to apply legal rules; which criminal laws might be applicable to foreign situations.

The technical legal process involved in international law may be frustrated with delays, costs, and differing interpretations, such as what is "binding" in international contracts. An experienced paralegal saves the government time and money by navigating through the myriad channels involved in international legalities.

c. Constitutional Law

Any appeal of an agency proceeding or decision that comes across an administrative agency paralegal's desk will undoubtedly cite a constitutional issue as its reason for appeal. Agency paralegals must understand the legal chain connecting modern cases with the nation's legal history — the grant of authority, the separation of government powers, the delegation to agencies. This knowledge is paramount as a paralegal works on constitutional issues such as search warrants (Fourth Amendment) or civil rights and discrimination (Fourteenth Amendment).

d. Mediation

There are presently a number of mediation positions in the federal government that utilize paralegal skills. Most of these positions relate to labor-management disputes. Paralegals need to familiarize themselves with prevention of labor dispute theories, settlement of labor disputes, collective bargaining practices, and the economic factors of today's industrial world.

CASE ABSTRACTS

The harsh reality of work in a law firm is that there may be conflict. The following is an agency decision and a court decision about such a conflict between lawyers and staff at a law firm.

The case is chosen because paralegals are not involved in the conflict. Therefore, your reading should be objective as you analyze the situations. What is important for you to note is the work environment of a law firm that is presented as the case unfolds. After reading the case, you should have shed any glamorous vision of the legal workplace.

Herrick & Smith and Mary M. Moran
Case 1-CA-21118

14 May 1985

DECISION AND ORDER

By Chairman Dotson and Members Hunter and Dennis

On 20 November 1984 Administrative Law Judge Mary Ellen R. Benard issued the attached decision. The Respondent filed exceptions and a supporting brief; the General Counsel filed the brief submitted to the judge, cross-exceptions, and a supporting brief; and the Respondent filled an answering brief.

The Board has considered the decision and the record in light of the exceptions and briefs and has decided to affirm the judge's rulings, findings,[1] and conclusions and to adopt the recommended Order.[2]

ORDER

The National Labor Relations Board adopts the recommended Order of the administrative law judge and orders that the Respondent, Herrick & Smith, Boston, Massachusetts, its officers, agents, successors, and assigns, shall take the action set forth in the Order.

DECISION

STATEMENT OF THE CASE

MARY ELLEN R. BENARD, Administrative Law Judge. The charge in this case was filed on June 17, 1983,[3] by Mary M. Moran, an individual, against Herrick & Smith (the Respondent). On August 11 the complaint was issued, alleging, in substance, that the Respondent had violated Section 8(a)(1) of the National Labor Relations Act by threatening Moran with discharge for making complaints about the terms and conditions of employment of the Respondent's employees and by subsequently discharging Moran because she engaged in concerted activities protected by the Act. The Respondent filed an answer in which it denied the commission of any unfair labor practices.

A hearing was held before me in Boston, Massachusetts, on October 31 through November 4, December 5 through 9, and January 4 and 6 and March 12 and 13, 1984. Thereafter, the General Counsel and the Respondent filed briefs, which have been considered.

---

[1]The Respondent has excepted to some of the judge's credibility findings. The Board's established policy is not to overrule an administrative law judge's credibility resolutions unless the clear preponderance of all the relevant evidence convinces us that they are incorrect. *Standard Dry Wall Products*, 91 NLRB 544 (1950), enfd. 188 F2d 362 (3d Cir. 1951). We have carefully examined the record and find no basis for reversing the findings.

[2]The judge found, and we agree, that the Respondent violated Sec. 8(a)(1) of the Act by warning employee Moran, in retaliation for her protected concerted activity, to refrain from making negative comments about the Respondent or to seek employment elsewhere and by thereafter discharging her. Accordingly, we find it unnecessary to pass on the General Counsel's contention that the Respondent's warning and discharge of Moran additionally were unlawful as being based on an overly broad restriction of employee rights.

[3]All dates are in 1983 unless otherwise indicated.

On the entire record in this case and from my observation of the witnesses and their demeanor, I make the following

FINDINGS AND CONCLUSIONS

B. *The Employment of Mary Moran*

1. Moran's employment as a floater

Charging Party Mary Moran began working for the Respondent in April 1976 as a legal secretary. For the first 5-1/2 years of her employment she was a floater, and credibly testified that as a floater she had worked for just about every attorney in the firm, that there was a tendency to assign her to the more senior attorneys and the more "difficult" ones, and that about 1980 the Respondent's personnel director, Susan Beranyk, told her that she was one of the best floaters in the firm and that consequently the Respondent preferred for her to work for the partners and the more difficult attorneys.

. . .

Anninger testified that after Moran said that the firm should hold a communication seminar for the attorneys as well as the secretaries, she went on to say that she was no longer working for Whitlock and something to the effect that although had liked working for him she "just couldn't take it anymore." According to Anninger, Moran also said that she had asked to be reassigned to a floating position because she did not want to work with Whitlock any longer, she looked "very intense" when she talked about Whitlock, and he felt that he was getting involved in something he would rather avoid. Anninger further testified that Moran then said something about he must be sorry he ran into her and he just shrugged his shoulders and walked away. According to Anninger, he was not upset about the conversation and he did not think he could have projected the image that he was.

. . .

According to Moran, sometime early in the first week that she worked for Anninger he called her into his office and said that he knew they would be working together for at least a week and asked Moran if she realized that the arrangement would not "work out over the long run." Moran said that she did. Anninger testified that he did not think he would have told Moran that the arrangement would not work over the long run, but that he may have referred to his understanding that the assignment was not permanent but was to last only until a secretary was found to replace Hanlon. I credit Anninger, who seemed to testify candidly on this point, and conclude that he did not make the specific comment Moran attributed to him. However, it is clear that Anninger emphasized the temporary nature of Moran's assignment to work as his secretary.

Moran credibly testified that about a week after she started working for Anninger he told her that he was pleased with the arrangement, that he would be traveling frequently to Washington, D.C., and that he felt very comfortable with her being there while he was gone. He then asked Moran if she would mind working for him indefinitely until a replacement for Hanlon was hired and she indicated that that would be all right. In consequence, Anninger arranged with the personnel department that Moran would be assigned to him indefinitely as a floater.

According to Cashman, about a week after Moran began working for Anninger, Cashman asked him how the assignment was working and he told her that things were going pretty well but that Moran did not have Hanlon's technical skills. It appears that this was the conversation in which Anninger asked to retain Moran indefinitely; however, Anninger testified that in the conversation in which Cashman asked him how the assignment was he replied that he would keep Moran until a replacement was found for Hanlon, but that he would watch the situation to make sure that it continued to be satisfactory. I do not credit Anninger on this point, for he did not appear candid when giving this testimony, but rather seemed to be consciously tailoring his testimony to fit the Respondent's position in the case.

6. The incident of May 3

Moran credibly testified that late in the morning of May 3 Anninger told her that he had some work that had to be completed that day, and that she responded that she could not stay after 5 p.m. According to Moran, Anninger gave her some work about 4 p.m. After she had done the typing, Anninger made some revisions, which she also typed. When Anninger gave her a second set of revisions, Moran concluded that she would not be able to finish the job by 5 p.m., so she called the personnel department to have someone do the work after she left. At 5 p.m. the other secretary arrived. Moran testified that while she was standing with her coat on explaining what needed to be done, Anninger came out of his office and she told him that the other secretary would finish the work. According to Moran, Anninger "got very upset and very red in the face" and yelled "Shit, shit, shit!" Moran testified that she just thanked the other secretary, said, "Good night," and left. It is undisputed that this was the only occasion that Anninger ever used crude language to Moran.

Anninger testified that he had had something difficult to write that afternoon and that about 4 p.m. he asked Moran if she could type his longhand draft so that he could make revisions. About 4:45 p.m., according to Anninger, Moran asked if she could get someone else to finish the work and he asked if she could stay because he did not think it would take more than an extra 20 minutes. Moran replied that she could not. Moran then, according to Anninger, tried to find someone else, but told Anninger that no one was available and he should take the work to the word processing department. That suggestion was not satisfactory to Anninger, and eventually someone else did come to finish the work. Anninger testified that, when he saw at 5 p.m. that getting his work done was going to be more difficult than he had thought, he turned on his heel, pounding the fist of one hand into the palm of the other, and said "Shit, shit, shit!" in frustration. Anninger further testified that he was not facing Moran when he uttered the expletive, and that the job was finished by 5:20 or 5:30 p.m.

I credit Moran's version of this incident over that of Anninger, for Moran seemed to testify forthrightly about the matter, while Anninger appeared less than totally candid. Further, as the General Counsel has pointed out in his brief, Anninger testified that, when Cashman, as discussed below, talked to him about the incident a few days later, he had to make an effort to recall what had happened.

Moran credibly testified that she was upset by the incident because, although she had heard attorneys use foul language on other occasions, Anninger had directed his words at her, and she did not think anyone should talk to her or to any secretary in that manner. It is undisputed that about the next day Moran placed the following memorandum on Cashman's desk:

TO: Mrs. Cashman
FROM: Ms. Moran
RE: *Thomas Anninger*

On Tuesday, May 3, 1983, at 2:30 p.m. Mr. Anninger told me he had something that had to go out by 5:00 p.m. I waited until 4:30 p.m. for the work to make various revisions—I told him I had to leave at 5:00 p.m. When I realized it would take longer than 5:00 p.m. to finish the job I called Personnel to find someone to complete the task. When Mr. Anninger came out and found me explaining to the woman taking over and putting my coat on he proceeded with "shit, shit, shit." This Mrs. Cashman is what we as secretaries, have to contend with.

Moran told Denise Allen, the only other secretary who worked in her area, about the incident and that she had written a memo to Cashman about it. Allen advised Moran that she thought that sending the memo was a good idea and that Anninger should not have used such language to Moran.

About May 5 Cashman called Moran into her office. Moran testified that when she went in, Cashman held up the memo and said she wanted to discuss it. Moran said that she had not been sure whether Cashman would want to discuss the memo or file it, and Cashman asked, "What would I file this for?" and then threw the memo on her desk and said she did not want any more memos from Moran and that if she had a problem she was to handle it herself. According to Moran, Cashman also said that perhaps this was Anninger's way of handling things; when Moran said that she would not have been able to get by with speaking to an attorney that way and that she was a professional and wanted to be treated as such, Cashman told her that she was inflexible, that if she did not like the firm she could leave, and that this was probably not the field for her. . . .

5. Cashman's reaction to the Anninger evaluation

Cashman first saw the evaluation when she arrived at work on Monday, June 13. According to Cashman, she had no reason to disbelieve Anninger's evaluation of Moran, and, although she could not evaluate Moran's performance herself, she believed that Anninger had done so to the best of his ability. Cashman also testified that she looked through Moran's personnel file to see if anyone else had had an experience similar to Anninger's with her, and came to the conclusion that there were periods when Moran had not performed as well as she had at others but that there were also times when she had done very well. However, it is undisputed that Cashman did not talk to Bohlen about Moran's work, and, although Cashman testified that she thought Bohlen was on vacation during one of the weeks at issue, Bohlen did not testify, and there is no documentary evidence or other testimony as to whether he was available to discuss Moran's situation. In any event, Cashman conceded that she did not even consider the question of Bohlen's view of Moran's work.

Under the circumstances, I do not credit Cashman's testimony that she had no reason to feel that Anninger had not evaluated Moran as accurately as he could. It is undisputed that Cashman knew that Anninger's conduct had been discussed at the secretaries' May 11 meeting with Remis, and she was, of course, aware that Moran had made an issue of Anninger's behavior on May 3. Anninger impressed me as a man who does not take criticism lightly, and I cannot believe that Cashman, an expert on personnel matters, did not recognize that Anninger might have evaluated Moran more harshly in retaliation for her criticism of him. Further, although Cashman testified that she considered Anninger's evaluation in light of other information in Moran's personnel file, I find it noteworthy that she nonetheless operated solely on the premise that Anninger's evaluation was justified, without taking it with the proverbial "grain of salt," and without discussing Moran's performance with any of the other attorneys, such as Wexler, Fishkin, or Bohlen, for whom she had recently worked.

The same day there was a meeting of the Respondent's salary committee, which is composed of Remis, Cashman, and Clark.[24] Cashman credibly testified that in the course of that meeting she told Remis that she had received a "scathing" evaluation of Moran from Anninger and that she intended to discuss it with Moran later in the week. Cashman testified that she also advised Remis and Clark that she had received an anonymous memo to the effect that Moran had been "badmouthing" the firm, and that she might discuss that with Moran at the same time as the evaluation. According to Cashman, she had received the note 2 or 3 weeks earlier through the interoffice mail, but had made no attempt to ascertain its author or to talk to Moran about it.

E. Moran's Discharge

1. The events of June 16

It is undisputed that on Thursday, June 16, Cashman called Moran and said she wanted to talk to her. Moran testified that when she arrived at Cashman's office Cashman told her that she had received various

[24]The salary committee is responsible for deciding the amount of salary increases the secretaries will receive on the basis of their annual evaluations. It is undisputed that although Remis is a member of that committee he does not attend all of its meetings. Indeed, Clark testified that for the year preceding Clark's testimony in this case Remis had not been directly involved in salary committee meetings unless specifically asked to be.

reports, including one from Whitlock, that Moran had been "bad mouthing" the firm. Moran said that Whitlock was entitled to his opinion but she had never "bad mouthed" the Respondent. According to Moran, Cashman then accused her of not being a loyal employee of the firm, and Moran denied the accusation. Cashman then said that she was not saying that Moran was disloyal, but repeating Anninger's comments,[25] and showed Moran the anonymous memo she had mentioned to Remis and Clark at the salary committee meeting. Moran repeated that everyone was entitled to his opinion, and at that point Cashman held up Anninger's evaluation of Moran and read excerpts from it.[26] It is undisputed that Moran denied everything she heard and said the evaluation was "ludicrous." According to Moran, Cashman said that if Moran did not like working at the firm she could leave and that she was in the wrong field and Moran replied that she had been working for lawyers since 1964. Cashman, however, testified that she told Moran that if she could not refrain from making negative remarks about the firm she should look for work elsewhere.

According to Moran, Cashman further told her that she would prepare a memorandum for Moran to sign and that if Moran did not change her attitude and receive better performance evaluations she would be terminated. Moran responded that she would not sign any memorandum and Cashman then said, according to Moran, that that would determine her employment and further said that Moran had stopped working with Whitlock because of a personality conflict. Moran replied that that was not the reason and that the correct reason was "on the record."

Cashman, however, specifically denied telling Moran that Whitlock had advised her that Moran had been "bad mouthing" the firm, or that she advised Moran that if she did not change her attitude and receive better evaluations she would be terminated. However, Cashman conceded that she told Moran that if her performance did not improve she would be discharged. Cashman also testified that, when she read to Moran, Anninger's comment about her attitude and loyalty, Moran protested that Anninger's remarks were foolish and that she had always been loyal to the firm and had worked hard for Anninger as well as for Whitlock. According to Cashman, at that point she said, "That may be, but what about this?" and showed Moran the anonymous note.

Cashman testified that, although she told Moran that she would prepare a memo for her to sign noting that she had read and understood its content, she did not say that whether Moran signed the memorandum would determine her employment. Cashman further testified that she believed that she told Moran that she was not asking her to agree with the substance of their discussion, but only to acknowledge what had

[25]Moran initially testified that she did not recall Cashman saying that she was only referring to what Anninger had said, but later conceded that Cashman had made this comment.

[26]Cashman credibly testified that she does not read all of an appraisal to its subject if she does not feel that reading the entire document will result in the employee viewing the evaluation session as a positive one.

been discussed and that she understood it. However, although I have credited much of Cashman's testimony, her demeanor at this point did not favorably impress me, for she seemed evasive and only made this comment in response to a leading question on direct examination. Further, Moran credibly testified that she did not recall Cashman telling her that she only wanted Moran to sign a memo to acknowledge that the conversation took place, and not as an indication that she agreed with the substance of what she had been told.

Finally, Cashman testified, she did not tell Moran that Anninger had recommended her discharge, but did tell her that she would look for a significant improvement in her performance over the next 30 days. According to Cashman, she did not tell Moran of Anninger's recommendation because she did not intend to do what he had suggested.

To the extent that there is a conflict between the versions of Cashman and Moran as to what was said at this meeting, I credit Cashman, except, as noted, with respect to her assertion that she told Moran that she would be asked to sign a memo only to acknowledge what was discussed. Although I have generally credited Moran's testimony in this proceeding, certain portions of her account of this discussion, particularly her statement that Cashman told her that her continued employment would depend on whether she signed the memo, seemed to me to be more of an attempt to bolster her theory of why she was ultimately discharged than to accurately recount the events at issue.

Cashman credibly testified that immediately after meeting with Moran she prepared the following memo:

June 16, 1983

To: THE FILE
Re: *Miss Mary Moran*

Today I spoke with Miss Moran regarding the following matters:

(1) Performance evaluation of Mr. Thomas Anninger for period 05/02/83–06/10/83.
(2) Reports that Miss Moran had been "bad mouthing" the Firm.

Performance Evaluation — I told Miss Moran that Mr. Anninger rated the quality of her work only satisfactory, the quantity unacceptable, and her personal characteristics such as judgment, initiative, dependability, cooperation, etc. as average or below average.

I read excerpts from Mr. Anninger's evaluation, such as "the first few weeks went fairly well. . . . However, with time her personal life began to interfere with her work. . . . She needs direction for every decision. . . . Her attitude is her biggest problem. She is not loyal to this office, and has the sense that we owe her more than she owes us. She complains constantly to me or others walking by and willing to listen. . . ."

Miss Moran took exception to all these remarks, said the comments were untrue, unfair, disgraceful and ridiculous.

Negative Comments on the Firm — Miss Moran denied "bad mouthing" the Firm. I told her nevertheless not only I, but partners [in the firm] had been told that Miss Moran had been making negative remarks, and that this would have to cease immediately. I showed Miss Moran the anonymous note I had received.

To sum up, I advised Miss Moran that her performance would be evaluated again over the next thirty (30) days, and that the evaluations would have to come through a lot better. I reminded her that she was earning $370.00 a week to be a floating secretary, and that if her performance did not improve we would be forced to terminate her employment.

I also told her that as long as she is employed by the Firm, we expect her to refrain from negative comments. If she cannot, she should seek employment elsewhere.

I told Miss Moran that Mr. Remis is aware of what I had discussed with her, and is in full agreement.

/s/ Gertrude M. Cashman
Gertrude M. Cashman
Director of Personnel

MC/bg

June 17, 1983

I have read, and understand the contents of this memorandum.

/s/ Mary M. Moran

Cashman testified that her only reason for meeting with Moran on June 16 was the Anninger evaluation, and that she felt that that evaluation was based on a short period of time and should be viewed against the long period when Moran's work was satisfactory, and Moran should be given an opportunity to improve her performance. Cashman also testified that if Moran had recognized the validity of Anninger's evaluation of her no written warning would have been issued to her and she would not have been asked to sign any disciplinary document. According to Cashman, if Moran had said that Anninger was right or that although he was wrong there were areas where she could improve, or if she had taken note of what Cashman said, Cashman would not have prepared a memo. However, according to Cashman, even if Moran did not acknowledge the validity of Anninger's complaints she should have been willing to discuss them, but instead Moran took the attitude that Anninger had no right to evaluate her performance and that Cashman had no right to convey Anninger's views to her.

Cashman further testified that in her tenure with the Respondent no other employee had refused to sign an acknowledgement of a summary of a discussion involving his or her work. However, according to Cashman, as of June 16 she had decided that if Moran refused to sign the memo she would have noted that fact on the document, and would also have noted that the conditions stated in the memo would nonetheless go into effect, i.e.,

Moran would still have been expected to significantly improve her performance in the next 30 days.

According to Cashman, her comment in her June 16 memo about having been advised by "partners" that Moran had been making negative remarks referred to a conversation with Whitlock sometime between the middle of April and the first of May. Cashman testified that in that conversation Whitlock told her something to the effect that Moran constantly told other secretaries, while they were at their desks, that the Respondent was a terrible place to work.

Cashman further testified that Laura Chasnov, the supervisor in the word processing department, told her in early May that, while she was in a crowded public elevator in the building where the Respondent is located, she overheard Moran say that everyone was leaving, that the secretaries were not treated right, and that the Respondent was an awful place to work. However, Chasnov did not testify, although there was no indication that she was unavailable to do so; there is no evidence that either Chasnov or Cashman prepared any memo documenting this incident; and at the hearing counsel for the Respondent specifically disclaimed any contention that this conversation with Chasnov was included in Cashman's reference in the June 16 memo to Moran's negative remarks.

Cashman testified that the anonymous memo played no part in her decision to talk to Moran on June 16 because she felt that a complaint submitted anonymously did not merit investigation. Cashman also testified about her comment in the June 16 memo that she had discussed the action she proposed to take about Moran with Remis, conceding that her only discussion with Remis about the Anninger evaluation was that on June 13.

2. Moran's response to the meeting with Cashman

The evening of June 16 Moran wrote a memo to Cashman which she left on Cashman's desk the next morning; she also left copies for Remis and McLauglin. The text of the memo read as follows:

> With regard to our conversation earlier today in which you alleged that I "bad mouthed the firm," had a poor evaluation by Mr. Anninger and in addition you quoted Mr. Whitlock as also having said that I "bad mouthed the firm" is not surprising to me. I knew it was only a question of time when you would set up a meeting between us to initiate action against me.
>
> 1. You are aware that I went in with a group of other employees to the Managing Partner to express my dissatisfaction with your lack of support to the secretaries in this firm;
> 2. In light of the fact that I have already written you a memo in regard to Mr. Anninger's inconsiderate, poor attitude towards me (his secretary left him for the same reasons) it is just a natural progression for you to eventually meet with me. It is on record about Mr. Anninger and the working relationship that we have;
> 3. The reasons why I did not want to work for Mr. Whitlock are on record as well as is my job performance during that time — which

is totally contradictory to statements you have made to me this morning;

4. The fact that you mentioned I am an unloyal employee of Herrick & Smith is ludicrous, inasmuch as I cared enough to have a meeting with the Managing Partner along with some other secretaries to try to straighten things out, i.e., the following:

   (a) The large number of secretaries that *have* and *are* continuing to leave the firm;
   (b) The *lack* of support from Personnel when secretaries have problems; and
   (c) The *intimidation* that other secretaries, and now myself, have to contend with.

My loyalty to the firm is of the highest quality. I have always done a good job here at Herrick & Smith and have always enjoyed working at the firm — over seven years speaks for itself.

Your comments and demand that I sign a warning notice not only is an insult but also a clear blatant act on your part to set me up to be fired. Now, for the record, I deny *all* your accusations and those of Messrs. Anninger and Whitlock and reaffirm in writing that I have never "bad mouthed the firm" but have spoken my personal feelings to my friends (and fellow workers) about your lack of support and if my *private conversation* about Personnel is misconstrued as against the firm, then it is obvious to me that you have a problem and not me.

cc: Edward F. McLaughlin, Jr.
    Shepard M. Remis

3. The events of June 17

Cashman credibly testified that she saw Moran's memo on her desk when she arrived at work the next morning and that after she read the memo she went to Clark's office and asked him to read both her memo and Moran's. After Clark had done so Cashman asked him to be present at her next conversation with Moran and he agreed. They then had a secretary call Moran and ask her to come to Clark's office.[27] . . .

. . . and by discharging Moran on June 17, the Respondent violated Section 8(a)(1) of the Act. In support of these contentions, the General Counsel argues that (1) it is unlawful under the Act for an employer to tell an employee that he or she must refrain from criticizing the employer or to condition continued employment on compliance with such a prohibition; and (2) Anninger's unfavorable evaluation of Moran, the warning Cashman gave to Moran at her meeting with her on June 16, and Moran's discharge were all prompted by Moran's protected concerted activity of complaining with other secretaries to Remis

[27]The following account of this meeting is a composite of the credible portions of the testimony of Moran, Cashman, and Clark. None of the three witnesses was totally credible on this issue, but, rather than detail all the conflicts in their testimony, I have noted only those which I consider the most significant.

and McLaughlin about working conditions in the firm. Thus, the General Counsel argues that the reasons given by Anninger, Cashman, and Clark for their actions were pretextual, as demonstrated by Moran's satisfactory work performance and the disparate treatment accorded to her as compared to other support staff with poor work performance and/or attitude.

The Respondent, on the other hand, contends that (1) neither Moran's involvement in the May 11 meeting nor her complaints about various matters at the firm constituted concerted activity protected by the Act; (2) even if she engaged in protected concerted activity, that conduct was not a motivating factor in her discharge; (3) Cashman's June 16 memo did not state any unlawful conditions of employment; and (4) Moran was not discharged for refusing to sign that memo.

H. *Analysis and Conclusions*

1. The warning

It is well established that a warning to an employee that he or she should either refrain from making protected concerted complaints or look for employment elsewhere violates Section 8(a)(1) of the Act.[49] However, as noted above, the Respondent asserts that Moran did not engage in any protected concerted activity, and, thus, that Cashman's warning to her about making negative comments was permissible. In support of this contention, the Respondent asserts that its evidence regarding Moran's complaints demonstrates that the complaints did not constitute protected concerted activity but were, instead, mere "chronic griping ... not intended to initiate or induce group action or even to advance the common interest of the secretaries."

The evidence on which the Respondent relies is the testimony of Whitlock, Anninger, and Wexler that they heard Moran complain frequently, Cashman's testimony about the purported report to her from Laura Chasnov about hearing Moran make a comment in the elevator, and the anonymous memo to Cashman which she mentioned to Moran during their meeting on June 16. However, I find that the record does not support a finding that Moran did as much complaining as the Respondent contends.

First, I have specifically discredited Whitlock's testimony about the alleged deterioration of his working relationship with Moran and her alleged complaining. In addition, given the circumstances under which Moran stopped working for Whitlock and Cashman's knowledge of those circumstances, I find that Cashman's purported reliance on what Whitlock told her was not in good faith. For, as with Cashman's testimony that she had no reason to believe that Anninger had not evaluated Moran as well as he could, it strains credulity that Cashman would take Whitlock's

---

[49]See, for example, *Steinerfilm Inc.*, 255 NLRB 769 (1981), enfd. in relevant part 669 F2d 845 (1st Cir. 1982), cited by the General Counsel.

comments at face value. Moreover, the only specific complaint by Moran that Whitlock could recall related to the unavailability of mag machines, a complaint which can hardly be construed as an expression of disloyalty to the Respondent.

I have similar difficulty with the Respondent's stated reliance on Anninger's statement in his evaluation of Moran that "[s]he complains constantly to me or others walking by and willing to listen" and on his testimony in explaining that comment that Moran was a "chronic malcontent, somebody who really was never very happy with any situation." Anninger testified specifically that Moran complained about a broken typewriter, a photocopying machine, and the bookkeeping department. However, I have credited Moran's denial of Anninger's testimony about bookkeeping, and I have also credited Allen's testimony that she never heard Moran make any remarks that could be construed as disloyal to the firm. Further, I note that Anninger did not testify that he referred to Moran's complaints in his discussions about her with Cashman; if the complaints were as distressing as he indicated in his testimony, it seems unlikely that he would have failed to include them in his listing to Cashman of the reasons for his dissatisfaction with Moran.

With respect to Cashman's alleged conversation with Chasnov, as noted above, Chasnov did not testify, although as a supervisor employed by the Respondent she could presumably have been produced as a witness. As also noted above, the Respondent has disclaimed any contention that the reference in the June 16 memo to negative remarks was based in any way on Chasnov's report.

As to the anonymous note, Cashman stated in her testimony that the memo did not enter into her decision to speak to Moran on June 16. Accordingly, the Respondent cannot properly rely on that note as justification for the warning given to Moran. Similarly, although Wexler testified that he overheard Moran make remarks which indicated "strong dislike for the way the firm operated and the way people were treated," he did not advise Cashman of Moran's comments. Thus, Cashman could not have relied on any information received from Wexler in deciding to issue a warning to Moran.

The foregoing discussion leads me to the conclusion that the Respondent's witnesses considerably overstated the nature and extent of Moran's complaints, and that, although Moran, as she stated in her June 16 memo to Cashman, had "spoken [her] personal feelings" to other staff, Cashman's warning to her in the course of the June 16 meeting was not based on "negative remarks" or "bad mouthing" by Moran. To the contrary, I find that the asserted reason for the warning was pretextual, and the real purpose behind it was an attempt either to force Moran to resign or to provoke her into some conduct that might arguably provide a legitimate basis for her discharge. I therefore find that the warning was in retaliation for Moran's protected concerted activity and thus violated Section 8(a)(1) of the Act.

Accordingly, I further find that by discharging Moran the Respondent violated Section 8(a)(1) of the Act.

On the basis of the above findings of fact and the entire record in this case, I make the following

CONCLUSIONS OF LAW

1. Herrick & Smith is an employer engaged in commerce within the meaning of Section 2(2), (6), and (7) of the Act.

2. By first threatening employee Mary Moran with discharge and later discharging her, the Respondent has violated Section 8(a)(1) of the Act.

REMEDY

Having found that the Respondent engaged in certain unfair labor practices, I shall recommend that it be ordered to cease and desist therefrom and to take certain affirmative action designed to effectuate the purposes of the Act.

Having found that the Respondent unlawfully discharged employee Mary Moran, I shall recommend that the Respondent be ordered to offer her immediate and full reinstatement to her former job or, if that job no longer exists, to a substantially equivalent job, without prejudice to her seniority or other rights and privileges previously enjoyed. I shall further recommend that the Respondent be ordered to make her whole for any loss of earnings she may have suffered as a result of the discrimination against her by payment to her of the amount she would normally have earned from the date of her termination until the date of the Respondent's offer of reinstatement, less net interim earnings, in accordance with *F. W. Woolworth Co.*, 90 NLRB 289 (1950), to which shall be added interest, to be computed in the manner prescribed in *Florida Steel Corp.*, 231 NLRB 651 (1977). See generally *Isis Plumbing Co.*, 138 NLRB 716 (1962). Finally, I shall recommend that the Respondent be ordered to expunge from its files any reference to the unlawful warning and discharge of Moran.

On these findings of fact and conclusions of law and on the entire record, I issue the following recommended[51]

ORDER

The Respondent, Herrick & Smith, Boston, Massachusetts, its officers, agents, successors, and assigns, shall

1. Cease and desist from
   (a) Threatening employees with discharge because they engage in concerted activities protected under the National Labor Relations Act.

---

[51]If no exceptions are filed as provided by Sec. 102.46 of the Board's Rules and Regulations, the findings, conclusions, and recommended Order shall, as provided in Sec. 102.48 of the Rules, be adopted by the Board and all objections to them shall be deemed waived for all purposes.

> (b) Discharging or otherwise discriminating against employees because they engage in protected concerted activity.
>
> (c) In any like or related manner interfering with, restraining, or coercing employees in the exercise of their right to engage in or refrain from engaging in any or all of the activities specified in Section 7 of the Act.

2. Take the following affirmative action necessary to effectuate the policies of the Act.

> (a) Offer Mary Moran immediate and full reinstatement to her former job or, if that job no longer exists, to a substantially equivalent position, without prejudice to her seniority or other rights and privileges previously enjoyed, and make her whole for any loss of earnings she may have suffered as a result of the Respondent's discrimination against her in the manner set forth in the section of this decision entitled "Remedy."
>
> (b) Remove from its files any reference to the warning to Mary Moran on June 16, 1983, and to her discharge on June 17, 1983, and notify her in writing that this has been done and that the evidence of this unlawful warning and discharge will not be used as a basis for future personnel actions against her.

HERRICK & SMITH v. NLRB
802 F2d 565 (1st Cir. 1986)

On petition to review Board Order

Before CAMPBELL, Chief Judge, ALDRICH and
ROSENN,* Senior Circuit Judges

565

BAILEY ALDRICH, Senior Circuit Judge: On May 11, 1983, charging party Mary Moran, a legal secretary employed by the now dissolved Boston law firm of Herrick & Smith, accompanied by a small number of other secretaries, met, at the suggestion of one of the partners, with the firm's managing partner, Remis. The purpose of the meeting, for which Moran had prepared an agenda, was to voice dissatisfaction with employee relationships, and to air specific complaints. The National Labor Relations Board warrantably found that this was activity protected by Section 7 of the Act. 29 USC §157. The meeting was pleasantly conducted on both sides,

---

*Of the Third Circuit, sitting by designation.

and, even on the firm's evidence, there were airable grievances.[1]
On June 17, 1983, Moran was discharged. The ALJ, although, at one
point, finding that petitioner did have a valid complaint, found that the
real reason for the discharge was her having "engaged in concerted activities." Stating that it had carefully examined the record, the Board affirmed
the findings and

566

proposed order without opinion. Petitioner seeks review.

Whether the ALJ was correct or not, on this single question of fact this
is the most inflated case about a minimum matter — one secretary, no general course of improper conduct, no union, and no novel principle — that it
has ever been our misfortune to encounter. The ALJ, who never once
suggested curtailment, permitted the trial to extend over 14 days between
October 31, 1983 and March 13, 1984. The resulting transcript ran to 2400
pages, "abbreviated" for us to 1072 pages. Even thus abbreviated, we are
treated, not only to endless repetition, but to pages of whether a partner
signed two overtime slips, or three, or whether an absence was on a
Wednesday or a Thursday, all of no conceivable significance except to
demonstrate that memories were not perfect, and that no detail of office
life was too unimportant to escape minute and unrestricted exploration.
This was not foot dragging by petitioner. General Counsel introduced 52
exhibits, of which those reproduced fill 156 pages of appendix, giving us a
total of 1344 pages to review in addition to the ALJ's decision.

On June 16, Cashman met with Moran to discuss Anninger's unfavorable appraisal, together with other matters, including reports that she had
been "bad-mouthing" the firm. Moran reacted very hostilely, saying it was
all "ludicrous," and wanting, instead, to discuss her own complaints. With
respect to this conference, and the one the next day, the ALJ credited Cashman over Moran in all respects but one. A memo was prepared of what had
been said, and, admittedly, Moran refused to sign it. The ALJ found,
"Moran credibly testified that she did not recall Cashman telling her that
she only wanted Moran to sign a memo to acknowledge that the conversation took place, and not as an indication that she agreed with the substance of what she had been told."

On June 17 there was a further meeting, this time including Michael
Clark, an administrative manager of the firm. We again quote from the
ALJ's Decision.

---

[1]Summarizing the agenda, after a very courteous introduction thanking the managing partner for receiving them, the general matters presented were the secretaries'
alleged low morale (noting the number who had recently left); the feeling that the
lawyers did not treat them with courtesy and respect (to which partner Anninger
contributed, post); that Cashman, post, did not give them sufficient response and
that her assistant was highly disliked, and that they were asked for uncompensated
overtime on account of pro bono work.

According to Moran, Clark then told her that he wanted her to sign the memo and she either did not respond or refused to sign. Moran testified that Clark then told her again to sign the memo and when she refused he became 'very red' and, leaning over his desk, pointed his finger at her and 'screamed' that she was fired. However, both Cashman and Clark credibly denied that Clark had acted in this way.

In view of the exhausting work we have been put to we feel justified in saying that General Counsel may present any case he wants to, but, with all due respect, even had it been errorless, this had become a gross imposition that the Board, with its supervisory authority over trial counsel and ALJs, should never have inflicted on us. If its staff has nothing better to do, we have. We call its attention to a recent remark by the incoming Chief Judge of the D.C. Circuit. "A particular need in this circuit is for a special calendar for the

571

complex administrative law cases, which take so much of our time." *New D.C. Circuit Chief Judge Wald Interviewed,* Third Branch, July 1986, at 1, 6. Complex cases have to be complex. If we had not seen it, we would have found it difficult to think the present case was for real.

The petition for review is granted; the order will not be enforced. Costs are charged against the Board.

Glossary

adjudicatory. Resolving disputes.

administrative agency. A government body created by legislatures to implement laws.

administrative law. A collection of laws that delineates the legal powers and the legal limits of agencies.

administrative law judge. A hearing officer.

Administrative Procedure Act. A federal statute that gives guidelines for administrative agency decisions, hearings, judicial review, and rule-making. Passed in 1946, it has served as a model for similar state statutes.

advisory opinion. Issuance of an agency's interpretation of a regulation or policy.

affirm. A court statement that an agency order is sound.

appeal. A written request for review.

appeal council. Agency board that reviews decisions.

arbitrary. Capricious, unreasonable.

arbitration. Presentation of a dispute to a third party for a decision.

authority. Power given to the agency by the legislature.

bias. Partiality or prejudice.

board. Agency executive members.

capricious. Arbitrary, unreasonable.

checks and balances. The powers of the government are divided so that one branch may scrutinize the actions of another.

circuit. A division of the federal and state court systems.

claim. Assertion or demand of a right.

Code of Federal Regulations. Published compilation of agency rules/regulations.

complaint. A petition for relief.

court calendar. Schedule of dates for trials.

court of appeals. A court that reviews prior decisions or rulings.

criteria. Requirements.

decision. A conclusion reached after considering all essential elements.

delegation. A transfer of authority from a legislature to an agency.

Delegation Doctrine. Theory of government in which people transfer authority to the legislatures, and it is not then transferable except with limitations.

de novo. A new hearing or trial by a reviewing court.

discretion. Right to take reasonable actions.

discovery. Gathering and exchange of information during pre-hearing stage.

district court. Federal courts with jurisdiction over specified territory and states.

due process. Protection of life, liberty, and property.

enact. To make or authorize a law.

executive agency. An agency, the head of which may be removed by the executive branch at any time.

expert. Qualified person in a profession or field.

expertise. Quality experience or knowledge.

federalism. The division of government into national or state governments.

Federal Register. Publication of government rules and regulations.

Fifth Amendment. Amendment of the U.S. Constitution requiring due process in the federal government.

finding of fact. Decision on evidence presented.

findings. Reasons and results derived from analyzing facts presented at a hearing.

formal rulemaking. Procedures and hearings on the record.

Freedom of Information Act. Statute passed that allows access to government records.

hearing. Process in which facts and evidence are presented before a hearing officer for a decision.

hybrid rule. Rule combining legislative and judicial functions.

immunity. Protection from liability or prosecution.

independent agency. An agency, the head of which may be removed from office only for just cause.

informal rulemaking. Procedures of rulemaking such as notice, comment, and publication.

inspection. An examination or investigation by an agency.

intelligible principle. Test for measuring the appropriateness of the legislative criteria for setting standards given to the agency.

interpretive rule. Agency explanatory rule.

investigation. An inquiry.

issue. Disputed question of law or fact.

judicial review. Appeal from agency to the courts.

jurisdiction. The area under agency authority; authority to hear legal actions.

license. Permission to practice an activity or to engage in an occupation.

litigant. Party in a lawsuit.

mediation. Process in which an impartial third person reconciles a dispute in order to reach an agreement.

notice. Document stating intention to appeal an action.

opinion. Court's decision and reasons.

order. Decision of agency.

party. Litigant in legal action.

past practice. Culmination of similar decisions.

petition. A written request for action on a matter.

precedent. Decisions that become the legal foundation for future cases.

Privacy Act. Statute protecting privacy of records.

privacy rights. An individual's right to be left alone.

procedural due process. Standards set to ensure fairness.

procedural law. Law describing methods or processes.

procedural rule. Rule describing agency proceedings.

procedures. Methods or processes of an agency.

proof. The establishment of the validity of facts presented as evidence.

public rights. Legal issues involving government.

quasi. Resembling; almost.

record. Written document or account.

regulation. Standard or guideline established by an agency.

regulatory agency. An agency that requires compliance.

remand. Send back case or issue for more proceedings.

remedy. Methods used to enforce a right.

report. Record or explanation of records sent to an agency.

review. Examination.

rule. Standard or guideline established by an agency.

rulemaking. Agency function similar to legislative lawmaking.

scope of review. Extent and limitation of judicial examination.

search warrant. Written decree or order authorizing a search of premises or person.

separation of powers. The division of government into three branches: executive, legislative, and judicial.

settlement. Compromise or agreement between disputants.

social welfare agency. An administrative agency that provides basic services to people in need.

statute. A written law.

subpoena. An order to appear in person at an agency or in court.

substantive due process. Requires laws and actions of agencies to be reasonable.

substantive law. A law that defines rights.

substantive rule. An agency statutory rule.

sufficient standards. Test that the delegation of authority by the legislature provided adequate guidelines.

Sunshine Act. Statute demanding open government meetings.

testimony. Information given under oath.

Trade Secrets Act. Statute that protects the release of business records.

tripartite. Having three sections or parts.

witness. Person giving testimony under oath or affirmation.

Table of Cases

Index